THE SYSTEM

ALSO BY JEFF BENEDICT

Poisoned: The True Story of the Deadly E. coli *Outbreak That Changed the Way Americans Eat*

Little Pink House: A True Story of Defiance and Courage

How to Build a Business Warren Buffett Would Buy: The R. C. Willey Story

The Mormon Way of Doing Business: How Nine Western Boys Reached the Top of Corporate America

Out of Bounds: Inside the NBA's Culture of Rape, Violence, and Crime

No Bone Unturned: The Adventures of a Top Smithsonian Forensic Scientist and the Legal Battle for America's Oldest Skeletons

Without Reservation: How a Controversial Indian Tribe Rose to Power and Built the World's Largest Casino

Pros and Cons: The Criminals Who Play in the NFL (written with Don Yaeger)

Public Heroes, Private Felons: Athletes and Crimes Against Women

Athletes and Acquaintance Rape

ALSO BY ARMEN KETEYIAN

Raw Recruits (written with Alexander Wolff)

Rod Carew's Hit to Win: Batting Tips and Techniques from a Baseball Hall of Famer (written with Rod Carew and Frank Pace)

Calling the Shots (written with Mike Singletary)

Catfish: My Life in Baseball (written with Jim "Catfish" Hunter)

Big Red Confidential: Inside Nebraska Football

Ditka: Monster of the Midway

Money Players: Days and Nights Inside the New NBA (written with Harvey Araton and Martin F. Dardis)

Why You Crying? My Long, Hard Look at Life, Love, and Laughter (written with George Lopez)

THE SYSTEM

THE GLORY AND SCANDAL OF BIG-TIME COLLEGE FOOTBALL

JEFF BENEDICT AND ARMEN KETEYIAN

DOUBLEDAY

NEW YORK LONDON TORONTO SYDNEY AUCKLAND

All rights reserved. Published in the United States by Doubleday,
a division of Random House LLC, New York, and in Canada by
Random House of Canada Limited, Toronto, Penguin Random
House Companies.

www.doubleday.com

DOUBLEDAY and the portrayal of an anchor with a dolphin are
registered trademarks of Random House, LLC.

Jacket design by Michael J. Windsor
Jacket photograph © Steve Bronstein / The Image Bank / Getty Images

CATALOGING-IN-PUBLICATION DATA is on file with the
Library of Congress.

ISBN 978-0-385-53661-5

MANUFACTURED IN THE UNITED STATES OF AMERICA

10 9 8 7 6 5 4 3 2 1

First Edition

To our wives, Lydia and Dede,

who endured the two-year journey with us

CONTENTS

PROLOGUE GAME ON

From the blimp's-eye view high above sold-out Sun Life Stadium the helmets looked like metallic gold dots, bank after bank of thousand-watt halide lights adding an almost ethereal glow. As the view compressed, more colors came into focus—first the crimson, then the white, and finally the navy blue. It was January 7, 2013, a perfect night for football in South Florida—a balmy seventy-three degrees with winds out of the northeast at five miles per hour. A record crowd of 80,120 erupted as four Wings of Blue paratroopers stuck landings on the field. Another 26.4 million fans were tuned in at home, making it the second-largest audience of any program in cable television history.

On paper, the Discover BCS National Championship game was a match made in football heaven: No. 1 and undefeated Notre Dame (12-0) against No. 2 and defending national champion Alabama (12-1). After six weeks of analysis and hype the big boys were finally getting down to business. It had all the earmarks of a storybook ending to a wild, crazy roller coaster of a season that had driven the popularity of college football to dizzying new heights.

For fourteen consecutive Saturdays in the fall of 2012 college football *owned* the sporting public's attention from noon till deep into the night. Click and there was Johnny Football, on his way to Johnny Heisman, performing magic tricks for Texas A&M; click and there was Bill O'Brien's gritty Penn State squad rising from the ashes of the soul-crushing child abuse sex scandal to go 8-4; click and there was Ohio State bruising its way to an undefeated season while barred by NCAA penalties from competing in a bowl game; click, click, click, click, and there was Oregon, Stanford, West Virginia and K-State taking their turns on the national stage.

Off the field the news wasn't so good. A dozen programs were on probation for major NCAA violations, including USC, Ohio State, Tennessee, Boise State, LSU and Texas Tech. Graduation rates for African-American players continued to lag behind, highlighted by 2011 national champion Auburn, where only 49 percent of black athletes graduated, compared with a majority of white players. A 2012 study found that student-athletes in top football programs are more accurately *athlete-students,* averaging 41.6 hours per week preparing for football, compared with 38.2 hours in the classroom.

The economics of college football were upside down, too. The latest figures showed only 22 of the 120 top-tier programs broke even or made a profit in 2010–11. "If anybody looked at the business model of big-time college athletics, they would say this is the dumbest business in the history of the world," said Michigan's athletic director, Dave Brandon, the former CEO of Domino's Pizza. "You just don't have the revenue to support the costs. And the costs continue to go up."

Another study, released in 2012, found that Football Bowl Subdivision (FBS) schools spent more than $91,000 per athlete compared with just over $13,000 per student. Yet students across the country faced steep tuition hikes and increased fees. As colleges and universities absorbed painful cuts in funding and went deeper into debt to stay afloat, a nationwide building boom—an arms race—was under way when it came to stadiums, premium seating, weight rooms and football facilities.

At the same time, a seismic shift in conference realignment had schools bolting conferences and abandoning long-standing rivalries in order to capture a greater share of the multibillion-dollar television contracts. "I don't know where this all ends," NCAA president Mark Emmert said at the IMG Intercollegiate Athletics Forum in early December 2012. "But it does make clear that those moves are, if not entirely about money, predominantly about money."

The result, said Emmert, was the erosion of friendship and trust that existed for decades among college presidents, athletic directors and conference commissioners.

"I really don't know what to do, but I'm really concerned about it, really, really concerned about it," said Emmert. "It's not healthy at all."

As for the players, they have paid a heavy price for what has become a year-round job. A staggering 282 players from eight of the ten Bowl Championship Series (BCS) conferences and major independents suffered season-ending injuries. And those were just the officially reported ones. Plenty of other players were carted off practice fields, never to return to action.

Meanwhile, in March 2013, researchers at the Cleveland Clinic released a study showing that college football players are likely to experience significant and long-term brain damage from hits to the head even when they do not suffer concussions. The findings were based on blood samples, brain scans and cognitive tests performed on sixty-seven college football players before and after games during the 2011 season. As the debate over the long-term effects of head injuries in football continues to escalate, it is now an established fact that college football players who never make it to the NFL are at risk of being diagnosed with degenerative brain disease caused by repeated head trauma.

But none of that mattered as Notre Dame and Alabama squared off for the national championship on ESPN. The last time the two storied programs had met with so much on the line was the 1973 Sugar Bowl, remembered for the gutsiest call of Irish head coach Ara Parseghian's career, a third-and-eight pass from the shadow of his own end zone, enabling the Irish to run out the clock and outlast Paul "Bear" Bryant's Tide 24–23. Epic.

Four decades later, Brian Kelly and Nick Saban had come to power. Kelly, in his third year, was a former women's softball coach at Assumption College before making a name for himself at Grand Valley State University in Allendale, Michigan. Six hugely successful seasons at Central Michigan and Cincinnati helped propel the son of a Boston politician to South Bend. Kelly had more than a bit of the Irish in him and, like his father, was wise to the media game. He offered smooth, thoughtful answers to almost every question, even ones he had heard for the third time in an hour. He also spoke of the importance of "painting a vision" of success at Notre Dame.

"Your program is defined by consistency and Alabama is that model," he said two days before the championship game. "I concede that. It's where we want to be."

Saban, on the other hand, was the reigning heavyweight champ of college coaching, 60-7 since 2008, and gunning for his third national title in four years and his fourth in the last decade. His way had become *the* way in the game. Melding body and mind through "The Process" into a new breed of "Built by Bama" athlete, Saban had his players hardwired to perform at their best when it mattered most.

All of this had helped propel Saban to the front of the roaring, seemingly unstoppable race in coaching salaries. He had earned north of $5 million in salary, bonuses and other perks in 2012, just ahead of Mack Brown at Texas. By July 2013, at least seventy-nine head football coaches made $1 million or more annually. Fifty-two made more than $2 million, while sixteen cleared $3 million. Assistant coaching salaries had routinely reached into the high six figures or more.

"Athletics has gotten so disproportionate to the rest of the economy and to the academic community that it's unbelievable," said Dr. Julian Spallholz, a distinguished professor of nutrition and biochemistry at Texas Tech. "The students pay more tuition. The faculty pay for not having a pay increase. And the football coach gets a half-million raise. I think that speaks for itself, doesn't it?"

Well, not exactly. College professors have tenure, and they are not expected to single-handedly fill stadiums in order to offset the eight-figure investments being made these days in stadium facilities. On the other hand, a college football coach may be the most insecure job in America. Between 2009 and 2012, seventy-two Division I head football coaches were fired. Auburn's Gene Chizik was among those let go in 2012—following a winless season in the Southeastern Conference (SEC) and just two seasons after leading Auburn to the national championship. The pressure to win—and win right away—had never been greater, and it was getting worse. A four-team postseason playoff was finally here, with Cowboys Stadium selected to host the first national championship game in January 2015. The conference "pool" payout for the eventual winner tripled to $75 million.

It was against this ever-changing landscape—in arguably the most tumultuous period in college football history—that the authors secured an all-access pass inside several mega-programs. We spent months behind the scenes with the coaching staffs at Alabama and Michigan and with top recruits headed to Texas A&M and Utah. We went on the road with BYU, Washington State and even up-and-coming Towson University; we traveled on a team charter, listened and observed inside locker rooms and team meetings and from the sidelines during games and practices. We traveled with the game's most powerful booster and hung out with ESPN's *College GameDay* crew. We also dug into some serious dirt at Ohio State, Tennessee and Missouri. We talked with tutors, hostesses, college presidents, agents, walk-ons, strippers, trustees, fans, directors of football operations and even a "janitor."

In all, with the help of four additional reporters, we conducted more than five hundred interviews and logged well over two hundred hours observing programs at every facet and level of the game to gain a wider, deeper understanding of the power of The System and all its component parts.

In the end, we hope, we have produced an enlightening, unvarnished, deeply detailed look at the pageantry, pressure, pain, glory and scandal that make college football the most passionate, entertaining game in America today.

———

Green streamers and white hankies filled the stadium as Notre Dame lined up to kick off to Alabama.

"This crowd is ready," said ESPN's Brent Musburger against a deafening crescendo of "O-H-H-H-H-H-H."

The stadium fell instantly silent the moment Notre Dame's kicker Kyle Brindza sent the football sailing toward Alabama's Christion Jones.

"Game on," Musburger said.

1 THE COACH

Part I, Mike Leach after midnight

On Saturday afternoons in the fall of 1981 the roar of the crowd would echo across campus every time BYU scored a touchdown. It happened a lot that year. BYU led the nation in offense, scoring more than five hundred points, thanks to the arm of two-time all-American quarterback Jim McMahon. On his way to setting seventy NCAA passing records, McMahon had put Provo, Utah, on the college football map.

Twenty-year-old Sharon Smith hardly noticed. But one evening that fall she was outside her apartment when a rugged looking guy with wavy, shoulder-length hair approached. He introduced himself as Mike Leach, a twenty-year-old junior from Cody, Wyoming. He lived in the apartment complex next door. They even used the same laundry room. Turned out they had been neighbors for months.

Smith was surprised they had never crossed paths. But Leach traveled a fair amount. He was a member of BYU's rugby team.

She was intrigued. Leach didn't look like a BYU student. For one thing, his hair was too long. It should have been above his collar, according to BYU's honor code. But Leach ignored the rule. That got him repeatedly summoned to the dean's office. Still, Leach didn't cut his hair. He didn't talk like a BYU student either. His vocabulary was a little more colorful. So was his upbringing. He grew up in Wyoming with boys who spent Friday nights popping beers and getting in fistfights. Ranchers wearing sidearms would come into town for lunch at the local diner. *Gunsmoke* reruns were all the rage. Marshal Dillon was Leach's boyhood hero.

Smith had met lots of guys at BYU. None was as authentic—or as funny—as Leach. They ended up talking until after midnight, and she accepted his invitation to go out the following night.

Their first date was a meal at an A&W restaurant in Provo. That's when college football entered the picture. Over hot dogs and a couple cold root beers, Leach started talking about coaching. His idol was BYU's head coach, LaVell Edwards. During Leach's freshman year he had entered his name in a drawing and won season tickets on the forty-yard line. From that perch he began studying BYU's offensive scheme: a controlled passing game with somebody always in motion before the snap; lots of receivers running a combination of vertical routes and crossing patterns; throwing to the backs in the flat. Edwards's innovative system was a forerunner of the West Coast Offense ultimately popularized by Bill Walsh in the NFL. But at the college level in the early 1980s, no defensive coordinator in the country had figured out how to stop it.

To the casual fan BYU's system looked pretty complicated. And to a certain extent, it was. But Leach had figured out that the genius of Edwards was the way he packaged his plays. He used an endless number of formations to disguise about fifty basic plays. That made it easy for the offense to memorize and difficult for defenses to recognize.

Smith had no idea what Leach was talking about. But one thing was obvious to her: the guy sitting across from her sipping root beer through a straw was no casual fan of the game. He wasn't some armchair quarterback either. In high school Leach had started a "coaching" file, filling it with newspaper clippings from the sports pages and schematic ideas he scribbled on loose sheets of paper. By the time he got to Provo and could watch LaVell Edwards up close, he was mapping out his future. "BYU had a state-of-the-art offense," Leach said. "The best in the country. I started studying it very closely. LaVell Edwards had a major impact on me."

After one date with Leach, Smith never saw anyone else. "Of all the people I dated at BYU, he was the only guy who knew exactly what he wanted to do," Smith said. "He told me right away that he knew he was going to be a lawyer or a college football coach. I found it very attractive that he had a plan and was very confident about achieving it."

Never mind that Leach had never played college football and his only coaching experience was as a Little League baseball coach back in Wyoming. Smith wasn't worried. "He could analyze the game and the way coaches were coaching, and he had it in his mind that he could do it better at a young age," she said. "Confidence is a very attractive feature."

In June 1982, Mike and Sharon were married in St. George, Utah. After BYU, they moved to Southern California, and Mike attended law school at Pepperdine. But just before he got his law degree, he posed a practical question to Sharon: "Do you want me to come home miserable and making a lot of money or come home happy and not earning as much money?"

She told him that being happy was more important than making a lot of money.

Leach didn't bother taking the bar exam. Instead, he and Sharon headed to Alabama so Mike could attend the U.S. Sports Academy. After he obtained his master's, they returned to California, and Mike talked his way into a part-time assistant's position with the football team at Cal Poly San Luis Obispo, then a Division II school. The fact that Leach had a law degree intrigued the head coach enough to offer him a job helping out for $3,000. Sharon figured that was a monthly salary. But it was $3,000 for the season.

With a one-year-old baby, the Leaches moved into campus housing. Their bed was a floor mattress. They didn't own a television. Their motto was "Opportunity trumps money."

After one season, the head coach at Cal Poly San Luis Obispo predicted that Leach would develop into a big-time college football coach. Over the next decade Mike and Sharon crisscrossed the country, taking coaching jobs at College of the Desert in California, Iowa Wesleyan and Valdosta State. Leach even spent a year coaching football in Finland. He held every position from offensive line coach to linebacker coach to quarterback coach. He even served as sports information director and equipment manager at one school. And when all the other coaches left at the end of the day, Leach stayed behind to watch film—always alone, sometimes until dawn—night after night.

———

For the first fifteen years of marriage, Sharon made more money doing clerical work and miscellaneous jobs than Mike made coaching. They were happy but broke. Plus, they were up to three kids with a fourth on the way. Then things changed in 1997. Kentucky's head coach, Hal Mumme, hired Leach as his offensive coordinator. Suddenly Leach jumped from small schools in the middle of nowhere to the SEC, the best conference in college football. His offensive scheme—referred to as "the spread"—would be tested against Florida, Alabama, Georgia, LSU, Tennessee and Auburn.

Working under Mumme and drawing from the BYU offense he'd studied in the early 1980s, Leach added new wrinkles that opened up the field even more, making it easier for his quarterback to throw into open passing lanes. "I spend more time trying to make my offense easy for the quarterback to memorize than anything," Leach said. "I want to make it as simple as possible because I want guys to trigger as quick as possible. The key isn't finding good plays. The key is packaging."

One of the most revolutionary aspects of Leach's system was spacing the offensive linemen three feet apart. At first glance, it appears to give pass rushers a clear shot at the quarterback. But the result was fewer sacks and cleaner passing lanes for the quarterback. The SEC had never seen anything like it. In Leach's first season as offensive coordinator, Kentucky upset Alabama and finished the year with the No. 1 offense in the country, led by quarterback Tim Couch. The following year Kentucky knocked off LSU; Couch threw for more than four thousand yards and went on to become the No. 1 pick in the NFL draft. Meanwhile, Leach's offense set six NCAA records and forty-one SEC records. The Wildcats had a winning record in the toughest conference in the country.

Coaches in the SEC weren't the only ones who noticed. Coaches from around the country—including Urban Meyer at Notre Dame, Tommy Bowden at Tulane and Mark Mangino at Kansas State—traveled to Kentucky to learn more about Leach's system. Even a number of NFL coaches made the trek to Lexington. The interest level was so high that Leach made an instructional video on the finer points of throwing and receiving techniques. It sold thousands of copies.

After two seasons at Kentucky, Leach accepted the position as offensive coordinator at Oklahoma. He was there less than one year before he got offered the head job at Texas Tech. The opportunity had some downside. It was 1999 and Tech was on academic probation for recruiting violations, academic fraud and unethical conduct. Eighteen scholarships were stripped from the football program between 1999 and 2001. Not only would Leach be competing against Texas, Oklahoma and Texas A&M, but he'd be doing it with eighteen fewer scholarships for his first three seasons.

There were other problems. Tech's graduation rates were among the lowest in the nation. Leach held two advanced degrees and had no interest in a football culture that ignored the importance of academics.

Plus, there was the unenviable task of replacing Tech's Spike Dykes, who had won more games—eighty-two—than any football coach in the history of the school. In Lubbock, where football is right beside God in importance, Dykes was beloved.

Despite all this, Leach said yes. At thirty-eight, a guy who never played college football was off to Lubbock to coach the Red Raiders in the Big 12.

Six years later, a cup of coffee in one hand and a remote control in the other, Mike Leach was alone in his office going over game film. *Play. Pause. Rewind. Play. Pause. Rewind.* Next sequence.

It was after midnight when he stood up to stretch his legs. He parted the blinds on his office window that overlooked the Texas Tech practice facility. That's when he spotted a shadow moving across the field. It was a human shadow. "Who in the hell is that?" he mumbled.

The facilities were locked, the lights off. The place was deserted. Leach wondered if it was a prowler. He headed downstairs to have a look.

Approaching the field, Leach spotted tiny orange cones. They were arranged in rows. Someone was darting in and out of them. Suddenly the figure came into focus.

"Michael?"

"Oh, hey, Coach."

It was Tech receiver Michael Crabtree, considered the top wideout in the country.

"Michael, what are you doing?"

"I got to thinking about the corner route," he said in between deep breaths. "If I come out of my cut like this"—Crabtree pointed his toes and jigged hard to the right—"I'll be open every time."

Impressed, Leach folded his arms and nodded.

"So," Crabtree continued, "I set up some cones, and I'm out here working on it."

Leach's eyes went from Crabtree to the cones and back to Crabtree. The most talented wide receiver in college football was alone in the dark. There was no ball. No quarterback. No position coach to tell him what to do. It was just Crabtree in his stance, doing starts and stops, running in and out of cones.

The truth was that Crabtree worked out alone at night a lot. He lived across the street from the practice complex and would sneak in after dark. "I always worked on my game," Crabtree said. "Coach Leach just happened to catch me that night."

Determined not to disrupt hard work, Leach turned and headed back inside without saying another word.

Leach and Crabtree had the kind of relationship that didn't require much talk. When Leach arrived in Lubbock six years earlier, Tech didn't land blue-chip recruits like Crabtree. A star quarterback at David W. Carter High School in Dallas, Crabtree was also one of the top high school basketball players in the state. Bobby Knight offered him a basketball scholarship. And Texas, Oklahoma, Texas A&M and LSU were all over him with scholarship offers to play football. Tech's facilities couldn't compete with those schools'. And Leach's budget was a fraction of his rivals'.

Still, Leach was winning with guys who had been passed over by the Longhorns and the Sooners and the Aggies. In Leach's first six seasons, Tech had gone 49-28, appeared in six straight bowl games and finished in the top twenty in both 2004 and 2005. But the thing that really got Crabtree's attention was Leach's Air Raid offense. "They threw the ball every play," Crabtree said. "Leach had the whole program going. I said to myself, 'Man, if I go to Tech, it's gonna be on.'"

Tech indeed had the most explosive offense in the country when Leach started recruiting Crabtree in 2004. That year, Tech's football scores often looked like basketball scores. The Red Raiders put up seventy points against TCU. Then they put up seventy against Nebraska, marking the most points scored against the Cornhuskers in the program's 114-year history. Virtually every Tech game was an offensive exhibition, and Leach's quarterbacks were leading the nation in passing year in and year out.

But Leach told Crabtree up front that he planned to play him at receiver, not quarterback. Crabtree had been the best athlete on his high school team, and—as is often the case for superior high school athletes—he got asked to play quarterback. But Leach saw in him all the raw materials to make a great receiver—breakaway speed, great leaping ability, big hands and fearlessness. He went as far as to tell Crabtree that he could see him playing wideout in the NFL.

Crabtree had never played receiver. But it didn't take much to convince him to switch. "I didn't want to stay in college that long," Crabtree said. "I wanted to get on to the NFL. If I played quarterback, I'd be at Tech for five years. I figured if I played receiver at Tech, I would tear it up."

The chance to play receiver at Tech also made it easier not to choose Texas or Oklahoma. "I didn't want to go to Texas or OU and just be another guy," Crabtree said. "I wanted to go somewhere to make a name for myself. With Leach at Tech, I had a chance to take it to another level."

All he told Leach, however, was one thing: "I want to score touchdowns."

Leach redshirted Crabtree his first year, giving him time to learn a new position. Then Crabtree started as a freshman in 2007. That year he became the first freshman since Herschel Walker named to the AFCA Coaches' All-America Team. He was also the first freshman to win the Biletnikoff Award, establishing him as the best receiver in the nation. Crabtree started his sophomore season as a projected Heisman candidate.

Yet Leach never gave him star treatment. Once, when Crabtree missed a couple of blocks during a scrimmage, Leach stopped play.

"Crabtree," Leach shouted. "Are you gonna block or just get your ass kicked all day?"

Crabtree didn't say a word.

Leach purposely called another running play to Crabtree's side. On the snap of the ball, Crabtree exploded into the cornerback, got underneath his shoulder pads, lifted him off the ground and drove him out-of-bounds. The defender's feet still off the ground, Crabtree kept pumping his legs, taking his man past the bench. By the time Leach blew the whistle, Crabtree had driven the defender up against a fence.

"I was there to catch balls and score touchdowns, not block," Crabtree said. "But coach was talking about my blocking. So I showed him that blocking was nothing by driving that guy all over the field."

About the only player who worked harder than Michael Crabtree was quarterback Graham Harrell. Leach demanded it. "The quarterback has to work harder than everyone else," Leach said. "He has to be the first one on the field and the last one off. If he's not willing to do that, I will find another position for him. But he won't be a quarterback."

Harrell came out of high school as the top quarterback in Texas. In one season he threw for 4,825 yards and sixty-seven touchdowns. His father was his high school coach and pushed him hard. But it was nothing like his experience playing for Leach.

"He is extremely tough on his quarterbacks," Harrell said. "There were days when I'd come off the practice field thinking I hated him. He can be extremely critical. But he did it because he expected a lot out of me."

Leach didn't just expect a lot from his players on the field; he demanded excellence off it. By the time Crabtree and Harrell arrived at Texas Tech, Leach's team had the highest graduation rates at any public institution in Division I football, peaking at 79 percent from 2006 to 2008. He achieved this by benching players who didn't perform academically. "I don't want my players missing classes and doing fourth-quarter comebacks academically," Leach said. "They are here to get a degree, and I reinforce that by holding them accountable for grades."

He also held them accountable for what they did off the field. He came up with his own code called the Three Queen Mothers. Players who were caught stealing, hitting a woman or smoking marijuana were kicked off the team, no questions asked.

"Players who steal can't be trusted, and trust is very important in football," Leach explained. "Any man who hits a woman is a coward. And I don't need cowards on my football team. Smoking dope—or any other drugs—is just selfish. It indicates that your partying is more important than your team. So any player—no matter how talented—is cut if he violates those rules."

From the outside looking in, playing for Leach sounds like a grind. He was a tough taskmaster who demanded excellence. "He cussed me out plenty of times, and I respected him for that," Crabtree said. "Some guys are soft and can't deal with it. But I realized he just wanted to teach me. He has a great mind, and he helped me understand the game."

Leach had his own way of making football fun, too.

"College football is like a job in many respects," said Harrell. "It's full-time. It's demanding. But Coach Leach made it feel more like a boy's game."

One way Leach accomplished this was with his dry sense of humor and a vocabulary that would make a sailor blush. "There is foul language everywhere, especially in football," Harrell said. "But Leach is more colorful than anyone. That was another reason the guys loved being around him. Sometimes he'd put words together I'd never even heard. But his language never offended us. We all laughed. That's just Coach."

Leach's reputation for using four-letter words was so notorious that it even reached the attention of Harrell's mother. "Graham, do you talk like that?" she asked her son at one point. He laughed. "Mom," he replied. "No one really talks like that but Coach."

Harrell's parents had raised him not to swear. And he rarely did. His backup Taylor Potts was even more conservative. A practicing Christian, Potts had a reputation for never using four-letter words. So Potts and Harrell got a kick out of the things Leach would say in quarterbacks' meetings. Eventually, Harrell decided to have some fun with Leach's colorful quips. It was January 2008, and daily planners had just arrived from the school. A stack was on Leach's desk. They were designed to help student-athletes budget their time. But Harrell had another use in mind. He handed one to Potts and told him to start writing down all of Leach's most colorful quotations.

It was a tall order for a kid who never used the f-word. Potts ended up recording pages of quotations littered with "f***." He never spelled out the word. One day the quotation book got left behind, and an assistant coach found it. He took it to Leach, informing him that one of the quarterbacks had been writing down everything he said. When Leach saw that the f-word wasn't spelled out, he knew it had to be Potts.

The following day when the four quarterbacks came in for their meeting with Leach, he had the book in his hand. "I noticed you all are keeping a little quote book on me," he said.

The other quarterbacks glanced at Potts and Harrell.

"The only thing that really bothers me," Leach said, "is it seems that Taylor Potts doesn't know how to spell the word 'fuck.'"

Harrell covered his mouth. Potts turned red.

"Now grab a marker and get up on the board," Leach said.

Potts stepped to the whiteboard.

"Okay, now write the letters I tell you," Leach said. "*F-U-C-K.* Now that says 'fuck.' So if you ever want to know how to spell it, just turn around and it will be right there on the board."

The quarterbacks erupted.

By the 2008 season, Leach had become a cult hero in Lubbock. His quarterbacks had won six national passing titles in eight years, and he had the most prolific offense in the nation. Harrell and Crabtree were the best quarterback-receiver tandem in college football. And only two teams in the Big 12 had a better cumulative record since Leach joined the conference. Needless to say, every home game at Tech's stadium was sold out.

Word of Leach's success went well beyond Lubbock. The author of *Moneyball,* Michael Lewis, had profiled him in the *New York Times Magazine.* And national sportswriters had dubbed him The Mad Scientist of Football. No one doubted that Leach was a first-rate college coach. The only question that remained was whether his unorthodox system was capable of contending for a national title.

The turning point came on November 1, 2008. That night, the No. 1–ranked Texas Longhorns came to Lubbock undefeated. Tech was ranked No. 7 and also undefeated. The two programs were bitter rivals. "I deeply hope we beat their ass today," Texas Tech's basketball coach Bobby Knight said hours beforehand on ESPN's *College GameDay.* ABC showcased the game in its prime-time Saturday night slot, and announcer Brent Musburger opened the broadcast by saying it was the biggest game in Texas Tech history.

A record crowd—56,333 fans in black and red, carrying swords and wearing eye patches and bandannas—was on its feet throughout. Texas trailed the entire way until late in the fourth quarter.

With 1:29 remaining in the game, the Longhorns scored a touchdown to go up 33–32.

Graham Harrell was on the Tech sideline, looking up at the clock. He had led ten scoring drives in 1:30 or less that season. But this felt different. The stakes had never been so high. The audience had never been so big. The chance to beat the best team in college football was in the balance. Tech had only one time-out left.

"Hey," one of his teammates yelled. "Leach wants to talk to you."

Harrell hustled over to Leach, prepared to hear something profound. The tension in the stadium was palpable. But Leach was relaxed and showed no emotion. He didn't even raise his voice.

"Now listen to me," he said. "Just make routine plays."

"I got ya."

"Everybody needs to get out-of-bounds. But don't be afraid to throw over the middle. Late in the game the middle is exposed."

Harrell nodded.

"Now come here," Leach said, his voice getting even quieter.

Harrell took a step closer.

"Listen to me. There's gonna be guys out there that don't believe we can march down and score. You need to get these guys going and make them believe we can score."

"No doubt," Harrell said, bouncing up and down on his toes. "No doubt."

"You make 'em believe. Huddle 'em up. Make sure everyone believes."

"We're ready to go."

"All right. Now let's go out there and shove it up their fuckin' ass and score a touchdown."

Harrell grinned. "All right, Coach." He trotted onto the field.

So much for profound. Harrell had heard that same late-game speech so many times he could recite it, right down to the last sentence. Even Leach's tone was the same. "He was really good about staying even keel no matter the situation," Harrell said. "It helped me to see him so calm. He doesn't have a football background. So football was never an emotional game to him. It was always analytical. With Coach Leach, when the offense gets the ball, you are supposed to score. That's it."

Over the next minute and twenty-one seconds, Harrell completed his first four passes—one over the middle and three toward the sidelines. He drove his team all the way to the Texas twenty-six-yard line before throwing an incomplete pass that stopped the clock with eight seconds remaining. Tech had a decision to make: attempt a long-distance field goal, or run one more play in hopes of getting closer for the kicker. But if Harrell completed a pass and the receiver didn't get out-of-bounds before time ran out, Texas wins.

Harrell ran toward Leach. "Wanna take a shot?" he shouted.

Leach was calm. "Just run four vertical."

It was Leach's favorite play—all four receivers running vertical routes. It gave Harrell options. If a receiver got past his man, he'd throw into the end zone. If the defense played back, he'd throw underneath, enabling the receiver to catch and quickly get out-of-bounds to set up the field goal.

Harrell relayed the plan in the huddle.

"Man, there ain't no way we can let the game come down to the kicker," Crabtree said.

Harrell agreed.

"Just throw me the damn ball," Crabtree said.

Harrell was sure Texas would double-team Crabtree, forcing him to throw to a different receiver. But when they broke the huddle, Texas was in man-to-man coverage. Harrell and Crabtree thought the same thing: *If the defender overplays, throw the back-shoulder pass.*

On the snap, Crabtree ran full speed straight at the defender, who backed off to protect against a throw to the end zone. Crabtree dug his toe into the turf at the eight-yard line and cut toward the sideline. The ball had already left Harrell's hand. Crabtree hauled it in and stopped on a dime. Two defenders ran past him, one of them trying to push Crabtree out-of-bounds. Tightroping the sideline, Crabtree kept his balance and scampered into the end zone. One second remained on the clock.

Fans stormed the field. Crabtree and Harrell were mobbed in the end zone. The goalposts came down. Cannons blasted. The band broke into the fight song. Texas Tech had knocked off the No. 1 team in the nation.

Amid the chaos, Mike Leach showed no emotion. He didn't even crack a smile. "There was a lot of drama and excitement, don't get me wrong," Leach said. "But this was pretty routine. If Crabtree was even with his man, throw it over the top. If they overplay him, throw the ball to his ass cheek, away from coverage, and he comes back and catches it. We practiced that all year. It's a safe play. They executed it perfectly."

———

That night, Leach stayed up until 5:00 a.m. talking with friends about the victory. By the time he woke up later Sunday afternoon, Texas Tech was ranked No. 2 in the nation. The victory transcended the sports page. Scott Pelley brought a CBS News camera crew to Lubbock and profiled Leach on

60 Minutes. Actor Matthew McConaughey, a University of Texas alumnus, started hanging out with Leach and his wife. Film director Peter Berg gave Leach a cameo role in *Friday Night Lights.* Mike and Sharon even accepted an invitation to take a private tour of the White House and meet with President George Bush at the end of the season. Graham Harrell went with them.

Leach's only regret was that his days coaching Michael Crabtree and Graham Harrell were numbered. A few weeks after knocking off Texas, his two star players started their final regular-season game as Red Raiders. It was at home against Baylor on November 29. Both got injured early. Crabtree ended up on crutches and did not return. Harrell's injury happened on a sack in the first quarter. When he got up and dusted himself off, he knew he was in trouble. Two fingers on his left hand were dangling. He knew they were broken.

Facing third and long, Harrell looked to the sideline. Leach called a running play, requiring Harrell to take the snap from under center.

Harrell turned his head from side to side and crossed his hands, indicating he didn't like the call.

Leach signaled time-out, and Harrell jogged to the sideline.

"What's wrong?" Leach said.

"My hand is messed up. I broke my fingers. I don't think I can take a snap under center."

The team trainer stepped in.

Harrell held out his hand.

"Your fingers are dislocated," the trainer said.

"Bro, I'm telling you. They are broken."

The trainer took a closer look.

"Don't mess with them," Harrell said.

The trainer yanked on both limp fingers, trying to set them.

"Dude!" Harrell shouted. "They're broken."

After being set, both fingers promptly went limp again.

"They're broken," the trainer said.

"No shit," Harrell said. "I just told you that."

Leach scowled at the trainer. "What are you doing?"

The referee jogged to the sideline. "C'mon, guys," he hollered. "It's time to play."

Leach looked at Harrell. "What do you want to do?"

"I'll play. Just don't call anything under center."

He trotted back on the field. A few plays later he threw a touchdown pass. For the rest of the second quarter Leach called nothing but pass plays out of the shotgun. At halftime, the medical staff took Harrell to the X-ray room. The technician, an older woman, smiled and handed him a candy. Harrell was her favorite player.

But after X-raying his hand, she started crying.

"Are they that bad?" Harrell said.

"You're not gonna like what you see."

"Then don't show them to me."

She handed the images to the trainer. Harrell had broken his hand in nine places. His ring finger and pinkie were shattered. After consulting with the rest of the medical staff, the trainer led Harrell back to the locker room. The team was ready to head out for the second half. Harrell and the trainer huddled with Leach.

"We looked at the X-rays," the trainer told Leach. "He probably shouldn't play."

"Well, what do you want to do, Graham?" Leach said.

"I can play."

Leach looked at the trainer. "Will playing make it worse?"

"Well, his fingers are shattered," the trainer said. "It can't get much worse."

"Tape 'em together and let him play," Leach said.

Harrell played the entire second half with his left hand wrapped in black tape. He completed forty-one of fifty passes, throwing for 309 yards and two touchdowns, while leading Tech to a come-from-behind victory in the final minutes.

"It was the most courageous effort I've ever seen," Leach said.

The following day Harrell underwent four hours of surgery. Seventeen pins were permanently inserted in his fingers.

"Leach made you tough," Harrell said. "And he made the game fun for me. Football is a kids' game, and he made it feel that way. I loved playing for him. All of us did."

═══

The 2008 football season was the best one in the history of Texas Tech. The Red Raiders won eleven games and finished in the top ten. Harrell won a slew of awards and was runner-up for the Heisman. After just two college seasons, Crabtree led the nation in receiving and entered the NFL draft, where he was selected tenth overall by the 49ers. And the nation's college football coaches elected Mike Leach as Coach of the Year.

The Leaches' financial situation had changed, too. At the end of 2008,

Leach had just one year remaining on his contract at Tech. Nine coaches in the Big 12 had higher annual salaries. Leach's agents had spent months trying to negotiate a contract extension that would have made Leach one of the highest-paid coaches in the conference. But the two sides were far apart, and the tenor of the negotiations got so ugly that Tech's athletic director, Gerald Myers, shut down the discussions altogether. That was before Tech upset Texas. After that game, Leach's name was floated to become the new head coach at Auburn. And Leach interviewed at the University of Washington, prompting the university's president at the time, Mark Emmert, to say publicly that the Huskies were well on their way to finding the right coach to take over the program.

The prospect of Leach leaving Lubbock for Seattle or anywhere else didn't sit well with the fan base at Tech. But the fact that Leach had interviewed elsewhere irked Myers. Shortly after the season ended, Tech's chancellor, Kent Hance, interceded and brokered a deal with Leach's agents that resulted in a five-year contract extension with a base salary of $12.7 million and bonus incentives of up to $800,000 per season based on performance. Hance boasted that Leach's new contract did not contain a buyout provision. "I know he's not leaving," Hance said.

For Sharon Leach, the days of sleeping on a floor mattress and living off $3,000 a season were ancient history. The kid who told her on their first date at BYU that he wanted to be a football coach had delivered.

2 THE CLOSER

The life of a college football hostess

Dictionaries generally define "hostess" as "a woman who entertains socially." Sounds simple enough. But the role of a hostess is a little more complicated in the college football lexicon. Officially, hostesses are university employees who typically receive minimum wage and work under the auspices of the admissions office, where they are responsible for promoting an institution's strong academic programs and rich traditions. The job description almost always mentions one other aspect: working with the athletic department to escort potential student-athletes on campus visits.

"Escort" is a bit of a misnomer. A hostess is the first—not to mention prettiest—face a recruit sees when making an official campus visit. Over the course of a weekend—the typical length of an official visit—a recruit spends far more time with his hostess than with anyone on the coaching staff. A recruit and his hostess go on campus tours together, take in a game, go to a movie, go out to eat and attend an official reception of some sort. A hostess may even take her recruit to an after-hours party. For a high school recruit, it is like having a weekend date with a college girl.

The idea of using pretty girls to entice the next big man on campus is not a new concept. In the 1960s, Alabama's legendary coach Bear Bryant had Bear's Angels. These hostesses were later renamed Bama Belles. Plenty of other programs, particularly in the SEC, followed suit. By the 1980s, Florida's Gator Getters, Clemson's Bengal Babes, Auburn's Tigerettes and Miami's Hurricane Honeys were somewhat notorious as recruiting tools.

But these days, hostesses are much more technologically savvy. Many of them spend countless hours communicating with recruits through text messaging, Skype, Facebook, Twitter and other social media outlets. This banter creates great expectations of what might be if a recruit commits to a particular school. The promise of an intimate relationship is the sort of thing that can trump sold-out stadiums, state-of-the-art facilities, Nike deals and schedules packed with nationally televised games, all of which are the norm in conferences like the SEC.

"All things being equal, in our conference hostesses can be a real difference maker," said one senior athletic department official in the SEC. "Let's not forget, these are college girls dealing with high school boys."

Yet fans—even the most ardent ones—know very little about the significant role that hostesses play in the system. Recruiting agencies never consider them when projecting where recruits might land. Even the NCAA has very little in the way of regulations to keep hostesses in check. For instance, hostesses are not subject to the contact restrictions with recruits that are imposed on coaches. For the most part, hostesses are a part of the system that gets very little scrutiny.

———

If there is such a thing as an über-hostess, Lacey Pearl Earps was it. A platinum blonde from outside Nashville, Earps had the usual prerequisites when she joined Tennessee's Orange Pride as a sophomore prior to the start of the 2008 season—good looks, a charming personality and boundless school pride. But Earps was hardly just a pretty face. She was a business major with unusual organizational skills, an indefatigable work ethic and a goal of one day working in college athletics. She figured that by going all out as a hostess in the hypercompetitive SEC, she'd learn the ropes while playing a pivotal role in convincing blue-chip athletes to commit to Tennessee. In the end, she hoped her efforts would be noticed and she'd eventually land a full-time job with her alma mater.

It was a good plan. And Earps couldn't think of a better person to work under than Tennessee's head coach, Phillip Fulmer, who had been with the school since 1992. Earps set out to be Fulmer's top choice as an escort for prized recruits. It was an ambitious undertaking, given that she was one of sixty hostesses and the best recruits were usually assigned to juniors and seniors. But when it came to recruiting, Earps was more competitive than most of the athletes Tennessee pursued, never mind her fellow hostesses.

"I would keep talking to a guy to get him to come," Earps said. "If texting was all we had to do, we did it. That was my mind-set. Let them think they have a chance with you once they get to school here. But in reality they don't."

Earps never had any interest in an intimate relationship with a football recruit. But she had no qualms about flirting. That was just part of the territory. "We are a few years older than these players," Earps said. "At that age that is a pretty substantial difference. They are juniors and seniors in high school. We are juniors and seniors in college. The thought of having a relationship with an older woman is appealing. But it never happened."

Earps stood out in her first year working with Fulmer and his staff. Recruits enjoyed their time with her, and she said the coaching staff told her they loved her work ethic. As a result, her peers elected her captain of Orange Pride. On top of that, the athletic department offered her a job as a student assistant helping out with recruiting. She was paid $7.50 an hour and assigned to work exclusively with the football team. Her office—which she shared with another student assistant—was down the hall from the coaching staff. She spent roughly twenty hours a week in the football complex. On weekends she continued as a hostess.

After going 5-7 in 2008, Fulmer was fired. On December 1, 2008, athletic director Mike Hamilton convened a press conference to announce the hiring of Oakland Raiders head coach Lane Kiffin.

"When it was all said and done, we felt like Lane Kiffin was a perfect fit for Tennessee," Hamilton told the audience. "He's energetic, charismatic, consumed with recruiting and has had a lifelong love affair with football."

Hamilton wasn't exaggerating when he said Kiffin was consumed with recruiting. Prior to joining the Raiders, Kiffin had been the offensive coordinator and recruiting coordinator on Pete Carroll's staff at USC for three years. In all three years, USC had the No. 1–ranked recruiting class in college football.

Hamilton introduced Kiffin to cheers. Kiffin wasted no time talking about where he planned to put his focus. "We will go everywhere to find the best players in the United States," he said. "We've got to find the best players, and we've got to get them to come to the University of Tennessee so we can do this thing and make a run for a long, long time."

After the press conference, Kiffin got on a plane and flew to Memphis to meet with a top recruit.

But it didn't take long for Earps to meet Kiffin. Given her personality and his enthusiasm to utilize Orange Pride, they hit it off right away. Kiffin and his staff were immersed in trying to commit recruits before the fast-approaching February 4, 2009, signing day. As captain of Orange Pride, Earps ended up working overtime on a flurry of official visits that took place in January. She became the go-to hostess for the top prospects that Kiffin and his staff were pursuing.

"Coach Kiffin was influential in the decision-making process for which woman is going to host a recruit," Earps said. "I got more official visits. And that was my ultimate goal."

The effort was a big success. Most notably, Kiffin and his staff convinced one of the top high school players in the country—Nu'Keese Richardson, a receiver from Florida with 4.4 speed in the forty—to break his commitment to the reigning national champion, Florida, and sign with Tennessee. On February 5, 2009, Kiffin talked about his first recruiting class with a group of nearly a thousand Tennessee boosters assembled at the Knoxville Convention Center. In his remarks he bragged about landing Richardson. In the process, he accused Florida's Urban Meyer of high-pressure tactics that crossed the line.

"This is a recruiting violation, and I'm gonna turn Florida in right here in front of you," Kiffin told the audience. "But while Nu'Keese was here on campus, his phone kept ringing. So one of our coaches said, 'Who's that?' And he looks at the phone and said, 'Urban Meyer.' Just so you know, when a recruit's on another campus, you can't call a recruit on another campus. But I love the fact that Urban had to cheat and still didn't get him."

The Tennessee boosters roared with laughter.

But Florida's athletic director, Jeremy Foley, was livid and demanded an apology. The SEC's commissioner, Mike Slive, not a man to be trifled with, didn't appreciate Kiffin's brash accusation either. Within hours Slive issued a public statement reprimanding Kiffin.

"Coach Kiffin has violated the Southeastern Conference code of ethics," Slive said. The bylaw "clearly states that coaches and administrators shall refrain from directed public criticism of other member institutions, their staffs or players . . . The phone call to which Coach Kiffin referred to in his public comments is not a violation of SEC or NCAA rules. We expect our coaches to have an understanding and knowledge of conference and NCAA rules."

Kiffin ended up apologizing less than twelve hours after accusing Meyer. But the Kiffin–Meyer flap made headlines for days, diverting attention from a much bigger recruiting battle that Kiffin was waging behind the scenes. The No. 1 recruit in the country at that time was running back Bryce Brown, a high school senior out of Wichita, Kansas. Virtually every recruiting service rated him as the best high school football player in America. As a junior, Brown had verbally committed to the University of Miami. It was believed to be a foregone conclusion that he would sign his letter of intent, officially committing to the Hurricanes, on National Signing Day. But at the last minute, Brown announced he would delay signing until

March 16, 2009. He also announced five new finalists in addition to Miami: LSU, Oregon, USC, Kansas State and Tennessee.

Brown's official visit to Tennessee took place on Valentine's Day and Kiffin asked Lacey Earps to be Brown's escort. "I was flattered," Earps said. "Official visits were the ultimate goal in Orange Pride. And Bryce was the No. 1 recruit in the country."

Earps was twenty-one at the time. Brown was seventeen. That weekend, she took him to a Tennessee men's basketball game against Vanderbilt. Afterward, they went to see the action movie *Taken*. Then Earps took him out for ice cream. They were together virtually the entire weekend.

The moment Brown returned home to Wichita, he and Earps started communicating daily during the period leading up to his decision day in mid-March. "I kept in contact with him the whole time," Earps said. "We Skyped. We texted a lot. We talked on the phone. Talked on Facebook."

One night Earps even stayed up until 4:00 a.m. Skyping with Brown. "We didn't have a relationship, but we were getting close," Earps said. "Actually, as I was recruiting him, maybe I did lead him on a little bit. Bryce wanted me to be single. It was more attractive to the guys if you are single."

In the vernacular of recruiting, "single" means a hostess isn't in a relationship with another player. The prospect of a long-term relationship with a hostess can be a powerful lure, one that hostesses are eager to perpetuate.

Brown notified Kiffin that he planned to return to Knoxville on March 13 for a follow-up visit, just three days before announcing his choice. Determined to close the deal with Brown while he was in Knoxville, Kiffin approached Earps and asked if he could speak with her. First he informed her that Brown was coming back to campus—a fact she knew before he did. Then Kiffin asked Earps for some help.

"I asked him what he wanted to do," Kiffin told Earps. "He said, 'Coach, all I want to do is hang out with Lacey.' So will you take him out?"

Earps agreed.

Then Kiffin gave her some money.

"I went into his office, and he handed me $40," Earps said. "It was enough to go to the movies and get ice cream."

Under NCAA rules, it was a violation to pay for recruits' entertainment and food on unofficial visits. But Earps didn't think much of being handed a few bucks for a night out. Kiffin was the head coach and certainly knew the rules. Besides, it wasn't the first time that members of Orange Pride had been given money by members of Kiffin's staff. On more than one occasion, coaches gave hostesses money for recruiting parties. Earps was personally handed $100 on one occasion and $200 on another. "I was given money by the coaches to get things for the party," Earps said. "The coaches aren't stupid. It's not like they didn't know what we were using the money for."

On March 13, Brown returned to Knoxville, and Earps accompanied him to a football scrimmage in Neyland Stadium. Afterward she took him to the movies. Then they went to Marble Slab Creamery, a popular ice cream shop at Market Square. It was another great weekend.

Two days after returning home, Brown held a press conference at the Kansas Sports Hall of Fame, where he announced he would attend Tennessee. "I feel that's the school that's gonna prepare me the best to go to the next level," he said.

"I had a big role in recruiting Bryce Brown," Earps said. "I was an influential part of his decision."

The press didn't pick up on Earps's role. But Kiffin's staff certainly did. After Bryce Brown signed with Tennessee, Earps got a new nickname. One afternoon Condredge Holloway, the director of student-athlete relations and lettermen, approached her. In the early 1970s, Holloway became the first African-American quarterback to play in the SEC. He was a legend around Knoxville. Earps knew and respected him. She was taking in a Tennessee practice when Holloway approached her.

"You know what you remind me of?" Holloway said.

She just looked at him.

"*The Closer*," he said.

"What do you mean?"

"Haven't you ever seen the TV show *The Closer*?"

Earps was confused. Holloway then described the television crime drama that starred Kyra Sedgwick as a tough LAPD interrogator with a knack for obtaining confessions that result in convictions. "She goes in and closes the case," Holloway told Earps. "Nobody can figure something out and they bring her in. She's the closer."

It was intended as a compliment, and that's exactly how Earps took it. The nickname stuck. From that day on, every coach and every member of Orange Pride knew Earps as The Closer.

When Bryce Brown committed to the Vols, Charlotte "Charli" Henry was a five-foot-six Tennessee sophomore with brown eyes and shoulder-length dark brown hair. She had grown up in a small town in West Tennessee famous for its Ripley tomatoes. One of her best childhood memories was spending Saturday afternoons watching Tennessee football games with her father. It was the Peyton Manning era, and Henry decided back then that one day she wanted to be a member of Orange Pride. In the spring of 2009—right after Lacey Earps officially took over as the captain—she got her chance. Henry was one of two hundred girls who applied for the twenty openings.

Beautiful and smart (her GPA was 3.77), Henry shone in her initial group interview, easily answering questions about UT history, naming the athletic director and head football coach and repeating her favorite UT chant. She got called back for a more rigorous individual interview with an athletic department official and two senior members of Orange Pride.

To make a good impression, Henry went to Banana Republic, where she purchased a baby-blue top, chocolate-brown pants, a big brown belt and some hot-pink heels. When she went to the interview, she also made sure to wear her pearls. The interview lasted thirty minutes. Her final question was whether she had ever quit anything. Henry had played volleyball and tennis in high school. Academically, she finished in the top 10 percent of her class. A classic overachiever, she couldn't think of any time when she had given up. "I'm a really honest person," she said. "I honestly said that I had not."

A month later, the list of twenty girls who had been chosen to join Orange Pride for Lane Kiffin's first season was posted outside the admissions office. The make-or-break tension felt just like trying out for an athletic team. Nervous, Henry ran her finger down the list. Her name was on it.

Orientation began immediately. There were packets to read and endless meetings with experienced hostesses and school officials. They suggested topics of conversation with recruits (Rule No. 1: Do not talk about the weather); how to conduct a campus tour; the importance of keeping a calendar; and instructions on how to dress, apply makeup and do their hair. In the ever-important quest to land top recruits, the athletic department wanted these girls to look as attractive as possible. There were also sessions on NCAA rules governing recruiting.

The hardest part for Henry was remembering the names and titles of all the coaches on Lane Kiffin's staff. To get them all down, she pinned each coach's name and title to a bulletin board above the desk in her bedroom. "I would study it every night before I went to bed," Henry said. "I wanted to know exactly who these coaches were because when an athlete comes in—especially a top recruit, like a potential quarterback—the quarterback coach would come in and talk with them. So I had to know their names."

Henry was a quick study. By the start of the 2009 season, she had found her groove with recruits. "I had no problem making these guys feel at home," Henry said. "There was flirting. Your goal or your job is to put all your attention on your recruit when he's there. The point of all this is no matter what the NCAA regulation is, when you have an official recruit that is torn between, say, Florida and Tennessee, your relationship is not to start and stop at the beginning of a football game. It just doesn't work like that."

By the start of the 2009 season, Tennessee had turned its attention to the top high school running back in the 2010 class—Marcus Lattimore from James F. Byrnes High School in Duncan, South Carolina. At the same time, Tennessee was after two of Lattimore's teammates, defensive stars Brandon Willis and Corey Miller. Both had attended a summer football camp at Tennessee in June 2009. Earps and another Orange Pride hostess, Dahra Johnson, met Willis and Miller at the camp. Earps and Johnson had become virtually inseparable. Johnson was the other member of Orange Pride who was offered a job in the football office. While Earps and Johnson were hanging out with Willis and Miller at the summer camp, Earps observed that one of the players had three championship rings hanging from his necklace. When she pointed that out, he responded, "You should come see us play sometime."

Earps and Johnson said they might just do that.

"Our job was to flirt with them, to be honest," said Earps. "So we said, 'Yeah, yeah, we'll come see you play.'"

But Earps and Johnson weren't serious about driving more than two hundred miles to Duncan, South Carolina, to watch a high school football game. They did, however, stay in regular contact with Willis and Miller through social media, building an online relationship much as Earps had done with Brown. By the third week of the 2009 season, the communication had intensified to a point where Earps felt as if both players were going to commit to Tennessee. They planned to visit campus on an unofficial visit on September 26 to watch the Vols play Ohio.

But the night before—a Friday—Byrnes had a home game. Willis and Miller wanted Earps and Johnson to attend. That Thursday night, Earps Skyped with one of the players until 4:00 a.m. The last thing he said to her was "Please come."

Earps didn't rule out the possibility. But after only a few hours of sleep, she was exhausted and had no desire to trek more than three hours to Byrnes. Johnson agreed. It wasn't worth the effort.

But when Earps and Johnson showed up for work at the football complex later that afternoon, Kiffin and his staff were having a luncheon. Earps and Johnson were invited. When they entered the room, Kiffin made an impromptu announcement: "These girls are going to Byrnes today."

The coaching staff, led by Kiffin, broke into applause.

"I guess I don't have a choice," Earps thought. "I'm going to Byrnes."

Johnson agreed—now they had to go.

"At this point I wasn't planning on going," Earps said. "I was exhausted. I had pulled an all-nighter. So this was not on the top of my list. But when Lane said, 'These girls are going to Byrnes,' I didn't want to look bad."

Earps and Johnson spent the early afternoon in the football office using colored chalk and poster board to make signs to hold up at the game. One said COME TO TENNESSEE. Another read MILLER & WILLIS HAVE OUR HEARTS. Numerous assistant coaches complimented them on their artistic touch. And at one point, Coach David Reaves, a brother-in-law to Kiffin who was in charge of recruiting in South Carolina, gave them some gas money—$40—for the trip. After Earps put on an orange outfit, the girls set out for Duncan, South Carolina, arriving just before kickoff.

Byrnes won big that night. But Earps and Johnson stole the show with their colorful signs and eye-catching outfits. The mother of one player called them "dolls" and asked to snap some pictures after the game. Earps and Johnson held up one of their signs and posed with Miller and Willis. *Sports Illustrated* senior writer Andy Staples, who had gone to the game to watch Lattimore, also snapped a picture. He had no idea that Earps and Johnson were from Tennessee and were part of Orange Pride.

Earps and Johnson made such a good impression that the father of one player invited them to spend the night with his family. But the Byrnes team mother stepped in. "Look," she told Earps and Johnson, "you girls need to get a hotel tonight and get out of town in the morning."

"If only Lane had given me his credit card," Earps joked.

The team mother didn't laugh. Instead, she led the girls to a local hotel and paid for their room. The following morning Earps and Johnson trekked back to Knoxville. But before they got home, they heard from Coach Reaves. He told them that the Byrnes coach had called him and expressed concern about Tennessee hostesses being at the game.

"Reaves said that we were basically too obvious," Earps said. "But he told us that he denied knowing anything about it."

Earps was puzzled. "I thought, 'And you are just going to cover it up?' I just felt, well, if he's going to play dumb, so will I."

Nonetheless, it didn't sit well with Earps. It was as if they were trying to hide something. If that had been the point, they would not have held up signs saying come to Tennessee. Earps and Johnson didn't think they were doing anything wrong. If the coaches knew otherwise, why did they compliment the signs? And why give them gas money for the trip? And why did Kiffin encourage the whole thing in the first place at the team luncheon?

Later that night, Miller and Willis traveled to Knoxville for the Tennessee–Ohio game. Earps and Johnson met up with them on campus. And they continued to maintain steady contact with both recruits through social media. Both players committed to Tennessee midway through the season. By that point, the trip to Byrnes High seemed like old news. Besides, the program had a more urgent public relations mess on its hands.

On November 12, three of Kiffin's prized freshman recruits—including receiver Nu'Keese Richardson—were arrested by Knoxville police for felony attempted armed robbery outside a convenience store. One of the players approached a parked car, opened the driver's-side door, brandished a weapon and told the individual in the driver's seat, "Give me everything you have." The other player opened the rear passenger's-side door and told the occupant, "Give us everything you've got." A store security camera captured the entire incident. And police recovered a powered pellet gun from the car driven by the players. Richardson pleaded guilty to reduced charges. All three players were kicked off the team.

At the same time, coaches continued to recruit players of questionable character, which put increased pressure on the members of Orange Pride. At one point, one of the assistant coaches approached Earps with a particularly onerous request. "One recruit was coming into town, and one of the coaches actually asked me if I knew any girls that would 'show him a good time.'"

Earps was not naïve. She'd certainly heard stories about hostesses having sex with recruits. But intimacy with high school athletes was something she never considered and never witnessed. Nor did she appreciate seeing a coach actively on the hunt for a girl to go to bed with a recruit. "He wasn't expecting an Orange Pride hostess to do that," Earps said. "He was looking for other girls that might do that."

Still, the whole idea turned her off, and she put the coach in his place. "No, absolutely not," Earps told the coach.

Charli Henry said she was never outright asked to sleep with a player either. But the expectation of sex to lure high school recruits was something she felt almost immediately after she joined Orange Pride. "I am a competitive person," Henry said. "I did not want to be a mediocre recruiter. I wanted to be a top recruiter."

Henry felt compromised, the reality far from the television fantasy she admired growing up. "It's kinda like a Catch-22," she said. "You wear high heels and your blazer. You look your best. I could always see myself as one of those beautiful women on the football field. But when you get into it and you learn the real reason you dress like that, the real reason your pants are tight, it's just warped. That was the reality for me."

As the 2009 season wound down, Henry began to question the whole idea of using hostesses to help recruit. "These are high school boys," she said. "They have one thing on their mind. So if you can show them that if you're a UT football player, this is what you get . . .

"What I realized in my experience was that it wasn't really what I expected," she said. "It really altered my opinion on the whole thing. From the athletic department's perspective it didn't matter how the recruit got there. Whatever it took. A lot of people turned a blind eye. That was very unsettling to me.

"I could recruit, but I couldn't do what I was supposed to do, something that was ethically wrong to me in my mind. So at that point I was just disgusted, completely disgusted."

Henry decided she would not return to Orange Pride after the season ended.

———

Tennessee played its final regular-season game on November 28, defeating Kentucky 30–24. The win gave Tennessee a 7-5 record and earned the Vols an invitation to a bowl game against Virginia Tech. As soon as the regular season ended, Earps turned her attention to final exams. On December 8 she was studying in the library when she got a message over Facebook from a friend: "OMG—did you see article?" The message contained a link to a *New York Times* story: N.C.A.A. PUTS TENNESSEE'S RECRUITING UNDER SCRUTINY.

Earps opened the link and began reading: "The N.C.A.A. is conducting a wide-ranging investigation into the University of Tennessee's football recruiting practices, according to interviews with several prospects, their family members and high school administrators. A significant part of the investigation is focused on the use of recruiting hostesses who have become folk heroes on Tennessee Internet message boards for their ability to help lure top recruits."

The article centered on the trip to Byrnes High to recruit Willis and Miller. The article named the players but not the hostesses. "It is not clear whether the university sent the hostesses to visit the football players," the *Times* reported. The piece also mentioned the recruitment of Bryce Brown and made reference to a picture of him with an unnamed hostess (Earps) that had surfaced on a social media Web site.

Earps was horrified. "The story didn't name me, but I knew it was about me," she said.

Unable to concentrate, she packed up her laptop and left the library.

The university promptly issued a statement acknowledging an NCAA review and promising full cooperation. "We are concerned about the alleged activities of some members of the Orange Pride," the university said. "Both university and NCAA guidelines are a part of the Orange Pride's orientation and training. If those guidelines were violated, we will take appropriate action."

The next day, Corey Miller's father spoke to the *Knoxville News Sentinel.* "Nobody put these girls on these boys," Miller said. "It wasn't like they came to our boys. Our boys started talking to them."

Miller said he was unsure whether his son was dating one of the hostesses. "They became friends," the elder Miller said. "I know they talk an awful lot. I don't know if he calls it dating or not. I don't think there's anything wrong."

Miller may have intended to downplay the situation. But by that point the story had legs. After Kiffin had accused Urban Meyer of recruiting violations, the specter of his program being caught playing fast and loose with the rules was garnering national attention. It was a particularly explosive story in Knoxville. Later that day, Earps went to a local supermarket to pick up some groceries. While checking out, the clerk recognized her. "Hey," he called out, "it's her." He held up the sports section of the Knoxville paper.

Mortified, Earps hurried out of the store. "I was on the front page of the sports section," she said. "I thought my life was over. I felt like people were staring at me everywhere."

Earps returned to her apartment and locked the door, afraid to show her face in public. She didn't even come out to take her final exam. More than anything, she just wanted the situation to die down.

But it didn't. Three days after the *Times* story appeared, SI.com published the photograph that Andy Staples had taken of Earps and Johnson standing with Willis and Miller. "I did not know who the women were at the time," Staples said in his SI.com piece, "and did not put two and two together until the *Times* published its story."

The SI.com photograph instantly went viral. The next morning Earps got a call from Lane Kiffin. "I didn't answer, because it was early in the morning," Earps said. "He left a message: 'Hey, Lacey, it's Coach Kiffin.' He said, 'This will pass. My dad has always told me to give it the forty-eight-hour rule. The media will talk about it for forty-eight hours, and then it will pass. It will go away.'"

Earps hoped Kiffin was right. "I just remember feeling the coaches are going to help us," she said. "Everything is going to be okay."

Lacey Earps never heard another word from Lane Kiffin. But just before Christmas, assistant athletic director David Blackburn called her and Dahra Johnson into his office. "I'm going to have to temporarily suspend you until this investigation is over," he told them.

The girls were crushed. "He asked me not to have contact with recruits," Earps said. "I couldn't work anymore."

Earps couldn't help feeling as if she'd been thrown under the bus.

"Orange Pride was something I loved," Earps said. "I never did anything to be ashamed of. I just wish I had never gone to Byrnes. And I would have never done that without being encouraged. That is the main reason I did go. I wasn't planning on going. Then I got talked into it. So I went."

A week after Earps and Johnson lost their jobs, Tennessee lost to Virginia Tech 37–14 in the Chick-fil-A Bowl, capping off a 7-6 season that included close losses to Alabama and top-ranked Florida. Kiffin pledged that he and his staff were just getting started. But on January 10, USC's head coach, Pete Carroll, announced he was jumping to the NFL to coach the Seattle Seahawks. Two days later, Kiffin accepted an offer to become the Trojans' new head coach.

Eight freshman recruits—the best players Kiffin and his staff had recruited—had just arrived on campus and enrolled in classes in order to be eligible to participate in spring practice. When Kiffin told them and the rest of his team that he was leaving, they were confused and angry. By signing letters of intent, they were not eligible to simply transfer to another school.

On the evening of January 12, Kiffin held a press conference at the Neyland-Thompson Sports Center. "This was not an easy decision," he said. "This is something that happens very quick. We've been here fourteen months, and the support has been unbelievable here. I really believe the only place I would have left here to go was . . . Southern California."

His remarks lasted fifty-nine seconds. He did not take questions.

As he turned to leave, a reporter shouted, "What does this mean for recruiting, Lane?"

Kiffin just walked off.

The news didn't go over well on the Knoxville campus. Students rioted outside the sports center, burning mattresses and trying to block Kiffin from leaving the building. Campus police had to drive him home, and police security had to be positioned around his home that night.

Suddenly the program was in shambles. Bryce Brown, after rushing for 460 yards as a freshman, transferred to Kansas State. Byrnes recruit Brandon Willis de-committed and signed with North Carolina instead.

As Kiffin and players he had recruited left town, NCAA investigators showed up. The university contacted Earps and Johnson, requesting that they turn over their cell phone records. It also informed the girls that an NCAA investigator wanted to talk with them.

Earps knew one thing: The forty-eight-hour rule may have worked for Kiffin. But it wasn't working for her. She figured she'd better find a lawyer.

———

Alan Bean is a medical malpractice attorney in Nashville. His specialty is defending health-care providers in negligence cases. But he got an intriguing call at his law office around the time that Kiffin left Tennessee for USC. One of Bean's friends knew Lacey Earps. He asked Bean if he'd be willing to give her some legal advice. Bean said to have Earps call him directly. He'd be happy to help her.

Bean, twenty-seven, had no experience with sports law or NCAA regulations. He'd been practicing law for only three years at that point. The first thing he told Earps was that he was no F. Lee Bailey. But the Vanderbilt Law grad had been following the so-called Tennessee recruiting scandal in the news. On the surface he thought Earps was caught in a situation similar to what nurses experience when a hospital gets sued. In multimillion-dollar malpractice cases, the real targets are hospital executives and physicians. They are the ones who set policy and prescribe treatment. Nurses, on the other hand, are on the low end of the totem pole, so to speak. Nonetheless, they get named in lawsuits and are served court papers along with everyone else. Bean figured that hostesses were a lot like nurses—caught up in an NCAA probe where the true target was Lane Kiffin and his staff, not members of Orange Pride.

Earps was immediately comfortable with Bean. At his invitation, she gave him a synopsis of what she had done as a hostess. She went into great detail with respect to the trip she took to Byrnes High. As he listened, Bean took notes. By the end of the session, he had a pretty good sense of what had transpired. "When it became clear there was an investigation going on, the coaches were quick to distance themselves from the students who had helped in that office," Bean said. "It didn't take them very long to say we didn't have anything to do with this. As opposed to defending the hostesses, the coaches pushed them to the front and suggested that students working under their control were responsible for all of this."

Bean was a huge Tennessee football fan. But he was hardly surprised that the coaches were letting the hostesses take the heat. "Coaches by nature are opportunistic, and I don't think that's a trait you can turn off," he said.

Earps asked Bean what to do about the university's request to see her phone records. Bean explained that neither the university nor the NCAA could compel her to surrender her phone records. But based on her story, he determined that Earps had done nothing wrong and had nothing to hide. All her phone records showed was that she made lots of calls to recruits. That didn't violate any NCAA rules. He advised her to cooperate fully with the NCAA.

Earps told Bean that her friend Dahra Johnson needed a lawyer, too. Bean agreed to represent both girls pro bono. One of his first items of business was to contact the NCAA investigator handling the Tennessee case.

Joyce Thompson had been out of law school for only three years when she joined the NCAA enforcement staff in 2002. But by the time the NCAA commenced its review of the Tennessee football program under Lane Kiffin, Thompson had become famous. In the motion picture *The Blind Side*—released in November 2009, just as the NCAA opened its inquiry into Tennessee's program—actress Sharon Morris plays the hard-nosed NCAA investigator who looks into whether Michael Oher—the main character—violated any recruiting rules when he signed his letter of intent to attend Mississippi. In one of the film's most memorable scenes, Sandra Bullock (playing Oher's adoptive mother) isn't allowed to sit in on an interview that Thompson conducts with Oher.

But in real life, Thompson's reputation was that of a personable, understanding professional. "Because of my background as a litigator, I expected her to be adversarial," Bean said. "But she wasn't. Joyce was open and pleasant."

Bean opened up to Thompson about the one thing about the case that angered him the most. Earps was taking a beating online. "Lacey had her picture plastered on the Internet," Bean said. "And she was the subject of message board topics being discussed in ways that no one would ever want their mother, daughter or sister described. Some of the stuff being said about her was just blatant defamation of character."

Bean even considered taking legal action against a few Web sites. He told Thompson that none of these rumors and sexual innuendos were true. Earps was willing to submit to questioning. But he didn't want her humiliated by inappropriate questions that dignified the lies being spread on the Internet. "I told Joyce that that issue concerned me a great deal and that I didn't want any questions about that," Bean said.

Thompson promised to tread lightly.

———

On March 16, 2010, Bean accompanied Earps and Johnson to the Andy Holt Tower on the UT campus. Before they sat down to face questioning by Joyce Thompson and Michael Glazier, outside counsel for the University of Tennessee, Bean gave his clients some simple advice: "Just answer the questions and tell the truth."

Nervous, Earps had no interest in lying. But due to her proximity to Kiffin and his staff, she had been privy to information about recruiting practices that other hostesses—not to mention the Tennessee administration—were not aware of. The last thing she wanted to do was implicate people.

"I didn't want to get anyone in trouble," Earps said. "Going in, I felt like I was being blamed for all of this. But I had a close relationship with the coaches and the staff. I didn't want to get them in trouble."

At the outset, Thompson showed Earps the picture that Andy Staples had taken during the recruiting visit to Byrnes High. "Is that you in this picture?" Thompson asked.

"Yes, it is," Earps said.

Then Thompson showed Earps another picture. This one appeared to depict Lane Kiffin at a party in Knoxville. He was standing next to a platinum blond woman who appeared to be in her early twenties.

"Can you tell me where this photo was taken?" Thompson said.

"Ah, that's not me," Earps said.

Thompson then asked Earps a series of questions pertaining to the trip she and Johnson took to Byrnes High. Earps told her the same thing she had told Bean: they went because they were encouraged to go by the coaches. The girls also admitted that they had received gas money from Coach Reaves.

Earps summed up what she told the NCAA. "The only inappropriate thing we did was lead on seventeen- and eighteen-year-old guys just to get them to come to the school," she said. "We are not the only ones who do that. That goes on with hostesses at lots of schools. And no one tells us to do that. We just did it."

Earps and Johnson never said anything to implicate Kiffin or his staff. At the same time, the NCAA never asked them about the money Kiffin had given Earps when Bryce Brown came to campus on an unofficial visit. Nor were there questions about the money that Kiffin's staff had given hostesses to put on parties for recruits. The NCAA simply didn't know about those things. Bean had instructed his clients to answer truthfully whatever was asked while refraining from offering information that went beyond the scope of the questions.

"I think that one of the systemic problems is that the NCAA and the enforcement staff doesn't have the resources or the people to do the enforcement side," Bean said. "They couldn't investigate this stuff."

Months after interviewing Earps and Johnson, the NCAA determined that the Tennessee football program committed secondary violations consisting of impermissible phone calls to recruits by coaches and inappropriate contact with recruits by more than one member of Orange Pride. In its Public Infractions Report on the University of Tennessee issued on November 16, 2012, the NCAA said, "The pattern of recruiting violations committed by the former football staff during its short tenure at the institution was, as stated in Infractions Report No. 342, troubling to the committee." The penalty was a reduction in phone calls to recruits and a ban on recruiting at one high school (Byrnes) for nine months.

———

Lacey Earps never got her job back at Tennessee. After graduating with a degree in business, she left the state and took a job in the insurance industry. She remained loyal to the university and Orange Pride. She just wished the university had contacted her at some point to say it didn't blame her for what happened on Lane Kiffin's watch. "I gave everything I had to the football program and the institution," she said.

Dahra Johnson also left Knoxville after graduating and entered the insurance industry. She also remained loyal to her alma mater and never spoke publicly about her experience.

After her sophomore year, Charlotte Henry transferred to the University of Memphis, where she earned a degree in journalism and public relations. She married, and she and her husband had a baby girl. Henry worked as a development coordinator for the mid-South chapter of the Make-A-Wish Foundation.

"This may sound so silly," she said, "but my experience with the Orange Pride really altered the way I thought of the university. And it altered it in a bad way. People there were crazy about sports. The reputation that Tennessee built was to bleed orange through and through. Integrity. Tradition. So when you get there and you're in it, the people that work there every day could care less about the colors they represent. It comes down to what's going to bring in the money.

"To be honest, people don't step back and say, 'At what cost?' Nothing came to be more important than winning football games."

3 THE BRAND

Going all in at Michigan

The Michigan–Alabama clash that kicked off the 2012 college football season was like a gigantic circus roaring to life. By Friday afternoon, August 31, the streets surrounding Cowboys Stadium, the billion-dollar state-of-the-art creation of Dallas Cowboys owner Jerry Jones crawled with cars flying favored-nation flags.

At 4:15 p.m., the University of Alabama arrived for a brief walk-through in three gleaming black Executive Coach buses escorted by a small squadron of motorcycle cops. Nick Saban led the procession of players. Looking sharp in a lightweight sport coat and contrasting slacks, he moved with a practiced economy into the locker room. He then headed onto the field, where Kirk Herbstreit and Brent Musburger, hoping for a few last-minute nuggets before their prime-time broadcast the next night on ABC, offered a congenial greeting. By now several of Saban's players, dressed in coats and ties, milled about, staring up at the mammoth video board, an alien auditory planet forty yards across, looming above the middle of the field. Pictures were taken. Offensive linemen bent down in three-point stances and tested the artificial turf.

Michigan's associate athletic director, Mike Vollmar, checked his watch for what seemed to be about the hundredth time in the last half hour. His Wolverines were running fifteen minutes behind schedule, and the director of football operations wore the look of a husband whose wife was a week overdue.

"We'll make it up, we'll make it up, we'll make it up," Vollmar said. His walkie-talkie crackled with an arrival update. He left to meet the buses.

Michigan had been priming for this moment for months. Ten days earlier, in Ann Arbor, the team had practiced with game-day intensity, three pristine outdoor fields humming with a relentless, unforgiving pace. A series of stations had been set up all over the fields—cone drills, fumble drills, long snapping. Coaches were all over players for the least bit of dogging or poor technique.

All the while, head coach Brady Hoke barreled around the place as if his blue *M* shorts were on fire, his sharp, insistent whistle piercing the air. Contact was frequent and often unrestrained: at one point, a smashmouth linebacker–running back tackling drill ran the width of one field; then first-team offense lined up against first-team D, half a dozen coaches within spitting distance of the line of scrimmage, coaching up the pitch even higher. When practice finally ended, linemen peeled off helmets, pads, shoes and socks and plunged into jumbo-sized tubs full of ice for a welcome, if brief, relief.

Unlike Alabama, when the Wolverines finally hit the field in Texas, the fifty-three-year-old Hoke had them in football mode—jerseys, shorts and helmets—running through plays. Deafening crowd noise pumped into the empty stadium. Coaches flashed signals from the sidelines. Hoke charged around like a kid at Christmas—playing quarterback one play, defensive tackle the next, sprinting fifty yards downfield on kickoff coverage. Giving off a vibe that seemed to say, Alabama, Sha-la-bama, we're ready to tee it up right now.

Few knew, but Hoke was suffering from a bad case of the flu.

"Sometimes," he would later say, "you just have to fake it."

In a profession oozing with false promises and dime-store sincerity, Hoke came across as anything but a phony. Instead, he seemed like a genuine guy who wore his emotions on his sleeve, who *cared* and who related to his players. He loved to tell recruits how his two big goals in college at Ball State were to play football and to drink every beer in Muncie, Indiana. In between those pastimes Hoke studied criminal justice and worked as an intern with the federal probation and parole office. After President Reagan was shot in 1981, he dreamed of becoming a Secret Service agent.

Instead, through a friend, he gravitated toward coaching. Working with parolees and wanting to protect presidents, he discovered, wasn't all that different from trying to help kids. Coaches at Ball State had straightened him out. He could do the same. Teaching high school athletes the importance of honoring your name, family and school.

In 1983, when Hoke was an assistant coach at Grand Valley State University in Michigan, he and his wife, Laura, snuck into an empty Michigan Stadium. They walked out of the tunnel onto the field. *This* is where I want to coach, Brady told her. And so he set out to accomplish his goal, spending eight years as an assistant under Gary Moeller and Lloyd Carr, before resurrecting the football programs at his alma mater and San Diego State.

———

In January 2011, Michigan's athletic director, Dave Brandon, found himself in the market for a new head football coach. The previous three seasons under Rich Rodriguez had dissolved into a frustrating snarl of missed opportunities that included an embarrassing NCAA investigation into excessive off-season workouts (later found to be minimal) and the worst defensive season in the 131-year history of the program. An athletic department known for its efficiency, stability and integrity was headed the wrong way in far too many areas. Worse, the game atmosphere had become as predictable as the fight song. The largest living alumni base in the world—at 450,000—was restless. Decades of fan loyalty had been put to the test.

Adding to the pressure was the fact U-M was truly a Big House divided on the man to replace Rodriguez. One alumni group pressed Brandon to reach into the past and hire former Wolverines quarterback Jim Harbaugh, then the head coach at Stanford; another group pulled for LSU's head coach, Les Miles, a former Michigan assistant. Hoke was seen as a long shot at best.

———

Prior to taking the Michigan athletic director job in March 2010, Brandon had served as chairman and CEO of Domino's Pizza for eleven years. He had been well schooled in the ingredients of marketing success, including a stint with the consumer giant Procter & Gamble. But he was a Michigan man through and through. A star at Michigan's South Lyon High School, he'd earned a scholarship at quarterback to U-M in 1970 but ended up playing sparingly as a tight end and defensive end under legendary head coach Bo Schembechler. His reward for sticking it out: three Big Ten championship rings—of which Brandon was immensely proud—and an enduring father-son relationship with Schembechler, a towering figure in Michigan legend and lore, a coach who believed, above all, in "The Team ... The Team ... The Team."

"One of the things I was looking for [in a head coach] was, who can be the unifier?" Brandon said. "Who is going to see the program is bigger than any one person? Who can put their arms around this whole *community* and say, 'Let's win football games'?

"So I had this form I put together. Listed the twelve things I wanted to rate each [potential head] coach on. Basic stuff. Track record in recruiting, track record in turning around a program; I was looking for someone with a passion and propensity for playing defense. Fund-raising, NCAA record, that sort of thing."

In Brandon's scoring system, candidates were ranked in each category on a scale of 1 to 10. When he sat down with Hoke, the coach was hot off the rebuilding of struggling San Diego State. Still, Hoke carried an under-.500 record as a head coach.

Brandon had never met the SDSU coach, so he allotted a couple of hours for the interview. Hoke went on about Michigan's unique culture, its storied football tradition (the most wins in college football history), iconic winged helmet and eleven national championships. He said he wanted to build a team that honored the past—tough, hard-nosed, competitive kids who loved the school and got chills running out of the tunnel.

By the time Hoke shook Brandon's hand and said good-bye, five hours had passed.

At that point Brandon pulled out his form, went to work and tallied up Hoke's score.

"I looked at the number, and I said, 'This can't be right, I added it wrong.' So I added it again," he said. "Then I took out a calculator and added it one more time because I thought I had miscalculated. The number was *so much larger* than anybody else I had met and, frankly, anyone else I thought I was going to meet. I just looked at it and said, 'Wow.'"

Still, Brandon knew he could ill afford to make a mistake. For an athletic director today there is no more important hire than that of a head football coach. Mess up and bowl and television revenue begin to dry up, donations drop, the entertainment and merchandising dollars find other outlets.

"You're dead," Brandon said.

———

At 9:00 a.m. on January 11, 2011, Michigan held a press conference to announce its new head football coach.

"I must have got four hundred e-mails telling me what an idiot I was," said Brandon.

Then Brady Hoke, he of the teddy-bear body and gravel-dusted voice, stepped up to the microphone. He said he would have walked from San Diego to Ann Arbor for the job. He spoke of "the game" and the days until they could beat "Ohio." Such was his distaste he couldn't bring himself to say the word "State." The "Go Blue!" nation could hardly believe its ears.

Then, during the Q&A, someone asked whether Michigan was still an elite job.

Elite?

Hoke's answer—as unrehearsed as it was unapologetic—was destined to earn a place in school history. In one single, unforgettable phrase, he declared how much the state, the school, the pride and the program meant to him, to anyone born to—or in love with—the maize and blue.

"This is Michigan fergodsakes."

"That press conference happened," said Brandon, "and I got four hundred e-mails from people saying, 'Thank God. We got a Michigan guy back.'"

───────

It was going on seven o'clock inside Cowboys Stadium when the "This is Michigan fergodsakes" guy rallied his team in the middle of the field. Brandon looked on from a few feet away.

"Nobody gives us a chance," he said. "I've been watching TV all day, and nobody gives us a chance."

In less than twenty-four hours the steel-and-glass palace would be filled with more than ninety thousand fans, at least half decked out in maize and blue.

"Well," he said, "I think we do."

───────

"When I came into this job, I knew how the business of athletics worked," said Brandon, who spent eight years as a U-M regent. "What you don't understand about the job is the *intensity*. One of the reasons it's so intense is because it's so competitive, it's so important to me. You don't take this job for the money. You don't take this job because it's easy. You take this job because you believe in the purpose of what we have to do."

It was Friday before the 2012 spring game, and Brandon, long and lean with close-cropped hair, looked relaxed sitting around a small circular table in his office on the second floor in Weidenbach Hall. An American flag fluttered in the breeze outside a large glass window overlooking the corner of Hoover and State. The place appeared to have been organized by a regiment of marines. Family photographs, a signed "Tribute to Bo" football and other personal mementos were neatly arranged around the room.

At heart, Brandon was a numbers guy. At the moment, in his mind, some of his most important were 109,901, 130, 29, 880, 15, 228, 5.8 and 22. The 109,901? Stadium capacity. Brandon had the biggest stadium in the country, complete with eighty-one luxury suites and thirty-nine hundred club seats. Michigan had led the nation in attendance for thirty-four of the last thirty-five years and needed to continue to fill the Big House to stay on top.

Why? Projected athletic department revenue was estimated to be around $130 million for the fiscal year 2012–13, second only to Texas. Given the full-throttle race his department was running, Brandon needed virtually every dollar to self-fund twenty-nine varsity sports and 880 student-athletes, including $18 million for financial aid, $44 million in department salaries and about $15 million in interest on the debt load associated with $228 million in upgrades and renovations to just the football and basketball facilities.

What kept Brandon—and so many other athletic directors up at night—was the razor-thin margin for error. Michigan's overall surplus for fiscal year 2012–13 was estimated to be just $5.8 million. The athletic department needed rivers of cash to stay out of the red. More than 70 percent of that money—or nearly $90 million—flowed from a single source.

"Michigan athletics cannot be successful if Michigan football does not lead our success, because the revenue it creates is what we live off of," said Brandon. "I think it was Mark Twain who said, 'If you put all your eggs in one basket, you better watch your basket.' That's our basket. It can't get sick. It can't falter."

That's where the number 22 came in. According to the latest NCAA figures, just 22 of the top 120 FBS schools had turned a profit in 2010–11. The average institutional debt of the other 100 or so schools was approaching $11 million each.

But Brandon didn't see it that way. He didn't see some unhealthy arms race behind the massive facilities boom sweeping across college athletics. Instead, he saw plain old American competition, with football as the economic driver to provide the coaching, the training and the academic and counseling support every one of his student-athletes deserved.

"I need that kid to get everything he or she deserves, just as if they're some star running back on the football team," he said. "Because if I'm not doing that, I'm doing a real disservice to that kid. Yeah, football is a huge driver for what we do, but we're here for a greater purpose."

At Michigan there was no question as to how that purpose would be accomplished. Plain and simple, it was Building the Brand. And nobody in college sports had proved more capable, more creative and, at times, more cutthroat in doing it than Brandon.

"Our plan is over there on the wall," Brandon said, pointing to the right side of his desk. "It's one sheet of paper."

Indeed, the Michigan Athletics Game Plan had been reduced to a single page, sectioned off into twelve distinct boxes. Running vertically, along the left side, were Long-Range Goals, Strategic Initiatives and SMAC Objectives, short for Specific, Measureable, Achievable, Compatible Objectives, a product of Brandon's days at P&G. Across the top of the page were four headings:

GROW IN EVERY WAY

BUILD THE BRAND

DRIVE CHANGE AND INNOVATE

TALENT AND CULTURE WINS

Listed inside the twelve boxes were forty-seven different goals and initiatives, such as "Achieve annual revenues of 160 plus million," "Own social media," "Encourage and reward risk-taking" and "Achieve #1 national ranking in licensing revenues and total football attendance in the same year."

For Brandon it all started with that block-*M* logo and what Michigan football meant to his alums. He was fearful of television's impact on game-day attendance. More than anything, he wanted that "wow" experience for his fans. So he upgraded the video boards, facilities and equipment inside Michigan Stadium, Crisler Arena and Yost Field House to the tune of $18 million. Out went the traditional pregame marching band music in the Big House in favor of a joint-jumping mix of hip-hop, rap and rock, as well as video board entertainment. Suddenly game balls were dropping out of the sky, delivered by "Rocket Man"; flyovers by stealth bombers kicked off games. Boring was out. Entertainment was in.

"We began to focus on what we call the 'driveway to driveway' experience," he explained. "Everything you see, from the pregame action on the field, to halftime, to postgame, to how we usher you out to your car and get you back to your driveway, every *step* of it, is going to drive your thinking about how many season tickets you want to buy next year. And what you'll pay for them. And my job is to get that ticket price as competitive as any other ticket price in the country."

At the spring game Brandon had barely slowed down—a nonstop sixteen-hour whirl of meet and greets, interviews and donor and sponsor work. Through it all, he moved with the natural ease and grace of an athlete. He honestly seemed to enjoy his game-day job—the endless shaking of hands, slapping of backs, chatting up alums, donors, sponsors and recruits.

Fresh off Hoke's spectacular first season—an 11-2 record complete with a win over Virginia Tech in the Sugar Bowl—about ninety former players had come back to the Big House to play in the alumni game. One of Michigan's greatest players, Desmond Howard, didn't suit up, but he was there, watching from the sideline, sporting dark jeans, white tennis shoes, shades and a black watch cap.

"I heard there was a Desmond sighting!" said Brandon with a laugh, wrapping his arms around the former Heisman Trophy winner.

"He's a game changer, that's what Dave Brandon is doing," said Howard a few minutes after the athletic director had moved on to shake yet another set of hands. "He understands the business side and he understands the athletic side and he understands the marketing side. He's a blend of all three."

As a self-described "left brain" guy, Brandon craved information, metrics and data. He barely slept and personally answered a couple hundred e-mails a day from friend and foe, often in exacting detail. His single-day record for meetings was seventeen, and his days often ran that long or more in hours.

"Truly a CEO, a man for our times, and I think it's great that someone with his acumen comes into our business," said Ben Sutton, president of IMG College, the sports business powerhouse that represented multimedia and marketing rights for more than forty BCS schools, including Michigan. "Our Michigan business, which, quite frankly, we've struggled with financially as a company, is getting between incrementally and exponentially better in large part due to the things he's done in and around the program."

When Brandon assumed ownership of Michigan athletics in the spring of 2010, about 275 people worked in the athletic department. Since that time about 80 had either voluntarily or not so voluntarily moved on. More than 300 people worked there now, but it was a completely different place—and pace. He lured Hunter Lochmann from his job as VP of marketing for the New York Knicks to be chief marketing officer for Michigan's athletic department. Twenty-two months into the job, Lochmann had redefined goals and cleaned up the school's sales, marketing, media, digital and social media platforms. Finding new ways, he said, to engage fans on Facebook and Twitter while optimizing ticket and merchandising sales on MGOBLUE.com, one of the top collegiate sites in the country.

"He just has this sixth sense," said Lochmann of Brandon. "In every conversation, in every meeting, in every phone call, I learn something. The way he analyzes a situation. He always has an idea for a solution or maybe a different question you didn't think of. Not many people have it."

"I tell our marketing team I want every Michigan home football game to feel like a Super Bowl," said Brandon.

By Saturday afternoon the lobby of the Sheraton Fort Worth was a nonstop parade of officially licensed products. Shirts, skirts and hats mixed with funky football fashion: crimson bow ties and madras shorts; cropped tops and cowboy boots; a hot maize mini ripped in all the right places.

Four hours before the early-evening kickoff, streets around Cowboys Stadium had a festive feel, the parking lots packed with tailgaters.

The good cheer extended inside the stadium as well. Fans from both teams bellied up, side by side, at bars soaking in the pregame festivities. The feeling was that of a giant indoor cocktail party, thirty thousand strong.

About forty minutes before kickoff, Hoke and his Wolverines took the field. The Michigan band blasted out "The Victors." Alabama's marching band matched the musical challenge as Saban and his Crimson Tide tore out of their tunnel.

As he stood on the field, Brandon's eyes told the story. *This* was the kind of memorable "wow" experience he lived—and loved—to create. Not the veiled corporate sell some NFL fans experienced on Sunday. No, on this night, college football was the greatest spectacle in sports. A regular-season record $10 million payout for both teams, an athletic director's dream.

"It's everything we could have hoped for," he said. "This game will sell merchandise. It will create interest for the tickets back home. It will hopefully get other networks bidding for these opportunities for us."

Brandon's first big "wow" had occurred on the night of September 10, 2011. When Brandon floated the idea of the first night game in U-M history, critics howled. Brandon listened and pushed ahead, breaking out new "throwback" jerseys for the occasion (on sale at an M shop near you). The team played its part, rewarding a record crowd of 114,804 with a thrilling, last-second 35–31 victory over Notre Dame. In yet another bold move, Brandon had authorized the purchase of ninety thousand yellow pom-poms. The resultant "Under the Lights" aerial photograph with those pom-poms pounding the air went up on the school's official site. Tens of thousands of people logged on and tried to pick themselves out of the crowd; the photograph hung like a trophy on the wall outside Brandon's office.

By the second series of the kickoff classic, Alabama had taken control of the game where it meant the most: in the trenches. Its massive, athletic offensive line—averaging six feet four inches and 320 pounds per man—simply overpowered Michigan's defensive front. What started out as a quick 7–0 lead methodically grew to 31–0 with less than five minutes left in the first half.

"Bigger, stronger, faster," said ESPN anchor Scott Van Pelt as he hustled down the 'Bama sideline. "I don't know what planet [D. J.] Fluker's from," he said, referring to Alabama's six-foot-six, 330-pound apartment building at right tackle, "but I know it's not one where you and I live."

The final score read 41–14. Michigan's electrifying quarterback, Denard Robinson, was bottled up all night. Michigan's offensive coordinator, Al Borges, seemed content to let him throw from the protection of the pocket, insulating, perhaps, his most important offensive asset for the long term. Afterward, Hoke took the long view. He saw the game as a "measuring stick" of how far his team still had to go to recruit the *athletes* needed to play with the big dogs.

But that was a problem for another day. On this night it was almost 11:00 central time when Michigan players began to filter out of the locker room and make their way to the team bus. They had been on the road for nearly thirty-six hours, at least five more to go before they would return to Ann Arbor around 5:00 a.m.

Brandon rode by in the passenger seat of a golf cart, his face set in stone. The stud left tackle Taylor Lewan limped by on an injured left knee. As the security line stretched out, Robinson and Hoke arrived after fulfilling their media obligations. During the game Robinson had gone down hard— twice: the first time following a helmet-to-helmet hit; the second time as the result of a desperate lunge for a failed first down that forced the star QB off the field. As he was helped to the locker room, thousands of Michigan fans stood as one and watched his every step.

But now there was Robinson, taking a bite out of a postgame sandwich while waiting to get on the bus—no worse, it appeared, for wear. His status was such he could have easily cut to the front and crashed out on the bus. Lord knows he deserved it. Instead, he waited like a walk-on, much like his head coach, who, in genuine sincerity, had found a spot in the middle of the line next to his wife: no special privileges; just a quiet, unmistakable message delivered by a coach living a life he loved.

Mike Vollmar looked over the scene. He had been the director of football operations for Saban at both Michigan State and Alabama before joining Hoke at Michigan. He knew more than a thing or two about big-time football. One of the biggest things, he said, was there was little or no time to wallow in the losses. Or savor the wins.

"Sunday is Sunday; Monday is Monday," said Vollmar. "You move on."

For Michigan that meant by the time the players arrived at Schembechler Hall early Sunday afternoon for treatment, weight lifting and meetings, BEAT AF signs had already been taped to the front door. Forget Alabama. Done and done. This week it was all about beating Air Force.

And beat the Falcons they did before more than 112,000 fans in the team's home opener. In doing so, Robinson broke out in vintage "Shoelace" style, amassing an incredible 426 yards in total offense (208 passing, 218 rushing), including 79-yard and 58-yard touchdown runs, the last one minus one of his famous untied shoes. It marked the fourth time in his career Robinson had passed the 200-yard mark in both categories in the same game, the most by any player in FBS history.

Still, the Falcons' unique triple-option attack gave Michigan fits, gashing its defense for 290 rushing yards and keeping the game on the line until the final two minutes, when a fourth-and-sixteen pass by Air Force came up empty, sealing a 31–25 win for the Wolverines. Brandon breathed a huge sigh of relief.

His day had officially begun about nine hours earlier, when he arrived at the stadium. "Good morning, are we ready to go?" he greeted some security personnel. Then he hopped into a golf cart and began his early-morning tour, checking everything from the cleanliness of the concession stands to the freshness of the cookies—"Hi, I'm with quality control"—to the color of the M&M's in the visiting athletic director's suite.

To his critics—and there was more than a chorus of those—the relentless nature of his search for fresh revenue—to build the brand—was hard to take. This was college *fergodsakes*, not the NBA. It seemed unseemly at times, charging for corporate events at the Big House, for school tours, the $6,000 wedding packages, the rising cost of season tickets and preferred-seat licenses.

Brandon didn't spend much time worrying about the naysayers. It was the cost of staying ahead, of "wow," the price mega-programs must pay for a seat at the table with Texas, Alabama, Georgia and Ohio State in the all-in, high-stakes game called college football.

Denard Robinson knew in the end that his senior season would not be judged by wins over Air Force or the mauling of UMass the following week. The true test of the quarterback's value to the team—to the athletic department—would come in the biggest games. Robinson all but disappeared against Alabama. The fourth game offered a chance at redemption— a Saturday night matchup in South Bend against Notre Dame.

But when the final gun sounded, Robinson's million-dollar smile was nowhere to be found. Instead, NBC cameras focused on a disconsolate twenty-two-year-old kid. The 13–6 loss would go down as the worst game of Robinson's career: four interceptions on four consecutive passes in the first half; a fumble on the Irish eight-yard line in the opening drive of the second; an all-around horror show of overthrown passes, missed reads and ill-timed mistakes. At the postgame presser Robinson issued an all-out apology to Michigan fans around the world.

"It won't happen no more," he said. "I'm going to be accountable for the rest of the season. I don't want to feel like this no more. In the 22 years I've been living, this is the most disappointed I've ever been in myself."

Like an inverted pyramid, the poker-game pressure to win in the mega-programs funneled down from athletic directors to coaches to players. No single athlete felt more of that pressure than Robinson. If Michigan football was the "front porch" of the university—and it was hard to argue otherwise—Hoke and Robinson were its welcoming committee.

With his shoulder-length dreads and infectious smile, Robinson was far and away the most recognizable—and popular—student on campus. He had met President Obama and LeBron James. His No. 16 game jersey was flying off the shelves and onto the backs of thousands of fans. A local comedian produced a hilarious music video titled "I Love You, Denard." Robinson had made a regional cover of *Sports Illustrated*'s College Football Preview issue as a leading candidate for the Heisman Trophy.

In fact, one could make the argument Robinson was far and away the MVP of college football, as in most *valuable* player to any single program in terms of dollars and cents. AJ McCarron at Alabama? Matt Barkley at USC? No way. Johnny Manziel? Not before the Alabama game. No, no school lived and died on the arm—and legs—of a single player more than Michigan did with Robinson.

The pressure was enormous. Robinson didn't like to talk about it, but he felt it. And the pressure was compounded by the unreal hours players were putting in. As much as the NCAA tried to monitor the hours spent on college football, there was no off-season, just a never-ending blur of conditioning and weight room workouts, meetings, physical therapy and training room treatment, practice, practice and more practice followed by film study and more practice, and don't forget travel and games.

"Oh yeah, it's a full-time job," said Robinson. "It's a grind. And it's a grind because you have to do this. Because those games you are going to face, it's going to take a toll on you."

Eventually, it did. After the dispiriting loss at Notre Dame, Michigan ran off three straight wins to up its record to 5-2, putting the Wolverines in the catbird seat for the Big Ten title and a trip to the Rose Bowl. Then, on the road at Nebraska, Robinson went down with a serious nerve injury to his right elbow. He never fully recovered. And as it turned out, despite Hoke's valiant effort, neither did his Wolverines. Partly due to his injury and partly due to the fact he was not perceived as a pure NFL quarterback, Robinson's draft position—at wide receiver—was projected no higher than third round and as low as sixth. (He would go in the fifth round to Jacksonville as a wide receiver.)

Michigan's final 2012 record turned out to be a disappointing 8-5, including a 33–28 loss to South Carolina in the final seconds of the Outback Bowl.

The Brand, however, had become virtually impossible to beat.

4 BIG MAN ON CAMPUS

A pretty awesome asset

When it comes to the cathedral of college football, seasoned travelers speak of pilgrimages to South Bend or Happy Valley when Father Joe held sway over his congregation. But when it comes to big money, there is just one church, one road leading in a single direction. To Austin and the University of Texas.

The UT football program is the mother ship of money, generating $103.8 million in revenue during the 2011–12 football season—nearly $20 million more than No. 2 Michigan. Even more impressive, it produced a reported $78 million in profit. Not $78 million in revenue—$78 million in profit.

To behold the nature of the machine at work, take a walk around Darrell K. Royal–Texas Memorial Stadium on game day or, better yet, on a quiet Sunday morning after a game. But give yourself some time. It takes a good half hour to circumnavigate the stadium alone, all 100,000 seats of it. The stone columns resembling hundred-year-old oaks only add to a percussive sense of size and strength.

Just inside an east-end entrance stands a statue of Royal, the certifiable Texas legend who died on November 7, 2012, at the age of eighty-eight. During his twenty years as head coach in Austin (1957–76) he won 167 games, three national championships (1963, 1969, 1970) and eleven Southwest Conference titles. The Sunday morning after his death, orange and red roses lay fading at the feet of his statue, the lone sound a state flag flapping in the breeze, clanging against a pole. A video board the size of a strip mall filled one end of the stadium. The day before, the Longhorns had honored Royal with, in part, moving videos on the giant screen. A white DKR logo was affixed to every player's helmet, and the marching band spelled out ROYAL during its halftime performance. The real tribute came on Texas's first offensive play—a razzle-dazzle pass out of Royal's fabled wishbone formation, players and coaches pointing to the sky following the forty-seven-yard gain. It marked the beginning of a textbook 33–7 blowout of Iowa State.

"A fitting way to honor him," said head coach Mack Brown after the game.

Fitting, too, that the statue right next to Royal's is that of Joe Jamail, as in Joe Jamail Field. Often referred to as the King of Torts, Jamail is regarded as the wealthiest practicing attorney in the country. His contingency fee alone for helping Pennzoil win a lawsuit against Texaco was reportedly in excess of $500 million. A Texas graduate, Jamail is beloved for his character and commitment to UT: the law school pavilion and the swimming center are named after him or his family, and the school has *two* statues erected in his honor on campus. He also happened to be Brown's personal attorney.

Ringing the stadium's upper level were the names and numbers of players who had carved their own legacy here—Bobby Layne 22, Tommy Nobis 60, Vince Young 10, Earl Campbell 20, Ricky Williams 34, Colt McCoy 12. Several were strung out below the Red McCombs Red Zone, courtesy of the San Antonio automotive magnate, co-founder of Clear Channel Communications and former owner of the San Antonio Spurs, Denver Nuggets and Minnesota Vikings. All along the stadium were names of other donors, who funded the field house and football complex, men with names like Tex and Doc, the loyalty and love for a football team running deep into their hearts. You need it, we build it. Like the time word got out Oklahoma might be sending some people to spy on practice and one donor was said to have ponied up $5 million on the spot to build an indoor facility.

To be a football star here has long provided an open invitation to enjoy the occasional company of such men—and women. Such largesse.

To be The Man here, well, that was something else entirely.

———

Texas had been The Man's final recruiting stop. Visits to two Big Ten schools had offered little more than what he had experienced in high school—standing around with a bunch of guys downing beers at somebody's house.

His first real taste of *recruiting* arrived on his official visit to Tennessee. It was there the unofficial SEC motto—"If you ain't cheatin', you ain't tryin'"—came into play. He had been flown into Knoxville on a private plane and ferried around town in a tricked-out van complete with flat-screen TVs playing continuous team highlights. A fellow blue-chip recruit that weekend wanted to keep anything and everything in sight—shoes, cleats, clothes, you name it. Tennessee officials had informed the future NFL All-Pro there was no need to worry; there would be a "big bag of things to take when you leave." And, oh, don't worry so much about going to class. If needed, they could take care of that as well.

As much fun as Tennessee turned out to be, it was Texas that set the standard for making an eighteen-year-old boy feel as if he were walking on air. "There was no hard sell," The Man remembered several years later. After the obligatory tour—only this time it was state-of-the-art facilities doing the talking—an assistant coach handed him a book. Inside was his personal rise to stardom mapped out in a four-year plan: play a bit as a freshman, start as a sophomore for a top ten team, Heisman Trophy candidate his third year with the team chasing a national title, then, win the Heisman his senior year while playing for a national championship. Sounded good to him.

And that was just football. The wining and dining had a Four Seasons feel, which just happened to be the host hotel. Friday night featured a visit to Coach Brown's house, where Mack worked his magic on the parents— "He could sell a Pinto to Donald Trump," said The Man—then dinner in a private room at the city's top restaurant. That's where he first met a few of the Angels, their female weekend hostesses, all smiles and creamy charm, the sexual tease heightened as they ditched the restaurant and the parents and headed to a Sixth Street bar. Forget the fact he was well underage at the time. He walked right in, no questions asked. Three-quarters of the team was already partying inside.

"That left a lasting impression," said The Man.

The energy of the place, he remembered, was off the hook: an intoxicating mix of alcohol, house music and hard-bodied girls, the sound system cutting out every half hour so the crowd could belt out—what else?—the Texas fight song.

His Angel that night was an African-American stunner. They didn't sleep together, but the message was sent, loud and clear: commit and there will be plenty of opportunities. Sure enough, he later learned firsthand, several of the Angels were sleeping with stars on the team.

Ah, sex, UT-style. After a huge showing in the spring game before his sophomore season, the girls came on to him in waves. "It would almost be you could pick the one you wanted to take home," he recalled. Some nights he simply doubled his pleasure—taking two back to his apartment.

By his junior year The Man was making national headlines, rolling up big numbers on the field and killing it in the campus haunts on Sixth. So he started to seek other action. He took to hitting the more "adult" clubs in

Austin. The women, many in their thirties, came on to him like the young ones—only more aggressive and less interested in small talk, more sophisticated and experienced. Plus, they had money.

Then things got really interesting. A teammate came home from one of the local strip clubs and handed him a phone number. The Man called the number. A stripper answered. They talked. She invited him to her upscale town house. He went on a weeknight. She answered the door wearing nothing but a robe. Moments later it was on the floor. She was in her twenties with dirty-blond hair, a doll-like face and a *Playboy* body.

"So do you want to fuck me now?" she whispered.

For the rest of his junior year The Man returned to her home regularly for sex with a woman far more sophisticated than any he met on the UT campus. She had more bling, too. She drove a fancy sports car, had plenty of cash and had a line to high-grade marijuana. She shared all of her toys with The Man.

"All through college it never ended," he said. "She was as cool as a girl could be. Pimped me out. Whatever I wanted—cash, a hundred here and there—she gave it to me. She let me drive her car whenever I wanted. If I wanted to smoke pot, she had that, too. Thinking back now, she was a pretty awesome asset."

These were the perks of being The Big Man on Campus—days focused on football, nights given to partying and sex.

———

Don King—no, not the boxing promoter—has been the king of the Austin strip club scene for thirty-five years. The Yellow Rose, Austin's first upscale "cabaret," was under his watchful eye for more than thirty years. On a Saturday afternoon in the fall of 2012, King was kicking back on the patio of a local sports bar, working on a perfectly executed afternoon buzz. Two of his best strip-club-owning buddies happened to be in town and were along for the ride. Over time what started out as a few icy drafts for King progressed to a carefully calibrated series of chilled vodka shots, fueling a natural, often hysterical, storytelling talent.

As he talked, King waved a cigar around with his right hand. His long gray-white hair was in a ponytail, a diamond stud in his left ear, a gold chain hanging from his neck. He wore jeans, flip-flops and an autographed Earl Campbell jersey. His car was just across the way—a burnt-orange Nissan 350Z complete with detachable steer horns built into the hood and an "Eyes of Texas" car horn that could be heard three blocks away.

"These kids would walk in gaga-eyed," King said of the Rose. "They're in one of the most famous titty bars in the world, and they're realizing if they go to Texas to play for UT, and we go into this place, we eat and drink for free and sit around VIP for free for the next four fucking years."

The Rose is still around today, 6500 block of Lamar, far from the prying eyes and maddening crowds of the downtown social scene. Low-slung, it sits between a liquor store and a collision repair shop, across the street from a tattoo joint. The decor leans toward rough cedar walls and maroon couches and booths. Most important, it has two corner VIP areas that became the home away from home for many a UT player.

"The players used to call it the office. They were going to the office," said King.

He started out in bars, working his way up to Austin's big live music scene and a club called Crazy Bob's, which night after night lived up to its name. "Three dollars at the door, five hours of happy hour, three for one, three full-sized drinks for the price of one. Two-dollar pitchers of beer. Three-dollar margaritas," recalled King. "It was crazy."

When Crazy Bob's went bust, King found work slinging drinks before managing a nasty little bandito biker hangout where strippers shared the billing with drugs, nightly fights and the Wednesday night special—the winning stub in the midnight ticket lottery earning a free massage, and negotiated happy ending, at the massage parlor next door. From there it was on to the Dollhouse. When it closed down, King moved to the Yellow Rose. That was 1981.

The thing about King was that right from the start the Rose had rules for football players. No underage drinking. None. Half-priced drinks when players turned twenty-one. Abuse the rules, act like an asshole—rip your shirt off and hop onstage to bump and grind with the girls, like one former Longhorn star—and you were headed to the office and a chat with Uncle Don.

"I told my waitresses and floor manager, don't let them drink, because I don't want the scandal," said King. "I don't ever want to challenge or ruin anyone's reputation." Down went another shot of chilled vodka. "It was safe for them," he said. "I wouldn't let anything happen to them. I would not let people come up to the tables and bother them. We'd treat them like VIPs, even though they didn't have money. But you know what? As soon as they graduated, that free ride was over. Full price."

For those who wore a Texas uniform on Saturday, the Rose was a gift that kept on giving—all the free soda and food you could eat, naked girls everywhere you looked. On any given Friday or Saturday night seventy of

King's finest dancers, culled from his "entertainment base" of three hundred girls, worked the floor. Single mothers, pros and more than a few UT honeys. A good six-hour shift left between $300 and $800 in their pockets, a far cry from forty hours a week behind the counter at Whataburger.

Somebody ordered another round. King took a sip of his draft and lamented the fact times had changed. UT football players didn't come around much anymore. Fact is, he had moved on as well. Not rich enough to retire, he managed another strip joint out near Round Rock. But he missed the old place and the chance to slip a bottle of vodka or two out the back door to a superstar after a national championship win or help reel in the next high school star with a complimentary evening at the club, watching some tasty little coeds do their thing. Run right, the system was nothing if not the sum of many moving parts. Quietly, professionally, one of its kings had done his part to give Texas an unseen edge.

"Over the years," he said, downing the last of an ice-cold Coors Light, "I've done more for recruiting at UT than Mack Brown."

THE VICTIM

"They had suffered enough. They lost their scholarships"

Two hundred and fifty-seven wins. Nineteen conference championships. Twenty-two bowl appearances. Those were the final numbers when LaVell Edwards retired in 2000 after twenty-nine seasons as head coach at BYU. Only six coaches in the history of college football had won more games. But one particular win in 1984 cemented Edwards's status as a coaching legend—a 24–17 bowl victory over Michigan to cap an undefeated season and secure BYU's only national championship.

The unenviable task of succeeding Edwards fell to Gary Crowton, an offensive coordinator with the Chicago Bears. Crowton arrived in Provo in 2001, and BYU appeared headed for another national title run. The Cougars got off to a 12-0 start behind running back Luke Staley, who led the nation in rushing that year with 1,596 yards and won the Doak Walker Award. Heading into the final game of the regular season, BYU was ranked seventh in the nation. But Staley broke his leg the week before the last game. Without him, BYU lost to Hawaii and then fell to Louisville in the Liberty Bowl, finishing 12-2.

Things went downhill from there. Despite a soft schedule, BYU went 5-7 in 2002, marking its first losing season since 1973. The 2003 season was even worse. BYU dropped to 4-8 and went 1-5 at home. Back-to-back losing seasons had never happened under Edwards.

"We had two losing seasons in a row," Crowton said. "I was under a lot of pressure from the administration to get back to the national championship and to get better players."

The pressure to win in 2004 was actually put in writing. "It happened after my third year," Crowton said. "I got a letter from the administration that said I had to be 6-5 the next year."

With his job on the line, Crowton changed BYU's recruiting approach. "I had to win," he said. "So I went out and recruited the best athletes."

Karland Bennett and B. J. Mathis were two recruits who Crowton and his staff felt could help change BYU's fortunes. They were the stars of Berkner High's football team in Texas. Bennett, a six-foot-one, 205-pound linebacker, was team captain. Mathis, a five-foot-seven, 170-pound running back, was an all-state kick returner. Both had scholarship offers from top programs—Bennett from Oklahoma, TCU and Arkansas; Mathis from SMU and Tulsa. But only BYU made offers to both players. So on the same day—January 22, 2004—they committed to the Cougars.

The duo was unfamiliar with the school's strict honor code, which prohibits alcohol, sex before marriage and pornography. But Crowton personally explained BYU's standards during his in-home visits. Most of what he told them about the honor code, however, didn't register. Bennett later said, "It was just on a sheet of paper with everything else that we had to sign, some religious thing."

That religious thing is actually a pretty big deal, seeing that the Church of Jesus Christ of Latter-day Saints owns BYU. The school's honor code mirrors the teachings of the church, which goes as far as forbidding its members to drink coffee and tea. Still, Crowton didn't foresee any problems. "Their high school coach told us that B.J. and Karland were 'angels,'" Crowton said. "Plus, I went to their homes and talked about the high standards and told them not to come if they couldn't do it."

One thing was abundantly clear: Bennett and Mathis would be racial minorities in Provo. Less than 1 percent of the city's 120,000 residents are black. But African-American college football players face a similar racial landscape at Nebraska, Oklahoma, Colorado, Kansas, Notre Dame and countless other powerhouse programs. Bennett and Mathis weren't worried. They had thrived as teenagers in Richardson, an affluent, predominantly white suburb of Dallas. Besides, they were focused on playing in the NFL, and they were convinced BYU gave them the best chance of achieving their dreams. BYU coaches pointed out that their program had more alumni in the NFL than any school in the West except USC. Bennett and Mathis were promised a lot of playing time and visibility: the first game in the upcoming season was on national television against Notre Dame. The campus was a draw, too. Everything was new, shiny and clean, especially the football facilities. Plus, people were ridiculously friendly. Mathis was so impressed that he told his high school teammate Trey Bryant, a 305-pound junior defensive lineman being aggressively pursued by

Baylor and BYU, that he should choose BYU. "This is the place," Mathis told him.

With BYU changing its approach to recruiting, Crowton turned to his close friend Bronco Mendenhall for help. Mendenhall was the defensive coordinator at New Mexico, where he'd spent the previous five seasons building the No. 1 defense in the Mountain West Conference. The idea of moving to Provo didn't thrill Mendenhall. His wife wasn't excited about trading Albuquerque for Provo, either. But Crowton was one of Mendenhall's closest friends, and when he said he needed a new defensive coordinator, Mendenhall felt obligated. His arrival coincided with the push to recruit more tough-nosed football players to Provo, a move Mendenhall supported.

"We clearly went after the athletes that year," Mendenhall said. "I remember the meetings. 'We need more athleticism.' 'We need more speed.' 'We need athletes.'"

Crowton was counting on Mendenhall to be his enforcer. "The reason I hired Bronco is because I knew he could help me honor the standards," Crowton said. "He was a real strong guy. He wanted to build the top defense in the nation. He was challenging me, saying, 'I can handle these guys. I can make sure they won't get into trouble.'"

Karland Bennett and B. J. Mathis arrived in Provo and became roommates at the end of July 2004, a little more than a week before the start of fall camp. Their apartment complex housed mainly freshmen football players, including eleven other African-Americans from Texas, California and Georgia. On August 8, a bunch of them ventured away from campus to the Provo Towne Center mall. It was a Sunday and there were few people at the mall. But a group of African-Americans in BYU football garb drew eyes. They were approached for autographs. Others wished them luck in the upcoming season. It felt pretty good.

Then the players spotted a cute girl. She was short but curvy, with dirty-blond hair. She didn't seem to mind that she'd been noticed. One player approached and said that one of his teammates wanted to get to know her but was a little shy. He pointed at Karland Bennett.

All the players were handsome, with athletic builds. But the girl quickly surmised that Bennett was the best looking one in the group. He looked like a *GQ* model. Before she knew it, he was approaching with his team-mates. One by one, they introduced themselves as BYU football players. She told them her name and her age—Jane Brown,[*] seventeen.

Like them, Brown wasn't from Utah and wasn't a Mormon. She had moved with her parents from Wyoming to nearby Sandy, a Salt Lake City suburb. But she certainly knew about BYU and its clean reputation. The idea that a group of its football players were paying attention to her was flattering.

Flattery, it turned out, was a healthy thing for Brown. Privately, she struggled with insecurities and was taking antidepressants. But all she felt was excitement when Bennett started talking to her. He suggested she get some of her friends and come by his apartment later that evening to hang out and watch movies. They exchanged cell phone numbers. Bennett said he'd call her around eight.

———

Brown didn't have many friends in the area, so she called her twenty-one-year-old cousin Kim Smith.[†] Basically, Smith was Brown's best friend and a big sister all in one. A six-foot-one basketball player at a small college in Wyoming, Smith was home for the summer. She lived in Salt Lake City. When she heard the enthusiasm in her cousin's voice, she said she'd be happy to tag along. At college she had dated a guy whose brother played football for BYU. Maybe he'd be at the party, Smith hoped.

———

It was 10:30 by the time the girls arrived at University Villa in Provo and made their way to the third-floor end unit, number 124. Bennett and Mathis showed them inside. To the left was a small kitchen area with a table and chairs. To the right four guys were huddled around a large television, playing video games on an Xbox. They were some of the same guys Brown had seen earlier at the mall. They said hello again.

Bennett offered the girls a seat on the long couch. He sat between them and grabbed a joystick. While he played, Brown made small talk, and Smith asked the others if they knew the BYU player who was the brother of the guy she used to date. None did.

After a while, a guy emerged from the living room closet wearing noth-

---

[*]Jane Brown is a pseudonym.
[†]Kim Smith is a pseudonym.

ing but SpongeBob boxer shorts and holding a drink. He was seventeen, the youngest player of the group. He was clearly the clown of the bunch.

Bennett turned to his guests. "Want something to drink?" he said.

"I'd love a glass of water," Brown said. Smith passed.

A minute later, the guy in boxer shorts came from the kitchen and handed Brown a cup. Without looking, she took a sip and nearly choked. The guy laughed. He had given her vodka. She set it down.

She repeated her request for a glass of water.

The guy in boxers disappeared to his apartment next door. He returned with a large bottle of Smirnoff. A couple players drank straight from the bottle. They offered the girls shots.

"I really don't want to drink," Brown said. "I just wanted water."

Smith said she didn't want any alcohol either.

The guys took a few more shots. Brown was surprised that BYU players were drinking. But it didn't change her opinion of them. Plenty of people she knew drank socially—not a particularly big deal.

"Why you not drinking?" one of them said to the girls. "You scared?"

"C'mon," another one urged.

"Fine," Smith said. "I'll take one shot. That's it."

Brown went along, taking another. With the players egging her on, she took one more for good measure.

Then one of the players suggested they all watch a "flick." Smith got suspicious. "Flick" was code for porn in her book. While a couple guys struggled to hook up a portable DVD player, Smith and Brown talked between themselves. Then they heard two women moaning. They were on the screen having sex.

"That's disgusting," Smith said.

"Like, you wouldn't do that?" one player said.

"You're right," Smith said. "I wouldn't ever, ever do that!"

A couple guys smirked but didn't challenge Smith.

Brown still hadn't figured out that a porn disc was playing. But she finally realized otherwise when she saw two black men simultaneously having sex with one white woman on the screen.

Embarrassed, Brown looked away.

"You'd like to do that, wouldn't you?" a player joked to Brown.

"No," she said, flashing an awkward smile. "I'm not that type of girl."

Smith and Brown turned their backs to the screen and made conversation with Bennett. He seemed disinterested in the porn. Other guys were coming and going. Bennett stepped out for a second, too. When he returned, he told Smith that one of his teammates wanted to see her on the balcony. He apparently knew the guy Smith used to date. Smith stepped out, and the guy invited her to go get some fast food. She ducked back inside to let Brown know. "We'll be right back," she told Brown. "Are you okay?"

"Yeah, I'm fine."

———

Brown stayed close to Bennett. He was the main reason she had gone there. At one point she told him that she wished they could go off to a late show or grab a bite to eat. But shortly after Smith left, Brown started feeling dizzy and nauseated. She had taken the antidepressant Paxil earlier that evening. Perhaps the alcohol had triggered an adverse reaction? She wasn't sure. All she knew was that she suddenly felt as if she were levitating. It was a strange sensation. Scared, she turned to Bennett. "I don't feel good."

First he got her some water. But she needed to lie down. He steadied her and led her to his bedroom. He told her nobody would mess with her in there. It was small and dark—a desk on the left, just inside the door, and a bed to the right. Bennett helped her to his bed. She sat and he stood while they talked for a few minutes. At one point, Bennett heard snickering. Three of his teammates had snuck in the room and were watching him. "Get out," he told them. They left. And a few minutes later, Bennett left to go find Smith. Brown passed out on his bed.

When Brown woke up a while later, she was no longer on the bed. According to police reports and grand jury transcripts, she was bent over Bennett's desk. A guy wearing no pants was seated on it. Her face was in his lap, pressed against his genitals. Her jeans and underwear were down around her ankles. Another guy was having intercourse with her from behind.

"No," she pleaded, trying to jerk her head away.

The guy on the desk tightened his grip, pressing his thumbs into her jaws, while moving her head up and down.

"Stop," she cried.

The guy behind her reached around and cupped her mouth. "Shut up," he said. Then the two men switched places.

The struggle continued, Brown crying while men kept switching positions. Her jeans and underwear came the rest of the way off. She could feel different sets of hands grabbing her from behind, along with different hands guiding her head up and down. But it was too dark to see who was doing what. And she was too weak to put up resistance.

Suddenly the bedroom door opened, and someone flipped on the light. Everyone stopped. The guy holding her head let go. She saw his face. She also turned and saw the other men in the room. None of them were wearing underwear except the guy in SpongeBob boxers.

"What the hell are you thinking?" one of them shouted at the one who had just entered the room. "Shut the lights off. Hurry."

Bennett started yelling, telling everyone to get out of his room and clean up the mess. There were used condoms on the floor. In the commotion, Brown wobbled out of the room and across the hall to the bathroom. She locked herself in and leaned over the tub, trying to gag herself. Her top was pulled down below her breasts. The rest of her clothes were missing.

Minutes later Bennett rapped on the door and insisted she open it. She did and he tossed her jeans at her. "Get dressed," he said.

A few minutes later Bennett led her out of the bathroom to the outside balcony. She promptly threw up. Using Brown's cell phone, Bennett finally tracked down Smith, who had experienced car trouble. He grabbed a couple buddies and drove Brown to the parking lot where Smith was stranded.

The moment Smith saw Brown she knew something had gone terribly wrong. Brown was crying and looked pale. While Bennett and his friends looked at Smith's car, she comforted Brown.

"You shouldn't have left me," Brown whispered.

"What happened?"

"They raped me."

Smith looked toward Bennett. Then she looked at his friends.

"They raped you or he raped you?"

"They raped me."

———

Scarcely a year goes by without one or more college football programs being rocked by sexual assault charges. In 2012, players at five BCS schools were charged with sex crimes, and two Texas players—Case McCoy and Jordan Hicks—were sent home before the Alamo Bowl when a woman told San Antonio police that she had been sexually assaulted. Both players were indefinitely suspended. But they proclaimed their innocence, and neither was charged with a crime.

This problem is not new. Nebraska's back-to-back national championship teams in 1994 and 1995 were tarnished by repeated police reports detailing violence against women. In the midst of the championship run, the Cornhuskers' top lineman pleaded guilty to sexually assaulting Miss

Nebraska, a fellow student. In 2002, four Notre Dame football players were accused of gang rape. One of them pleaded guilty to sexual battery; the other three were exonerated. In the past decade, Penn State, Wisconsin, Kansas State, Arizona, Miami, USC and Iowa were just some of the programs that faced publicized allegations of sexual abuse by players. Things got so out of hand at the University of Montana that it had to conduct its own investigation into nine sexual assaults by football players between September 2010 and December 2011.

But those are just the cases that make the news. Most incidents of sexual assault involving college football players never see the light of day. As a general rule, sex crimes are widely underreported. Even fewer of them are prosecuted. That's especially true when the accused are athletes. A comprehensive national study on the prevalence of sexual assault among male student-athletes sheds some light on this. The study—the only one of its kind—was done in the mid-1990s. Researchers targeted Division I colleges and universities with top twenty football and basketball programs to provide the following information:

total number of male students enrolled
total number of male student-athletes enrolled
total number of sexual assaults reported
total number of reported sexual assaults involving a student-athlete

Thirty institutions participated in the study. Information was gathered from twenty campus police departments and ten judicial affairs offices. In all, 107 cases of sexual assault were examined. The primary finding was that male student-athletes made up just 3 percent of the male student population yet were responsible for more than 19 percent of the reported sexual assaults on campus. Very few of these cases were publicly reported.

Subsequent research has suggested a range of factors contributing to why some athletes are more prone to abuse women, from a sense of entitlement to a higher frequency of casual sex with multiple partners to a warped sense of women as sexual prey. But the biggest factor may boil down to opportunity or access.

In the case of college football, there is no denying that just about everyone on campus is in awe of the young men who wear the uniform and fill the stadium on Saturday afternoons, including plenty of beautiful girls. The fact that some girls want to be seen with a football player does not, of course, necessarily mean they want to have sex with a football player.

But the lion's share of sexual assault cases against college football players—and athletes in general—usually involve a victim who willingly goes to an athlete's turf—his dorm room, apartment or hotel—and later claims that something happened that she didn't sign up for. In almost every instance, the accused player admits to sexual contact and claims it was consensual. It sets up the classic she-said-he-said scenario with a unique twist—when athletes are involved it is often she-said-they-said.

These cases usually come down to the freshness of the complaint, the strength of the physical evidence and, most important, the credibility of the accuser.

Detective DeVon Jensen is an investigator in the Special Victims Unit for the Provo Police Department. It was 5:30 p.m. on Monday when a desk sergeant notified him that a young girl, her parents and a cousin were in the waiting area. They wanted to file a rape report stemming from an incident the previous night. Jensen buzzed them in.

Through tears Brown gave a detailed account of what had happened in apartment 124 eighteen hours earlier. But she was pretty sketchy on names. She identified Bennett as the one she had gone to see and the one who had escorted her out afterward. She was pretty sure he had not assaulted her. She claimed his roommate, B. J. Mathis, had assaulted her. She only knew the faces of the others.

Jensen contacted BYU campus police and requested head shots of the African-American football players. He told Brown she could return the next day to ID them. He also took Smith's statement. She said that Brown had been pressured to drink and that porn scenes she had viewed mirrored the acts later performed on Brown. She also helped identify a couple more players. Jensen completed his report and called the hospital.

Dr. Sandra Garrard, a physician at a family practice clinic, performed an examination of Brown. Experienced in handling sexual assault victims, Garrard began by asking Brown about her medical history, noting the various medications she took—Paxil for depression; trazodone for sleeping; and Ortho Tri-Cyclen for irregular menstruation. Then Garrard went head to toe, documenting outward signs of trauma—abrasions on the left breast, a bruise on the right thumb, and tenderness along her neck and around her navel. She also noted two small lacerations on the outer area of the vagina.

The rape kit results were on Detective Jensen's desk by Tuesday morning, August 10. Across town, Gary Crowton and his team were in a meeting with Athletic Director Val Hale. It was the first day of fall camp, and Hale was lecturing the players about the honor code and the need to avoid trouble. He specifically warned the team against getting into compromised situations with girls that might lead to allegations of sexual assault. While that went on, Detective Jensen and two partners executed a search warrant at the apartment belonging to Bennett and Mathis. They immediately detected a strong chemical odor—cleaning solution of some sort. The place was spotless. Even the trash cans were empty. It was as if a maid service had just been through.

The first bedroom—Mathis's—was the one room in the apartment that Brown had not entered. It was also the only room that wasn't cleaned up. The officers gathered up the bedsheets and dusted the desk for fingerprints. There were dozens.

Bennett's room was a different story. It was immaculately clean. Even the desk was spotless—literally. When Jensen swept it for fingerprints, he found none. The surface had been wiped clean with bleach. They collected Bennett's sheets, a couple washcloths containing semen residue and a box of condoms found in his duffel bag. But there was no sign of alcohol—no empty bottles or plastic cups—anywhere in the unit. The officers checked the dumpster out back, but it had been emptied the previous day. Jensen did, however, find a pornographic DVD left on top of the living room television. He seized it as evidence.

At precisely 3:35 that afternoon, Gary Crowton started a meeting with his quarterbacks. Then there was a knock at the door. It was tight ends coach Mike Empey. "We have an issue," he said.

Crowton stepped out.

Empey, who was also the recruiting coordinator and oversaw housing for freshmen players, informed him that one of the apartment managers had just been by. He had reported that the police had just searched one of his units—number 124. They were investigating a sexual assault that allegedly took place Sunday night. They were also looking for evidence of alcohol consumption.

"Who's in that room?" Crowton asked.

Empey told him.

Crowton wanted both players in his office immediately.

Minutes later Bennett and Mathis showed up.

"Was there alcohol and a sexual situation in your room on Sunday night?" Crowton asked them.

Both players acted surprised. "No," they told him.

"Was there any kind of party at that house?" Crowton asked.

They told him there had been a Madden Football party.

"Was there any alcohol?"

"Coach, there was no alcohol," one of them said. The other agreed.

"Was there any sexual nature of any kind?"

They told him there was a girl present but insisted there had been no sexual contact whatsoever.

"I want you to go down to the police department and tell them your story," Crowton said.

Bennett and Mathis started talking over each other.

"Stop," Crowton said. "Just go tell the police your story."

He yelled for his secretary, gave her his car keys and told her to drive the boys to the station. The minute they left, Crowton rushed back to his quarterbacks meeting. By the time he got back to his office, his secretary had returned from the police station. She handed Crowton his keys and directed his attention to some paperwork that Bennett and Mathis had brought back—a copy of the warrant and an inventory of what was collected during the search.

Crowton scanned the evidence list for alcohol and found none. But he noticed that a pornographic DVD and condoms had been found. Not a good sign. The two players were waiting outside his office. He called them in and asked them how things had gone at the station.

They said they had told the police the same things they had told him: there had been no alcohol and no sex. Crowton asked them about the DVD. They said it belonged to someone else, and they denied watching it. They had an answer for the condoms, too. "Both of them explained that their mothers had given them condoms since they were fourteen years old because of all the teenage pregnancies in Texas," Crowton said. "Their parents wanted them to always have a condom with them."

Crowton took them at their word. Still, a criminal investigation was under way. He followed the protocol and telephoned Val Hale the minute Bennett and Mathis left his office.

Hale was in Crowton's office minutes later. They got on the speaker-phone with Steve Baker, the director of BYU's Honor Code Office. After getting up to speed, Baker gave Crowton some simple advice: *Don't say or do anything that can hurt the investigation.*

Next, Hale called the university's vice president, Fred Skousen, who subsequently notified the president. Late that night, Hale called Crowton at home with word from the top. "The athletic director told me that the president and vice president said . . . if these kids did anything, we need to get rid of these guys," Crowton said.

At that point, all Crowton knew was that an investigation was under way. The players were denying everything, none of them had been charged, and the Provo police were not talking. They weren't releasing any reports, either. The university was in the dark. So were the local media.

On August 19 the Associated Press ran the following headline: POLICE, BYU INVESTIGATING GANG RAPE ALLEGATION. Citing a police affidavit for the initial search warrant, the AP reported what little information was available—that a seventeen-year-old girl had been given alcohol, passed out and later woke up to being raped by a series of football players. None of them was named.

The news broke hours before a "meet the team" night at LaVell Edwards Stadium to kick off the 2004 season. It didn't go so well. Instead of pumping up the fan base, athletic director Val Hale got inundated with questions about an alleged gang rape. So did the university's communications office. Crowton issued an official statement: "Anytime allegations of misconduct surface regarding our players, it's a matter of serious concern for us. We want to get to the bottom of this and when we do, we will work with the University to do what is appropriate."

ESPN's *Outside the Lines* began working on a segment about BYU's troubles. It aired on September 3, the night before ESPN carried BYU's home opener against Notre Dame. By then, reports had surfaced that earlier in the year BYU had expelled its top running back and suspended three other players after another woman said she had been gang-raped at a party. She later recanted and said she had consented to sex with six of them. That was bad enough.

On September 8, one week into the season, BYU's vice president, Fred Skousen, fired athletic director Val Hale. He called the move an "important first step in creating a distinctive, exceptional athletic program that is fully aligned with the mission and values of Brigham Young University and the Church of Jesus Christ of Latter-day Saints."

After firing Hale, Skousen paid Crowton a visit at football practice. "He told me to be careful and make the right decision," Crowton said.

The only decision to be made at that point was whether to suspend the accused players. But the honor code review was not yet complete, and the police had still not charged anyone with a crime. "The police never told me what happened," Crowton said. "The next thing I know they are questioning every minority player on the team. If I knew a guy had done what they were accused of, I would kick him off the team in two seconds. But I didn't know. The players were saying they didn't do it."

Crowton chose a wait-and-see approach.

———

Since becoming a prosecutor in 1990, Donna Kelly had done nothing but sex crimes and child abuse cases. She'd handled more than three hundred in all, including roughly a hundred jury trials. She was among the more experienced sex crimes prosecutors west of the Rocky Mountains. And she'd spent her entire career in Provo. She fully appreciated the politics of a case against a bunch of BYU football players.

Kelly was convinced that a sexual assault had taken place. The question was whether she could prove it beyond a reasonable doubt. That's tricky when the crime scene is an athlete's bedroom and the accuser went there willingly.

A few years before Kelly got the BYU case, researchers studied 217 criminal complaints of felony assault attributed to college and pro athletes between 1986 and 1995. The outcome in those cases was compared with national arrest and conviction rates for sexual assault. Two key findings emerged:

1. A criminal complaint against a college or pro athlete for sexual assault is far more likely to result in arrest and in an indictment.
2. Athletes are significantly less likely to be convicted.

One way of looking at this apparent discrepancy is that law enforcement is overzealous when athletes are accused. But the research suggests the opposite. It's a well-known fact that elite athletes—like other celebrities—garner a disproportionate amount of publicity when accused of a crime. That cuts two ways. The image of an accused athlete takes a hit before anything has been proven. The flip side is that these cases put police and prosecutors under a microscope, too. Besides the glare of the press, law enforcement faces a team of top-flight lawyers when athletes are accused of sex crimes. Even college football players without resources inevitably end up with the kind of legal defense and support system rarely afforded to accused sex offenders.

As a result, prosecutors are much less likely to charge an accused athlete in a date rape case unless the evidence and the accuser are rock solid. Consider that of the 217 felony sexual assault complaints levied against athletes between 1986 and 1995, only 66 went to a jury trial. In other words, those were the cases with the most compelling evidence and the most credible victims. Still, only 10 of them (15 percent) resulted in convictions. That's far below the national average. There are a variety of reasons for this. But the big one is that jurors are reluctant to convict athletes of sexual assault when the accuser has willingly gone to a player's bedroom or otherwise put herself in a compromising situation. That raises doubt in the eyes of jurors.

Kelly faced that precise scenario with the BYU case. The accuser had gone there willingly, consumed alcohol and not bothered to leave when the players started showing porn. The defense was predictable—admit sex, deny force.

BYU's Honor Code Office didn't have to prove that a rape took place. It only had to find that sex occurred, not to mention that alcohol was consumed or porn was viewed. After a three-month internal review it became clear that players had lied to Coach Crowton. The university suspended Bennett and Mathis at the end of November. William Turner—the one with the SpongBob boxers—and Ibrahim Rashada were put on probationary status.

By that time, criminal investigators had questioned at least ten football players in connection with the incident and narrowed the number of suspects to the same four who had been disciplined by the school. Bennett and Mathis packed their bags and returned to Texas. Turner went home to the Bay Area. Only Rashada remained in Provo. He was still on the team.

On November 20, Utah blew BYU out 52–21 in the final game of the 2004 regular season, dropping the Cougars to 5-6 and marking their third consecutive losing season. A week later, Mendenhall ducked into Crowton's office to discuss a recruit. But Crowton looked preoccupied. Earlier he had met with Peter Pilling and Tom Holmoe, two senior associate athletic directors who were brought in to run the athletic department after the previous AD became a casualty of the gang rape case. Pilling and Holmoe told Crowton he had to resign. Crowton had refused, saying they'd have to fire him. But after talking to his wife and thinking it over, he came to grips with the fact that fighting to keep his job would be messy. The last thing he wanted was to embarrass the institution. He decided to bite the bullet.

"I'm not gonna make it," Crowton finally muttered.

Mendenhall didn't understand. Too numb to be angry, Crowton didn't elaborate.

"I'm not gonna make it," he repeated. "And I've recommended that you and Lance Reynolds be considered for the head job."

Mendenhall felt sick to his stomach. The next day—December 1— Mendenhall stood in the back of the room as his best friend held a press conference on campus. "At this time I feel it's time for me to step down and let the football program move on in a different direction," Crowton told the media. "I love this university. I wish we could have got more wins. In this business, that's what it's about—getting wins."

"Was it a forced resignation?" one reporter asked.

Crowton didn't want to point fingers or appear bitter. Instead, he thanked everyone and complimented his staff and players. Another reporter asked how much the off-the-field problems—most notably the alleged gang rape—had factored into the resignation.

"I was appalled by it," Crowton said. "I don't want to bring any embarrassment to the university as their coach and their leader, but there was some embarrassment to the university."

Crowton didn't say it at the time, but the rape case had placed him in a no-win situation. "That was the hardest thing I ever dealt with," Crowton explained. "BYU didn't want me to talk about it, and Provo police put a gag on it. I just followed what I was told to do. But as a father who knows how to treat my daughters and my wife, this was killing me. Yet I had recruited these kids as their head coach. For most of the season I didn't know who had done what. It broke my heart that that girl was harmed. But all I had to go on was he said, she said."

As Crowton left the press conference, it was all Mendenhall could do to keep his emotions in check. He felt the coaching staff had let Crowton down and the athletic department had thrown him under the bus. "There were kids who were making poor choices that we as assistants had brought here," Mendenhall said.

———

One day after Crowton stepped down, a Utah County grand jury indicted four players—B. J. Mathis, Karland Bennett, Ibrahim Rashada and William Turner—on rape charges, along with furnishing alcohol and pornography to a minor. Bail was set at $100,000 each. Turner, seventeen at the time of the incident, agreed to surrender and say what happened on the night in question in exchange for being prosecuted as a juvenile.

News of the indictments hit like a bomb in Provo. Rashada, the only one of the four still on the team, was arrested the following morning and thrown in jail. BYU immediately kicked him out of school. Bennett and Mathis returned from Texas and were jailed pending a bail hearing.

Salt Lake City defense attorney Greg Skordas got a desperate call from Karland Bennett's mother, begging him to represent her son. Before becoming one of the city's best criminal lawyers, Skordas had been a Salt Lake City prosecutor, where he was the Special Victims Unit chief. When Skordas visited Bennett in jail, he immediately observed three things: good looks, manners and, above all, fear.

"He was scared," Skordas said. "He's a very good-looking kid and extremely respectful. He called me 'sir' and had a southern way about him."

Skordas wasted no time getting to the facts with Bennett. "I had him describe the events," Skordas said. "The defense was consent, not that it didn't occur. This was a 'yeah, it happened, but' case."

For Skordas, it sounded all too familiar: horny jocks versed in the pickup game cross paths with a vulnerable girl who gets in way over her head. "It was the other guys that jumped in that caused the problem," Skordas said. "Karland wasn't an active physical participant. On a good day he was an aider and abettor. He supplied the bedroom and the condoms."

Eventually, Skordas called Kelly and started talking about a plea deal. Then, on March 17, 2005, Bennett went with his lawyer to the prosecutor's office and submitted to a lengthy interview. He was not put under oath. The prosecutors wanted him to speak freely, and Skordas didn't want anything he said to be used against him if a deal wasn't reached. First, Bennett told authorities that when Brown got sick, the reason he led her to his room was to protect her from the other guys. Second, he claimed that Brown had been taunted into drinking and that he later saw multiple teammates taking turns having sex with her.

On August 9, 2005, Bennett pleaded guilty to obstruction and dealing harmful material to a minor in exchange for the state dropping the sexual assault charges against him. He also agreed to testify against Mathis and Rashada. His sentencing was delayed until after their trial.

"The other lawyers were mad at me because my kid turned," Skordas said. "But it's business. It's what you have to do."

The trial against Mathis and Rashada opened two weeks later. There was plenty of drama. Brown described her assault. Medical and criminal investigators testified, as did football players and BYU officials. But the state's key witness was Bennett. He placed Mathis and Rashada at the scene and confirmed that they both had sex with Brown. But he did not go as far as to say it was the result of force.

"He was a star witness, and he didn't describe a rape," Skordas said. "In the end, the defendants were happy because his testimony helped them."

The jury acquitted Mathis and Rashada on all counts.

Mathis's criminal lawyer, Jere Reneer, said, "I've never felt prouder to be a lawyer."

Outside the courtroom, Mathis's grandmother cried and shouted: "Thank you, Jesus! Thank you, Jesus! Thank you, Jesus!"

Brown was devastated. After leaving the courthouse, she collapsed and started sobbing. "They raped me. They raped me. They raped me." She had to be carried to the car. Over the ensuing months, she became a recluse and gained seventy-five pounds.

The verdict stung Kelly, too. Despite her long career, she had never tried a case against college football players. She saw things in the BYU case that were completely foreign to her. "There was something obviously very different about prosecuting football players," she said. "The football dynamic was an undercurrent to everything we did. And it was ultimately football that had a very big influence on the jury."

After the courtroom cleared out, three jurors were still around. Kelly cornered them and asked why they had acquitted. "The jury said they had suffered enough," Kelly said. "They lost their scholarships. They were kicked off the team."

Kelly said it was the most bizarre thing she'd ever heard—the idea that the players had been sufficiently punished when they lost their opportunity to play football. "That's the power of college football," she said.

After the trial, B. J. Mathis and Ibrahim Rashada went on to play college football elsewhere. Mathis became a standout kick returner at Midwestern State, and Rashada went to Southwest Mississippi Community College.

Karland Bennett never played football again. After watching his teammates go free, he withdrew his guilty plea on obstruction and dealing harmful material to a minor. Prosecutors threatened to try him. But Brown had no interest in taking the stand again. Ultimately, the state dropped the charges against Bennett, wiping his record clean in Utah.

But back in Texas his life went downhill fast. He accumulated a lengthy criminal record, including multiple arrests for aggravated robbery, unlawful possession of a handgun, theft and possession of a controlled substance. Then, on April 16, 2010, a Dallas man was abducted, shot and killed in a drug deal that went bad. Bennett was arrested, jailed and charged with capital murder. On January 25, 2013, he pleaded guilty to murder and was sentenced to forty years in prison.

6 THE COACH

Part II, Terminated

The 2009 season was Mike Leach's tenth at Tech. When it ended, Tech got invited to the Alamo Bowl to face Michigan State. It would mark Tech's tenth straight bowl appearance under Leach.

With less than two weeks remaining until he would take his team to San Antonio, Leach held a night practice on December 16, 2009. Afterward, reserve wide receiver Adam James tracked down Mark "Buzz" Chisum, one of the team's athletic trainers. James said he had been injured on one of the final plays of scrimmage and felt dizzy and disoriented.

Chisum took James to his office, pulled out a Sports Concussion Assessment Tool 2—known in college athletics as a SCAT 2—and recorded the time: 10:52 p.m. Then he asked James a series of questions and documented the following symptoms:

mild headache
very mild neck pain
moderate blurred vision
moderate balance problems

Along with instructions to take Tylenol for pain, Chisum gave James his cell phone number and told him to call if symptoms got worse overnight. James went out that night with a friend. They ended up at IHOP. It was after midnight by the time James went to bed. The following morning he saw team physician Dr. Michael Phy and Tech's head trainer, Steve Pincock. He reported that his headache had subsided a bit. But he said he had thrown up some time after eating at IHOP and he still felt a little nauseated. His dizziness hadn't completely subsided either.

Phy administered a standard diagnostic test, and James lost his balance. That, along with everything else Phy had heard and seen, led him to his diagnosis: mild concussion.

With Pincock looking on, Phy instructed James not to practice for seven days. But he was cleared to follow the team's protocol for players with a mild concussion—dress in team-issued workout clothing and walk laps around the field during practice. But no running or other strenuous activity that might elevate James's heart rate or increase his stress level.

That afternoon, practice had been under way for about twenty minutes when James showed up wearing street clothes, a blue bandanna, a backward baseball cap and sunglasses. Leach spotted him walking nonchalantly around the practice field. Irritated, he turned to Pincock.

"Why's he dressed like that?" Leach said.

"I don't know," Pincock said. "He just got here."

"Why's he wearing sunglasses?"

Pincock revealed that James had been diagnosed with a mild concussion. The shades, he said, were no doubt intended to deal with his sensitivity to light.

The injury was news to Leach, but his dissatisfaction with Adam James was not. Just three days earlier, Leach had stopped practice and removed James and a few other receivers from the field for poor effort. In spring practice, Leach had kicked James off the field in an incident that was captured on tape. "I can't even stand to watch you fucking stumble around," Leach told James during a drill. "Shitty fucking effort. Like you fucking accomplished something."

Then, at the start of the regular season, James's position coach, Lincoln Riley, called him into his office to inform him that he was being demoted to third string, citing poor effort in practice. James disagreed. So Riley showed him practice film to prove his point. When James left the office that day, he took his anger out on the door.

Another coach confronted him. "Why did you break the door?"

"What the hell do you think?" James said.

Leach thought about kicking him off the team then but didn't.

Complicating the relationship between James and the coaching staff was the presence of Adam's father, Craig James. The former NFL player was a college football analyst for ESPN. It wasn't unusual for him to attend Tech practices and cover Tech games. Leach felt he meddled too much. "I heard more from Craig James than I did from the other 120 parents of players combined," Leach said.

Right after Adam got demoted to third string, he texted his father: "Bummer news. I'm third string."

Later that day, Lincoln Riley got a voice mail from Craig James: "If you have the balls—and I don't think you do—call me back."

Leach found out and didn't like it. "He was a helicopter parent," Leach explained. "It was all about trying to get more playing time for his son."

———

Pincock's report that James had a concussion guaranteed that he wouldn't get much practice time leading up to the Alamo Bowl. Fed up, Leach told Pincock to isolate James from the team for the duration of practice.

"Put his fucking pussy ass in a place so dark that the only way he knows he has a dick is to reach down and touch it," Leach told Pincock.

At Leach's insistence, Pincock shared that statement with James. Then he led him off the field to a shed that housed blocking dummies, watercoolers, an ice machine and an ATV. Injured players would sometimes go there to ride a stationary bike. Virtually spotless, the brand-new structure had a tacky, rubberlike floor and an overhead, garage-style pull-down door, as well as a man door on the side. There were overhead lights but no windows. Aided by freshman student-trainer Jordan Williams, Pincock removed anything that James could sit on and made sure the lights were off. He told James that Leach wanted him to remain standing in the dark for the duration of practice. Then he closed the door.

Pincock had Williams remain outside the shed to monitor James. "Leach had also instructed me to have a student trainer sit outside the shed to make sure he was standing and that he did not leave," Pincock said. At one point, however, James did leave after requesting permission to use the bathroom. Otherwise, he stayed put for the duration of practice—roughly two hours. During that time he sent his father a text message: "You're going to like this. Leach thinks it's impossible for me to have a concussion. And I'm just being a pussy. So for punishment he had me locked in a pitch black shed for the whole practice."

Later, when asked to explain why he sent that message to his father, James said, "We have the same sense of humor and personality, and I thought it was funny. So I said, 'You're going to like this.' I did find humor in it."

But Craig James wasn't amused. It was the first he'd heard that his son had a concussion. He took exception to his treatment. He texted back to his son, "Think about what you will allow me to do."

"Okay, I'll call you when I get out," Adam texted. "Don't do anything yet though."

Later that evening, Craig spoke to Adam, obtaining more details. But Adam made clear that he didn't want his father intervening—that would only make things worse. Nonetheless, he told his father about the colorful language Leach had used with the trainer.

As a former player, James was used to profanity from coaches. But as a father, he felt Leach had crossed the line. "You hear the f-bomb on the practice field all the time," James said. "It just rolls off your back. But this here is an injured student-athlete with a concussion. Adam was humiliated."

Nonetheless, at Adam's insistence, Craig promised to stay out of it.

That night, Craig and his wife, Marilyn, couldn't sleep. In high school Adam had sustained a concussion playing baseball. They worried about the effects of a second one. Lying in bed, staring at the ceiling, Marilyn peppered Craig with questions.

"Why is he in a shed?"

"Why isn't he in the training room?"

"What if he had fallen down and passed out?"

Craig had the same questions. And he couldn't help wondering what was in store for their son at the next practice.

The team didn't practice the following day. But on December 19, Tech practiced at Jones AT&T Stadium. Adam James felt much better, and this time he showed up in appropriate attire. But the doctor still hadn't cleared him to practice. When Pincock asked Leach what he wanted done with James, he said to do the same thing.

This time Pincock led James through the stadium tunnel to the media room, a space reserved for reporters to conduct postgame interviews. It contained numerous television screens, a table and some chairs. It also had a cramped electrical closet with wires, a panel of circuits and a pile of electronic devices. After removing the chairs from the media room, Pincock inspected the electrical closet and told James that the closet was off-limits.

Over the next two hours, James remained alone, standing in the darkened media room. At one point, unbeknownst to anyone else, he entered the electrical closet, closed himself inside and used his phone to record a short video of himself. "I'll turn the lights on real quick," he said into the microphone on his phone. "So I got to be . . . I got to be fast." When asked later why he made the video, he responded, "So I could show my friends."

Early that evening, Craig and Marilyn James had just sat down for dinner at a restaurant when Marilyn got a call from Adam. She asked how things went at practice. He reported that he'd been confined again. This time she put her foot down.

"This will stop," she told Adam.

Craig looked on.

"You're an adult," Marilyn continued. "But you are still our child. We are going to put a stop to this."

Craig agreed. "We never dreamed he would put him back in dark, solitary confinement," he said.

They decided to approach Tech's chancellor, Kent Hance. Earlier in the season James had met Hance briefly after a game, but he didn't know how to reach him. However, Marilyn had a connection to the vice chairman of Tech's board of trustees, Larry Anders. She called a friend, and within thirty minutes Craig received a call from Anders. He was at a wedding reception in Dallas at the Belo Mansion & Pavilion for Texas governor Rick Perry's son. Kent Hance was there, too. James told Anders that his son had been mistreated twice and he wanted the chancellor to put a stop to it.

After speaking to James, Anders cornered Hance. "We've got a problem," he began.

Hance said he'd handle it. It wasn't the first time he had dealt with a situation involving Leach. Back in 2007, after Texas beat Texas Tech 59–43, Leach called the officiating crew "a complete travesty" in his postgame press conference. He pointed out that one official was from Austin and suggested that the Big 12 Conference take a serious look at using out-of-conference officials for future Texas–Texas Tech games. Commissioner Dan Beebe fined Leach $10,000 for questioning the integrity and competence of game officials. It was the largest fine in conference history. But Leach refused to back away from his comments. He also didn't pay the fine. To resolve the matter, Hance paid the fine out of his pocket.

Hance ducked out of the reception and called Leach. He explained that the James family had made a complaint. The idea that Craig James had gone to the board of regents set Leach off. He decided he'd had enough of Adam James. "I'm going to kick him off the team tonight," Leach said.

"You can't do that," Hance said.

Leach rattled off a series of issues with Craig and Adam James, including the time Adam broke a door at the coach's office.

"Well, hell, you should have kicked him off the team back when he did those things," Hance said. "But you can't do it now."

The longer the conversation went, the more adamant Leach became.

Hance, a former lawyer and congressman, was looking for a quick solution. He proposed some options for Leach to consider:

1. Adam James could stay on the team if Craig James promised to stop calling and interfering.
2. Adam could leave the team but remain at Tech as a student, and the university would honor his scholarship.
3. Adam could withdraw from Tech, and Tech would release him from his scholarship, enabling him to transfer to another school, where he could begin playing the following season.

"If he will transfer, I will give him a release," Leach said.

Hance said he would talk to Craig James. In the meantime, he wanted Leach's assurance that Adam would not be put in any kind of confined areas during the next practice.

———

It was midnight by the time Hance reached James, who had waited for the call. He gave Hance an earful. "He tells the trainer put his fucking pussy ass in a place so dark the only thing he can do is reach down with his hands and touch his dick to know he has one?" Craig said. "I've been in this business all my life, and I've never heard a coach anywhere at any level put someone in confinement like that, especially with a concussion."

"I've spoken to Leach," Hance told James. "He said this is all about playing time and you're a helicopter dad."

James was incredulous. As an ESPN analyst, he hung around lots of teams and attended plenty of practices. It wasn't unusual for coaches like Mack Brown at Texas, Pete Carroll at USC and Urban Meyer at Florida to invite him on the field. "But when I went to Tech practices, I made a point to stay on the sidelines and away from the football kind of stuff," James said. "Adam would not have wanted a perception by his teammates that anything was going on."

Hance offered up the same three options that he had previously discussed with Leach. But James said his son had no interest in leaving the program—he loved Tech and his teammates. Rather, Craig wanted Leach held accountable.

Getting nowhere, Hance decided to conduct an internal investigation.

———

Charlotte Bingham didn't work directly with athletics at Texas Tech. A former trial lawyer with the Lubbock firm Crenshaw, Dupree & Milam, she joined the Texas Tech University System as assistant vice chancellor for administration. She reported directly to Hance, and her responsibilities included oversight of any employee complaints related to discrimination or violations of university policy. On the afternoon of December 20, Bingham received an urgent call from Hance. He told her about Craig James's allegations. He asked her to get to the bottom of the matter.

Over the ensuing forty-eight hours, Bingham interviewed Craig and Adam James, the team doctor, the team trainer and members of the football staff. Leach was the last person she interviewed. While Bingham questioned Leach on December 22 in Lubbock, Craig James flew to San Diego to work the Poinsettia Bowl. That night over dinner he told a colleague at ESPN what was going on. His colleague gave him one piece of advice: consider hiring a PR firm. "This will be a big deal if it breaks," his colleague told him.

James didn't hesitate. Already weighing a run for U.S. Congress, he called his political consultant back in Texas as soon as he got to his hotel room that night. His consultant recommended Spaeth Communications in Dallas. Spaeth's Web site said it specializes in "mastering the media," "witness preparation and trial support" and "crisis management."

The following day, James authorized his lawyer James Drakeley to retain Spaeth.

Meanwhile, Charlotte Bingham met with Kent Hance, university president Guy Bailey and athletic director Gerald Myers and gave an oral summary of her findings:

1. Mike Leach did not require Adam James to stand in an electrical closet. James entered the closet voluntarily and without the knowledge of anyone on the football staff. Nor was Adam James locked in a shed; in fact, the door had no lock.
2. Adam James was mistreated by being required to stand in a darkened, enclosed space on two occasions.
3. Mike Leach was extremely profane in how he dealt with the situation.
4. The team physician concluded that the coaches' handling of Adam James posed no harm or health risks.
5. Craig James threatened to sue the university and dispatch a team of lawyers "and depose everybody at Tech."

Bingham's findings were also shared with two senior members of the board of regents—Larry Anders and Jerry Turner, a prominent attorney who had been the captain of the Tech football team in the late 1960s. Disturbed, the trustees wanted Craig James's complaint handled swiftly.

Hance called Craig James in San Diego and told him that his complaint had been "substantially verified" by Bingham's investigation.

"Okay," James told Hance. "What's going to happen?"

"Tell us what you guys are looking for," Hance said.

"He needs to apologize for what he's done," James said. "And he needs to be held accountable."

After hanging up with James, Hance received a text message from him that left no doubts about James's stance. "Adam's claim has been verified," James texted Hance on December 23. "If any person or organization associated with Tech did what Mike did to Adam, they would be fired, which is exactly what we expect to happen to Mike."

The decision whether to fire the head football coach rested with the athletic director, who reported to the president. But neither Myers nor Bailey wanted to fire Leach. They thought it was unnecessary and suggested some ways to resolve the matter that weren't so extreme.

———

Hance called Leach and suggested three things that would put James's complaint to rest: pay a fine, perhaps as much as $60,000; apologize to the James family; and sign a statement saying that he would not punish anyone under a doctor's care.

"The main thing is we wanted him to apologize," Hance explained. "Surely when you're wrong, you say, 'I'm sorry for any misunderstanding.'"

But Leach had no intention of paying a fine or apologizing. "I'm not going to do any of those things," he told Hance, "because I haven't done anything wrong."

Hance felt Leach was being unreasonable and suggested he give serious consideration to acting on his recommendations.

"Well, if I don't do it?" Leach said.

"I'll probably have to terminate you."

Up to that point, Leach hadn't sought any legal advice. The bowl game was a week away, and his focus had been solely on Michigan State. But after hanging up with Hance, Leach called his attorney.

———

After graduating from the law school at Texas Tech, Ted Liggett went to work for a small firm in Lubbock. He ended up representing lots of Tech student-athletes who had issues with eligibility. He also represented the athletic department during numerous NCAA investigations. When Leach arrived in 2000 Liggett became his personal attorney. They were polar opposites politically. Leach is conservative; Liggett a far-left liberal. But they became fast friends. Liggett had never attended a Tech football game until Leach became his client. Before long, he never missed a game. Leach gave him a sideline pass to every home game.

It was late in the afternoon on December 23 when Liggett's home phone started ringing. He was in bed recovering from back surgery. But he took Leach's call.

"I might have a problem," Leach said.

"What's going on?" Liggett asked.

Leach brought him up to speed on the incident and the investigation.

Liggett was familiar with all the players. He had known Charlotte Bingham for more than twenty years. He was on good terms with Hance and Myers, and Bailey was a close family friend.

"We'll get this worked out," Liggett told Leach. "But I need to start by talking to some of these people."

After an initial conversation with Charlotte Bingham, Liggett called Guy Bailey. They both felt they could resolve the matter and agreed to meet the following day—Christmas Eve—at Bailey's office. Bailey said he'd make sure Gerald Myers attended, and Liggett agreed to bring Leach.

But a blizzard hit Lubbock on December 24, pushing the meeting to the day after Christmas. The delay gave Bailey plenty of time to think through the situation. Bailey liked Leach a great deal and admired the excitement his coaching style had brought to Lubbock. He and his wife, Jan, went to every home game. They had even gotten to know many of Leach's players on a first-name basis. It was Bailey's sense that Leach and his players had a strong bond and that the incident with Adam James was an isolated one, not a systemic problem.

Nonetheless, Bailey was uncomfortable with the way Adam James had been treated. After all, he had been diagnosed with a concussion. The dangers of concussions among pro football players were starting to attract national attention. That fall Congress had convened hearings on head injuries in the NFL. Public awareness around sports-related brain injuries was starting to pick up. Bailey felt it was only a matter of time before the NCAA faced similarly difficult questions about whether member institutions were adequately addressing the risks associated with concussions in football.

Less than two months before Adam James sustained a concussion, researchers at Boston University School of Medicine documented the first case of chronic traumatic encephalopathy (CTE)—better known as degenerative brain disease—in a college football player who did not play professionally. Mike Borich, a wide receiver at Snow College and Western Illinois University in the 1980s, died from a drug overdose on February 9, 2009. He was forty-two. During his college football career Borich sustained at least ten concussions. After college he had no concussions or head injuries. Yet by his late thirties he displayed many of the symptoms found in NFL players diagnosed with degenerative brain disease caused by head injuries. So Borich's father donated his son's brain for research. After diagnosing Borich with CTE, a leading sports concussion expert said, "Brain trauma in sports is a public health problem, not just an NFL problem."

Bailey had read about Borich's case in the *New York Times*. He also felt the university had an obligation to answer concerns and complaints from parents, whether over grades, housing or, in the case of Adam James, the standard of care afforded to a student-athlete following an injury. Over the weekend he drafted a letter that he hoped Leach would sign. He and Myers planned to present it to him at the meeting.

"Gerald and I are going to talk to Mike," Bailey told his wife as he left the house.

She asked when he'd be back.

"It shouldn't be very long," he told her. "I think we can get this done in half an hour."

There was one problem: Bailey had no idea that Hance had already called Leach and given him an ultimatum. Hance hadn't told Bailey.

When Liggett and Leach arrived at Bailey's office, Bailey asked Liggett to wait in the reception area. "We want to meet with Mike alone," he said.

Leach entered and took a seat opposite Bailey and Myers.

"We're here to help you, Mike," Bailey began. "We want to work through this and get to a solution."

Then Bailey handed Leach the letter and asked him to read it.

Dear Coach Leach,

As you know, we have been conducting an inquiry into allegations by a student athlete that your treatment of him, subsequent to his being diagnosed with a mild concussion, may have been injurious to his health and served no medical and/or educational purposes.

The letter went on to outline five guidelines that the university wanted Leach to follow:

1. All practices and team meetings would be monitored by the athletic director.
2. All injured players had to be cleared in writing by a physician before being eligible to practice or play.
3. Leach had to acknowledge an obligation to treat student-athletes with respect.
4. Leach had to treat all student-athletes at all times in a fair and responsible manner and cease any actions not in compliance with his employment contract.
5. Leach would not retaliate against any student-athlete who suffered an injury.

"Well, I already do these things," Leach said. "They're in my contract." He pushed the letter back across the table.

"Mike, if you will sign this letter and make an apology to the James family," Myers said, "we will get this situation behind us."

"Listen," Leach said, "if you don't want me here, let's negotiate an exit strategy and I'll leave."

"There's not any reason to talk about that," Myers said. "We have no interest in that."

"I will find another job," Leach continued. "And you can hire somebody that you're more pleased with. But you're not going to railroad me with false charges."

The bad blood between Leach and Myers stretched back to the previous year's difficult contract renegotiations. Bailey, on the other hand, had a good rapport with Leach. "Look," Bailey said, "concussions are a serious issue. It needs to be addressed. It can be addressed through an apology or some kind of letter of explanation that shows you were doing what you felt was in his best interest or welfare. But somehow we have to demonstrate that we had the welfare of the student-athletes covered."

Leach didn't argue with Bailey. But he didn't back down, either. "First of all," Leach explained, "Adam James was treated as if he had a concussion. Two, I did the same thing with Adam James that I did with other injured players: I told the trainer to handle him. Did I tell him to get him off the field? Yeah, I told him to get him off the field.

"He had him stand in the garage," Leach continued. "I found out half an hour later that this is where he had him stand. I don't have a problem with it. But since when have I ever commanded a trainer or doctor to do anything? Nor do I have the ability to. They don't answer to the head coach. They answer to the assistant AD."

Bailey repeated that he simply wanted Leach to explain that in writing.

"We were not asking necessarily that Mike say he was wrong," Bailey explained. "But say, 'Here is why I did this and here is why I think my actions were in the best interests of your son.'"

After making his request, Bailey asked Leach to step out and send in Liggett.

When Liggett came in, Myers handed him the letter he had prepared for Leach. "Ted, if you can get Mike to sign this letter," Myers said, "we will get this situation behind us."

Liggett looked it over. He wasn't surprised that Leach had refused to sign it. "I don't think he thinks he's done anything to apologize for," Liggett told them.

Bailey said he understood that and made clear that he wanted Leach to remain the head coach. But the university needed something in writing from Leach. Otherwise, it was going to be very difficult to prevent the situation from going public. Then all bets would be off.

"I'll see what I can do," Liggett told them.

While Bailey and Myers met with Leach and Liggett, Kent Hance was communicating with Craig James. "Mike Leach's actions with Adam were inhumane and dangerous, designed to inflict punishment and create great mental anguish," James wrote in an e-mail. "Action must be taken to not only insure the safety of Adam but to protect his teammates from this and other forms of abuse Coach Leach inflicts on his players.

"Kent, I ask you and the board members this: Have each of you seen the shed and electrical closet Adam was confined to? I'd recommend each of you visit the places—walk in them and turn the lights off. NOW, imagine standing there for three hours in the cold without being allowed to sit down or lean against the wall. This story will become public at some point and you can count on the fact that some television cameras will show this picture."

The regents were getting antsy, too. So was the university's legal team, led by general counsel Pat Campbell. In consultation with the lawyers and the trustees, Hance told Bailey and Myers that they needed a letter from Leach by noon on Monday.

Craig James wanted answers by Monday, too. "They were getting ready to leave to go down to the Alamo Bowl," James said. "He is still the head coach and our son is about to go and be under his guidance again on the football field. We hadn't heard back with certainty what the procedures would be."

Mike Leach spent the remainder of the twenty-sixth trying to prepare for the bowl game. Liggett told him to focus on football; he'd handle the ongoing Adam James matter. In the back of his mind, Liggett was convinced that Leach was going to have to make some kind of concession to get the problem behind him. But he was hoping to delay any action until after the bowl game. He called Charlotte Bingham, updated her on the meeting with Bailey and Myers and said he would continue to work toward a resolution.

The following morning Liggett got a voice mail from Bingham.

"Hi, Ted. This is Charlotte. Sorry to call you on a Sunday morning. I did want to touch base with you. Actually, after our conversation last night I did visit with both the chancellor and the president. Here's where I think we are. One, a number of . . . things just keep happening in terms of . . . let's just put it [at] outside pressure. And so what I really think needs to happen, if there's not just some incredible objection Mike needs to sign the letter that he . . . sign the letter that he was presented with. Return that to . . . return it to Pat or return it to the president, and then he needs to work on some sort of apology. And also the chancellor would like you to get that either to the president or to Pat on Monday."

Reading between the lines, Liggett determined that the reference to outside pressure was code for Craig James. It was Sunday night before Liggett reconnected with Leach and told him about Bingham's voice mail and the Monday deadline to produce a letter of apology.

"If there was a Monday ultimatum," Leach said, "they should have told us that at the Saturday meeting. They never told us that."

Liggett agreed. But that no longer mattered.

"If you don't sign the letter, Kent is going to come after you," Liggett told him.

"Yeah, well, I'm not signing it," Leach said.

Once Leach left for San Antonio without providing the letter, Gerald Myers told Guy Bailey he planned to suspend Leach. Bailey pledged his support. "But we need to make sure we've got the backing of everybody above us," Bailey told Myers.

They quickly convened a phone conference with Hance and board members Anders and Turner. One of the issues they discussed was the ramifications of suspending Leach on the eve of a bowl game. That step was sure to achieve the one thing they had been trying to avoid—bad publicity. But the board members were beyond that issue. One of them asked Bailey a simple question: If a dean had refused to cooperate with your request to write a letter to a parent who had complained, what would you do?

"He wouldn't be dean anymore," Bailey responded.

That sealed it. They all agreed that Leach shouldn't coach the game. As soon as the meeting broke up, Anders sent Hance an e-mail: "Kent, I agree with Jerry and you. He will not coach the Alamo Bowl while this is ongoing."

"Our hope," Bailey explained, "was that the suspension would send a strong enough message that we really had to have the letter."

The responsibility to inform Leach fell to Myers.

———————

Sharon Leach had invited practically every relative on both sides of the family to the Alamo Bowl. A virtual Leach family reunion was set for San Antonio. As soon as Mike and Sharon reached the hotel room, she started calling family members to double check arrival times. Her ten-year-old daughter, Kiersten, and thirteen-year-old son, Cody, were unpacking. Mike went off in a corner and began scribbling notes for the team meeting scheduled for later that afternoon. It was roughly 2:00 p.m. when his cell phone vibrated. It was Myers. He didn't bother with pleasantries.

Sharon immediately knew something was wrong. Mike was pacing with the phone to his ear.

"Why?" he finally said, breaking the silence.

The kids looked at Sharon.

"None of it's been proven," Leach said to Myers. "And it didn't happen."

Sharon put her arms around Kiersten.

"Who is *they*?" Leach said.

There was another long pause.

"I'm not signing a letter that said I did something I didn't do," Leach told Myers.

Myers was through talking. "Mike, the administration, the board, supports this. It's a done deal. You're suspended."

Leach hung up and turned to Sharon. "I've been suspended."

Sharon covered her mouth. The in-laws had just landed at the airport. They would be at the hotel soon. "What do we do now?" Sharon asked.

"Fight."

Leach called his defensive coordinator, Ruffin McNeill, and told him he'd have to run the team meeting. Then he called Liggett back in Lubbock.

"They are not gonna let me coach," he began.

"What?" Liggett asked.

"They suspended me."

"What? Shit."

"What are my options?"

"Mike, I'm going to have to hang up and think about this for a second. I have to absorb this before I counsel you."

———

Minutes after Myers had hung up with Leach, Kent Hance telephoned Craig James.

"Craig, I want to read a statement that will be coming out from the university here in the next thirty minutes. 'Tech University recently received a complaint from a player and his parents regarding Red Raider Head Football Coach Mike Leach's treatment of the athlete after an injury. At Texas Tech all such complaints are considered as serious matters, and as a result, an investigation of the incident is underway. Until the investigation is complete, Texas Tech University is suspending coach Leach from all duties as Head Football Coach effective immediately. The investigation into this matter will continue in a thorough and fair manner. Coach Ruffin McNeill will assume duties as Interim Head Coach and will coach the team during the Alamo Bowl. The decision to take these actions was made in consultation with the Texas Tech University president, and the Texas Tech University System chancellor, and Board of Regents chairman and vice chairman. Because this is a personnel matter no further comment will be forthcoming.' "

James thanked Hance for the heads-up.

Meanwhile, the video that Adam James had shot on his cell phone in the electrical closet was turned over to Craig's PR firm. After viewing Adam's video, one Spaeth associate e-mailed another: "I think the sound adds to the drama. He's turned on the lights but is afraid he will get caught." The firm started making plans to release the footage to national media, as well as post it on YouTube.

———

Ted Liggett never expected Tech to suspend Leach. Not after he and his family had flown to San Antonio. Not on the eve of a bowl game. Not when they had a strong ally in Guy Bailey, the university's president. Liggett was convinced of one thing: Bailey and the athletic director weren't calling the shots. That left Kent Hance and the board. And Liggett was convinced they were listening to Craig James. The suspension, Liggett felt, looked like a compromise move by Hance. It didn't go as far as James wanted, but it punished—and embarrassed—Leach.

Pissed, Liggett ran through Leach's options. One was to simply sign some sort of apology letter. Another was to ask a judge to issue a temporary restraining order (TRO), effectively freezing the suspension until a full hearing could be held to determine whether the suspension had merits. The chances of getting a TRO, Liggett believed, seemed pretty strong. Leach's contract gave him a ten-day cure period for any disputes pertaining to employment.

But Liggett couldn't help wondering how Tech officials would react if he took them to court. They might just fire Leach.

He called Leach and gave him his options: sign the apology letter and keep his job, or go to court and risk getting fired.

"You might want to think long and hard about doing what they want you to do," Liggett said.

Leach held his ground. He wasn't signing the letter.

"Mike, I'll file the TRO. But it's going to be a big fucking deal. It will force their hand."

"File it."

By the evening of the twenty-eighth, speculation was rampant among the Lubbock media about the identity of the player who had accused Leach of mistreatment. But by the following day, it was a national story. Craig James's ESPN colleague Joe Schad named Adam James. So had the Associated Press. The ESPN story cited an unidentified source close to the family who said James had sustained a concussion and "Leach told the trainer, two days later, to 'put [James] in the darkest, tightest spot. It was an electrical closet, again, with a guard posted outside.'"

Shortly after the ESPN story broke, Kent Hance heard that Ted Liggett planned on asking a judge to block the suspension. An emergency hearing had been scheduled for the following day. It was hard to predict how a judge in Lubbock might rule. But there was no question what the court of public opinion in Lubbock thought. Fans and alumni were in an uproar. They wanted Leach back. They wanted Adam and Craig James jettisoned. And they wanted Hance and Myers fired. The comment pages on the Lubbock news Web sites were flooded:

I literally cannot fathom how the board of regents can allow this injustice to occur. I will never attend another athletic event or donate to the Red Raider Club again if Coach Leach is fired. I encourage others to do the same.

I am a Texas Tech alumnus. Here are my thoughts: Give Leach a bonus. Fire Kent Hance.

Mike Leach has done wonders for this university and its football program. I would hate to see Mike Leach fired. I am sure that my loyalty to this university and its sports program would go elsewhere if that happens.

I have been a season ticket holder for many years, but if this situation results in Coach Leach leaving, I will not renew them. Furthermore, I will not support Tech athletics in any monetary way until Gerald Myers is dismissed.

If Tech fires Leach over this, there will be a mushroom cloud over Lubbock that will be visible for thousands of miles and a likely revolt of Tech fans, alums, and former players.

Leach has helped fill the seats at the stadium the administrators continue to expand. I am quite sure that most of those seats will not be filled should Leach be let go. This will be a huge setback not just for the Texas Tech but also the city of Lubbock.

The local media had clearly sided with Leach, too. Hours after the suspension was announced, the *Lubbock Avalanche-Journal* ran an article featuring a slew of former Tech football players—including star quarterback Graham Harrell, who had played with a broken hand—who had come to Leach's defense. "Leach doesn't deviate from the rule book at all and wouldn't do anything to put a player in harm," one former player told the paper.

But Hance wasn't talking to alumni, fans or former Tech players. He was talking mainly to two regents—Turner and Anders. Both were determined to keep Leach out of the game. "He's not coaching the game," Turner told Hance in an e-mail. "Hope we don't have to fire him to prevent him from doing so. But he's not coaching the game."

There was another thing to consider. Leach had just earned an $800,000 performance bonus, based on how well he had coached during the regular season. But regents and university lawyers were looking at a provision in his contract that said the lump payment was contingent on Leach being "the Head Football Coach at University as of December 31, 2009." In other words, if the university fired him on December 30, Tech didn't have to pay him the bonus.

Not all of the regents were comfortable with the direction things were heading. "I am pleading that the course we are on wait until Monday after the game," wrote regent Nancy Neal in an e-mail to Jerry Turner. Neal was on the audit committee and had previously overseen fund-raising for the university. "If we owe the $, let's not be so cheap that it isn't paid . . . that being said, wait until Monday to act if still necessary."

Bailey felt as if the situation were spiraling out of control. "The whole purpose of the suspension was to get Mike to work with us to resolve the issue," Bailey said. "When it became clear that that wasn't going to happen, we had two choices: either we say we really didn't mean it, or we take the next step."

While Texas Tech officials figured out the next move, Craig James gave his PR firm permission to post Adam James's cell phone video on YouTube. A Spaeth employee provided the following description: "This video was taken by Adam James, a player on the Texas Tech Red Raider football team, on Saturday, December 19th, after being confined by Coach Leach in an electrical closet off the press room at Jones AT&T Stadium."

Spaeth also sent out an internal e-mail to some of its employees, encouraging them to take steps to help the video go viral.

Leach was holed up in his hotel room in San Antonio, working on an affidavit to accompany his application for a TRO. That's when his cell phone began blowing up with phone calls and text messages about a video on the Internet that showed Adam James in a closet. It was the first Leach had heard of it. He called Liggett, and by that night Liggett was on KCBD-TV in Lubbock, giving a local television reporter a guided tour of the shed where James had been put.

That same night, Craig James was in San Diego preparing to provide color commentary for the Holiday Bowl. Before the game he did an interview about Leach's actions with ESPN's Steve Levy on *SportsCenter*. "ESPN made me go on the air and do the Steve Levy interview," James said. "They said, 'We won't let you announce the Holiday Bowl if you don't address this.

You've become the news. If you want to work the game, do the interview.' [It was] the hardest interview of my life."

———

Judge William "Bill" Sowder presided over the district court in Lubbock. Mike Leach's fate rested in his hands. A Texas A&M grad with a law degree from Baylor, Sowder fully appreciated the significance of college football in Texas. A poster of Robert Griffin III running out of the tunnel at Baylor hung on the wall in Sowder's chambers. His son Andrew Sowder is right behind RGIII in the poster. Andrew was Griffin's tight end. Judge Sowder was intimately familiar with just how seriously folks in Lubbock took football.

But even he didn't expect the scene that greeted him when he showed up at court at 5:30 in the morning on December 30. Television satellite trucks were in front of the building. Reporters were outside. He ducked in through a side door and spent his morning preparing for the hearing. By 9:00 it was standing room only in the courtroom. The gallery was packed with Red Raiders fans, none too happy.

Tech sent a team of lawyers, led by general counsel Pat Campbell and deputy general counsel Victor Mellinger. Deputy Attorney General Dan Perkins was also on hand. They were all waiting in the judge's chambers when Liggett drove up to the courthouse. He had not been told in advance that the hearing was going to be in open court and was surprised by the media circus outside. He telephoned Judge Sowder from his car.

Sowder explained that the media had petitioned to have the hearing in open court and he'd granted it.

"Shit! You're kidding me," Liggett said.

"I'm not kidding."

Liggett was wearing jeans and a camouflage coat. "I've gotta go home and get a suit on," he said.

"Just come in," Sowder said.

"My ass. I'm getting dressed."

More than an hour later, Liggett returned. The people in the courtroom had grown impatient. So had Judge Sowder. He wanted a word with the lawyers in his chambers before starting the hearing.

"Is there anything I need to know before we go out there?" Sowder asked. "I don't like any surprises."

"Well, Judge, there is," Campbell said. "Even if you grant the TRO, we're not going to let him coach."

"So what are you saying?" Sowder asked.

"The decision has been made to terminate Mike," Campbell said.

Sowder was speechless.

Liggett was incredulous. "Win, lose or draw?" Liggett asked.

"Win, lose or draw," Campbell said.

"Why have a hearing if what I do isn't going to make a difference practically?" Sowder asked.

"That's why I'm telling you," Campbell said.

Campbell reached into his jacket pocket, removed a letter and handed it to Liggett.

Dear Coach Leach,

This letter shall serve as formal notice to you that, pursuant to Article V of your Employment Contract, you are terminated with cause effective immediately, for breach of the provisions of Article IV of that Contract.

That was it. One sentence. Tech's president, Guy Bailey, had signed it.

Liggett handed the letter to Sowder. He read it and handed it back.

"What do you want to do?" Sowder said.

Liggett asked for a moment. He stepped into a private hallway and called Leach at his hotel room in San Antonio. "Mike, they fired you."

Leach was reserved. "Yeah, well . . ." His voice trailed off. Liggett couldn't help thinking back to the final minute of Tech's dramatic victory over Texas a year earlier. He was on the sideline that night, standing just a few feet behind Leach, when Michael Crabtree got into the end zone with one second remaining. Leach showed no emotion then. He expressed no emotion now. He just quietly hung up the phone.

Sharon Leach didn't need to ask what happened. She knew. And as soon as Mike and Sharon started packing their suitcases, the kids figured it out too—Dad was out of a job.

"What does this mean?" Kiersten asked, tears running down her cheeks. "Are we still going to be living in Lubbock?"

Sharon put her arms around her daughter. "Shhhh."

———

"We're gonna sue those sons of bitches," Ted Liggett muttered to himself as he trudged back to Judge Sowder's chambers. "There is no point in having the hearing," he told the judge.

Sowder agreed.

"Can I use the courtroom to speak to the media?" Liggett asked.

"I don't have any problem with that, Ted," Sowder said.

As Liggett stepped into the courtroom, Tech's lawyers quickly filed out through a back door to avoid the public and the media. Sowder sat alone in his chambers. Moments later he heard a collective gasp from his courtroom. Liggett had just read Leach's termination letter. "No!" someone screamed. The courtroom erupted in anger. "You can stuff my season tickets," a man shouted. The fury quickly spilled into the hallway and out into the street. Cars circled the courthouse. Horns honked. People shouted obscenities.

It was chaos in Lubbock, and Tech fans and alumni weren't the only ones upset. Some regents were angry, too. The governor had appointed Windy Sitton, mayor of Lubbock, to the board of regents. Hours after Leach was fired, she e-mailed her fellow regent Jerry Turner.

"How in the world can the Regents justify suspending, much less firing Mike Leach, over this issue?" she said. "Mike Leach is not perfect by any means but he cares about his students, he wins games, he fills the seats . . . Everyone sees through this injustice to Mike Leach and Texas Tech. The Sitton family has given scholarships and has had multiple seats since 1976. We will not renew our options [on] our 12 seats or for that matter our PSLs for basketball. This whole thing smells, and we do not want to be part of this blight on Texas Tech."

Guy Bailey regretted the way it ended. But he wasn't surprised. "Mike's whole personality is to be aggressive and to take the offense, not the defense," Bailey said. "If you watch Mike's teams, he just scores as many points as he can. He just wants you to score one less. Part of the way this case worked out was just personality."

Adam James suited up for the Alamo Bowl. The following season he was booed every time he caught a pass. But he stuck with the program and became one of the team's standout players—and a team favorite—in his senior year before graduating and taking a job in the oil and gas industry.

"At some point I had hoped that Mike would just man up and take ownership of what he did," said Craig James. "It was wrong."

————

Mike and Sharon Leach returned to Lubbock just long enough to pack a week's worth of clothing. Then they took the kids and headed to the vacation home they had purchased in Key West a year earlier. By the time they arrived, Craig James had authorized his PR firm to give the video Adam James had made of himself in the closet to CNN, along with permission for CNN to broadcast it on all its networks and affiliates worldwide. "We wanted to prove, to show that our son had been confined, ordered and confined twice to be by himself," James said.

Meanwhile, Tech withheld Leach's $800,000 bonus, as well as the remaining portion of his base salary that was owed for the 2009 season. Leach sued Tech for wrongful termination. And after a week in Key West, he and Sharon decided not to leave. They enrolled their kids in a school on the island, purchased four bicycles for transportation and began the process of trying to figure out what to do next with their lives.

"Mike had been in coaching forever," Sharon said. "The hardest thing about living in Key West was not having a team. All of a sudden we were all alone."

7   THE SACRIFICIAL LAMB

Towson University plays with the big boys

In a downstairs meeting room at the Crowne Plaza Baton Rouge hotel, Towson University quarterbacks coach Jared Ambrose had a few final words. It was Saturday afternoon, September 29, 2012. In a little less than four hours the Towson Tigers, twelfth in the NCAA's second-tier Football Championship Subdivision (FCS) rankings, would play undefeated LSU, ranked third in the Bowl Championship Series (BCS) rankings, in Baton Rouge. To come here to "Death Valley," the recognized funeral home for nonconference opponents—LSU had won a record forty such games in a row—Towson was being paid a school record $510,000. That amounted to a full 25 percent of its annual football budget.

Staring back at Ambrose were twenty-five members of the Towson offense. Most had no idea of the financial stakes at play. No clue as to the physical and emotional price they were about to pay.

"All right, listen up, I'll be quick," Ambrose began. "Who here's nervous? Hands in the air."

Not a single hand shot upward.

"No?" he said, his eyes scanning the room. "How long you been driving a car, Tyler?"

"Four years."

"How long you been dating girls, Joe?"

No answer.

"The point is," said Ambrose. "Football's the one thing in your life you've been doing longer than anything else. Now, this is a big stage [but] football is the one thing you know best. Find pride in that. Not nervousness."

Jared Ambrose is the younger brother of Towson's head coach, Rob Ambrose. And like his brother he could breathe his fair share of fire.

"There are three things we're going to do," he said, voice rising. "Play fast and smart. Play *physical*. And play *relentlessly*."

Another hard look around the room. Nobody uttered a word.

"Now, there are a couple of things we have in our favor," said Ambrose. "Number one, they don't fucking respect you. Number two, they're the No. 3 team in the nation and they don't fucking respect you. Number three, they're *Parade* all-Americans, blue-chippers. These motherfuckers never have gone through during the dark hours of this program. They've never gone somewhere and had to *build something*.

"So here's what we're going to do. We're going to punch them in the mouth. And then we're going to do it again. And again. And again.

"Now let's go whip their fuckin' ass at home. Got it?"

"Yes, sir!"

———

In the world of twenty-four-thousand-square-foot weight rooms and twenty-four-carat donors, there are few absolutes. But there is this: no mega-program can physically survive a dozen heavyweight fights a year. The players are just too young, the bodies too fragile, the depth chart too thin, to handle the load and still be fresh when it comes to crunch time late in the season. So a smart athletic director—in concert with his head coach—concocts a regular-season schedule peppered with a couple of patsies. More often than not the pain relief comes in the form of home games against lower-division opponents or "directional" schools. The various sacrificial lambs are lured to slaughter by so-called guarantees—payouts that run from a few thousand dollars to several hundred thousand or more.

Over the years these money games had served but a single purpose: the visitors take a beating, take the check and use the funds to help balance deep athletic department deficits. So if that means the Savannah States of the world become roadkill at Oklahoma State (84–0) or Florida State (55–0)—a combined score of 139–0—as they did in 2012, so be it. Or if Idaho State gets run through a 73–7 meat grinder at Nebraska, take heart in the news that the Bengals athletic department took home $600,000 for the mugging—or about 5 percent of its entire athletic department budget.

But more and more lately, for the designated losers these guarantee games have morphed into marketing plans, a way for college presidents and athletic directors (and even boards of trustees) to raise the promotional flag, to showcase the "brand." And while the move can occasionally surprise—witness Central Michigan's upset of Iowa and Northern Illinois knocking off Kansas on the same September weekend in 2012—the unwritten contract remains clear: You come into our house. We kick the shit out of you and rest our starters. You take home a nice fat check for playing the Christians to our Lions. Or Tigers.

Or so LSU figured.

The forecasted rain had begun in earnest by the time the Towson buses snaked their way into Tiger Stadium. A Scottish mist hung in the lights, adding to the ominous air. At LSU the road to the underground visitors' entrance runs a gauntlet of tailgating fans and hairpin turns, allowing lubricated locals unfettered access and the chance to scream "Ti-ger BAIT! Ti-ger BAIT!" at the tops of their lungs. It also allowed—in a sight, one suspects, unique to this part of the South—a father and towheaded son to stand together on the sidewalk and flip off each and every bus as it crawled by.

Prior to September 29, 2012, odds were that few in Baton Rouge—and across the country for that matter—could tell you where Towson was located. If they could, more than likely they pronounced it "Toe-son" or "Townsend" or called it Towson State. For the record it has been Towson *University* since 1997. Located about twenty minutes north of Baltimore, the leafy campus is home to some twenty thousand commuter and residential students. Its forty-four-year football history, while no Notre Dame, featured the likes of Super Bowl champions Dave Meggett and Sean Landeta of the New York Giants and former Pittsburgh Steeler standout Chad Scott. But lately its claim to athletic fame had leaned more toward lacrosse than football.

"All right, dim the lights," barked Coach Rob Ambrose. The clock on the locker room wall read 14:30 before kickoff. He had an energy drink in one hand, a chunk of chewing tobacco in his cheek and his starting center holding a sledgehammer down at his feet.

The 2012 football season marked Ambrose's fourth as the man in charge at Towson. Intense and deeply organized, he checked off all the right coaching boxes. The son of one of Maryland's most successful high school football coaches and athletic directors, he'd been a three-sport star in high school, twice an all-county quarterback, before making his mark as a wide receiver at Towson. After a knee injury cut his senior season short, head coach Gordy Combs offered Ambrose a spot as a student assistant—beginning a career that would take him from Towson to Catholic University to the offensive coordinator job at UConn in the Randy Edsall era, where Ambrose played a pivotal role in the development of quarterback Dan Orlovsky, a fifth-round pick of the Detroit Lions.

The best days of Towson football were fifteen years in the rearview mirror when Ambrose took over in 2008. He would become only the fourth head coach in Towson history after a call from Mama. That's what he called it at his first press conference. A call from Mama.

"Although I've never been a fan of Bear Bryant's, I agree with him on one topic," Ambrose said. "In 1958, Bear Bryant was asked why he left his coaching job at Texas A&M to become the coach at Alabama. He responded, 'My school called me. Mama called. When Mama calls, then you just have to come running.' That's how I feel about Towson."

Ambrose took over a team that would have made Mama anything but proud. Its record the previous two seasons was 6-17. It had won only two of sixteen Colonial Athletic Association (CAA) contests and finished dead last in the conference both years. Ambrose's first two years were actually worse, a combined 3-19. This dismal record belied a major rebuilding job that saw several bad actors run off and a sense of toughness and pride instilled in the program. "In our first year, there were a number of games against CAA teams that were decided long before halftime," Ambrose once recalled. "In 2010, I think most of our games were decided in the fourth quarter. Even though we didn't win any of them, we knew we were more competitive."

The ridiculous hours and relentless work ethic paid off in 2011. The Turnaround Tigers, as they were known, turned out to be the most improved team in Division I football. From 1-10 they went 9-3 and finished as the eighth-ranked team in the FCS and won their first CAA title in school history. Despite the heartbreaking loss at home (40–38) to sixth-ranked Lehigh in the second round of the playoffs, the sellout crowd at Unitas Stadium had seen the future . . . and it was Ambrose, honored that year as the FCS National Coach of the Year.

"Not only am I proud to be the coach here," Ambrose told a sellout crowd before the Lehigh game. "I'm proud to be a part of this community."

Towson came into the LSU game 2-1, hot off wins over William & Mary and St. Francis University, in Pennsylvania. But after getting a good long look at what the SEC was bringing to the table, Ambrose had emerged, in the words of one observer, "ashen-faced" from the film room.

"I've been watching them on offense, defense and special teams, and I've been looking for any holes I can find. I can't find any," he said. "This is the most athletically talented, technically sound football team I've ever seen on film."

LSU presented problems everywhere he looked. Its starting defensive ends were top five NFL prospects; its strong safety a predicted top twenty pick. It had speed to burn at wide receiver and a massive, mauling offensive line. (Eleven LSU underclassmen would eventually declare for the NFL draft.)

But Ambrose knew he had some *players* too—eleven Division I transfers to be exact—a quarterback, running back and defensive linemen and backs good enough to be recruited by any Division I school. If his Tigers were going down, they were going to go down swinging.

"Come on, get in here," he told his team in the locker room before the game. Fourteen minutes and counting to kickoff.

The lights dimmed. Up came a video. Muhammad Ali, in the ring, shouting, "I'm going to shake up the world, shake up the world," giving way to these words from the narrator:

> Here's the thing that makes life most interesting. The theory of evolution claims the strong shall survive. Maybe so. Maybe so. But the theory of *competition* says, "Just because they're the strong doesn't mean they can't get their asses kicked." That's right. See, what every long-shot-underdog-come-from-behind will tell you is this: the other guy may, in fact, be the favorite. The odds may be stacked against you. Fair enough. But what the odds don't know is that this isn't a *math* test. This is a completely different kind of *test:* one where *passion* has a funny way of trumping logic. The results don't always add up. No matter what the stats may say, and the experts may think, and the commentators may have predicted, when the race is on, all bets are *off.* And then, suddenly, as the old saying goes, we got ourselves a game.

The driving music ended, the lights came up, and Ambrose took over. Crammed into every inch of the tiny locker room were kids with no clue as to what waited outside. But they sure as hell were feeling something *inside.*

"You are the walking epitome of shitting on the impossible," Ambrose began. "You are no good. You can't win. Can't win in this league. Can't win a conference championship. No way in hell can you go to Division I playoffs."

He took a swig from the Monster can.

"Fuck 'em."

He was in a zone now; the system running on red. You wanted to see, to feel, where this was headed.

"A tough-ass attitude," said Ambrose. "An *extreme* attention to detail. And a *relentless* belief in each other." Swig. "They bench four hundred. So do we. They run 4.5. So do we. They squat five hundred. So do we. The only thing makes them different than us is them ugly-ass purple uniforms.

"So . . . we don't wait. This time we don't wait. Ain't nothing to be worried about. When tonight is over, you're going to leave a lasting impression on the United States of America, and no one will ever say Towson State again. They will know exactly *who* and *what* this university is."

You wanted to put on a uniform.

"HEY, WHY THE FUCK DID WE COME ALL THE WAY DOWN HERE? WHY'D WE COME DOWN HERE!"

"TO WIN!!"

"CAPTAINS! LET'S GET OUT . . ."

Standing in the crush right by the door was star defensive end Frank Beltre, he of the multicolored Mohawk. Beltre bounced up and down on the balls of his feet. When he spoke, he seemed to be speaking to no one but himself.

"God, I love football," he said. "I swear to God it's better than sex."

The first sign this could be Towson's night came as the team stormed the field. A cold, persistent rain had thinned the home crowd by a third. So the infamous full-throated, beer-soaked Death Valley roar was down a decibel or two.

But that low-key atmosphere went only so far once the game began. On LSU's second possession wide receiver Russell Shepard exploded along the right side on his way to a seventy-eight-yard streak into the end zone. There was 10:24 remaining in the first quarter. You could almost hear the Colosseum crowd beseeching the Roman emperor to send in more Christians.

But then a funny thing happened on the way to the slaughter. While its offense struggled for every yard, Towson's disciplined, hard-hitting D was playing its ass off. At the end of the first quarter the score stood at 7–0.

"That's what the world is going to see!" screamed deputy athletic director Devin Crosby from the sidelines. "All this is working in our plan!"

And it kept working.

Two minutes into the second quarter—in a sight that must have shocked those watching on ESPNU—Towson kicked a short field goal to cut the lead to four: LSU 7, Towson 3.

It got even crazier when tailback Terrance West slammed into the end zone moments after Towson's quarterback Grant Enders had scrambled forty-three yards to the LSU one.

Suddenly, impossibly, the nobodies from North Baltimore were leading mighty LSU 9–7 with 5:15 left in the first half. The crowd sat in silence. On the Towson sideline, athletic director Mike Waddell could barely believe his eyes. He whipped out his phone and clicked a commemorative shot.

But there are fairy tales, and then there's the SEC. Right before halftime LSU had used its speed and a shanked Towson punt to push ahead 17–9.

Still, it was a jacked-up Towson locker room. "Twelve rounds, baby, that's only six," shouted all-conference free safety Jordan Dangerfield. "They're going to come out and try and bully us."

Ambrose stuck a stake in the celebration.

"Now, any of you sons of bitches that are smiling 'cause you think we did something, I'm gonna kill ya. It's a fifteen-round fight, not five. You got it?"

"Yes, sir!"

"So what the hell we waiting for? Let's go!"

———

Some on campus had openly questioned the wisdom of becoming Tiger bait for LSU. The most visible anger was evident in the Friday afternoon TU 'PROSTITUTES THEMSELVES' FOR LSU headline in the school newspaper. In the accompanying article, the author charged the school was "sacrificing the health of our players and reputation of our program" for a paycheck. Others, like athletic director Waddell, took a broader view. "I think what it means for the university is a branding opportunity," he said. "It's another national television appearance. It's another chance for people to get to know who we are. Hopefully, within a few years of doing this kind of thing, we won't have other schools saying, 'Where are they? Are they in Arkansas? Nebraska? North Dakota?' It's branding. Everything we do has to, in some way, build to the brand."

Waddell's résumé showed a broadcasting background leading to athletic administrative stints at Virginia, at Akron and, most recently, five years at Cincinnati. (In May 2013 he would accept a job as senior associate athletic director at Arkansas.) One of his first acts after taking over as AD at Towson in September 2010 was to fill the slot on LSU's schedule that had just opened after Texas Christian University, believing it was headed to the Big East, pulled out.

"You think Les Miles didn't do a dance in his office that day," Waddell said, laughing. "Go from TCU to Towson."

He conceded Ambrose and his boys were essentially taking one for the team—the team, in this case, the entire university. He carried no grand illusions. This was a money play, needed and necessary, balanced by the opportunity to play before ninety thousand fans; the chance for coaches and players to learn something about themselves; to be part of something that would never be forgotten.

"Hey, you look back on our last ten years, we've taken a lot of poundings and not gotten paid," said Waddell. "So if you look at it at that level of analysis . . . it's not uncommon. That's what it is."

"It's really about the marketing of the institution," said David H. Nevins, the chairman of the school's board of visitors, its de facto board of trustees, as well as the owner of a strategic communications company. "It's really about being on [national TV], being in the papers on Sunday. People will read the name Towson, people who have never heard of it. Hopefully, we won't lose by the biggest number in college football history, and hopefully we won't lose any players. But that's really what this is about."

As Nevins spoke those words, he was sitting in the middle seat of the sixth row of the Friday afternoon charter flight down to Baton Rouge. In the row behind him was a well-heeled contractor; across the aisle, the executive vice president of a large health-care concern; two rows up, the president of several eye-care companies. Even though the football team was an enormous financial drain on the university, its $2 million budget funded in large part by $800 in annual student fees, recent success in football had reenergized the alumni base.

"Football is vital," declared Nevins. "Not so much from an economic standpoint. Frankly, it's a drain financially . . . it's never going to be an economic driver at our level; it's always going to be more expensive than the revenue it produces. So why do we do it? Hopefully, the answer is because football gives our campus something to rally around, to boost the spirit of our community. Football does that six or seven times a year. We believe at a school like Towson, transitioning to a big-time residential campus, football plays a critical role.

"Look," he continued. "We've been a quite extraordinarily solid institution for several decades now. We train a plurality of the state's teachers, a majority of the state's nurses, a plurality of the state's technology professionals. But, you know, we've never had the spotlight shine on us for much of anything.

"Winning is really important. It also matters who you win *against*. At Towson we are changing the way teachers are taught to teach. Hopefully, in a few years, we will invent a new way to teach. That gets us an article on page 2 of the newspaper.

"Nothing drives attention to this university like winning the Colonial Athletic Association football championship. It was *that* that caused the articles about the teacher's program to be written. It's unbelievable. That's the reason we put so much emphasis on football . . . It's time to step it up. Athletics is the most visible way to do it. We want to get on TV, tweeted about . . . [But] there's definitely risk involved. If it's 42–14, between you and me, I'll take that."

———

From the opening drive of the second half Towson got a full dose of a different LSU. By the end of the third quarter—after another long bomb to wide receiver Odell Beckham Jr.—it was 31–9. The rout, it appeared, was on.

But then Towson did in Death Valley what nonconference opponents rarely do. Like Ali, it got up from the canvas, squared its shoulders and punched back. As the fourth quarter began, the Towson Tigers put together their best drive of the night, a gritty, clock-grinding, in-your-face testament to toughness and will. On third and two from the LSU four-yard line quarterback Enders stuffed it right down to the one. A moment later it was 31–16 with nine minutes left. Ball game.

Again LSU responded. Running no huddle, it pounded away on the ground and attacked through the air, scoring again: 38–16. In response, Towson's offensive line and tailback Terrance West pounded back, producing another long, never-say-die drive that ended with a nine-yard circus catch in the end zone right in front of Waddell, who looked as if he'd just won the lottery. And maybe he had.

The final score read 38–22. A sixteen-point loss on paper. But a win in every other way.

"You couldn't buy this type of advertisement nationally," said Waddell after the game. "I could not be more proud."

Later, in a locker room brimming with pride, Ambrose told his team, "I've been doing this since I was about four years old, and I'm telling you the truth: of all my time in football I've never seen a team put in that kind of effort and belief. This team believed in each other and tuned out what everyone else had to say."

He took a breath and looked around at a roomful of sweaty, dirty, half-dressed athletes. They had escaped without serious injury. They had done their university proud.

Within minutes, the name Towson was trending on Twitter. The game highlights were in regular rotation on ESPN, its anchors singing the school's praises in the same breath as the eight touchdown passes by West Virginia's quarterback Geno Smith and Texas's last-second win at Oklahoma State. Towson *University* had arrived, even if the team was still trying to depart Baton Rouge . . .

It turned out that the charter company, Miami Air, had two runs that day. In addition to the Towson trip, it was ferrying the Cincinnati football team back from Virginia Tech. So by the time the charter arrived in Baton Rouge, it was 1:30 in the morning. Not a word was uttered as the players piled off buses and onto the plane. Within minutes the entire travel party was sacked out save a couple of graduate assistant coaches huddled over computers finishing up scouting reports on James Madison.

It was 5:30 in the morning when the team buses finally pulled in to a university parking lot. Some players drove away in cars. Others began a zombielike walk to their apartments or dorms. Waddell headed to Denny's for breakfast. In six short hours, the system required quarterbacks, wide receivers and defensive backs to report for treatment. By 4:00 p.m., the team would assemble for unit meetings. The schedule listed a walk-through/practice at 6:20.

Physically and emotionally drained from the LSU game, Towson lost 13–10 the following weekend at James Madison, a critical conference defeat, before dropping another crucial game, this time at home, to Old Dominion, 31–20, two weeks later. The team went on to win its final four games to finish 7-4, including rolling up 660 total yards in a 64–35 season-ending win at New Hampshire. Still, it wasn't enough to make the postseason playoffs.

But as Waddell suggested, in the long run the LSU game lived on. Few would forget the sight of that scoreboard: Towson 9, LSU 7, 5:15 to go in the first half. *In the lights.* On national television. Towson *University.*

8 OHIO STATE V. MICHIGAN

The return of "The Senator"

A chilling northwest wind sliced across the campus of Ohio State University on the final Saturday in November. It was The Game day—the 108th revival of the border war between the Buckeyes and their neighbor to the north.

By 8:45 the four cash registers at College Traditions were humming a pricey little tune. It was near freezing outside (thirty-three degrees), so the scarlet-and-gray hooded sweatshirts and fleece blankets flew off the shelves. With every purchase buyers received a commemorative BEAT MICHIGAN button. One fanatic bought fifty.

Up in Section 39A at the south end of the Horseshoe, twenty-one-year-old Cayla Hellwarth passed a box of Donatos pizza around. She and about three hundred of her fellow students had been inside since 8:00 a.m., setting color-coded flash cards on every seat in the section. On the back of one card were directions explaining exactly how they were to be used for a series of stunts during the game. "Every week, since we're here so early, we get free pizza for everyone that's on setup," Hellwarth explained. "I mean we're here for eight hours if you include game time, so we offer some incentive to sign up and help out."

Hellwarth was vice president of Block O—the largest student organization on campus and one of the finest student-run sports organizations in the country. Founded in 1938 by the former head cheerleader Clancy A. Isaac Jr. in support of the team, today Block O numbers nearly twenty-six hundred students. The group is funded largely by a $20 surcharge on twenty-one hundred first-come, first-served season tickets that sell online faster than seats to a Taylor Swift concert.

Block O was far from some "hey, dude, let's hang out" operation. It organized viewing parties for away games and pep rallies, where head coaches spoke, bands played and actual cheers and songs were learned.

There was something called Blockie points for attending games and meetings. Earn enough and you could score a seat on a special bus trip to Ann Arbor or Madison. And it wasn't just football. Block O supported all sports, with directors of operations for volleyball, soccer, baseball and many other teams. Elections were no beauty contests; if they were, odds were that Hellwarth, a stunning senior blond marketing and international business major, would have won, as she was, well, an actual beauty queen. The reigning Miss Miami Valley 2013, she came to Ohio State as a legacy; there was no other choice.

"I'm actually the sixth person in our family to attend Ohio State," she said a few days before The Game. "My mom was the only one that didn't go. She didn't go to college either, so we kind of already included her as a Buckeye. It was a tradition to go; I didn't even bother to visit here. I just knew it was the place for me to go."

Hellwarth fell in love with Block O her sophomore year after she "painted up" for the first time. "I think we won 65–0, and I think it was the best game I've ever been to as a home game," she said. "The experience is just so different."

So, it appeared, was the experience behind Section 39A. That's where sophomore Trevor McCue and a bunch of his Block O buddies were getting their game faces on. College girls with sponges—always a good thing— were busy painting a variety of Os and Hs and Ss, in gray and scarlet, on the chests and backs of shirtless boys. Hard to believe, but McCue and his buds actually had to *sign up* for this kind of work. McCue has done it every home game the last two years, even on frigid days like this. Normally, McCue said, he was a U. Today he settled for an S.

"You just have to stay active and move around," said our boy McCue. "Plus, the adrenaline from the game helps."

Ah, The Game.

The first one was played on October 17, 1897, a 34–0 Michigan victory. The Wolverines led the overall series 58-44-6 on the morning of November 24, 2012. By that night, it was 58-45-6, thanks to a gritty 26–21 comeback win by OSU that would have made Woody Hayes proud.

But as joyous as the score was, the game would long be remembered not for the fourth-down stop by the Buckeyes or the four Michigan turnovers, but rather for the celebration of the 2002 national championship team between the first and second quarter.

Ten years earlier in the Arizona desert, Ohio State had knocked off heavily favored Miami 31–24 in double overtime in the most memorable title game of the BCS era. And here they were again. Cheers rang out as the team was introduced. Maurice Clarett was among them.

As a freshman, the talented but troubled running back had carried the Buckeyes to the 2002 crown. A year later he was a pariah to the program. A year after that Clarett extracted a shocking form of revenge. He buried Ohio State in a carpet-bombing story written by Tom Friend in *ESPN the Magazine*. In chapter and verse Clarett revealed what Friend described as a system full of "free rides, free cash [and] free grades" for the star running back. A place where eligibility problems magically disappeared, tutors wrote research papers, and Clarett lived the life of a rap star.

"I had the money I wanted, the car I wanted. I literally, literally, had everything," Clarett told Friend.

And then, suddenly, it was gone.

In the week leading up to the win over Miami, Clarett said he was led to believe he would be able to travel back to Ohio to attend the funeral of a childhood friend. But then OSU said no, citing a paperwork problem. Clarett was angry and called out school officials.

In the *ESPN* article, Clarett said it was head coach Jim Tressel who set up the buffet table of mouthwatering perks—"thousands" in cash from boosters, free loaners from car dealers, phony jobs, no-show classes, whatever he needed. In the spring of 2003, the NCAA got wind of the cars and cash. Questioned that summer, Clarett kept answering, "I don't know" or "I don't remember" or "I magically got them." Protecting his head coach, he said. By the fall of his sophomore year, however, he was done, suspended for the season. And Tressel, he said, had stopped taking his calls.

"I think he knows in his heart he sold me out," Clarett told Friend. "He sold me out to keep his integrity . . . Coach Tressel, he made everything easy . . . until he wanted to make it hard."

Crisp in tone, polished in nature, a stickler for detail, Tressel had earned the nickname The Senator. He had guided Ohio State to three BCS title games and won 81 percent of his games in ten years. He had won or shared six straight Big Ten titles and sent the Wolverines home with their tails between their legs nine times.

Tressel's epic fall from grace was quick and painful just eighteen months after it was discovered that the coach lied to the NCAA and Ohio State on several occasions while being questioned about the "tattoo-gate" scandal in which more than twenty players, including star quarterback Terrelle Pryor, received free tattoos in exchange for memorabilia. But inside the Horseshoe, in the Church of the Scarlet and Gray, all seemed forgiven on game day. The 2002 team received a special blessing. Cheers rolled out of the stands. Chants of "Tress-el! Tress-el!" and "We love Tress-el!" thundered across the stadium.

Ohio State fans had plenty to cheer about on this afternoon. After new savior Urban Meyer led Ohio State past Michigan the Buckeyes had reached perfection again, this time finishing 12-0. But it ended there. No Big Ten title game. No bowl. No possibility of another national championship. Among the NCAA penalties for Tressel's lies and "tattoo-gate" was a postseason ban.

"I wasn't actually affected all [that] much that there was no postseason for us," said Ohio State senior Tim Collins, president of Block O. "Probably because I've had a year to process this and fully expected it. The perfect season probably won't hit me until I'm telling nostalgic stories to friends or children, that I was at Ohio State during one of its most tumultuous yet simultaneously terrific times in our athletic history."

———

From the headlines it appeared that the Ohio State football scandal had broken new ground. Not so. On paper it looked pretty familiar—free stuff for athletes, some memorabilia sales, a little cash courtesy of a deep-pocketed booster, the failure to properly monitor his activities. The suspected criminal drug connection of the tattoo parlor owner was the wild card.

In its Infractions Report dated December 20, 2011, the NCAA laid out the allegations:

- Between November 2008 and June 2010 eight football student-athletes had received more than $14,000 in cash payments or preferential treatment from tattoo parlor owner Eddie Rife in the form of free or discounted tattoos or cash for things like championship and bowl rings, game-used pants, jerseys and shoes.
- One player was given an estimated $2,420 discount on the purchase of a used car and an $800 loan from Rife to fix his car.
- Between the summer of 2009 and the summer of 2011 nine football players received a total of $2,405 for work not performed (five players, $1,605) and "impermissible extra benefits" (four players, $200 cash each) from a "representative" of the university's athletics interests to attend a charity event in the Cleveland area.
- Unethical conduct charges against Tressel.
- Failure to monitor charges against the school.

To soften the coming blow, Ohio State did what every school does these days: it self-reported. The school launched an internal investigation, then proposed a series of penalties—harsh but not too harsh—in hopes of appeasing the NCAA's powerful Committee on Infractions. During its self-report investigation OSU never discovered that its upstanding head football coach knew about the memorabilia-for-tattoo problem as far back as April 2010. OSU penalized itself with two years' probation, the loss of five football scholarships over three years, vacating all wins associated with its tainted 2010 season and the forfeiture of more than $388,000 in revenue from the 2011 Sugar Bowl. It also took the preventive step of disassociating the booster involved, Robert "Bobby D." DiGeronimo, from the athletics program for ten years.

The Infractions Committee was not moved. It focused on the "failure to monitor" DiGeronimo and the fact that several Buckeyes linked to the violations, particularly Pryor, had played in the Sugar Bowl with Tressel's full knowledge of their transgressions. In December 2011 the committee came down hard on Ohio State.

It hit the Buckeyes with three years' probation beginning in December 2011 (not two) and the loss of nine scholarships (not five) while vacating the wins and forfeiting the bowl revenue. Most significantly, the committee banned the team from a bowl game in 2012 and expressed particular displeasure with The Senator, slapping a "show cause" penalty on Tressel, essentially removing him from major college coaching for five years.

Ohio State athletic director Gene Smith described the university as "surprised and disappointed" at the ruling.

It's a new day in Columbus. Under Urban Meyer the school had a renewed energy and fresh commitment to learn from past transgressions. A stellar 2013 recruiting class and a slew of returning stars, like quarterback Braxton Miller, had the Buckeyes on the short list of teams with legitimate BCS title hopes in the 2013–14 season.

But those inclined to plumb the "tattoo-gate" scandal at greater depth discovered that what happened at Ohio State offered sobering lessons in how the system could be used and abused. Used to protect those familiar with its levers of power and control. Abused to punish those caught up in its clutches. A system where the athletic director who can't remember in an NCAA interview what month it is ("Where we at? October?") and cannot, for the life of him, remember specific times and dates, is allowed to slide on his answers. While a student-athlete is expected to have an extraordinary memory—to reconstruct days and hours worked two years past. Where cell phone records read one way confirm guilt, while read another confirm innocence; a place where the qualifiers "around," "near," "likely" and "estimates" are strung together to devastating effect.

––––––––

Two days before Easter Sunday 2010, Jim Tressel received an e-mail from someone named Chris Cicero. It arrived at 2:32 on Friday afternoon. As best Tressel could remember, Cicero was a former walk-on football player, a mid-1980s guy when Tressel served as an assistant coach under Earle Bruce. Tressel could not recall Cicero's position—linebacker, it turned out—but knew he was a local criminal defense attorney. Five or six years earlier, he recalled, Cicero had been part of a group that put on a seminar on law enforcement issues for his team.

Ten months later, on February 8, 2011, Tressel was interviewed for five hours by NCAA investigators Chance Miller and Tim Nevius. Several Ohio State legal and compliance officials and outside enforcement consultants were also in attendance. About a half hour into the interview Tressel was asked about Cicero's first e-mail. Tressel said one of his first thoughts was, "What in the devil are you sending this to me for? This is not in my league."

But then he looked at the bullet points, and the words "Federal government raid" registered. At the bottom of the e-mail he noticed the words "homicide" and "drug trafficking." And this: Cicero said he had been told the federal government had hit the house of a former client, Edward "Eddie" Rife, owner and operator of Fine Line Ink. In 2001, Cicero said, Rife had been convicted of felony forgery and possession of criminal tools. Cicero wrote he was being told Pryor and "other players" had taken signed Ohio State memorabilia (shirts, jerseys, footballs) to Rife, who was selling them "for profit."

At 11:20 a.m., Tressel responded to Rife: "I hear you!! It is unbelievable! Thanks for your help . . . keep me posted as to what I need to do if anything. I will keep pounding these kids hoping they grow up . . . jt."

In the NCAA interview Tressel described himself as "scared" and "frightened" at the "magnitude" of the e-mail.

"This is frightening," he said. Because what he was reading, he said, "was way beyond" an NCAA rule.

"I mean, it was a security issue," he said, according to the 139-page transcript of his interview. "It was a federal criminal issue. It was a narcotics issue . . . where do you turn?"

Where to turn? At this point Tressel had been the head football coach at Ohio State and Youngstown State and in the college game for decades. Of all the things The Senator was, naïve wasn't one of them.

The NCAA would later point out that Tressel could have turned to it, to local law enforcement, to university legal counsel or to his compliance department for help or guidance. Tressel did not see it that way. He told investigators the "gravity" of the situation involving Rife "trumped" any such action. A cynic might suggest the sale of a boatload of memorabilia to a suspected drug dealer by several current players—including his star quarterback—trumped *every* other action. But spring practice was about to begin. The Buckeyes were one of the favorites to win another national championship, and starting quarterback Terrelle Pryor was being hailed as one of the best ballers in the country.

But that's not to say Tressel took no action. The next day he forwarded Cicero's e-mail to Ted Sarniak, a trusted adviser and mentor to Pryor. The two had met during Pryor's freshman year in high school in Pennsylvania, a relationship that in 2008 earned a serious look by the NCAA. Tressel expressed concerns about Pryor's safety, and Sarniak was the only person, he believed, capable of telling Pryor "the right things for the right reasons."

Here's what Tressel told Sarniak: "Hey, look, you know, I heard [Pryor] was out, you know, and he's got to—he's too visible. You gotta remind him, you know, that he's under the microscope. And, you know, it—I know it's not fair 'cause forty thousand other students are allowed to be out and all that. But life's not fair. You know, just, you know, bring that one into the discussion, you know?"

NCAA investigator Chance Miller, a former claims litigator for the City of New York, asked Tressel if he ever thought of following up with Cicero to determine whether Pryor or other players were involved with criminal issues.

"You know, I didn't," Tressel answered.

On April 16, Tressel received two more e-mails from Cicero. The first came in at 9:43 a.m., the other at 2:24 p.m. Two weeks had done little to calm Tressel's sense of fear and helplessness. Now Cicero was telling him Rife had been in Cicero's office for ninety minutes the night before and he "really is a drug dealer." What's more, Rife had about fifteen pairs of cleats (with signatures), four or five jerseys (all signed) and nine Big Ten championship rings and a national championship ring in his possession.

Four bullet points down in his morning e-mail Cicero had written this sentence: "What I tell you is confidential."

"And in there, he said, you know, 'What I tell you is confidential,'" Tressel said in his NCAA interview. "And so now I'm thinking, 'Okay, I gotta ask him what the heck, you know, what should I do? Now you've—you know, you pulled me into this operation.'"

That led to this exchange with NCAA associate director of enforcement Tim Nevius:

NEVIUS: And you've pointed to specific names or references to potential criminal activity. The e-mails from Mr. Cicero appear to emphasize the sale of memorabilia, though.

TRESSEL: Mm-hmm, mm-hmm.

NEVIUS: . . . There's nothing in the emails that mentions or references that any of the Ohio State football student athletes were involved in criminal activity.

TRESSEL: Right. That's right.

NEVIUS: Did you follow up with him [Cicero] in any regard to inquire as to whether or not they were involved in criminal activity?

TRESSEL: No. 'Cause, I mean, I don't know that I thought this through from that standpoint.

Instead, Tressel said he began "pounding" away at his team in "awareness" meetings, telling them he was hearing things, bad things; they had to "stay away from the wrong people." He admitted to the NCAA he never mentioned just who those wrong people might be; never once mentioned the seized memorabilia, the tattoo parlor and potential NCAA violations. Or Rife.

Asked why, Tressel responded: "Not sure. Probably reluctance of—I wanted it to be vague about, you know, who we were talking about yet. I guess I wanted it to be all-inclusive."

"Did you ever ask them [players] if they sold their memorabilia?" asked Nevius.

"No, no," answered Tressel. "And why didn't I? I don't know? I didn't really didn't ask 'em anything. It was not an asking situation. It was a 'Hey, I've heard.' 'This one's serious, you know . . . You better stay away.'"

About three-quarters of the way through the five-hour interview, Nevius cut to the chase.

NEVIUS: Do you understand that it is an NCAA violation not to report information concerning violations?

TRESSEL: Yeah.

NEVIUS: —you thought the most appropriate thing was not to do anything?

TRESSEL: Right. It was to let the federal investigation happen, you know . . .

NEVIUS: And you felt that even though you knew that NCAA violations had occurred, and that you were gonna go forward with those student-athletes participating in the 2010 season.

TRESSEL: Yeah.

NEVIUS: I guess what the problem is that there was no action taken on either the NCAA issues or the federal investigation.

TRESSEL: Right.

NEVIUS: So despite the concern that one of these issues being more problematic than the other—

TRESSEL: Mm-hmm.

NEVIUS: —the facts are you didn't address either.

TRESSEL: Right.

NEVIUS: But it is important for a head coach to recognize that if student athletes had engaged in violations and they're aware of that, that that information needs to be reported, and the student athletes have to go through the appropriate channels to be reinstated before they can participate in competition. You're aware of that, too, right?

TRESSEL: I am, yeah.

NEVIUS: And you were aware of that at the time?

TRESSEL: Yeah. I don't know that I was thinking of it that way.

———

On September 13, 2010, Tressel signed what turned out to be his own death certificate. It came in the form of the NCAA's certificate of compliance. By signing and dating the form submitted by Ohio State to the NCAA, Tressel declared he had informed "appropriate individuals" of his knowledge of any violations of NCAA rules.

He had no knowledge.

Again, Nevius bored in.

"When you signed it, did you think about the e-mails and the—all the discussions with Cicero?" asked Nevius.

"Probably not."

Then, a few questions later:

NEVIUS: You know, you've acknowledged that you didn't report the information. But then you suggest, though, that that might have had to do with the fact you anticipated consequences.

TRESSEL: Mm-hmm.

NEVIUS: And you anticipated NCAA consequences.

TRESSEL: Right.

Tressel's attempts to skirt the truth almost certainly would have worked if not for a letter the Department of Justice sent to Ohio State in early December 2010. As part of their investigation into Rife, the feds informed the university that dozens of signed football-related items had been seized during a raid of Rife's home and office. That certainly was news to Ohio State. Did Tressel know? No, he said. He didn't. At that time Ohio State was 11-1 and ranked No. 6 in the country. It was on its way to a BCS matchup with Arkansas in the Sugar Bowl, a game it would win. Pryor was named MVP.

On page 114 of the transcript, Miller bluntly asked Tressel the following question: "If that letter would have never been received by Ohio State, would you have come forward with these violations?"

In response, The Senator offered an answer straight out of a Washington filibuster, truly worthy of the Hypnotic Hall of Fame.

"Never is a long time. I don't know. I don't know," Tressel began.

I mean, the easiest for me to say is, "Yeah, I had set a deadline of, you know, whatever, January 14, 2011." I hadn't. I had confidence in the federal government that they were gonna do what they were supposed to do. They didn't need my help to do it, nor did they need my interruption to do it.

And that when that was completed, that I had confidence that they weren't gonna throw our stuff in the dumpster. I had confidence that they weren't gonna confiscate it and put it in their own man caves. You know, that they were gonna return it to us. And we were gonna deal with it, you know, from that standpoint.

You know, I suppose things could take two years. It wasn't my impression on June 1. My impression on June 1 was, "Hey, they said this guy's going to prison," you know. Now, obviously, as the days got closer to him going to prison, he said, "No, no, wait a minute. Let me tell you—I'll help you." And so I guess that's what happened.

So I don't know the answer to your question.

———

The litany of lies that began on Easter weekend 2010 lasted until Memorial Day 2011. At that point Tressel had outlasted additional violations involving extra benefits, a five-game suspension and $250,000 fine and a knockout March 2011 *Yahoo! Sports* investigation by Charles Robinson and Dan Wetzel charging Tressel knew about the scandal in April 2010. But in the end, he could not survive a withering *Sports Illustrated* cover story that opened another huge can of worms. The linchpin of the piece: the memorabilia-for-tattoos party had started as far back as 2002 and involved at least twenty-eight players—twenty-two more than previously acknowledged by the university.

Tressel was out the door by Monday.

In their official response to Notice of Allegations, Case Number M352, Tressel's attorneys finally acknowledged he broke a cardinal rule of coaching—Unethical Conduct Bylaw 10.1. Tressel offered "no excuses" for his decisions.

In its official response, Ohio State said its former coach had paid a "terrible price" for his mistakes.

In February 2012, Tressel was hired by the University of Akron as its vice president of strategic engagement, a position created just for him. His main focus at the school would be working with students and alumni to foster better relationships with the community. His base salary was a reported $200,000 a year, some $3 million a year less than he earned annually at Ohio State. At his introductory press conference Tressel made clear he felt fortunate to have this opportunity.

"This," he said, "is a second chance."

9 THE JANITOR

"I fix shit"

They are the unseen, unsung heroes of college football. Seated up front on every bus or plane, walkie-talkie in hand, eyeing the road, checking a watch and anticipating trouble. Getting things *done*.

The official title of these problem-solving point men is director of football operations (DFO). It might as well be director of *detail* operations. For eighty hours or more a week they are consumed with nothing but *details*. Team travel. Game management. Seating charts. Rooming lists. Hotel buffets. Academic support. Law enforcement. Ten thousand and one things in their hands alone.

"We're facilitators," said Mike Sinquefield, the highly respected DFO at Texas Christian University. "That's what we do. Coaches expect things. Athletic directors expect things. You can't anticipate everything, try as you might, [but] you just have to be ready to think on your feet."

In 2012, Stanford's DFO Matt Doyle was honored as the Operations Director of the Year by his peers. It said something about the nature of his job that Doyle could not remember how old he would be in May of that year—thirty-six, it turned out. But he knew precisely the number of goblets (two) and drinks (six) and the type of bread (sourdough) and ketchup (Heinz 57) he wanted set on a breakfast table at away hotels.

"For the most part it's because we want to eliminate distractions that exist," said Doyle. "What we don't want is for things to be different. We don't want a guy after three weeks finally getting into a routine of eating eggs and cheddar for breakfast and all of a sudden we don't have eggs and cheddar. Sounds silly, but that's how it is."

That's exactly how the game is run these days, because if you can't *systemize* life for coaches consumed by Xs and Os, by one thing and one thing only—winning—you're working Division IV football, which, by the way, does not exist.

"I always think if something goes wrong, somehow it's my fault," said Doyle. "If the sprinklers come on in the middle of practice, that's probably my fault. If the plane is delayed, there's nothing I can do about it. But it's nobody else's fault but mine."

––––––

In the spring of 2012, about one hundred and fifty DFOs from across the country converged on the Omni Fort Worth for their annual convention. Had some wayward soul stumbled into the second-floor ballroom and listened to a panel discussion, he would have thought it was a taping of the *Dr. Phil* show.

"I don't see my family, ever," said Luke Groth with a sigh, then in his second year as DFO at Division III power Wisconsin-Whitewater. "I don't see my mom. I don't hardly ever talk to my mom. I feel terrible."

Like virtually every other member of his profession, Doyle had paid a steep personal price. A few days after the Fort Worth meeting, during a two-hour drive to speak at a donor luncheon in Sacramento, Doyle laughed at the notion he was enjoying his so-called downtime.

"Downtime is an interesting definition because right now I'm traveling like fourteen of the next eighteen days," he said. "So that's not really my downtime.

"This is fun for me; I like doing it," he added. "But the reality for me is what would I be doing if I decided not to go to Sacramento to speak? If I don't speak, I'd be teeing off at two o'clock. Or heaven forbid, I might pick up my daughter at lunchtime."

After graduating from college, he found work as a teacher and coach at his alma mater, St. Francis High in affluent Mountain View, California. Several of his students had parents who were coaches or worked at Stanford, including the son of then Cardinal head football coach, Tyrone Willingham, and the daughter of former athletic director Ted Leland. A member of the football staff was leaving and wondered if Doyle would be interested in the job. He was. Doyle applied, got it and over the years, through five head coaches, had seen his role steadily expand into assistant AD, director of football operations.

From the first of August 2012 and the start of training camp until the Rose Bowl on New Year's Day 2013, Doyle had worked 153 days in a row. "There's no day off to go to the dentist," he said. "There's no mowing your lawn. You can only get a haircut because Supercuts stays open until ten. But for the most part there's not all this stuff that regular people do on weekends."

Instead there was a list of duties and responsibilities Doyle had compiled in the winter of 2012 for national comparison with other DFOs:

PRIMARY DUTIES
Day to Day Management of the football program
Team Travel
Budget Manager
Summer Camps and Clinics
Summer Jobs Program
Summer Housing Program
Football Alumni Coordinator
Support Coaches and Staff in all areas of need
Supervise Office Staff, Interns and Volunteers
Pre-Season Training Camp
Bowl Game Management
Event Management/Stanford Football
• Alumni Relations (Fall and Spring)
• Season Kickoff Dinner (Aug)
• Starting 11 BBQ (May)
• LOI Reception (Feb)
• Pro Timing Day (March)
Stadium Design Projects
Football Office Redesign Projects

MISCELLANEOUS DUTIES
Game Day Management
New Hire Coordination
Future Scheduling
Pac-12 Conference Championship Committee
Big Game Committee
Rose Bowl Advisory Committee
Football Operations National Committee

LIAISON DUTIES
Strength and Conditioning
Equipment Room
Sports Medicine
Facilities
Marketing
Ticket Office

Football Sponsorship and Trade Out
Development Office
Media Relations Department
Faculty and University Staff
Campus and Community Police
Dean's Office
Office of Judicial Affairs
NFL/Pro Scouts
Agent Relations
Pac-12 Officials
Pac-12 Office
Parent Organization
Housing and Dining

For those scoring at home, that is forty-five different areas in which Doyle had some control or input. In answer to the frequent "What do you do?" question posed three years earlier, he had compiled another list. Jim Harbaugh was the Stanford head coach at the time. "A Day in the Life" was how Doyle described it. The day in question, a Monday following a heartbreaking loss on the road at Arizona. He had already worked his regular twelve-hour day on Sunday. Monday had started bright and early, at 7:00 a.m., with a quick stop for coffee. By 7:04 he had unlocked some meeting rooms for NFL scouts who wanted to watch film. Nearly sixteen hours later, at 10:45 p.m., Doyle's list ended with this notation: "Day is done, heading home." In between his timeline showed no fewer than a dozen different meetings ranging from game management to the equipment manager, head trainer, offensive and defensive coaches, to finally Harbaugh himself, at 10:00 p.m. Sprinkled throughout was a daily dose of multitasking combined with crisis management—making sure the ryegrass inside the stadium looked just right for the upcoming game against Arizona State on national TV; tracking down a player's lost wallet; responding to a flood of e-mails that had poured in overnight; helping a graduate assistant fill out an application to a coach's academy. Just one more day of driving the locomotive that was only picking up speed. Fueled by what Doyle saw as a "major inflation of self-importance" rippling its way through top-tier programs.

"There's a football program in the Big 12 where they have an equipment manager going to each coach's home and packing his bag before they leave on Friday for the away game," he said with more than a touch of disgust in his voice. "You're telling your coaches they don't have the wherewithal—they're too *busy* to pack their own bag and bring it in with them on Friday to the office. Have the *staff*, have the equipment manager, go to a guy's home and pack their bag?"

———

In Fort Worth the impromptu therapy session eventually evolved into a nuts-and-bolts Q&A. How best to nurture alumni help? What's best—training table or university food service? Clearly the bane of every DFO's existence was finding the best way to communicate with 105 players in a constant state of social media flux, ever-changing cell numbers, oblivious to university e-mail. One DFO said he still relied on old-fashioned notes stuck on lockers to update a change in practice time. But in reality, at football powers with robust budgets, old-school ways were quickly being replaced by cutting-edge communication and organizational systems like Scoutware and ACS. Doyle said Stanford used a program called Teamworks, produced by Logistical Athletic Solutions (LAS).

"Totally changed the way we do business," he said.

A voice rose from the back of the meeting room. "Come see the big Greek guy, we'll take care of ya!"

Zach Maurides was, indeed, a big, outgoing Greek guy. A former left guard at Duke, he had founded LAS in 2005 with $300,000 in seed money. "Human beings are the least efficient solution to your problem, especially when it's rote work, repetitive tasks, like data entry," he said. "Why should you have a coach sit and individually text 105 kids? That can all be done programmatically; it can be scripted."

In 2006, Maurides brought in computer programmer Shaun Powell, now a partner in the company, to design a Web-based platform geared to streamlining communication and the convergence of data. "The concepts aren't new," said Maurides. "They've been applied to every other industry. It's just that athletics is finally to the point now where it's a big enough operation, there's enough money involved, you have to start looking at these things and organizing ourselves."

Teamworks offered eight core modules. There was a mass-messaging system; another eliminated the need for paper and paperwork. A Profiles module stored biographical information, family contacts, addresses, academic information and notes. A Time Management module synthesized practices, workouts and appointments.

By now the big Greek had fired up his laptop. Multicolored, password-protected files and pages danced on his screen. "Take a look at this," he said. He clicked on a sample Mass Communication page. The options appeared endless—immediate messaging via text, voice or mail by grade, group or position within ten seconds. Real-time feedback as to whether the message had been received or not. To demonstrate, Maurides sent a voice mail to a reporter's phone. Ten seconds later it appeared: "You're late for a meeting."

The jaw-dropper was the Athlete Record Management module. In addition to centralizing all medical and academic records, biographical data and financial and personal information, it provided a metrics component. For example, Player A's entire weight room and conditioning history could be inputted by a staff member, and then, with the click of a mouse, the staffer could run a regression analysis to see if the player was improving or had flatlined in his bench, squat or forty-yard dash. What player had made the biggest percentage increase in strength at tight end? One click and the answer appeared.

Duke was one of the first schools to buy into the program. In 2011 it purchased all eight modules (Maurides said, depending on the size of the team, the cost ran between $450 and $18,000 per module; an entire athletic department priced between $35,000 and $70,000). A return-on-investment study conducted by LAS and approved by Duke showed in 2011 the athletic department saved more than eighty-eight hundred man-hours that year and more than $244,000. Teamworks had since expanded to more than forty FBS programs; Nebraska, Oregon, Notre Dame, Miami (Florida) and Texas had all bought into the system within the system.

"If you look at *Moneyball* and the way people look at baseball teams, it's the same thing here," said Maurides. "A lot of things are still gut decisions. This is what I *think* I should do. But then we can change it to this is what the *data* is telling us, this is what the data said."

Maurides made no bones about the fact much of the data collection—the personal info, roommate and girlfriend contacts—was mainly about "risk management." In an emergency it enabled a DFO to find a player as quickly as possible.

"A guy's in trouble, he's hiding out," said Maurides. "That's a reality."

During the question-and-answer period Mack Butler, the silver-haired DFO at Oklahoma State, had touched on that topic. He was looking for suggestions on the best ways to handle what Butler described as "those probing eyes."

"Probably have a hard time getting anyone to do this," Butler said. "I think how you handle those things is a huge deal. One of the things that has been unique about this group is we all know ways to do things in which we stretch the envelope. We all know the NCAA doesn't necessarily agree with this, but we have found the words and the terminology to go beyond what they are trying to control."

———

Circumstances being what they were, the man best suited to address the issue of wayward players was not in Fort Worth but in Austin. In the insular world of football operations Cleve Bryant, the DFO at Texas from 1998 until 2011, was viewed as nothing less than a legend, lionized for his ability to *facilitate*, to stamp out fires before the first sign of smoke.

Bryant liked to say he could look into a player's eyes as he boarded the bus and *know* exactly what kind of practice he was going to have. Nothing got by Bryant—not a watch, not a vehicle, not the slightest change in lifestyle.

"Whose ride?" he'd ask a player suddenly driving a different car.

"My girl."

"Bring me the paperwork," Bryant would say. "No paperwork, that ride had better disappear."

To those who had butted heads with Bryant over the years, he was known as Dr. No, a backhanded slap at the force field he'd built up over thirteen years around Texas's head coach, Mack Brown. Bryant was perhaps best known for his unwavering radar when it came to issues that might eventually spread some mud on the Longhorns program.

Bryant's personal warning system began to buzz one year when the Longhorns checked into a hotel for a game with Oklahoma State. It was nearly midnight. Off in the corner of the lobby Bryant spotted a young, pretty girl in a miniskirt. Groupie, he thought. Then the tumblers clicked and he remembered how sports agents had turned to babes like this as "runners" to help entice top draft picks to sign. Either way she was a problem. Bryant turned to the Texas Ranger who always accompanied the team on road trips.

"Lance, check that out for me," he said, nodding at the girl. "Find out if she's a guest in the hotel."

Turned out she was.

"But that didn't matter to me," Bryant explained. "I didn't want her there. So I went to the manager of the hotel and told him he had to decide if he wanted to rent one room or a hundred rooms because either she's gone or we're gone. And like that, she was gone."

In a legal setting Bryant described himself as "a liaison guy for football operations," the messenger between Brown and the administration, his assistant coaches, trainers and staff. Officially, Bryant handled day-to-day football operations. Unofficially he was Mack's jack-of-all-trades: disciplinarian, teacher and father figure to every single player on the Texas roster.

"Shit happens," Bryant said. "And my job is to deal with the 'holy shit' moments. That way Mack can spend his time on football, and I can run the program."

He had been with Brown since they arrived in Austin in 1998 and for three years before at North Carolina. More than once Brown had acknowledged Bryant's friendship and influence, saying publicly, "If Cleve leaves, I'm leaving, too."

"He knows everything," said one former UT football star of Bryant. "He was the reason the program was indestructible. Why it never had a problem with the NCAA."

So how did Bryant see himself? Right-hand man? Buffer? Bad cop?

He paused, smiled and turned up his hands.

"I'm the janitor," he said. "I fix shit."

As Bryant, sixty-four at the time, spoke of his janitorial duties, he was sitting in a deserted restaurant on the lower level of the Austin Four Seasons in the fall of 2011. Tall and fit, he arrived wearing sweatpants and a crisp Polo shirt and carried a quiet, confident air. In 1967, Bryant was an all-conference quarterback at Ohio University, one of the first blacks to play that position in the Mid-American Conference. The next season he earned Player of the Year honors.

"Many people just didn't think blacks were smart enough," he said. "It was a challenge, and I was stubborn, bound and determined."

He was drafted by the Denver Broncos in the eleventh round in 1970 but never made the team. A twenty-year coaching career began a few years later, with stops as a quarterbacks and/or wide receivers coach at his alma mater, North Carolina, Illinois and Texas before Brown brought him back to Chapel Hill in 1995, adding recruiting coordinator to Bryant's growing list of responsibilities. He was forty-seven years old. At fifty, he told Brown he was giving up prostitution, a reference to the recruiting game.

"I don't give a shit," Bryant said Brown told him. "I want you on my staff."

In 1998, Brown got the call from Texas. Soon he and Cleve were headed to Austin to pick up the pieces of the broken John Mackovic era (1992–97). With Bryant at his side, Brown expanded the school's promotional and recruiting base, courted high-end donors, upgraded facilities and reversed the ratio of white to black athletes. Together they rebuilt a fading football power. Texas won nine games each of its first three seasons and eleven in three of the next four before striking it rich with the undefeated (13-0) 2005 national championship team. It didn't stop there. The Longhorns reeled off forty-five wins (against just seven defeats) over the next four seasons before a loss to Alabama in the January 2010 BCS championship game.

Brown got the accolades. But Bryant did the dirty work.

"I was always on call, twenty-four hours a day," he said. "During the course of the day you don't know what's coming at you. You just adjust on the run and go. My television never goes off. It's on all night. When a call comes into my house, it comes up on the TV. Two, three, four in the morning, my wife turns to me and said, 'Cleve, that's for you.' I can look at the TV and tell who is calling. I pick up the phone, 'Cleve, we arrested one of your boys.'

"In this town I know the UT police and the Austin PD. I met with them two or three times a year. I bring them our media guides. And I tell them: If one of my players shows up someplace they aren't supposed to be, you call me. I don't give a shit what time it is.

"My first question is, 'Where's he at?' I ask what's the situation, and the officer will tell me. Then I hang up and the process rolls from there. I take care of everything."

And no matter how sensitive or messy the crisis, Bryant never strayed from Rule No. 1: Never panic.

"As soon as the kid is released, he knows his ass is in my office. I'm going to hear his side of the story. I got his side, the police side, the truth is going to fall someplace in between. Once I have that, I call Mack and say, 'So-and-so has been arrested.' Mack may say, 'Do you believe him?' I tell him the same thing every time: 'Coach, I'm still gathering information.'

"After I see Mack, I see the AD. Then I call the SID [sports information director] and tell him to prepare a statement to the press for Mack. 'We are aware of the situation. We are monitoring the legal process.' The standard bullshit lines.

"Bottom line, these are my sons. Right, wrong, indifferent, I'm going to defend them. I tell them, 'I don't give a shit what you did. When you come into my office, you tell me the truth. If you lie to me once, I'm going to leave you out there on your own. Tell the truth.' I've never had a kid lie to me."

In all their years together Bryant and Brown acted like an old married couple—speaking in unspoken looks and shrugs. They had long since devised a way to deal with distractions and potential trouble. Cleve would handle it.

"Most schools have individuals to do each job," Bryant said. "It's really better when one person does it all. Mack said he didn't want a committee. I'm my own committee. Mack and I met every day.

"Mack can handle the bad news. What he doesn't like is surprises. He doesn't like people coming into his office if he doesn't know what it's about. Ninety percent of the day-to-day bullshit never made his desk.

"Mack doesn't like people getting mad at him. They get mad at Cleve. I can handle it. It's easier for me to say no, let me work on that rather than Mack. I don't give you a fast no. I'll give you a slow no. I may know in my mind it's not going to happen, but because of the sensitivity I'll give you the slow no.

"Sometimes we have pissed off parents. They call, demanding a meeting with Mack. 'I don't want to fucking talk to Cleve.' Okay. In my office I have a file on every player—scholarship, walk-on, manila folders, in alphabetical order. If a player is late for class, doesn't show for treatment, flunks a drug test, gets a ticket, I have all the paperwork in my file. Mack would not meet with the parent alone. I would be there with that file, and I'd pull that file out and start talking the truth."

The truth was, said Bryant, eighty percent of the kids did everything right. The thickest files were always the other twenty percent—the ones he would have to remind: "They were playing before you got here and when you leave they'll still be playing." That's why he created what he called the Newcomer List. It covered all the dos and don'ts—everything from how to handle a traffic ticket ("you don't pay, at some point it becomes a warrant") to time and money management.

"That's a tough one," he said. "Most adults in the country can't do it [and] we expect these kids to do it. NCAA only lets us provide one meal a day. For us, that's usually dinner. So the kids get a check for the other two meals [a day]. One check per month. The problem with the check is you give a freshman a check for $400, he's going to buy a phone, CDs, gimmicks. It's gone in one or two weeks. Now what's he left with? He's got one meal a day, and he's trying to survive off that until the end of the month. So halfway through the month he's hungry. He ends up eating at McDonald's and living on fast food. It's another reason the quality on the field is suffering. We take these guys to grocery stores and show them how to eat. They are told to eat healthy and why it's important. It doesn't matter. They get that check in the beginning of the month and they blow it."

Often Bryant dealt with problems that had nothing to do with the players. At the 2000 Holiday Bowl in San Diego, Texas was down late in the game to Oregon—it would eventually lose 35–30—when Arthur Johnson (now UT's associate athletics director for football operations) approached Bryant on the sideline.

"Cleve," said Johnson. "I've got some good news and some bad news."

"Give me the good news."

"The good news is the postgame snack is here."

"What's the bad news?"

"The plane we were supposed to take home right after the game is still in Minneapolis."

Shit, thought Bryant. Johnson's next question dealt with who was going to inform Brown. Bryant knew that answer. But first things first.

"Okay, call the hotel," he told Johnson. "I don't give a fuck what it costs, get Mack his room back. Then get a room downstairs and fill it with pizzas and food."

"Do you want me to tell you when the plane leaves Minneapolis?" asked Johnson.

"No, tell that son of a bitch to call me when he's on the ground in San Diego."

After the game Bryant walked up to Brown and delivered the bad news.

"You're shitting me," said Brown.

"You got your room, don't worry," Bryant said.

After the game the team and the travel party bused back to the hotel and hung out until the plane finally arrived. It was only after Bryant had every single player accounted for and every single person in the travel party on the bus that he knocked on Brown's hotel door.

"Okay, Coach," he said. "Let's roll."

————

At the time of his departure Bryant estimated Texas was netting at least $8 million per home game, plus concessions. The fifty-seven luxury suites surrounding the field go for around $56,000 a year, he said, not counting food and tickets. The fact the players, *his players*, didn't see a dime of that money, of any outside money, bothered Bryant.

"It's basically slave labor," he said.

To that end he explained how if he could find a way to skirt the rules from time to time, to put a little extra cash in a kid's pocket, he would. Sometimes it meant playing games with the way plane tickets were purchased. Sometimes it meant knowing a place where the star running back could buy a $500 suit for $50 to look good at an awards dinner or setting up a good deal on a used car.

It's in those ways, and countless more, that Bryant's loss to the Longhorns program cannot be measured. Those in the know argued the early-morning incident involving quarterback Case McCoy and linebacker Jordan Hicks, accused of sexually assaulting a twenty-one-year-old woman in a hotel room at the Alamo Bowl at the end of the 2012 season, would never have happened under Bryant's watch (no charges were filed in the case). He would have seen trouble coming three steps ahead and put an end to the party before it started.

Which makes his personal undoing all the more ironic.

———

"I got terminated on March 23 [2011]," he said. "A young lady in the athletic department asked me for an $11,000 raise. I told her it wasn't going to happen. She went to the AD and others and was told no."

That "young lady" was twenty-four-year-old Rachel Arena, a former Angel, UT's version of a recruiting hostess, who, shortly after graduating from Texas in 2008, had been hired to work as an administrative assistant in the football office. Bryant was her supervisor.

It was August 2010 when Arena first alleged that during the two years she worked in the football office, Bryant had made repeated sexual advances in the form of unwanted texts and verbal and physical acts of sexual harassment, charges Bryant vehemently denied at the time.

In its "Summary of Investigation," the university reported that in October 2010 it received a formal letter of complaint from attorneys representing Employee 1 (Arena). One of those attorneys was Gloria Allred. Known for teary-eyed press conferences and her fearless, brass-knuckle approach, Allred only added to the anxiety brought on by Brown's first losing season in Austin.

According to documents obtained by ESPN's *Outside the Lines,* in her formal complaint Arena charged the harassment began with inappropriate texts from Bryant and escalated from there. "It progressed to more and more personal questions and at all hours, including weekends," *Outside the Lines* reported Arena had said. "He would ask me when I was going out, where I was going, and what I was wearing. He would ask me if I went home with anyone and about my sex life." She told investigators he would repeatedly text her. At least one of the texts allegedly read "IW2KY"—short for "I want to kiss you."

In September 2011, *Outside the Lines* reported Arena told Linda Millstone, the school's associate vice president for institutional equity, that she showed some of Bryant's texts to her mother the previous April but never informed Longhorns head coach Mack Brown of the unwanted advances.

"I was upset," Arena was said to have told investigators, "but I couldn't bring myself to tell him [Brown] what had happened."

In her complaint Arena charged the harassment continued until July 2010. On July 15, she alleged, during a closed-door meeting in Bryant's office dealing with her request for a raise—to $38,000 a year—that Bryant, whose wife works in the athletic department's athletic services unit, pulled down the top of her dress and bra and fondled her breast. She also charged that another time, in a break room, Bryant came in, stood in front of the door and, as Arena started to leave, kissed her neck.

Bryant insisted the allegations were untrue. "I'm guilty of a lot of shit," Bryant said. "But I'm not guilty of this."

About a month later Arena would take a paid leave of absence from her job.

According to documents obtained by ESPN, the formal university investigation uncovered at least two other female office workers who charged Bryant had attempted to kiss them as well. Another woman described Bryant to investigators as "old-freak-nasty."

A formal interview with Bryant took place on November 3, 2010, at the office of his Austin attorney, Tom Nesbitt. Bryant repeatedly denied any form of verbal or physical harassment had taken place or sending inappropriate text messages, including the one that allegedly read "IW2KY."

Late in the sixty-five-minute interview Nesbitt asked university attorney Jeff Graves a rather important question: "Has anyone told you they have seen text messages from Cleve Bryant that were of an inappropriate, sexual or romantic nature?"

Responded Graves, "Well, this is not the appropriate time for information to go that way." He then moved on to another subject.

Based upon that interview and those with some sixteen other individuals, on November 29, 2010, investigators working on behalf of the university submitted an "initial written review" to President William Powers Jr. The review found that "sexual harassment had occurred."

Mediation between university counsel and Allred began almost immediately. On January 11, 2011, according to the summary report, a formal settlement was reached, and Arena was paid $400,000, a figure that included a full release for the university and all officers and employees.

Two months *after* that agreement was completed, Powers met with Bryant and Nesbitt to discuss their concerns about the university's conclusion. Three weeks after that meeting, on March 23, 2011, Powers wrote to Bryant and advised him that "sufficient reasonable and credible evidence" existed that Bryant had sexually harassed Arena. The most compelling evidence, Powers wrote, was the interview investigators had conducted with Arena. Bryant, who had been on voluntary leave, was immediately terminated. At the time of his dismissal Bryant was the highest-ranking African-American employee on campus, earning around $250,000 a year.

Oddly, it wasn't until five months later—on August 17–18, 2011—that a "full evidentiary hearing" was held in the case. In that hearing both sides were given "a full opportunity" to present "all evidence and testimony." That hearing took place more than eight months *after* the university had already paid $400,000 to Arena.

"UT rushed to settle the claim before it even finished its investigation," Nesbitt said. "Having paid a fat settlement, the university could come to but one conclusion."

Nesbitt added: "I never saw any allegedly inappropriate texts between Cleve and the complainant. There never were any. All texts I saw were routine business communications related to athletic department business. The complaining party never produced any texts to UT or to us. Not one. No witness ever said they had seen inappropriate texts from Cleve. The complainant ultimately claimed that she deleted the allegedly incriminating texts. Our view is that is ridiculous. You get these texts. You hire Gloria Allred to seek a cash settlement. That person deletes the texts? Not likely."

University officials declined comment on the case. In response to several Open Records requests the Texas Attorney General's Office ruled the university "must release" both the summary of the investigation and the statement of the accused. Despite such an order the University of Texas withheld Arena's statement, citing privacy issues.

"It will always be a privacy issue," said a legal spokesperson for the school. "The privacy of the victim or alleged victim must be protected."

In October 2011, shortly after news of the settlement was released, Gloria Allred told ESPN, "I am very proud of my client and the courage that she demonstrated to stand up for her rights in this case. Her willingness to do the right thing has benefited other women and the University as well."

As for Bryant, he said the university never asked one person about his character and did not allow Brown to speak on his behalf. And despite his oft-heard comment about leaving if Bryant ever did, Brown remained firmly entrenched at Texas.

10 REBUILDING A PROGRAM

"There is no gray with Bronco"

BYU's football program was reeling after the 2004 season. Two players were in jail awaiting trial on rape charges. The head coach had been forced out. And it had been three years since it had posted a winning record. Adding insult to injury, its archrival, Utah, under head coach Urban Meyer, had finished the 2004 regular season ranked No. 5 in the country with an 11-0 record. Dubbed the original "BCS Busters," Utah was the first team from a non-BCS conference to get invited to a BCS bowl game.

While Utah basked in the national headlines as it prepared to face Pittsburgh in the Fiesta Bowl, BYU was desperate to get its program back on track. The task of finding a new head coach fell largely to Tom Holmoe, a BYU alum who had won two Super Bowls as a defensive back with the San Francisco 49ers before becoming a head coach at Cal. Holmoe was chosen to lead a transition team put in place after BYU fired its athletic director at the outset of the gang rape investigation. Holmoe had no interest in hiring anyone from Gary Crowton's staff. There was only one man Holmoe wanted—Utah's defensive coordinator, Kyle Whittingham.

Holmoe and Whittingham went way back. In 1981 they were the two best players on BYU's defense: Holmoe a gritty corner; Whittingham the team's intense, emotional leader and captain. He had that same fiery brand of leadership as an assistant under Urban Meyer at Utah. Hours after Crowton resigned, Holmoe offered Whittingham the BYU job.

———

But that same day Whittingham got offered the head job at Utah. Urban Meyer had announced he was heading to Florida to become its new head coach right after Utah played in the Fiesta Bowl. Whittingham had been chosen as his successor.

Whittingham felt torn. "Anytime you are talking about your alma mater, there is a pull and a certain allure to that," he said. "There was so much to the decision—bitter rivals; same conference; same state. That's why it was such a gut-wrenching experience."

After days of mulling it over, Whittingham called Holmoe and told him he was coming to BYU. But he couldn't stop thinking about the relationship he had formed with his players. Plus, he and his family were firmly entrenched at Utah. "For my wife it was: 'Why are you even thinking about this? It's Utah.'"

Persuaded, Whittingham called Holmoe back and told him he had changed his mind: he was remaining at Utah.

Later that night, the phone rang at Bronco Mendenhall's home. It was Holmoe. He asked how Mendenhall was doing. Mendenhall said he and his family were packing.

"Not so fast," Holmoe told him.

———

On December 8, 2004, Utah announced Kyle Whittingham as its new head coach. That same day, Bronco Mendenhall trudged into his job interview with Tom Holmoe and a number of other BYU administrators. He went in with a chip on his shoulder.

"I only came to BYU for one reason, and that was to help a friend—Gary Crowton," Mendenhall said. "And I saw the relationship between him and the athletic department leadership as adversarial. So all of those feelings were pretty raw when I went in. I was defending Gary."

An introvert by nature, Mendenhall was tight-lipped throughout the interview. It left a poor impression on Holmoe.

"He wouldn't say anything," Holmoe said. "He was so loyal to Gary because Gary had hired him. I was trying to draw out of him a vision for the program. I asked what things he would do differently and how he would make it better. He said he didn't think there was much that could be done to make it better. I was like, you gotta be kidding me."

By the time the interview ended, Holmoe had decided to pursue other candidates, and Mendenhall didn't care.

But when BYU players got wind that other candidates were being considered, a bunch of them went to see Holmoe. "About twenty-five guys came into my office to tell me—plead with me—'Please let it be Bronco,'" Holmoe said. "They were all defensive players, not one offensive player."

It was the kind of input Holmoe couldn't ignore. At the same time,

BYU's president privately reached out to Gary Crowton and asked for his recommendation. He made a case for Mendenhall. "I recommended Bronco because he would be very disciplined in exercising what he felt was right," Crowton said. "There is no gray with Bronco. It's black-and-white."

Under the circumstances, that was music to the ears of the top brass at the university. On December 13, BYU introduced thirty-eight-year-old Mendenhall as its new coach, making him the second-youngest head coach in Division I football.

In his first full day on the job, Mendenhall arrived at his office before 5:00 a.m. No one was around. Mendenhall had tossed and turned all night, unable to stop thinking about the task ahead. He looked around his new office. The walls were bare. The top of his desk had lists of recruits. There was a couch with Nike gear on it. A pile of messages was next to the phone. He started making a to-do list. An hour later he was still writing. There was so much to do he didn't know where to start. Hire assistant coaches? Meet with the team? Call recruits?

All of a sudden he felt as if he were in over his head. He knew football. He knew BYU's strict honor code. But he didn't know how to meld the two in a way that would return the program to the national prominence it had achieved under LaVell Edwards. Worse, he had no one to turn to for advice.

Desperate, he knelt beside the couch and prayed. "I needed help, and I was seeking guidance," Mendenhall said.

His quiet prayer eventually transitioned to prolonged, silent meditation. He lost track of time until he was stirred by a knock on the door. He checked his watch; it was nearly 8:00 a.m. He opened the door and discovered LaVell Edwards.

"I had a feeling you'd be here early," Edwards said in his signature raspy voice. "I just came by to wish you luck."

Mendenhall was speechless. He hardly knew Edwards. But he revered him.

"Please come in," Mendenhall said.

Nursing a bum knee, the seventy-four-year-old legend limped toward a chair and took a seat opposite Mendenhall. Then he just stared at the young coach. Mendenhall met his gaze.

"You've got a tough job," Edwards finally said.

"I just realized that over the past two hours."

Edwards grinned. He knew Mendenhall hadn't even begun to realize how tough it would be. "You've got one of the hardest jobs in the country," Edwards continued.

Sober, Mendenhall nodded.

"But you've also got one of the best jobs in the country," Edwards said.

For the next thirty minutes, Mendenhall listened as Edwards shared ideas. When it was clear that the visit was coming to an end, Mendenhall asked if he had any parting advice.

"Don't try to be me," Edwards said. "Don't try to be anybody else, either. The best way to success is be yourself. Just be yourself and set your program in that direction."

Then he disappeared.

⸻

That afternoon Mendenhall called a team meeting. In no uncertain terms, he let everybody know that the game at BYU was about to change. Players would be expected to meet an exceptionally high performance standard on the field—unparalleled conditioning and exceptional technique—and an even higher standard off the field. No aspect of the honor code would be optional.

At the end of the meeting, three players trailed him to his office and announced they were quitting the team. The following day three more players quit. That only emboldened Mendenhall. Over the first ten days of his tenure he came up with a five-point mission statement for himself. He listed the points in order of priority:

1. Help develop each BYU player spiritually.
2. Help each BYU player grow intellectually.
3. Develop character in each player.
4. Enable every player to provide public service.
5. Finish in the Top 25 every season.

None of these were expectations placed on him by the university. Mendenhall came up with these on his own. The first four were based on his reading of BYU's handbook and the university's instructions to faculty and staff. "I considered myself an employee of the institution," Mendenhall said. "I figured if those objectives applied to everyone that teaches and works at this university, they probably ought to apply to me, too."

The fifth one—finishing in the top twenty-five—was Mendenhall's self-imposed goal for greatness on the field.

Then he told his staff that he wanted to change the profile of their recruits. "National-championship-caliber athletes that are exceptional students and who are either Mormons or who want to live the Mormon standards," Mendenhall said. "That is what we want. Otherwise you should not play football at BYU."

To ensure they were recruiting student-athletes who fit the mold of a faith-based institution, Mendenhall also told his coaches that he wanted them to use new recruiting protocols:

- All recruits would be subject to background checks.
- Recruits' parents would be invited to accompany their sons on official campus visits.
- No recruit—Mormon or otherwise—would receive a scholarship offer without being interviewed and endorsed by an ecclesiastical leader from the Mormon faith to ensure the recruit was living his life in accordance with the BYU honor code.

There was one other thing. Mendenhall wanted recruiters to be much more explicit about the honor code when making in-home visits to recruits, especially when visiting homes of non-Mormon athletes who had little or no familiarity with the church's teachings. "They don't have to believe what Mormons believe," Mendenhall said. "But they need to know that Christian values are expected to be lived on our campus."

Some of his assistants thought he was crazy. "Nobody is going to come here," one of them said.

Others agreed.

But Mendenhall had a different perspective. "I don't want these kids to come and not know what they are getting into," he said. "If you don't acknowledge and aren't pretty clear about what they are getting into here, I think it borders on exploitation for the sake of playing a game. I've seen young men make mistakes and come and go here. And I don't want that to ever happen again."

The changes in recruiting tactics had an instant impact. The year before Mendenhall took over, BYU pursued 1,000 recruits. In Mendenhall's first season, BYU recruited just 125 players. A fraction of them received a scholarship. The culture of the team changed overnight. Its record improved pretty fast, too. In Mendenhall's first season, BYU finished 6-6. The next year BYU opened the 2006 season by losing the first two games. Then the Cougars ripped off ten straight wins to close out the season 11-2. Along the way they knocked off fifteenth-ranked TCU in Fort Worth and hammered Oregon 38–8 in a bowl game. In 2007, BYU went 11-2 again, going on another ten-game winning streak that included a bowl victory over UCLA.

After back-to-back eleven-win seasons and three straight trips to a bowl game, Mendenhall wasn't hearing any complaints from coaches or anyone else about his system. BYU was winning. The stadium was full. The university administration was thrilled, and Mormon Church officials were undoubtedly relieved. Those embarrassing headlines were long gone. Most important to Mendenhall, though, his players were thriving on and off the field.

———

On April 29, 2008, Bronco Mendenhall stepped to the pulpit at a Mormon church in Reno, Nevada. He wasn't there to talk football. His topic was faith. But the event had been billed as an evening with BYU's head football coach—a devotional. On that night in Reno, as Mendenhall looked out at hundreds of kids—girls in modest dresses and boys in white shirts and ties—his eyes were drawn to the one at the very back of the hall. He looked different from the others in every way—taller, well built, sporting an Afro, and wearing a long black peacoat. When Mendenhall made eye contact, the boy returned his gaze with a skeptical, hard stare. It was clear this kid didn't want to be there.

That boy was Kyle Van Noy, then a sixteen-year-old junior linebacker and wide receiver at Reno's McQueen High. Arguably the best all-around athlete in the state of Nevada, he had recruiting letters from the top football programs in the country—LSU, Nebraska, Oregon, UCLA and twenty others. BYU had written and called him, too. But he had ignored the Cougars. Despite being a Mormon, Van Noy had zero interest in playing for his church's university. "I didn't like anything that had to do with BYU," Van Noy said.

Nor did he care to hear what Mendenhall had to say. "I didn't want to be there that night," Van Noy recalled. "My parents made me go. I figured it was going to be another talk about church stuff."

Instead, Mendenhall talked about geese flying in V formation, taking turns at the point and never abandoning a member of the flock. He had Van Noy's undivided attention.

"He taught us that if one goose fell off and was unable to fly, another goose would wait with him until he either died or was able to rejoin the group," Van Noy recalled. "At that time I felt so alone. And it felt like he was talking directly to me. I had never heard a football coach talk like that."

Afterward, Mendenhall introduced himself. A friendship was struck.

"I had a clear impression when speaking and looking at him that night," said Mendenhall. "I said to myself: 'He needs to be at BYU.'"

Months later Mendenhall made an in-home visit. There he met Kyle's parents, Layne and Kelly. In 1991 they adopted Kyle weeks after he was born in Las Vegas. Devout Mormons, the Van Noys were living in California when they received a call from LDS Family Services, which assists Mormon families with adoption.

For the first two years of Kyle's life he wore corrective leg braces. At night he wore a bar fastened to his shoes in order to keep his legs apart. In the morning the toddler would climb out of his crib, crawl down the hall GI Joe–style and enter his parents' bedroom, the bar still fastened to his shoes. The impediment forced him to use only his elbows to pull himself from one end of the house to the other. That's when Layne and Kelly realized that their adopted son had an unusually determined spirit.

Eventually, the leg braces came off, and the Van Noys relocated to Reno, where Kyle blossomed into a three-sport star athlete. While he remained close to his parents during high school, Kyle became less comfortable around his fellow Mormon teens. Instead, he ran with kids who partied and drank. He felt more accepted by them.

Van Noy shared all of this, as well as other personal challenges he was facing, with Mendenhall during the in-home visit. "He didn't hide anything," Mendenhall said. "He was sincere and truthful. He just said, 'I've done this. I've done this. I struggle with that.' He was very blunt."

Mendenhall was equally blunt, telling Van Noy that he would be required to live every aspect of the honor code if he accepted a football scholarship to BYU. "BYU is a unique place," Mendenhall said. "I told Kyle who we are and that it's not for everyone. I was pretty clear about what he was getting into if he chose BYU."

———

Jim Snelling was Van Noy's defensive coordinator at McQueen High. A former player at Nevada, Snelling had coached plenty of kids who earned Division I scholarships, including a couple who went on to successful careers in the NFL. But he had never seen a player quite like Van Noy. "His acceleration from a standing-still position is remarkable," Snelling said. "At the snap of the ball he just explodes. All the college recruiters saw this when I sent out film on him."

By his sophomore year, Van Noy had a scholarship offer from Colorado. UCLA and Boise State were right behind it. By the start of Van Noy's senior year in the fall of 2008, Snelling felt as if top recruiters across the country had him on speed dial.

Oregon, in particular, was putting a lot of heat on Van Noy to commit early. It was hard to overlook the appeal of playing there. The team played a lot of games on national television. It had the coolest uniforms. And it was sure to be in the mix for the national championship. But Van Noy's top priority for choosing a team was much more personal.

"I wanted to play for a coach who cared more about me as a person than a football player," Van Noy said.

Eight weeks into the season BYU was 7-1, losing only to nationally ranked TCU. On October 31, Mendenhall was with his team in Fort Collins, preparing to play Colorado State the following day. That same night back in Reno, Van Noy was in his bedroom, alone. "I was sitting there thinking about all the things I had done," Van Noy said. "I was thinking, 'I have to get out of this. I need a way out.' As a sixteen-year-old, I was pretty lonely."

Unsure where to turn, he picked up his cell phone and called Mendenhall. He was at the team hotel. It was late. After saying hello, Van Noy got to the point. "Hey, I have these issues," Van Noy told him. "I know you have standards. I don't know if I will fulfill the standards. But I will try."

At the same time it was recruiting Van Noy, BYU was in the hunt to land Manti Te'o, another Mormon who was the nation's top high school linebacker. The prospect of Te'o and Van Noy playing side by side had put BYU in position to have the best linebacking corps in the country. Although Van Noy didn't have as much fanfare as Te'o, Mendenhall had concluded he had just as much talent. Van Noy was a bit smaller—six feet three inches and 209 pounds. But in terms of raw athleticism, he was actually faster and quicker. He ran the forty in 4.5, and he started both ways. While leading his team to a state title and a perfect 14-0 record as a senior, he terrorized quarterbacks and caught thirty-five passes for 731 yards and eighteen touchdowns on offense. On defense he made seventy-nine tackles, fourteen sacks and forced six fumbles.

"With Kyle all you had to do was watch a couple series of film and you knew," said Mendenhall. "I thought very early on that there was no limit on how good he could be."

On January 10–11, 2009, Te'o and Van Noy both made their official visits to BYU. Every detail had been considered to persuade Te'o to join Van Noy by committing to BYU. Even his cousin Shiloah, already a member of the team, had been assigned to be Manti's host for the weekend. But things didn't quite turn out as planned.

At the end of the visit Van Noy reaffirmed his commitment to BYU, pledging to sign with the Cougars on National Signing Day. "I didn't want to go to a school where I knew I'd face challenges and temptations," he said. "I knew I needed an environment like BYU."

But before Te'o left Provo, he met with Mendenhall. The conversation was cordial and respectful. But BYU stopped recruiting Te'o after that weekend. Two weeks later, Te'o called Mendenhall a couple days before National Signing Day to say he was going to Notre Dame.

Later that day Mendenhall also got an unexpected call from Van Noy.

"I messed up," Van Noy began, his voice cracking.

Mendenhall took a deep breath.

"I got arrested," Van Noy continued.

Mendenhall felt sick.

It happened the night before. Van Noy had been out and got arrested for drunk driving. He was underage. So the case would be disposed in juvenile court. But Mendenhall had a policy that prohibited him from offering scholarships to players who weren't living in compliance with the honor code. He didn't make exceptions—not even for the best recruits.

"You understand you can't come to BYU under these circumstances?" Mendenhall asked.

Van Noy was silent.

"Kyle, I love you just the same," Mendenhall told him. "I'll release you from your commitment to BYU."

More silence.

"You can choose any of the schools that were recruiting you," Mendenhall said. "My guess is that they will want you in a second."

"But that's not what I want," Van Noy said.

Mendenhall didn't expect that. "I was absolutely ready to release him at that point because of the honor code," Mendenhall explained. "I told him I'd help him go anywhere he wanted to go. But he kept saying he wanted to come to BYU."

Mendenhall wasn't optimistic. But he told Van Noy to give him the rest of the day to explore options. They agreed to talk again later.

Kelly Van Noy was heartbroken. Her son's arrest was all over the news in Reno. Juvenile arrests are supposed to remain confidential. But a reporter found out that the city's top athlete had been charged, and the news spread fast. Friends and neighbors were talking. Plus, it looked as though all hope of her son attending BYU had been dashed.

While the Van Noys waited for Mendenhall to call back, other coaches who had seen the news of the arrest on the Internet started calling the house. "Kyle had coaches call him after the arrest and say you come here and you can play right now," said Kelly Van Noy. "That is appealing to a seventeen-year-old kid. So is not having to face the music and not being on a campus where you feel judged and all they know about you is that you are the kid who got the DUI."

Mendenhall went to see athletic director Tom Holmoe. They put together a scenario where BYU could still honor Van Noy's scholarship. He'd have to agree to sit out the 2009 season and go a full year without violating the honor code. At that point, he'd have to get the endorsement of an ecclesiastical leader who could vouch that his personal life was in line with BYU's standards. In other words, he'd have to live the honor code for a full year—whether at home or on campus—before he'd be eligible to be a student-athlete.

Holmoe was convinced Van Noy would never go for it. "That just doesn't happen," Holmoe said. There were too many top schools willing to overlook the DUI and play him immediately.

Mendenhall agreed. But he was also convinced that he would not be helping Van Noy by glossing over the arrest and making an exception to the rule. Besides, what message would that send to the rest of the team?

They took their proposal to BYU's dean of students, Vernon Heperi. He signed off. Then Mendenhall called Van Noy and told him his options.

The prospect of sitting out a year had not entered Van Noy's mind. He had every intention of starting as a true freshman. He wanted some time to think it over.

Later that evening Mendenhall's phone buzzed. "I'll do it," Van Noy told him. "I'll sit out a year."

"I honestly don't know what made me say yes to that," Van Noy said. "But I did, and once I gave my word, I was committed to it."

The next day—February 4, 2009—when BYU announced its recruiting class for 2009, Mendenhall read off Van Noy's name. Then he brought the media into a private room and read them a letter Van Noy had written the night before: "This past weekend, I received a DUI citation, which will delay my arrival. I know that I have disappointed you, my family and friends. You have my firm commitment that I will do what it takes to earn back your trust and be part of BYU's winning tradition."

———

One month later Van Noy went out with friends. They had alcohol. It got late. Van Noy didn't go home. He ended up on a park bench on the streets of Reno, where he fell asleep. The next thing he remembered was waking up to police sirens and flashing lights. Scared, he took off running. Officers gave chase. Trapped in an alley, Van Noy shrugged off an officer and broke free. Then from behind he heard the clicking of a Taser gun. He dropped to the ground. Before he knew it, he was in police custody for a second time in a one-month span, this time cited for eluding an officer.

He was not charged with an alcohol offense this time, however. And when the authorities considered his juvenile status and the fact that he was already facing DUI charges, they opted not to bring a second case against Van Noy. Charges were dropped. And this time the local press did not find out. Under Nevada law, the report in the second incident was sealed. Fortunately for Van Noy, no one would find out about his second arrest, especially not Coach Mendenhall.

But Van Noy was uneasy. Mendenhall had given him a second chance. He felt he owed it to him to come clean, even though he knew that would likely end his football career at BYU before it started.

He talked to his parents and decided to fly to Provo and confess to Mendenhall.

"Up until that point I didn't want to be helped," Van Noy said. "But suddenly I felt like a kid who needed help. I wanted help."

He went straight to Coach Mendenhall's office. The door was ajar. He knocked and Mendenhall looked up and grinned. "C'mon in, Kyle. Why are you here?"

Van Noy looked away, biting his lip.

The grin left Mendenhall's face as he stood and walked toward him.

Van Noy's eyes welled up. So did Mendenhall's.

"Kyle, talk to me. Let me help you."

Van Noy took a seat. His voice shaking, he revealed every detail about the second run-in with the law. "I need help," he said.

Mendenhall recalled the opening lines to a favorite speech by BYU's former president Jeffrey R. Holland: "It is the plain and very sobering truth that before great moments, certainly before great spiritual moments, there can come adversity, opposition, and darkness. Life has some of those moments for us, and occasionally they come just as we are approaching an important decision or a significant step in our life."

He looked Van Noy in the eye and told him not to worry about the second incident. "That's why I gave you the one-year plan," he told Van Noy.

"There are no words to describe how bad I felt before I got to his office," Van Noy said. "And no words to describe how good I felt when he accepted me."

Mendenhall and Van Noy put their arms around each other.

———

After reaffirming his commitment to Van Noy, Mendenhall informed the athletic director and the dean of students. Both had reservations. But Mendenhall held his ground. "He never hides when his mistakes come," Mendenhall said. "He has been honest from the minute our relationship started. I'm always the first to know when he makes a mistake."

The dean had two simple questions: "Is this someone you believe needs to be at BYU?"

"He needs help," Mendenhall told the dean and the AD. "He wants help. I want to help him. And I believe he can make it. He's giving up a chance to go elsewhere."

"Is this someone you believe will represent this institution and our faith?" the dean asked.

"Unlike so many people I deal with that will hide behind texts and e-mails and half-truths, he admitted what he did," Mendenhall said. "Not only is he trying to do something about it, he's already done something about it. He's here."

The dean and the AD signed off.

"Our administration knew the situation," Holmoe said. "When you bring someone here who is high risk, you have to wonder. This is a different culture than Kyle was used to. But we trusted Bronco. And Kyle made a commitment to hang in there. That was Bronco's risk, not mine."

———

BYU opened the 2009 season in a nationally televised game against third-ranked Oklahoma at Cowboys Stadium. It was precisely the kind of stage that Van Noy had always longed to play on. Instead, he was back home in Reno, preparing to start school in January. All he could do was watch on

TV. That only made things harder as BYU pulled off a big upset, winning 14–13. For a kid who always started and never missed games, he was finding accountability to be a bitter pill to swallow. He couldn't get over the idea that he could have been on the field making plays.

One BYU linebacker who was there making plays was Shiloah Te'o. But a week before the Oklahoma game, Te'o had been arrested for DUI in Provo. Police pulled him over on August 29 after he pulled out of a liquor store parking lot without stopping. A field sobriety test indicated his blood-alcohol level was over the legal limit.

Mendenhall didn't know about the arrest before taking his team down to Arlington. It hadn't made the local papers. But weeks later Mendenhall heard a rumor that Te'o might be in trouble with the law. By that time BYU had played five games, and Te'o had been on the field in all of them. Mendenhall confronted Te'o about the rumor. He denied any involvement. But a couple nights later Mendenhall learned otherwise. And on October 8, Mendenhall kicked Te'o off the team for violating team rules.

Te'o ended up transferring to Oregon State.

11 THE BOOSTER

What $248 million will buy you

C ollege football has a long, checkered history with boosters. Back in the 1980s, the NCAA issued the death penalty—a one-year ban—to SMU's football program after athletic department staffers paid twenty-one Mustang players from a secret slush fund set up and funded by boosters. The total amount of money involved was $61,000.

The SMU scandal seems quaint by today's standards. In 2011, the NCAA began investigating University of Miami booster Nevin Shapiro for allegedly spending hundreds of thousands of dollars on seventy-two Miami football players between 2002 and 2010. Shapiro claimed he gave players money for everything from big hits against opposing teams (bounties) to cover charges at nightclubs and entertainment at strip clubs. He claimed he even paid for an abortion after a Miami player impregnated a stripper.

Yet something as innocuous as giving student-athletes grocery money or treating them to lunch violates NCAA rules. Those rules define "boosters" as "any individual, independent agency, corporate entity, or other organization" that promotes or makes financial contributions to athletics, assists in recruiting or provides benefits to student-athletes or their families. Under this broad definition, everyone from a season ticket holder to a nonprofit that prints and distributes T-shirts that say GO BUCKEYES is a booster.

In other words, there are hundreds of thousands of boosters or, in NCAA parlance, "representative[s] of the university's athletic interests." The overwhelming majority of them—easily 99 percent—are rank-and-file supporters whose school spirit and financial backing form the backbone to every college football program. They are students who paint their faces and purchase season tickets all the way up to wealthy alumni who shell out thousands of dollars for luxury suites and donate to nonprofit fund-raising organizations set up to support the athletic department. Boosters from this group are rarely the subjects of NCAA investigations.

The remaining 1 percent of boosters fall into four basic categories:

POWER BROKERS. Few individuals have more power than Jimmy Rane and his counterpart at Auburn, Robert "Bobby" Lowder. Rane, sixty-eight, is a self-made multimillionaire who made his fortune at Great Southern Wood Preserving Inc., building its signature product, YellaWood, into the world's best-selling pressure-treated pine. Rane has been a trustee at Auburn, his alma mater, since 1999. Lowder, a former banking executive, spent two decades on Auburn's board of trustees. Guys like Rane and Lowder are insiders who raise money, influence decisions and have direct ties to the university or to private foundations that raise money for athletics. And they rarely, if ever, speak to the press. "I'm not a big man on campus and I have no intention of portraying myself that way," Rane said. "I am not a power broker. I'm trying to do good. I don't need the money. I don't need anything. I'm trying to leave the world a better place than I found it."

JOCK SNIFFERS. These are boosters who have no direct ties to a university and tend to give money directly to players. Their primary motive is to gain access to student-athletes, particularly ones with the promise of becoming future pros. Nevin Shapiro at Miami was a prime example of this type. This group is most often responsible for scandals.

BUILDERS. These guys write eight-figure checks and have their names on things—stadiums, practice fields and statues erected on campus in their honor. This group includes James "Bill" Heavener, a member of Gator Boosters Inc. and the CEO of the Heavener Company. Florida's football complex is named after him. At Tennessee, Jim Haslam is the most prominent booster. The founder of Pilot Oil gave $32.5 million to the university in 2006, the largest single donation in the school's history. Part of that gift was used to renovate Neyland Stadium. And Tennessee's practice field is named Haslam Field. Michigan has Stephen M. Ross, a global real estate developer. Among the many properties he developed was the Time Warner Center in New York, and he is the owner of both the Miami Dolphins and Sun Life Stadium. The Ross name is on the academic center for athletes at Michigan as well as its school of business.

TURBO BOOSTERS. This is the ultimate exclusive booster club. It's so exclusive that only two billionaires belong—Nike's chairman, Phil Knight, and oil and gas tycoon T. Boone Pickens. These two march to a very different drummer. They have the deepest pockets, and they are driven to single-handedly catapult their respective alma maters—Oregon and Oklahoma

State—to college football relevance. Prior to their arrival on the scene, Oregon and Oklahoma State were afterthoughts in the Pac-10 and the Big 12. But in recent years both schools have been in the running for the national title.

Knight began bankrolling Oregon athletics in the 1990s. Eventually, he donated $100 million to the University of Oregon's Legacy Fund, the single largest gift in the university's history. He also contributed between $50 million and $60 million for the football stadium expansion, along with another $68 million for the construction of Oregon's new football operations facilities.

Pickens got in the game after Knight. In 2006, Pickens, the CEO of a Dallas-based hedge fund, gave a $165 million gift to Oklahoma State athletics. It was the largest single donation for athletics to an institution of higher education in American history. That was in addition to the $83 million he put into overhauling OSU's football stadium between 2003 and 2008. The combined $248 million in gifts produced a new baseball stadium; new soccer, track and tennis facilities; an equestrian center; various outdoor fields; and a multipurpose indoor practice complex.

The crown jewel, however, was Boone Pickens Stadium, a sixty-thousand-seat state-of-the-art facility ringed by 101 luxury suites and four thousand club seats that opened on September 5, 2009. The field and the amenities set the gold standard for college football:

- spacious football offices adjacent to the stadium
- a twenty-two-thousand-square-foot weight room
- a sprawling training table area that offers buffet-style dining rivaling the Ritz-Carlton
- a team room that accommodates 220 people and offers plush leather furniture, each piece embossed with OSU's logo

But Pickens's record-setting gift did more than overhaul the football stadium. It touched off an unprecedented fund-raising drive dubbed The Next Level. More than $1 billion was raised, which led to one of the largest building projects in recent NCAA history.

Why spend a fortune on football?

"What I keep coming back to is we're in the Big 12 and it's a tough conference," Pickens said at the time of the record-setting gift. "I want us to be competitive."

At the time he was also asked whether he thought his investment would pay off. "I'd bet my ass on it," he said.

It turned out to be a good bet. OSU has done more than become competitive. Since the infusion of Pickens's money, it has become a national power in football. In 2010, the team won eleven games for the first time in school history and finished the season ranked thirteenth in the nation. The following year it won twelve games, captured the Big 12 Conference championship and defeated Stanford in the Fiesta Bowl. It almost won the national championship, too, finishing third in the country at 12-1.

There is a lesson in this that Knight and Pickens understand: the best facilities in college football attract the best talent. Oregon competes for the national title virtually every year. Meanwhile, in 2012, more than twenty-five OSU players were on NFL rosters. That put OSU in the top fifteen schools in the country for producing elite NFL talent. Before Pickens came along, OSU had a losing program and was a financial drain on the athletic department.

Rivals like to joke that Oregon and Oklahoma State have the only two college football teams with an owner. The irony is that Pickens didn't set out to turn around the fortunes of OSU's football team. He just got tired of the team losing its annual homecoming game. So he quit going. Then someone with no ties to the football program challenged him to do something about its losing ways.

Mike Holder wasn't an obvious choice to start a fund-raising campaign for the Oklahoma State football program. As OSU's golf coach, he had won eight national championships and led a capital campaign to finance the construction of a world-class golf course outside Stillwater. Over the years he had gotten so good at raising money for the golf team that he had a surplus of $31 million.

The golf team was in great shape. But OSU's football team was a mess, losing lots of games and lots of money. In a conference like the Big 12, where football is king, a losing program can be a financial drain on all other sports. That's what worried Holder.

In 2001, Holder was invited to go quail hunting with Boone Pickens. They became friends and would talk from time to time about OSU's athletics and what it would take to make the football team competitive. Eventually, Holder pitched Pickens on the idea of contributing $20 million to upgrade the stadium.

It wasn't the first time that Pickens had been asked to give money to football. Back in 1987, when Oklahoma State had two future NFL Hall of

Fame running backs on its roster—Barry Sanders and Thurman Thomas—Pickens was approached by an assistant football coach and asked to funnel money into a secret slush fund. A couple installments of $25,000 would have been pocket change for Pickens while going a long way to quietly helping the team.

"Hold it," Pickens told the coach. "When I give, every check will be made out to the OSU Athletic Department and marked for golf, football, basketball or whatever."

The coach persisted. "You know all the schools are cheating," he said.

"They probably are," said Pickens. "But you can't do that indefinitely. You'll be found out, embarrassed and penalized."

Instead, Pickens gave $57 million over a number of years to various academic initiatives, including the Boone Pickens School of Geology.

Two years later, in 1989, the NCAA put Oklahoma State's football program on probation for more than forty recruiting violations that included improper payments to players.

But Holder wasn't talking about secret slush funds. He suggested the stadium be renamed after Pickens in exchange for the $20 million gift for a face-lift. Pickens liked the idea, and in March 2003 he made the donation. The money was used to upgrade the south side of the stadium and add some suites and club seating, which were completed in 2004.

Holder knew Pickens was capable of doing a lot more, though. He said as much to Pickens. The conversation continued for a year. Pickens was still mulling over Holder's request for a bigger gift to athletics when OSU's athletic director, Harry Birdwell, announced he was stepping down in June 2005.

Shortly after Birdwell's announcement, Holder got a call from Pickens, who suggested Holder apply for the job.

"I don't want to be AD," he told Pickens. "I am perfectly happy in the life I have right now."

"I understand that," Pickens told him. "It's because you are coasting through life on your handlebars. You are winning in golf. But you need a new challenge."

"Well, I don't want to be the AD," Holder said.

"Well, I don't want to give the money unless you are the AD," Pickens said.

With Pickens poised to become the largest donor in the school's history, it was hard to ignore his wishes. In mid-August 2005, Holder notified the search committee that he was interested in the job. Two weeks later he was one of eight candidates invited to interview.

OSU had invited Pickens to be on the hiring committee for the AD. But he was too busy running BP Capital, the energy hedge fund he started after selling his oil company. He didn't have time to get into the details of OSU athletics. Instead, he informed the university that he had designated someone to stand in his place.

Robert "Bobby" Stillwell was a partner at the Houston law firm Baker Botts when Boone Pickens became his principal client in 1963. Eventually, Stillwell became a director at Pickens's Texas-based oil company Mesa Petroleum, where Pickens made a name for himself on Wall Street as a hostile-takeover specialist. When Pickens left Mesa Petroleum to start BP Capital, Stillwell joined him in 2001 as the company's general counsel. Pickens also appointed Stillwell to be chairman of his charitable foundation, a move that essentially made Stillwell the gatekeeper to all the groups and individuals approaching Pickens for money.

As a result, Stillwell worked very closely with Holder on the initial $20 million gift that Pickens gave for the stadium upgrade. He had also been intimately involved in talks between Holder and Pickens for a second, much larger donation to OSU sports.

At Pickens's request, Stillwell joined OSU's hiring committee for a new AD. And in August 2005, he was on hand when the committee interviewed eight candidates over a two-day period at Addison Airport, north of Dallas.

When the interview process ended, Stillwell brought Pickens up to speed. Holder, it turned out, was the only candidate without experience as an athletic director or assistant athletic director. The consensus was that he wasn't the best choice for the job. Lack of experience was the primary knock against him. Thirty-two years as a golf coach didn't necessarily prepare someone to run an athletic department in the Big 12, where football rules. At least that was the conventional thinking.

Pickens disagreed. He made his case for Holder to Stillwell.

"What I want is a leader," Pickens said. "And Holder is an obvious leader."

The message got through to OSU. On September 15, 2005, Mike Holder was introduced as the new AD at OSU.

"If I was going to commit $100 million or whatever, I had to have someone I was comfortable with spending the money," Pickens explained. "I said that's the way you get the money. So they went along with that."

Hours after his press conference, Holder got a congratulatory call from Pickens, who also asked him how much it would cost to make the football team competitive in the Big 12.

Holder spent his first week on the job running numbers and preparing spreadsheets. Then he flew to Dallas to meet with Pickens and Stillwell. There he made his case for a massive stadium renovation, including the installation of ninety-nine luxury boxes. That alone, he projected, would cost $100 million. But Holder had also built in funding for a new baseball stadium, practice fields and training facilities for other sports. A lot needed to happen, he argued, to put OSU in position to beat Oklahoma and Texas. The total price tag was $365 million.

"You don't just want to put a name on your stadium," Holder told Pickens. "You have to have the resources to put a competitive team in that stadium."

"Mike, I'm not going to give $365 million to be competitive," Pickens said.

"Well, you wanted to know what it would cost. That's what it will cost."

"That's too much," Pickens said. "If I give you $365 million, everybody else will stop giving. It will stifle all fund-raising."

Holder left Dallas empty-handed and confused. He and Pickens had been talking about a substantial gift for years. Now that he was AD, he figured it was a sure thing. "I went to Dallas to see him, and I was disappointed and shocked that I didn't make some headway," Holder said. "I thought it would be $100 million to finish the stadium and then a whole bunch of other things, like a new facility for a lot of sports that didn't have a facility and an operating budget to go out and compete with the other schools that were winning national championships. That's why the number was so big—$365 million."

Bobby Stillwell knew that Pickens wanted to make a big gift. But the number had to make sense, and $365 million didn't make sense. "That was a shockingly large sum," Stillwater explained. "Nobody went around giving that kind of money, certainly not to athletic programs."

Over the following three months, Stillwell talked regularly with Holder. Then, in December, Pickens gave OSU athletics $6 million. He also told Stillwell he was leaning toward tacking on another $100 million. But he was planning to give the money through his will.

Privately, Holder and Stillwell agreed that Pickens should make his $100 million gift right away, not after he had died. But getting Pickens to see it that way required understanding how he thinks.

"Boone is an all-in competitor," Stillwell said. "He goes all in on every hand. He never plays it safe. He likes high risk."

Stillwater had a heart-to-heart with his friend.

"Boone, you've got a lot of money now," he told him. "You like to play big. Why wait another twenty years when you have the money now? Why wouldn't you want to see the results of what you give?"

"I never thought of that," Pickens said.

The idea of being around to watch the impact that big money could have on an institution appealed to Pickens. On a broader scale, the chance to shake up the status quo in college football had a certain surface appeal. But the idea of parting with $100 million or more all at once still gave him pause.

"It's such a large amount of money," he told Stillwell. "It is hard to give it. Maybe the prudent thing is—"

"Screw prudent," Stillwell said. "You don't have to be prudent. Think of how much fun this will be and what this will mean to the students and the alumni at Oklahoma State."

Pickens did some quick figuring. "You know, we can have a lot of fun with this," he said. "I'm seventy-eight. I'm going to live to be ninety at least. If it takes us three to five years to get this going, I'll still have almost ten years to have a lot of fun."

Stillwell smiled.

"I want to kick OU's ass," Pickens said.

That's what Stillwell was talking about.

"And by the way, Bobby," Pickens said. "UT, too."

Stillwell had deep ties to Texas and had been invited to join its board of regents. "Texas probably won't be happy if I help arm OSU," he said. "But I don't give a damn."

They both laughed.

———

Stillwell told Holder to rework his request from $365 million down to something more reasonable, something in the $100 million to $200 million range. Unable to think about anything else, Holder spent Christmas Day putting together a new spreadsheet.

"I tried to get down to a number that was more reasonable," he said. "I pared it down to $165 million. And I did a spreadsheet that showed we could build this stuff and put football where it needed to be."

He e-mailed the spreadsheet to Stillwell that evening. Days later Holder got invited back to Dallas to meet with Pickens and Stillwell. This time Holder brought along OSU's president at the time, David Schmidly, as well as V. Burns Hargis, chairman of the board of regents. They knew Pickens had just given $6 million and was contemplating another, more sizable gift.

Neither had any sense of what was being contemplated. And Holder didn't tell them how much he was seeking.

With Pickens and the others looking on, Holder put his spreadsheet numbers on a whiteboard in Pickens's conference room at BP Capital's headquarters. Then he broke down each item—building out the west end of the football stadium and adding more luxury suites, a new practice facility, new locker rooms, new training facilities and on and on.

"Now, what is it that you need to get this done?" Pickens asked after the presentation.

"One hundred sixty-five million dollars," Holder said.

Schmidly and Hargis braced themselves.

"Okay," Pickens said. "I'll give $165 million."

Schmidly and Hargis were speechless.

"They were flabbergasted," Holder said. "This was fantasy stuff. OSU is out in the middle of nowhere. OSU was the stepchild of the conference. Our alumni can't give large amounts of money to build beautiful stadiums. To think that someone would give our institution $165 million was shocking."

Holder looked at Stillwell. Both men were fully aware that the balance of power in the Big 12 and across college football had just shifted. It would take a couple years to complete all the construction. And it would take a couple more years for new crops of recruits to get into the OSU system. But the Cowboys were about to become players.

SEVEN YEARS LATER

Friday, September 28, 2012, began like any other business day for Boone Pickens. The eighty-four-year-old started with a 6:15 call with his two traders. They briefed him on how the world markets had performed overnight. At 6:30 the personal trainer arrived, putting Pickens through an in-home workout. After a shower, Pickens drove himself to his Dallas office. He was at his desk by 8:00. Thirty minutes later he met face-to-face with the chief operating officer of a major transportation company. Then it was a battery of phone interviews—*Parade* magazine, a radio station in the Midwest, another magazine—and meetings: one with a political strategist to discuss House and Senate races, another with his staff to look at investment opportunities. He hustled off to the Dallas Country Club for a lunch in his honor, hosted by the chairman of the Texas Railroad Commission, then returned to his office for another round of business meetings.

But at 3:15 sharp, everything came to a screeching halt. No more calls. No more meetings. No more talk of equities, natural gas and alternative energy solutions. It was the weekend of the Oklahoma State–Texas game in Stillwater, Oklahoma. Pickens had a plane to catch.

His assistants handed him last-minute messages while following him past framed pictures and autographed footballs decorating his office walls. Each one symbolized the great returns on his investment in OSU football. In 2010 the team set a school record for wins, going 11-2, including a particularly satisfying 36–16 shellacking of Texas. In 2011, OSU went 12-1, thumping both Texas and Oklahoma and winning the conference and the Fiesta Bowl. Only Alabama and LSU finished ahead of OSU in the national rankings. Pickens had been there for every moment, having a lot more fun than even he had anticipated.

He said good-bye to his staff, hopped behind the wheel of his car and sped off. Fifteen minutes later he pulled up to the gate at a private runway entrance. He pushed a button and announced his password into an intercom. The gate opened and Pickens eased his car to a stop alongside his Gulfstream G550. His pilot and co-pilot were waiting. So were a dozen passengers, all personal friends Pickens had invited to the game—the former mayor of Dallas and his wife, a retired CEO and his wife, an old grammar school mate and his wife. Most of the couples were Boone's age. Some were big OSU fans. A few had strong ties to the University of Texas. But guests of Boone's knew to root for OSU.

It's the least they could do. Boone treated game-day guests to Four Seasons hospitality. His Gulfstream—replete with leather seats, gold-plated fixtures and polished wood paneling—delivered them to Mesa Vista Ranch, a sixty-eight-thousand-acre pristine oasis that Pickens owned in the far northeastern corner of the Texas Panhandle. It's where he went before every home game, secluded by rolling hills, bluffs and twenty-eight miles of waterways with all sorts of wildlife, including lots of quail. Guests stayed in his twenty-three-thousand-square-foot lodge. The exterior was grand and muscular—stone façade with thick wooden doors bookended by nickel-plated longhorns mounted to the exterior. But the inside was perfectly appointed—leather furniture, western artwork, cathedral ceilings.

Cocktails were at 6:30 in the great room. At 7:30 guests filed into a dimly lit dining room with screened windows and doors that bordered an outdoor patio. The tables were candlelit and covered in white tablecloths. Pickens took his place at a corner table and tapped his wineglass with a spoon.

"Welcome to Mesa Vista," he said. "I have brought together people that are friends."

Guests nodded, expressing thanks.

He went over the menu: largemouth bass caught earlier in the day on the ranch, risotto, ham loaf, green beans and Napa Valley wine. It was all arranged buffet-style on a nearby table.

All of this was part of the buildup to the big game. It was a weekend excursion filled with exquisite food, fine wine, great companionship and resort-like accommodations.

———

Saturday was game day. Pickens followed his routine. The morning was spent tooling around the ranch. While his guests shot skeet, played tennis and took a helicopter tour of the ranch, Pickens inspected the oil exploration project under way on the far corners of his property. By noon the televisions around the lodge were tuned to college football games on ESPN, ABC and CBS. Ohio State faced Michigan State in one room. West Virginia versus Baylor in another. By 4:00, Pickens had reappeared in the library wearing orange leather boots and an orange sweater vest. Everyone knew what that meant—time to head to the main event.

The Gulfstream engine purred on the ranch runway as passengers filed on board. Pickens sank into his seat and fastened his seat belt. Georgia and Tennessee were knotted up 30–30 on the flat-screen monitor at the front of the plane. Disinterested, Pickens glanced out the window at a herd of black cows grazing on prairie grass beneath a wooden windmill off the runway. The pilot invited everyone to relax. It was 178 miles to Stillwater: flight time, thirty-six minutes. At 4:30 sharp, it was wheels up.

In the nineteenth century, the American author Washington Irving visited Stillwater and described it as "a vast and glorious prairie, spreading out beneath the golden beams of an autumnal sun." In many respects, that's how Stillwater looked as Pickens's jet approached Stillwater Flight Center, touching down shortly after five. Normally, the tiny regional airport was dead on weekends. But not on OSU game nights. The runway was stacked up with more than twenty private planes from Dallas, Houston, Austin, Tulsa and Wichita, all carrying well-heeled alumni from Texas and Oklahoma State. It was all part of the new economics of college football.

Pickens's jet was the biggest plane. And the ground crew knew him by name. "Mr. Pickens, welcome back to Stillwater," shouted a man in a green shirt, khaki pants and earplugs, wind whipping his hair as he clutched a handheld radio. "Your van is here for you and your guests."

Other similarly dressed workers served as ground escorts. Each smiled. The new stadium had brought more air traffic, which translated into overtime. Grateful for the work, they handed Pickens and his guests off to Jesse Martin, a stout associate athletic director standing in front of an OSU shuttle van parked on the runway.

On game day, Martin's job revolved around Pickens and getting him where he needed to be. The drive toward campus was scenic and quiet until the stadium came into focus. At that moment the impact of Pickens's money became obvious. Stillwater's total population is forty-six thousand. Yet close to sixty thousand people decked out in orange and black were trudging toward the stadium entrances. And those were just the ones with tickets. Thousands more had put down blankets and set up lawn chairs in the surrounding lots. They were in overalls and cowboy hats, Wrangler jeans and OSU sweatshirts. Smoke rose from the burgers and hot dogs on their barbecues and hibachis. Mini satellite dishes and televisions plugged into portable generators enabled them to see the game as their grass-stained kids tossed footballs. They had come to campus to be part of the experience.

Martin snaked the shuttle around pedestrians, easing to a stop at the only parking space right next to the stadium's main entrance. The sign above the space read GAME DAY PARKING. T. BOONE PICKENS. Moments later, Pickens was inside the stadium on a private elevator that delivered him and his guests to the skybox level. It was bustling with the luxury-suites crowd—prestigious alumni, big donors, corporate executives, real estate developers, construction contractors, bankers and lawyers. There were ice cream and popcorn vendors, bartenders, waiters, waitresses and cheerleaders. Everything was pristine—the Italian tile, the recessed lights, the mahogany trim around the individual suite entrances.

Pickens's suite was overlooking the fifty-yard line. Inside, two chefs prepared beef tenderloin, sautéed mushrooms, potatoes, beets, carrots and creamy spinach. There were hot hors d'oeuvres, cold beverages and plenty of glossy game-day programs sponsored by Verizon and Blue Cross Blue Shield. Additional VIPs milled around—friends like Steven W. Taylor, chief justice of the Supreme Court of Oklahoma. Taylor was more of a basketball fan. But he was Boone's special guest at all football games. A 1971 OSU graduate, Taylor had volunteered countless hours to improving and enhancing the university's academic programs. That's how he met Pickens.

In addition to the record-setting gifts to the football program and other sports, Pickens had given just as much—well over $200 million—to fund professorships, department chairs, scholarships and the Boone Pickens School of Geology. As a result, when the state cut OSU's general education budget by 4.7 percent in 2011, OSU didn't miss a beat, continuing to hire faculty and planning a new business school.

By hanging around with Pickens, Taylor became a big believer in the notion that a winning football team can lift a university's academic profile. "It was his philosophy that for this university to grow, the football team had to be competitive," Taylor said. "Boone told me many times, 'If we have a successful athletic program, then the giving everywhere else will increase— the chairs, the professorships and the buildings.'"

That's precisely what happened. In the four years prior to Pickens's gift, OSU received $327 million in donations. In the four years after his gift, the university took in over $1 billion in donations.

"It's all because he put the big money in and everybody followed," Taylor said. "He has changed this university."

As soon as his guests were settled, Pickens grabbed Taylor's arm. "Come with me," he said, hustling down to the field for a pregame interview with a local television station. The minute he reached the field, Pickens walked past the student section. Shirtless guys sporting giant cowboy hats and orange-painted chests chanted alongside girls wearing black bra tops and jean shorts: "T-Boone. T-Boone. T-Boone." Of the nearly fifty thousand season ticket holders, more than eleven thousand were students who paid a reduced rate—$200—for a season pass. That's nearly half of the entire student body. Many were holding orange wooden paddles that said POKES. Others had orange wigs. But every one of them was jubilant, and they all knew the man responsible for the surge in campus spirit. "T-Boone. T-Boone. T-Boone."

He went up to the stands and shook their hands.

"We love you, Boone," one guy in an orange tuxedo jacket and orange bow tie said.

"Thank you, Boone," another yelled.

A group of army reservists from the ROTC wanted in on the act. They were wearing their military fatigues, standing behind the sideline, right in front of the student section. They all recognized Pickens and lined up to shake his hand. One by one, he greeted each of them.

Chief Justice Taylor stood back and watched Boone work the student section of the stadium. "If you could have seen this when it was Lewis Field," he said to a reporter, "it looked like a medium-sized Texas high school football stadium. Exposed iron. Bleacher seats. No suites. It was just a big iron football stadium that had been dubbed 'Rustoleum' because it was so rusty. Before Boone came along, an OSU game against Texas would draw twenty-five thousand on a good night. Tonight there were over fifty-eight thousand people in attendance. The alumni spirit and student pride is off the charts. This is a different university. And it's just because one guy decided to do something."

After Pickens finished his television interview, he and Taylor left the field and headed up the tunnel. "Mr. Pickens," someone shouted. Pickens looked up. A man in his sixties was on the other side of the chain-link fence that prevented spectators in the bleacher seats from falling into the tunnel opening. He had a game program in his hand and was wearing blue jeans and an OSU football jersey and baseball cap. "Mr. Pickens, I just wanna thank you," the man said, "for what you've done for this community, for your generosity. This is a magnificent stadium."

A number of senior couples seated within earshot of the man stared at Pickens. "You have given us something to cheer for," the man continued. "You've brought us together. We thank you."

Pickens reached up to shake the man's hand. "Well, thank you," Pickens said. "I appreciate it."

More than seeing his name on the stadium, Pickens got a lift from the heartfelt expressions of appreciation from students, veterans, retirees and the thousands of blue-collar people who came together around OSU football.

Suddenly a security guard ran up from behind, waving a radio. "You've either got to go or stay," she yelled at Pickens, "because they are coming. But you gotta decide right now."

He looked over his shoulder. The Longhorns had just come off the field and were headed back to the locker room for final preparations. They were running right toward him and Taylor.

"Let's go," Pickens said. He took off running up the tunnel, Longhorns at his heels.

At 6:34, Boone stood, placed his hand over his heart and stared in silence during the national anthem. Then the crowd chanted:

"Orange!"

"Power!"

"Orange!"

"Power!"

A black stallion ran down the field, and the OSU team raced out of the tunnel, through a smoke screen and onto the field.

"We welcome you to Boone Pickens Stadium," the PA announcer said. "Ladies and gentlemen, it's a beautiful night in Stillwater, Oklahoma. Are you ready for Cowboy football?"

More noise.

Pickens grabbed his binoculars.

On the second play from scrimmage, OSU's running back broke loose for a sixty-nine-yard run. Less than one minute into the game, OSU was up 7–0.

"Pretty good," Boone said.

Ozzy Osbourne thundered through the PA system. "All aboard! Ha, ha, ha, ha." The crowd went into a frenzy.

But minutes later, Texas quarterback David Ash tossed a forty-four-yard touchdown pass to Jaxon Shipley, tying the game and silencing the crowd.

"That shut them up," Pickens said.

Another CEO entered Boone's suite. James "Jim Bob" Moffett was listed as one of the twenty-five-highest-paid men in America on the *Forbes* list. His total compensation in 2010 was $35 million. He had barely taken a seat next to Pickens when Ash threw another touchdown pass to Shipley—14–7 Texas.

Five minutes later OSU's quarterback tossed a forty-four-yard touchdown, tying the game at 14.

———

The game was a barn burner, both teams marching up and down the field, putting up points, giving fans their money's worth. With 9:36 to play in the fourth quarter, OSU's running back barreled into the end zone, giving the Cowboys their first lead since the start of the game—33–28. Pickens rose to his feet to applaud. Everyone in his suite followed. Cannons blasted. The black stallion charged across the field, his masked rider hoisting an OSU flag. Cheerleaders kicked and flipped. The army reservists banged out thirty-three push-ups in the OSU end zone while the eleven thousand students in the student section cheered them on. And in the suite next to Boone's—the one occupied by OSU's president, V. Burns Hargis, and his wife—twenty-four VIPs jumped up and down, hollering with excitement.

Hargis had plenty to smile about. On the one hand, revenue had poured into the athletic program. OSU sold forty-six thousand season tickets in the first year of the new stadium. That number had risen to nearly fifty thousand by 2010. On the other hand, student enrollment had skyrocketed 44 percent in the four-year period since the stadium upgrade. Annual giving was off the charts, too.

———

By midway through the fourth quarter the sky was dark. Moths flooded the stadium lights. Texas was driving. In the bleachers beneath the suites, bowlegged men in cowboy boots and cowboy hats were on their feet, hands on their hips. But their hands went to their heads as Texas running back Joe Bergeron punched it in from one yard out, putting Texas back up 34–33 with 5:48 left. But they grabbed their hats and waved them in a circular motion above their heads when Texas failed to make a two-point conversion. OSU had life.

Pickens stayed on his feet as OSU drove deep into Texas territory. With 2:34 remaining, Quinn Sharp nailed a field goal. OSU was up 36–34. The crowd noise was deafening.

But with time running out, Texas made a last-ditch drive deep into OSU territory. Pickens had seen enough. He stood and everyone in his party quickly gathered their jackets. It was time to roll. OSU still had the lead. But Boone was a betting man, and he didn't like OSU's hand. By the time he reached his shuttle van, Texas had gotten in the end zone to go back up 41–36 with twenty-nine seconds to play.

Final score: Texas 41, Oklahoma State 36.

Pickens hated to lose, but he couldn't complain. As his Gulfstream took flight a few minutes later, he looked down on streams of car lights that stretched for miles. All of them led back to Boone Pickens Stadium. The crowd was emptying out. Texas had won the game, but Oklahoma State had clearly become one of the top programs in the nation.

"Wherever you are and whatever you are doing, you are making a record," Pickens said. "I've always been sensitive to my record. I want people to see me as a hardworking guy and that I am a serious person whatever I'm doing. At the same time, I have a lot of fun doing it."

12 THE TUTOR

Friends with benefits

In March 2012, the NCAA sanctioned the University of North Carolina for academic fraud and impermissible benefits to student-athletes. The scandal centered on Carolina's football program. In a lengthy Public Infractions Report detailing the most serious violations, the NCAA zeroed in on three primary culprits: a sports agent, an assistant football coach and an academic tutor.

The agent and the coach were working in concert. It took lawyers and investigators looking at bank records to verify that the agent had paid the coach for access to players. The tutor, on the other hand, acted alone and was far less sophisticated. She basically did schoolwork for football players and gave a couple of them a modest amount of money.

As a result, the university was censured, fined and placed on probation until March 2015. The football program was stripped of fifteen scholarships and banned from postseason play in the 2012 season. The university also vacated the football program's wins from the 2008 and 2009 seasons.

The transactions between the agent and the coach involved significant sums of money. Plus, thousands of dollars in impermissible benefits were given directly to football players. The actions of the agent, the coach and a handful of top football players prompted the NCAA Committee on Infractions to write: "This case should serve as a cautionary tale to all institutions to vigilantly monitor the activities of those student-athletes who possess the potential to be top professional prospects."

The NCAA and member institutions have gone to great lengths in recent years to tamp down improper relations between sports agents and student-athletes. But there are just as many minefields inherent in the relationship between student-athletes and tutors. Only elite athletes are at risk of getting in trouble with an agent. On the other hand, every freshman football player and many upperclassmen spend significant time with tutors. Most regulations for tutoring address academic fraud. But the NCAA seldom mentions the elephant in the room—widespread opportunities for intimate relations between athletes and tutors that can lead to abuse, heartache, tarnished reputations, lawsuits and criminal prosecutions.

But NCAA investigators steered clear of the real danger zone. According to the NCAA, the tutor at the center of the probe "committed multiple major violations involving football student-athletes." Those so-called major violations consisted of writing paragraphs for papers, revising drafts and composing "works cited" pages. She also paid $1,789 in outstanding parking tickets for one player and helped another purchase an airline ticket. Pages and pages of evidence support these violations in the NCAA report.

But you have to dig deep to find this passage about the tutor: "Her supervisors in the academic support center began having concerns that the former tutor was possibly socializing with the student-athletes off campus, which was prohibited for tutors in the program." The truth is that every tutoring program for student-athletes prohibits socializing between athletes and tutors. The reality, of course, is that socializing is near impossible to regulate. In the end, socializing—not academic fraud—is what caused the tutor at North Carolina to lose her job.

Yet other than a one-line reference to rumors of her being "too friendly" with football players, the NCAA report avoids this issue. The only other mention in the entire report was this one: "Because of the rumors, the institution in July 2009 made the decision not to renew her employment contract. No further investigation into her activities was conducted at that time."

The bottom line: There is plenty of gray area when a tutor has to show an athlete how to properly compose a "works cited" page. Showing can easily entail doing. Sex between athletes and tutors, on the other hand, is pretty black-and-white. In plenty of programs it is quite common, too.

But a far more serious issue is nonconsensual sexual contact between student-athletes and tutors.

Teresa Braeckel was simply following the advice of a professor. The twenty-year-old junior was majoring in hotel and restaurant management at the University of Missouri. She had stellar grades and an outgoing personality—a perfect combination, her professor insisted, for tutoring student-athletes. "The schedule's flexible," her professor said. "Would you be interested in taking an interview?"

Braeckel was already working twenty hours a week at the university's recreational center, mainly as a swim instructor and lifeguard. She also helped out with swim meets. That was on top of her full course load. But she was putting herself through school, and a little extra money wouldn't hurt. Besides, she was an overachiever. With her professor's help, she landed an interview with one of the academic coordinators at the university's Total Person Program, the outfit that oversees tutoring for all Missouri student-athletes.

The job description sounded pretty straightforward—roughly ten hours per week doing one-hour, individual sessions with a handful of athletes. The pay was minimum wage. After completing some paperwork, Braeckel was offered the job.

A compliance officer went over the guidelines governing proper relations between tutors and athletes:

Do not lend money to student-athletes.
Do not offer them rides.
Do not bake them cookies or cupcakes.
Conduct all tutoring sessions in the academic center.
Never engage in improper relations with student-athletes.

Braeckel was the type who wouldn't think twice about offering someone she tutored a lift. She'd also been known to make cookies for her friends on the swim team. When she signed the agreement promising to abide by the rules, she made a mental note—*never give an athlete a ride and no more warm plates of cookies*. A week later she reported to the academic center and was paired with athletes from numerous teams. One of the names on her list was Derrick Washington, a freshman football player. He needed to maintain a 2.0 GPA to remain eligible to play. Braeckel was assigned to help him with an entry-level agriculture class.

———

In the summer of 2007, Derrick Washington arrived in Columbia with great expectations. Rated by Rivals.com as one of the top high school running backs in the nation, he had rushed for over fifty-five hundred yards and scored eighty-three touchdowns at Raymore-Peculiar, a top Kansas City area prep school. Missouri was primarily a passing team. Tigers' coaches assured Washington that the offense would become more run-oriented. It was some of the coaches' other promises, however, that resonated with Washington's parents.

"They told Derrick it was like a family atmosphere," Sarah Washington said. "And they assured us they were going to take care of him and he would get his education. They explained the tutoring situation and that it was mandatory for freshmen to have tutoring."

Derrick's grades meant more to Sarah and Donald Washington than how many touchdowns their son scored. Sarah was a systems administrator at a hospital. Donald was a benefits specialist for the government. Derrick was the second oldest of their five children. The family lived in a blue-collar neighborhood, and every Sunday they attended the Emmanuel Baptist Church. Their life revolved around family, religion, school and sports. Derrick's scholarship to Missouri was a source of pride, both in their congregation and in their neighborhood.

But Donald stressed that football would take his son only so far. He spoke from experience. Donald had played college football for Louisiana Tech in the 1980s. He graduated with a degree and wanted his son to do the same. Academics were high on Sarah's priority list, too. That's why she favored Missouri over the other schools that recruited her son: Missouri stressed its academic support system for athletes. And support was exactly what Derrick needed to get him through the transition from high school to college.

"The first year was kind of rough," Sarah said. "Even though they had tutors and he went to class, the first year academically was tough."

———

One reason Derrick Washington made it through his freshman year was Teresa Braeckel. She met with him regularly, encouraged him and helped him through a couple classes. The sessions always began with some small talk, usually consisting of him telling her how he had done that week on the field. Then they'd get down to business. She was professional, and he was polite and earnest. They respected each other.

Then, in 2008, Washington's college football career really took off. He led Missouri in rushing as a sophomore and established himself as one of the top backs in the Big 12 Conference. By the fall of 2009—Washington's junior year—he was an offensive star and a household name on campus. He also had women vying for his attention.

Braeckel tutored Washington for the last time in spring 2010. Her interest in tutoring had diminished. For one thing, she was turned off by all the off-color jokes and sexual innuendos between student-athletes and tutors.

The guidelines called for all tutoring sessions to take place at the academic center. But the atmosphere there was hardly conducive to learning.

Male athletes would show up in small groups, physically exhausted and totally disinterested in studying. Instead, they'd sit around, egging each other on with vulgar cracks about anatomy or the lyrics from the latest music booming through their headphones. Girls who got into tutoring for the wrong reasons played along, flirting and dressing provocatively for tutoring sessions. The place had become a hotbed for hooking up.

The situation was not unique to Missouri. The long hours and intense physical demands placed on football players are not conducive to sitting through tutoring sessions. A former tutor at the University of Georgia described how football players there would show up for tutoring sessions completely drained after workouts and practices. "The tutoring center has nice leather couches and chairs," the tutor said. "You would see these six-foot-five, three-hundred-pound guys sprawled out on the couch because that's the only sleep they were going to get. Tutors had a hard time motivating their students."

One result of this situation, according to a tutor at the University of South Carolina, was that tutors would end up doing the work for the athletes. "Some tutors would complete homework assignments for the football players," the South Carolina tutor said.

Even more common, tutoring sessions would morph into flirting sessions. "The undergraduate female tutors liked the flirting going on as someone recognizable on campus was noticing them," the tutor from Georgia said. "The players took advantage of the female tutors in that they could skirt by without doing a whole lot of work or not showing up for a meeting when they were supposed to."

In a twist on the sexual theme, tutors at some schools were the ones making the advances on players.

A former tutor at the University of Miami said that sex between football players and tutors was not uncommon. Things got so out of hand that Miami's tutoring coordinator told female tutors to minimize the amount of makeup they put on and to stop wearing skirts and low-cut shirts to tutoring sessions. The big concern was that tutors who slept with athletes would cheat for athletes. "There was definitely cheating that took place," said a female tutor at Miami. "There were female tutors who would offer sexual favors to the athletes in return for doing a paper. Miami was big for that."

———

At Missouri, sex between athletes and tutors was common enough that the participants had a name for it: "friends with benefits." But the idea of casual sex with athletes had no appeal to Teresa Braeckel. She was a virgin, a fact that made her the subject of ridicule among some athletes.

Meanwhile, Braeckel's close friend and roommate Lauren Gavin was also a tutor, and she was caught up in the friends-with-benefits system. Derrick Washington was one of the athletes Gavin slept with. Washington had a steady girlfriend, but once or twice a week he would drop by Gavin's apartment for sex.

Braeckel didn't meddle in Gavin's business. They'd met when they were freshmen and had been tight ever since. But the situation eventually became awkward. Braeckel had become Washington's tutor and Gavin's roommate. Since she was rarely home, Braeckel had never crossed paths with Washington when he was at her place to see Gavin. Nonetheless, Gavin would report that Washington sometimes made jokes about having a threesome with them. Braeckel didn't find that funny. But she didn't find it alarming either. She'd been around athletes enough to know that was par for the course. "Things like that get said in the locker room, on the practice field, on the team bus and in other situations," Braeckel said. "I think men bring up threesomes just to see what they can get away with. So I didn't let it bother me."

Nonetheless, Gavin reminded Washington more than once that Braeckel was a virgin.

<hr>

June 18, 2010, was a Friday. That evening Teresa Braeckel met up with some girlfriends at Harpo's, a popular bar in Columbia. It was dollar-beer night, and Braeckel had at least seven beers. Around midnight the group walked to a nearby Mexican restaurant to get a bite to eat. It was around 1:00 a.m. when a friend brought Braeckel home.

She had planned to go right to bed; she was beat and had to be at the rec center in the morning to teach swim lessons. But she noticed that Gavin's bedroom door was ajar and the light was on. Braeckel peeked in. Gavin was on her bed, worn out from a long day of babysitting. But she wanted to hear about the girls' night out. Braeckel gave her a quick rundown, then asked why Gavin was still up.

"Derrick Washington might be coming over," Gavin said.

Braeckel knew what that meant. "Then I think I'm going to go ahead and get ready and go to bed," she said, exiting the room.

The apartment had suites of two bedrooms at each end, with bathrooms connecting them. Gavin and Braeckel were suite mates, their rooms separated by a bathroom. After removing her contacts, Braeckel washed her face and put in her night guard: she had a terrible habit of grinding her teeth in her sleep. Then she stepped into her bedroom, closed the door, undressed and slipped into a pink lace tank top and an extra-large pair of plaid boxer shorts. She didn't bother with panties. After plugging in her cell phone and setting her alarm clock, she turned off the light and climbed into bed. It was around 1:30.

Banging on the front door to the apartment woke Gavin at 2:30. She checked her phone and noticed a series of missed calls and texts from Washington. He'd been trying to get in for a while, but Gavin had fallen asleep waiting for him. Groggy, she went to the door and let him in, not bothering to turn on the lights. He followed her to her bedroom. After a few minutes, he stepped out, saying he had to use the bathroom.

———

Suddenly Teresa Braeckel opened her eyes. It was pitch-black. But she felt something in her vagina. Fingers. She tensed up. Lying on her left side, she was facing her bedroom door. It was partially open.

Terrified, she didn't make a sound. Neither did the individual behind her, not even as he pulled away from her bed and left the room. She never saw his face, just his figure. But as she remained motionless on her bed, she felt pretty certain of his identity. Afraid to cry or scream, she just waited. Finally, after roughly twenty minutes, she heard the front door to the apartment slam shut. He had left.

Braeckel fumbled for her glasses, got out of bed and threw on some clothes. She walked out of her room just as Gavin exited the bathroom.

"What are you doing up?" Gavin said.

"I woke up to Derrick fucking fingering me," Braeckel snapped.

Gavin froze.

Braeckel started shouting, blaming her. Gavin said nothing. She was in shock. So was Braeckel. The friends-with-benefits system suddenly had serious consequences. Braeckel grabbed her car keys and cell phone, then stormed out of the apartment.

———

After driving aimlessly around Columbia, Braeckel pulled in to the parking lot of a twenty-four-hour supermarket around 4:00. She spotted a police officer in his patrol car. Her adrenaline rushing, she reached for her phone to call a friend. That's when she noticed a missed call from Derrick Washington. They had exchanged cell numbers back when she tutored him; it was required in case one or the other had to cancel a session at the last minute. But they hadn't talked in many months. She noticed that his call had come in at 2:19, about the time he showed up to have sex with Gavin. She figured Washington had been unsuccessful in reaching Gavin to let him in, so he tried her number. Never mind that it was the middle of the night. Typical, she thought.

Crying, she started calling and texting friends for support. But nobody was awake. Desperate, she called her home back in Winston-Salem, North Carolina.

Joe Braeckel was in bed when the phone awakened him. Half-asleep, he picked up and immediately recognized his daughter's voice. She was crying hysterically. In between sobs, she told him what had happened.

The first thing he wanted to know was whether she was in a safe place. She told him she was in a parking lot with her doors locked and a police officer was parked about fifty yards away.

Joe Braeckel took a deep breath. He and his daughter were extremely close. He was always there for her. But nothing in his life experience prepared him for how to handle news that his daughter had been violated in her bed. He was heartbroken. She was inconsolable and alone. All he could think to do was keep her on the phone. Thirty minutes later they were still talking.

"Dad, what do I do? Do I go up to this officer in his car and tell him?"

"What do you want to do?"

"I don't know."

She started sobbing again.

———

Later that morning, Braeckel showed up to teach swim lessons. She hadn't slept and looked like hell. Her boss sent her into the swim office, and Braeckel called the women's shelter. A counselor referred her to the hospital, where a nurse trained to deal with sexual assault victims performed an exam. The hospital also notified the police. Before long, Braeckel was in a room with an officer. She gave a statement, detailing what happened.

The rest of the weekend was a blur. On Monday morning Detective Sam Easley showed up at Braeckel's apartment. He photographed the crime scene and had Braeckel walk him through the events of the previous Friday night. Then he talked to Gavin.

It wasn't the first time that Gavin and Easley had met. Six months earlier—on January 11, 2010—Gavin filed a police report of her own, alleging another Missouri athlete—the basketball standout Michael Dixon—had raped her in her apartment. Gavin underwent a rape kit at the hospital, and Easley conducted the criminal investigation. In his report, he noted that "she was afraid of what might happen" if she pressed charges. Ultimately, Gavin declined to cooperate with prosecutors, choosing instead to meet with the head basketball coach, which led to Dixon issuing her an apology. She dropped her complaint at that point. (Dixon would later withdraw from the University of Missouri after a second woman on campus accused him of rape in November 2012.)

Gavin's ordeal turned out to be the tipping point for Braeckel. "Lauren and I never went to another basketball game after that," Braeckel explained. "And I quit tutoring at that point. It was no longer worth it to me." And Gavin went to the head of the tutoring program and said she no longer wanted to tutor basketball players. But she continued tutoring football players.

Sensitive to Gavin's history, Detective Easley went gingerly when he questioned her about Derrick Washington. But Gavin was mortified and said little to help the investigation. She confirmed that Washington had been at the apartment on the night in question. But when Easley asked if Washington had said anything incriminating about Braeckel that night, Gavin told him, "Derrick didn't say anything to me."

"How could I tell the detective that I knew this guy did this, but I slept with him?" Gavin explained. "Plus, there was the huge embarrassment that I was still hanging around with these types of guys. So I lied to him."

———

The next day—June 22, a Tuesday—Derrick Washington was at his apartment when one of his roommates told him there were two police officers at the front door to see him. Puzzled, Washington nonetheless had been coached on what to do in such situations. Every year during fall camp, Washington had listened carefully as attorney Bogdan Susan (pronounced su-zon)—a leading criminal defense lawyer in Columbia—paid a visit to the football team and talked about what to do if approached by law enforcement: *Say you want to talk to your lawyer.* Naturally, Susan and his firm represented Missouri athletes who ran afoul of the law. On the firm's Web site, Susan's bio states: "Because of his successful representation, and despite the heightened intensity of media attention, athletes have been able to continue both collegiate and professional careers."

Washington stepped outside on the porch and faced the officers.

"Can you come down and talk to us at the police station?" Easley said.

"I would rather talk to my lawyer," Washington told them. "What is this about?"

Easley said there had been an incident at the Campus View Apartments recently. He did not elaborate any further.

Washington said he didn't remember being at the Campus View Apartments, a point that Easley noted in his report. He advised Washington to stay away from that complex. Washington politely said he understood.

After hearing from the police, Washington called one of his coaches, who gave him Bogdan Susan's number and advised him to contact him right away. "Susan was the team lawyer," Washington said. "He came in and spoke to the team every year since I was a freshman."

———

Teresa Braeckel talked to Detective Easley after he visited Washington's apartment. She wanted the investigation to go forward, but she was scared, especially since Washington had been contacted. Easley told her about the option of taking out a restraining order against Washington. It would put him on notice to stay away from her. She went to the courthouse and filled out an application. In it she detailed what had happened to her. A restraining order was issued against Washington, and a sheriff notified him. Any questions about why the police had been at his door a couple days earlier had been put to rest. That made Braeckel even more nervous. She ended up packing her bags and heading for the security of her parents' home in North Carolina.

The results of Detective Easley's investigation landed on the desk of prosecutor Andrea Hayes. The minute she read the reports and spotted the name Derrick Washington as the accused in a sexual assault, she knew what to expect. Hayes was a huge Missouri football fan. But she was a bulldog when it came to going after sex offenders, and she had previously prosecuted a Missouri student-athlete for sexual assault. "It's a nightmare when we get one of these cases," Hayes said. "It's the big story. The local press starts calling me at home. And it's very unpopular to accuse a football player."

Hayes tracked down Braeckel in North Carolina. By telephone, she went over the ramifications of pressing charges against Washington. They also talked about the strengths and weaknesses of the case. The upside was that Braeckel had been consistent in her telling of the facts to everyone she had talked to—her father, the hospital nurse, the police officer who took her initial report, the detective and Hayes. Consistency builds credibility. So does reputation. On that front, Braeckel was in great shape, too. She had graduated with excellent grades. She had glowing reports from her employers. She'd never been in trouble with the law. Most important, she had no history of sexual liaisons with athletes. The fact that she was a virgin would make it very difficult for defense lawyers to convince jurors that she had pursued Washington for sex or had somehow invited him into her room.

Rather, the defense was likely to be that she had fabricated her story, made it up. After all, no semen or other body fluids had been recovered. No hair fibers. Nor did Braeckel show signs of physical injury. As is typically the situation in cases of digital penetration, the physical evidence was scant. Complicating matters further, there was nothing to corroborate Braeckel's claim that Washington had entered her bedroom, much less assaulted her. As things stood, the case would boil down to Braeckel's word against Washington's.

Braeckel couldn't imagine going to trial. The last thing she wanted was for the public to find out what had happened to her. She got embarrassed and humiliated just thinking about it. Yet she wanted him held accountable.

Hayes had been through this with many sexual assault victims. After a series of phone conversations, she laid out the cold, hard facts. "You're accusing one of the top players on the football team," Hayes said. "Your identity will get exposed. You're going to have to talk about your vagina in front of strangers."

It was a lot to process for a twenty-one-year-old woman who had grown up in Catholic schools and lived a pretty conservative college life. Braeckel wished there was another alternative. Hayes said there was—a plea bargain.

———

The Missouri athletic department has a policy that prohibits student-athletes charged with a felony from competing. Braeckel's allegation certainly constituted a felony. If Hayes brought felony charges against Washington, he'd be forced to sit out until the matter was resolved. In theory, he'd miss the entire season if the case went all the way to trial. Not a very good prospect for a guy with hopes of getting drafted into the NFL at the end of the season.

Hayes figured that the threat of being removed from the team was a pretty big carrot to get Washington to the negotiating table. Her offer was simple: plead guilty to misdemeanor sexual assault, and the state will forgo felony charges.

If he accepted, he could play his senior season, and Braeckel would be spared from testifying.

Braeckel liked it.

Hayes believed timing was on their side. It was mid-August, and the start of the season was just two weeks away. She told Braeckel she'd pursue the plea deal.

———

Sarah Washington was trailing her husband, Donald, into a meeting with a high school principal back in Kansas City when her cell phone began vibrating. She looked at the number and noticed it was one of Derrick's coaches. He always called whenever Derrick had a problem, such as poor grades or a minor injury. "Coach," she said jokingly, "if you're calling, something must be going on."

But the smile quickly left her face as the coach explained that Derrick had been accused of sexual assault. There was talk of a possible plea deal. The team had hooked Derrick up with a criminal lawyer. They were reviewing Derrick's options. The situation was quickly coming to a head. He suggested Sarah and her husband come fast.

The minute Sarah got off the phone, Donald knew something was terribly wrong. Sarah looked sick. She told him what was going on. They canceled their meeting and started driving to Columbia.

Neither of them could get beyond the shock. They had taught their son values. They were a God-fearing family, not perfect, but earnestly striving to live the Golden Rule and treat others with respect and compassion. Hearing that their son was the subject of a sexual assault probe was like a kick in the stomach.

"I was floored," Sarah said. "My first thought was that he didn't do it. But I wanted to sit down and look him straight in the eye."

It was Monday, August 23, 2010. Two months had passed since their son had told his coaches and a lawyer that the police had shown up at his door. Two months had passed since the restraining order had been issued. Yet Sarah and Donald were hearing about the situation for the first time. They couldn't help thinking the worst.

"As African-Americans, we have to teach our boys that this happens," Sarah said. "We always teach that you have to be careful. As a mother, that is always going through your head. It is almost like a black mother's worst nightmare. You know what could happen, and you try to avoid it. Sometimes you can and sometimes you can't."

Sarah was heartbroken. Donald was frustrated. In his college football days he had seen players accused—sometimes falsely—of taking advantage of women. To help his son avoid getting into trouble with girls, he had given him some simple advice before leaving home. "I told him to leave them alone," Donald explained.

Yet they found themselves rushing to the University of Missouri to deal with a crisis that involved a girl and an accusation.

———

When Derrick Washington had a football under his arm, he was elusive. He had visions of running through NFL defenses. But all of a sudden he felt trapped. Prosecutors were threatening to indict him. His coach might suspend him. Worse still, his parents had been notified and were en route. Facing them was going to be the hardest part.

"I didn't know how to tell my mom," Washington said. "I was scared. I didn't know what to say."

When Sarah and Donald reached the Missouri campus, they huddled alone with Derrick. They wanted to know what had happened.

"Just tell the truth," Donald said. "Don't make us look like no fool."

Washington faced his parents.

"I was there to see the victim's roommate," Derrick Washington later recalled. "Lauren let me in and we went in her room. She started giving me oral [sex]. I stopped her and went to the restroom. Before I left the room, she [Lauren] said: 'Can you check on Teresa?' So I went to the bathroom and washed my hands and then peeked my head inside Teresa's room. That was as far as me going anywhere close to Teresa. Then I went back into Lauren's room. 'She's in there, knocked out.' That's what I told her [Lauren]. After that we did what we did. She led me out. I left. That was that. I think it was a Friday night."

Washington gave his parents essentially the same account, minus the bit about the oral sex. "He said he went to see the other girl," Sarah recalled. "He went to the bathroom and then went back and had sexual intercourse, and then he left twenty minutes later. He said, 'Mom, I never stepped a foot in her room. I did not touch her.'"

Sarah and Donald believed their son. But they knew he needed a top-notch criminal lawyer. "Try to get a misdemeanor," one of the coaches encouraged them. "Try to get a misdemeanor."

The Washingtons were bewildered. When their son left home to play college football, they never anticipated he'd end up in the criminal justice system. Suddenly his freedom was in jeopardy, never mind his career. After meeting with Derrick and his coaches they went to the law office.

———

Christopher Slusher is the firm's senior trial lawyer. He's smart, tough and a seasoned negotiator. Although he and his firm are connected to Missouri's athletic department by way of referrals, their priorities are not exactly the same. Washington's coaches were hoping to get their star back in uniform for the season opener. Slusher was looking a little further down the road: Washington's ability to earn a living as a professional football player was at stake. His bottom line was to fend off any criminal charges that would result in Washington having to register as a sex offender. Even a misdemeanor sexual assault conviction would put a blight on his name for years to come and put at risk his prospects for making it to the NFL.

Slusher got back to Hayes with an answer to her plea offer—no deal.

That put Braeckel in a tough spot. "I felt very weak at the time," she said. "But I wasn't going to roll over and play dead. I was going to fight this."

Missouri coach Gary Pinkel had no choice. On August 26—just nine days before the season opener against Illinois—he indefinitely suspended Washington. He gave no explanation. "I don't ever talk about those issues," he told reporters.

Rumors swirled. Four days later Hayes formally charged Washington with felony sexual assault, and Washington surrendered to police. After the arrest, Sarah got a call from Coach Pinkel.

"Coach Pinkel called and told us he was permanently suspended," Sarah said. "He said he fought for Derrick for over an hour. But he said the curators, essentially the school's trustees, called him in and told him what they were going to do. He said he wanted to redshirt Derrick until after the trial. And if the trial went well, he'd reinstate him and play him the following year. But the curators wouldn't go for that."

Then Pinkel issued a brief statement. "I'm kind of embarrassed," he told a reporter. "We've worked real hard to develop a program that has a very good reputation for being first-class and disciplined. We've taken a few hits. And the only way you're going to get that back is to earn it back, and that's what we intend to do."

Two other Missouri football players—a linebacker and a reserve tight end—were arrested for drunk driving within a week of Washington's indictment. Plus, an assistant coach was arrested in the parking lot of the football facility when police found him behind the wheel of his truck. He was intoxicated at the time. But it was Washington's arrest that drew national attention.

Braeckel was still at home in North Carolina when the news hit. Her phone immediately began buzzing: the *Kansas City Star,* the *St. Louis Post-Dispatch,* the AP, ESPN and every newspaper and television station in Columbia. She had listed her cell number on the restraining order she had filed back in June. Suddenly every journalist covering the story wanted to talk to her.

She also started receiving menacing text messages. Some Missouri football fans blamed her for destroying the season before it started. Others called her vile names. Some even threatened her.

Braeckel never responded to a single call, and she got rid of her phone. She also started second-guessing her decision to press charges. It felt as if her life were upside down.

––––––

Lauren Gavin was having trouble looking in the mirror. It had been more than two months since the incident, and she and Braeckel were still not on speaking terms. The prosecutor had left multiple phone messages. But Gavin had been too scared to call back. All she could think about was the fact that she hadn't told the police the truth. "I had this huge guilt," Gavin explained. "I didn't want to say anything. I didn't want to get pulled in to testify. I didn't want to deal with any backlash from the athletes."

Most of all, Gavin didn't want to deal with the humiliation and embarrassment that would come when her friends and family found out about her intimate relations with more than one student-athlete. "I had this huge fear," she explained. "I didn't want to feel awkward going out in public, running into people."

At the same time, the lie she had told was gnawing at her, especially when she thought back to her Methodist upbringing. She started praying for guidance, pleading for courage. "What have I done?" she asked herself.

After some soul-searching, she was determined to face her fears.

"It was just a voice inside my head," Gavin said. "I just kept thinking, the truth will set you free. I have made a lot of mistakes. But I knew what I had to do."

On September 7, Gavin went to see Andrea Hayes. At first, Hayes suspected that the football team had gotten to Gavin. That wasn't it, though. On the contrary, it was one of Washington's teammates who encouraged her to come forward. Sitting in the prosecutor's office, Gavin confessed that she had withheld some information from Detective Easley when he questioned her days after the incident. Washington, she told Hayes, had in fact said something incriminating about Braeckel that night. It happened after he had briefly stepped out of Gavin's bedroom.

"He came back in and I asked him what he was doing, and he said he just went to go say hi to Teresa," Gavin said.

"And what did you say?" Hayes asked.

"I said, 'Are you kidding me? You went to go say hi to Teresa? It's 2:30 in the morning.' And we just started arguing. And it escalated a little bit. And he's like, 'You want me to leave? Like, whatever, Lauren. I just played with her cooch.'"

Hayes knew that "cooch" was slang for "vagina."

"When he told me that," Gavin said, "I didn't believe him. I thought he was just trying to upset me. And after that, we ended up sleeping together."

After having sex, Gavin reported, Washington left. That's when she got up to use the bathroom and bumped into Braeckel coming out of her room. "She said that she woke up to him trying to finger her," Gavin said. "And that's when I knew that he wasn't just saying it."

Hayes believed every word of Gavin's story, especially her explanation for why she had initially withheld information from the police. The other thing Gavin explained was that the environment in the tutoring program was hot-wired for sexual abuse. She fully admitted that the tutors shared in the blame. It wasn't just the athletes. It was a mutually destructive situation. But Braeckel, she assured Hayes, was never involved with athletes and never wanted to be. She was just there to tutor.

Gavin said she would testify to all of this at trial.

———

After meeting with Gavin, Hayes expanded her investigation. She interviewed more girls affiliated with the tutoring program. The deeper she dug, the worse it looked. "Listening to what the girls were saying, people have a real 'thing' with football players," Hayes said. "Too many tutors were having sex with the athletes, and really filthy conversations were going on between players and girls. It was a sexually charged environment. It was a joke—the whole tutoring situation."

Five days after Hayes met with Gavin, police responded to a disturbance call at an apartment complex in Columbia at 1:30 a.m. on September 12. Upon arrival they found Washington's girlfriend—identified in police records as GR—with blood on her nose and shirt. Her forehead was swelled, and her left eye was hemorrhaging. She told police that they had been arguing when Washington grabbed her by the throat and pinned her down on her bed, struck her multiple times and pressed two fingers on her eyes.

Two hours later Washington was arrested. According to the arrest report, he told police, "I did not hit her because if I did she would still be asleep."

News of his domestic violence arrest turned the tide for Braeckel.

By the time she flew back to Columbia to provide a pretrial deposition on January 11, 2011, Washington was the one looking for a plea deal. But now it was Braeckel's turn to say no deal. "He was willing to plead to felony burglary," Braeckel said. "But his lawyers wanted me to drop the sex offense part. But that's what this case was about. So even though I was a wreck at the time, I was unwilling to accept that."

With Derrick Washington's trial set to begin in four days, Judge Kevin Crane convened pretrial proceedings in his Boone County courtroom on September 16, 2011. The defense had filed a last-minute motion. The prosecution wanted it denied. In a closed-door session, Washington's attorney, Christopher Slusher, and prosecutor Andrea Hayes appeared before Judge Crane.

"Okay. What's up?" Crane began.

"The testimony in the case has been that the complaining witness in this sexual assault case was a virgin," Slusher said. "She worked in the tutoring program over at the athletic department and that she was teased by people about being a virgin. I had discussions with the state and it came to my attention that they intend to bring out that fact that she was a virgin. Our motion is filed to keep that evidence out."

Crane turned to Hayes.

"The state does plan to introduce evidence that the victim is a virgin, and we would also be able to establish Mr. Washington was aware that she was."

"What's the relevancy?" Crane asked.

"It's relevant because the other girl isn't a virgin, and this is a joke, it's funny, it's an accomplishment, it's an achievement," Hayes said. "She's a virgin. He's made jokes about that before. It's a common thing at the athletic department. 'Teresa is a virgin.' It's like this big feat."

Crane turned back to Slusher. "Let me ask you this. Insofar as the defendant's state of mind is concerned, whether or not she's a virgin, he seems to think so, right?"

"Well, there is evidence from the roommate that he was told she was a virgin," Slusher said.

"And—" Crane said.

"Yes," Slusher said.

"He finds that attractive?" Crane asked.

"That would be our evidence," Hayes said.

The thing that had Crane scratching his head was that Slusher was using the rape shield law in his attempt to keep the victim's virginity out of evidence. But the rape shield was intended to protect victims, not defendants. Its purpose was to keep victims from having irrelevant aspects of their sexual history paraded before a jury. Braeckel had no sexual history. And there was no provision in the rape shield law enabling defendants to invoke it in their own defense.

"Have you got any case law where the defendant in a sex case has ever invoked the rape shield in the history of the planet?" Crane asked.

"No," Slusher said. "But our objection is it's not relevant."

"So your real objection then is relevance."

"Yes."

Crane turned back to Hayes. "Are you going to have the locker room talk in front of this jury about this gal being a virgin?"

"It is so pivotal in our case with motive," Hayes said. "She tutored the athletic department. And that was something that people did kind of give her a hard time about."

"How would people know that?"

Hayes explained that the victim's roommate was also a tutor to the athletes and she frequently had sex with Derrick Washington and other athletes. "So a lot of athletes were at my victim's apartment and would make comments about Teresa not having guys over and stuff, and they would make comments about threesomes. And she'd say, 'Teresa doesn't do that. Teresa is a virgin.' And they were thriving on that."

"How are you going to get that in?" Crane asked. "That he knew she was a virgin?"

"Because Lauren Gavin, her roommate, told him that she was a virgin. And they had conversations about it."

"And what did he say?" Crane asked.

"'Tell Teresa I fuck,'" Hayes said.

"Oh, she's a virgin, so let her know—" Crane said.

"'I fuck,'" Hayes said, quoting Washington.

"Hmm," Crane said.

"I know," said Hayes, "it's not, you know, conversations I'm having with people. But that was . . ."

"You'd almost think telling that to a virgin would be a negative," Crane said.

It was all a little bewildering to the court. Who knew that top football players at the state's flagship university were engaged in such vulgar behavior toward female academic tutors? Crane was a University of Missouri alumnus. Unsure what to do, he said he'd wait to make his ruling until hearing some testimony.

Days later, when the trial started, Braeckel was the first witness. Hayes wasted no time getting her to describe the incident.

> HAYES: How did you know someone was in your room?
> BRAECKEL: I woke up. I felt weight behind me and then I felt fingers inside of me.
> HAYES: And what did you do?
> BRAECKEL: I tensed up. I realized what was happening. I had no reaction. I've never been so scared in my whole life.

On cross-examination, Slusher asked Braeckel questions that explored a number of theories: she invented the story; she invited the sexual conduct; and she did not know who was in her room. The shotgun approach did little to shake Braeckel. But it convinced the judge to allow the state to bring in evidence that Braeckel was a virgin. When Gavin took the stand, she told the jury what she had told Hayes months earlier: that she had slept with Washington on the night of the incident and that at one point he left the room and returned, claiming he had played with Braeckel's cooch. She also confessed to withholding that information from the police when she was first interviewed.

In an attempt to discredit Gavin, Slusher asked her difficult questions about the tutoring program on cross.

> SLUSHER: Did you feel that there was a sexually inappropriate environment in the tutoring program?
> GAVIN: Yes.
> SLUSHER: Now, college students, people your age during this time period, pretty open about sex?
> GAVIN: Yes.
> SLUSHER: And true with respect to the athletes in the tutoring program?

GAVIN: Yes.

SLUSHER: When you entered the program you had to sign an agreement?

GAVIN: Yes.

SLUSHER: And part of that agreement that you signed was that you not have relationships outside of the tutoring context with athletes.

GAVIN: Correct.

SLUSHER: You violated that pretty quick, right?

GAVIN: Yes.

SLUSHER: But it wasn't just with Derrick. There were other athletes.

GAVIN: Correct.

SLUSHER: And you described this as friends with benefits, right?

Gavin cried as she testified and said she was not proud of her behavior. She also said that Braeckel was the one who never participated in the friends-with-benefits system that was prevalent in the tutoring program. Her unwavering testimony won over the jury. "I was really nervous," she said. "I knew I was doing the right thing. But I really didn't want my family to know. That was hard. My mom knows now. But after I told the truth, I had peace."

On his lawyer's advice, Washington did not testify in his own defense. The jury deliberated for less than three hours before announcing the verdict: guilty of deviate sexual assault, a class C felony. His lawyers vowed to appeal. Meanwhile, sentencing was scheduled for November. Until then Washington was released into the custody of his parents. Later that day, Donald and Sarah Washington drove their son back to Kansas City. He cried the entire way home.

———

Andrea Hayes pushed for Washington to receive prison time. But she recognized that the university bore some responsibility for what had transpired. "The university has created this environment," Hayes said. "When you put a room of athletes together with attractive girls, some of whom like to sleep with athletes, you are just asking for trouble. It creates a sexually charged environment, and athletes get an opinion of girls that is skewed. Tutors who are in it for the right reasons get lumped in with the others. [Their] tutoring program needs to be revamped."

On November 15, 2010, Judge Crane sentenced Washington to five years in prison. But as a first-time offender, Washington was eligible for early release after 120 days. He also had to register as a sex offender. He left the courtroom in handcuffs.

Two days after Washington headed off to prison, Missouri's head coach, Gary Pinkel, was arrested for drunk driving, and the university suspended him for that weekend's game. In a statement released the next day, he expressed remorse for his actions and apologized to the team and the university.

In the meantime, while Washington was in prison, he pleaded guilty to domestic assault against his ex-girlfriend. His ninety-day sentence for that offense ran concurrently with his sexual assault sentence.

Teresa Braeckel never returned to Columbia. "I think I'm one of many girls that had something happen to them," she said. "After seeing what I've seen and knowing what I know, I think there are better places than the tutoring program to make an extra dollar." She resides in North Carolina, where she works in athletics.

Lauren Gavin graduated from Missouri. Her experience prompted her to pursue a life of service. So she entered nursing school. She works at a hospital. Her friendship with Braeckel is tighter than ever.

On March 16, 2012, Washington was released from jail after serving 120 days. "Fresh Out!" he tweeted. With his parents' help, he got accepted to Tuskegee University in Alabama, where he joined the football team. In the fall of 2012 he rushed for 1,494 yards and fourteen touchdowns, leading the team to a 10-1 record. He was named the Southern Intercollegiate Athletic Conference Player of the Year. At the end of the season—on January 8, 2013—the Missouri Court of Appeals affirmed his sexual assault conviction. Three months later, Washington was not selected in the NFL draft.

Part I, "We have no money. Nobody is giving money. We are not on TV"

Bill Moos couldn't imagine how life could get much better. At fifty-nine, the retired former Oregon athletic director had his health, a happy marriage and a six-figure pension, and his son Bo was playing football at Arizona State. Best of all, Moos finally had time to check off the item at the top of his bucket list—build and operate his own cattle ranch. The minute he stepped down at Oregon in 2007, he and his wife, Kendra, broke ground on Special K Ranch near Spokane, Washington. They did everything themselves, from dig the wells to erect the fences to develop the strictly organic diet for their herd of Black Angus cows. Moos's suits and ties were packed away in storage, replaced by Wrangler jeans, cowboy boots, leather gloves and a denim coat that fit snug across his thick chest and square shoulders.

In many ways, Moos was poised to finish out his life the same way it had begun. He had grown up on a wheat farm and cattle ranch in eastern Washington. Then his father got into state politics, serving in the legislature before being named director of agriculture and eventually running the state's fisheries. As a boy, Bill Moos dreamed of being a cowboy like his dad. But he also loved football and ended up with a scholarship to Washington State University. He became team captain and in his senior year—1972—was an All-Pac-8 offensive lineman. That experience propelled him to a career in college athletics as an administrator. He climbed the ladder for two decades before landing the athletic director's job at Montana. Then, in 1995, he took over as AD at Oregon. Under his leadership Oregon's annual budget for athletics grew from $18 million to $40 million. The school built state-of-the-art athletic facilities, expanded the football stadium and increased the number of women's sports. But the hallmark of Moos's leadership at Oregon was that the football team went from being an afterthought in the Pac-10 Conference to being a national powerhouse.

Nike co-founder Phil Knight fueled Oregon's rapid ascension under Moos. An Oregon alum, Knight pumped hundreds of millions into athletic facilities, and Nike outfitted Oregon teams with everything from footwear to uniforms to gear. Unlike NFL teams, college football programs don't have owners. Not officially, anyway.

But it's impossible to ignore the will of someone who almost single-handedly underwrites the construction of new and updated stadiums and practice facilities. Moos knew that from firsthand experience. On the one hand, his job as AD was made a lot easier thanks to Knight's giving. But when Knight's vision clashed with Moos's administrative approach, the job lost its luster. It was a battle Moos knew he couldn't win. So he reluctantly announced in November 2006 that he would step down in March 2007. In Moos's final press conference at Eugene, a reporter asked him why on earth he'd walk away from one of the premier programs in college athletics to work with cows. Moos famously said, "I guess I'm at a point in my life where I'd rather step in it than put up with it."

The upside to early retirement was that he finally had time to be a cowboy. Ranching was hard work. But it lacked the stress that comes with the bang-bang demands of big-time college athletics. He no longer began his mornings reading the sports pages. His days were spent in the quiet, wide-open spaces of the western prairie. Life was good.

But in mid-February 2010, an old friend called and reported that WSU's athletic director had abruptly resigned to take the AD job at San Diego State. WSU was on the hunt for a successor. Moos immediately felt restless. For the first time since leaving Oregon, he had the itch to get back in the game. The chance to be AD at his alma mater would be nothing short of a dream come true. Plus, Pullman wasn't very far from his ranch.

For the next few days, Moos scoured the sports page of the *Spokesman-Review* for any news on WSU's plans. Then his phone rang. The call was from the president's office at Washington State University.

"Bill, this is Elson Floyd."

Floyd had an unmistakable deep voice that resembled that of singer Barry White. Moos recognized it immediately. Since leaving Oregon, he had consulted for Floyd on some athletic department issues and knew him on a first-name basis.

"Hello, Elson."

"I want to cut to the chase," Floyd said. "I want to know if you are interested in serving as the athletic director."

"I am."

Floyd had been caught off guard by his previous AD's sudden departure. A national search committee had already been assembled. But Floyd had been privately polling key alumni, boosters and top administrators in athletics to get their input on whom to hire. The feedback was unanimous: Bill Moos. Floyd planned to let the national search run its course. But he already had his target in his sights.

"Bill, I have to go through a process," he said. "It's going to be a very public process. But you are my guy."

They agreed to meet on campus within days.

———

Tall, with imposing broad shoulders and big muscular hands to go with his tightly cropped salt-and-pepper Afro, Elson Floyd could be easily mistaken for a retired pro football player. But engage him in conversation, and he comes across like a mix between a polished diplomat with old English manners and a CEO with a practical can-do approach. The fact is that he never played football and is less than a casual fan of the game. He's an academic to the core. His top priorities were increasing enrollment and building on WSU's reputation as a leading academic institution. He viewed football as a ticket to both.

"Like it or not, football serves as the front door to institutions, with the exception of the Ivy League," Floyd explained. "The reputation of a school is predicated on athletics. Football is first. Basketball is second. If you have a successful football program, it will support all the other revenue and non-revenue sports."

Floyd's view of college football is consistent with more and more presidents and chancellors at leading colleges and universities in America today. But the reality is that very few football programs are profitable. At that point, only 20 of the top 120 Division I football programs were in the black. The remaining programs were losing on average close to $10 million per year. But it's reached a point where virtually every college president has bought into the idea that in order for a university to be successful, it must have a successful football program.

Before taking over as president at WSU in 2007, Floyd spent four years as president at the University of Missouri, a school that competed against Texas, Oklahoma, Oklahoma State and Kansas in the Big 12 Conference.

When Floyd got to Washington State, he immediately noticed that the Pac-10 was way behind the Big 12 and other conferences like the SEC and the Big Ten in terms of how much money is invested in athletics. It was a point he stressed when he and Moos met face-to-face to discuss the vacant AD position.

Seated in a high-back leather chair in the wood-paneled living room of the president's home on WSU's campus, Floyd made no bones about his desire to see the resurgence of the football program become a top priority.

"Football is an area where WSU has to make a much more strategic and important investment," Floyd explained. "Our performance has not been what we would like. The only way to change that is to make investments in the physical facilities and the personnel."

Moos could not have agreed more. To attract the best athletes, WSU needed great facilities and a great coach. That was the philosophy that Oregon had adopted before turning its fortunes around.

The other point Floyd stressed was that he had no plans to look over Moos's shoulder. He had neither the time nor the interest in micromanaging the athletic department, particularly with respect to personnel decisions. Moos would be free to hire and fire coaches. Floyd's only input was that he wanted to start attracting the best in the business to Pullman, even if that meant spending more money than in the past.

It all sounded perfect to Moos. There was just one hitch—the noncompete contract he had signed when he left Oregon. His generous severance package—$3.5 million—was spread out over ten years. Moos received annual $350,000 payouts. But they were contingent on his not taking a job with a BCS program west of the Mississippi. Accepting the WSU job was a definite breach. He'd have to forfeit the remaining seven years of severance money. That amounted to $2.45 million.

It was a potential deal killer. But Floyd didn't want to dwell on it. He reiterated his hope that Moos would be the new AD. Then he sent him on his way for a full day of meetings and interviews on campus with other WSU officials and administrators.

———

Days later Bill Moos delivered some steers to Sandpoint, Idaho. He was headed back to Spokane, pulling an empty trailer behind his pickup truck, when Floyd called him. "Bill, you did an excellent job down here," he said. "People were very impressed. I want to make you an offer to be the athletic director."

Cell reception was spotty. But before dropping the call, Moos heard the annual base salary: $350,000.

Moos had already made up his mind that he was going to take the job, regardless of the money. He called Floyd back and told him he would accept.

"I wish something could have worked out with Oregon on your severance," Floyd said.

"Well . . ."

"How many years did you have left?" Floyd asked.

"Seven. So I lose some security."

"No," Floyd said. "I am going to give you a seven-year contract."

Under Floyd's offer, Moos would end up making exactly what he would have received from Oregon. When he got back to the ranch, he told his wife it was time to dig his suits out of storage.

———

Bill Moos's first official day on the job as AD at WSU was April 10, 2010. After hiring a ranch hand to help his wife run their ranch, Moos moved into a town house in Pullman and started working days, nights and weekends. There was a lot to do and little to work with. WSU had the smallest budget in the Pac-10, and the football team had become a serial loser. The Cougars had gone 2-11 in 2008 and 1-11 in 2009. Attendance was down. Fan apathy was up. Giving had come to a standstill. Meanwhile, the stadium was in dire need of improvements and expansion.

Moos made a list of top priorities:

1. Branding
2. Facilities
3. Better infrastructure
4. Better salaries
5. Better recruiting budgets

Then he made a list of obstacles:

1. We have no money.
2. Nobody is giving money.
3. We are not on TV.

The question was, where to begin? Then he got an unexpected call. "Moos?"

"Yes."

"Philip Knight."

"Hey, how are you?"

"I'm good. I just want to congratulate you."

"Thanks."

"College athletics needs you. The Pac-10 needs you. I think it's super that you are back in it."

"I really appreciate that, Phil."

The conversation went on for fifteen minutes. Moos told Knight that one of his first orders of business was to work with Nike to rebrand WSU. The Cougars desperately needed an identity. Knight understood. He had a favorite saying he had shared with Moos many times back at Oregon: "You don't need a sign on the Eiffel Tower. When you *see* the Eiffel Tower, you *know* that it is the Eiffel Tower. Now when you see the *O*, you know it is Oregon."

By the time the two men hung up, Moos knew the hatchet had been buried. Knight had pledged to send his best design team at Nike up to Pullman.

One thing Moos had going for him was experience. The minute he took over as AD at WSU, he became the senior AD in the Pac-10 Conference. This immediately thrust him into a leadership role right as the conference was undergoing seismic changes. For starters, the Pac-10 was about to become the Pac-12.

By 2010, conference realignment was sweeping college football, and the Pac-10 was no exception. It had invited Utah and Colorado to join. The decision to expand was a financial one that made fiscal sense for everybody, but especially for schools with smaller athletic budgets like WSU. Under NCAA rules, only conferences with twelve schools can hold a conference championship game. There were obvious benefits for the two teams that play in a championship game. But even the conference's other schools stood to receive roughly $500,000 each from the game.

But expansion also created some challenges, like figuring out how to split the conference into two divisions. There was a lot to consider, such as geography, long-standing traditional rivalries and competition of schedules. All of that had to be sorted out fast. The Pac-10 television contracts with ESPN and Fox were about to expire in 2011. Commissioner Larry Scott was gearing up to negotiate new deals with both networks. But he also planned to launch a Pac-12 network. "We had a lot of inventory that wasn't making its way to TV," said the conference's chief operating officer, Kevin Weiberg. "Under the old deal with ESPN and Fox many of our basketball games and football games were not on TV."

The same month that Moos took the helm at WSU, Weiberg joined the Pac-10 to help oversee the launch of the conference network and serve as Scott's top deputy as he prepared for negotiations with ESPN and Fox. Previously, Weiberg had been VP of planning and development for the Big Ten Network. With the addition of Utah and Colorado, the Pac-12 would feature a conference network that included six regional networks. Pac-12 Washington, for example, would feature Washington and Washington State games, while Pac-12 Arizona would feature Arizona and Arizona State games, and so forth. That way, the Pac-12 Network in the appropriate regional markets would televise every football game that wasn't picked up by ESPN or Fox.

To fill additional programming space, the conference planned to tap its rich history with Olympic sports. In the 2008 Summer Olympics alone, the Pac-10 had 256 athletes compete, and they brought home eighty-nine medals. Yet for years, world-famous Olympic athletes from the Pac-10 such as Jackie Joyner-Kersee and Matt Biondi had gone virtually unnoticed until they left college. Scott wanted to change that.

"Our plan was to take inventory that wasn't generating net revenue for institutions and turn it into an additional revenue stream," Weiberg explained. "Plus, the conference network gives you a chance to expand exposure and brand reach for the conference generally. You've got a promotional vehicle out there 24/7, year-round."

———

Bill Moos was sure of one thing: conference expansion, new television deals with ESPN and Fox and the creation of a new conference network promised a flood of new revenue into the Pac-12. The question was how it would be distributed. Under the Pac-10's existing television contracts with ESPN and Fox, teams that participated in televised games shared 55 percent of the revenue. The remaining 45 percent was divided up equally among the other schools. Since USC or UCLA was on television virtually every week, the two of them were taking in the lion's share of the money. They resided in the second-largest television market in the United States, and both schools had rich football traditions and were a bigger draw for the national networks. WSU was in one of the smallest markets and seldom appeared on TV. The year Moos arrived, WSU received less than $2.5 million in TV money. USC and UCLA both received roughly eight times that much.

When he was at Oregon, Moos chaired the Pac-10's television committee and tried repeatedly to get the conference to switch to an equal revenue-sharing plan. But conference bylaws required eight votes to change any revenue policies. Naturally, USC and UCLA always voted no. University of Washington routinely joined them because the Huskies were on television a fair amount in the 1980s and 1990s and consistently had one of the strongest programs in the conference. But for WSU to turn its football fortunes around, Moos had to find a way to get eight votes before the new television contracts with ESPN and Fox were negotiated.

One weekend Moos left Pullman and went back to his ranch. He tended to get his best inspiration behind the wheel of a tractor. So he spent a day on his John Deere. At one point he turned off the engine and called the Pac-10 offices to inquire about voting rules. With Utah and Colorado joining, he wondered how many votes it would take to change revenue policy.

The answer was nine votes. If he could get Utah and Colorado on his side, it wouldn't matter how UW voted. He also learned that he had an ally in Commissioner Larry Scott. "Larry was a proponent for equal revenue sharing, and we put that on the table early on, based on experiences I had at the Big Ten Network," Weiberg explained. "If you are going to do complicated things in TV, you have to have all members participating as equal partners, and you need a grant of rights across the board. So senior and junior partners doesn't work."

Moos had a plan. He started laying the groundwork for it in July 2010 when the conference ADs met at the Peninsula hotel in Beverly Hills. UCLA's AD, Dan Guerrero, chaired the meeting. After a full agenda that included discussions on conference realignment, scheduling, bowl games and future media rights, the final agenda item of the day was a discussion on the composition of new conference divisions. That's when Moos raised an objection. He argued that it was ridiculous to discuss how to divide the conference until they determined how to divide the money from the new television contract. "The money," he said, "will dictate how we divide the conference."

Other ADs agreed. The matter was tabled, and the meeting was adjourned.

Over the remainder of the summer, Moos called every AD in the Pac-12, except for Pat Haden at USC and Guerrero at UCLA. His message to the other ADs was simple and direct: *This is our chance to get an equal share of the pie.* He already had the nine necessary votes to get equal revenue sharing passed when he called Washington AD Scott Woodward and secured an insurance vote. For years Washington had sided with USC and UCLA. But Moos had a hunch. Washington had reached an all-time low in its program's history in 2008, finishing 0-12—the only team in the country to go without a victory. It had another losing season in 2009. The Huskies were seldom on TV, and they had to pay for a huge stadium renovation. Equal revenue sharing suddenly sounded very appealing.

"I'd like to propose we carry the hammer," Moos told Woodward and the other ADs. "Let them [USC and UCLA] talk first. And we'll have a plan to slam them right in the face."

———

After a series of conference calls and additional meetings, the Pac-12 ADs reconvened on October 6, 2010, in San Francisco to vote on proposals to divide the conference and embrace equal revenue sharing. With Larry Scott about to begin negotiations with ESPN and Fox, it was imperative to settle these issues. A motion on conference divisions suggested the following plan:

SOUTH	NORTH
USC	Oregon
UCLA	Oregon State
Cal	Washington
Stanford	Washington State
Arizona	Utah
Arizona State	Colorado

On paper the South conference looked much stronger. When the ADs voted, they deadlocked 6–6 along division lines. Every school in the South Division supported the measure; every school in the North Division opposed it. Oregon, Oregon State, Washington and Washington State felt like second cousins under the proposed alignment. Those four schools wanted Stanford and Cal in the North Division, while placing Utah and Colorado in the South Division.

But during a brief recess, Moos had second thoughts. When the ADs reconvened, he invoked Robert's Rules and changed his vote, giving the South Division ADs a 7–5 margin. The motion passed.

"My northwest peers looked at me like I lost my mind," Moos said.

"Washington, Oregon and Oregon State each questioned me. But I got to thinking about the ultimate objective at WSU, which is to win the northern division, putting us in the championship game with a chance to go to the Rose Bowl. It is my belief that we have a better chance of achieving this objective if we've got Stanford and Cal playing USC and UCLA every year and we don't have to."

Once the divisions were established, the ADs turned their attention to revenue sharing. Things got much more testy. Right off the bat, USC and UCLA made it clear that they fully expected to have a higher share of the television revenue, based on precedent and the fact that they were in the most lucrative television market. "The L.A. schools were saying we're the ones driving it, so you are damn right we should get more," Moos explained. "My argument was that the New York Giants don't get more than the Green Bay Packers and they've got a pretty good league."

Everyone except USC and UCLA was with Moos. "USC and UCLA had received a larger share in the past," said Weiberg, "and were very cautious about schemes and plans that might change that dynamic unless they were going to be in a better position than they were before."

Haden and Guerrero held their ground. But Moos informed them that he had ten votes. That didn't go over well.

Haden hinted that USC might explore leaving the conference.

Stanford's AD, Bob Bowlsby, had no patience for Haden's bluster and called his bluff, saying everyone knew that wasn't going to happen.

Moos and his colleagues could have rammed the revenue-sharing plan through with a 10–2 vote. But that would have been a costly mistake. "If our television partners sensed a fracture, we would never be able to command the big money," Moos explained. "We had to come through with everybody happy."

USC and UCLA came around when they were each promised a $2 million premium in 2012–13. A sunset provision was also included, which stipulated that UCLA and USC would not receive the premium if the conference's yearly television revenue reached $170 million. With these two caveats, the ADs voted 12–0, endorsing equal revenue sharing.

———

Todd Van Horne is Nike's global creative director. He is to Nike what Jonathan Ive is to Apple. A constant innovator, Van Horne has been the genius behind Nike's ever-evolving development of the most advanced football uniform system ever assembled. And his flair for marketing helped him come up with names like Nike Pro Combat, a system of dress—from state-of-the-art helmets to lightweight, ultra-breathable jerseys that provide enhanced thermoregulation—that is revolutionizing the look and style of college football uniforms. Van Horne is also transforming the look of NFL uniforms. When Nike took over as the supplier to the NFL, Van Horne completely redesigned the entire uniform for teams like the Seattle Seahawks, overhauling everything from the color of the top of their helmets to the tips of their cleats. He even designed colorful gloves that formed the Seahawks logo when a receiver brings his hands together to catch a pass.

At Knight's request, Van Horne met with Bill Moos to figure out what could be done to reinvent the image at WSU. "We needed an identity," Moos explained. "A lot of people—young and old—want to wear the gear that their Saturday idols wear. Plus, partnering with Nike helps us immensely with recruiting. When football recruits visit our campus, I wanted to be in a position to talk up our partnership with Nike because today's recruits have grown up with Nike."

In their first meeting, Van Horne stressed the importance of uniforms and apparel that comport with modern fashion trends. "Today's fashion is dictated by youth," Van Horne told Moos. "You want something that is going to appeal to kids, something that makes them feel good, makes them want to come to your school. It needs to show well and show consistently."

The one thing Moos didn't want to do was fool with WSU's logo. "Our logo is seventy-five years old," Moos explained. "It has stood the test of time. It is recognizable."

WSU also has had the same colors—crimson and gray—for the same length of time. Van Horne opted to start there, maintaining a true crimson while developing fifteen shades of gray to reinvent WSU's athletic uniforms.

The practice of creating uniforms that change from week to week is a pattern that Nike started at Oregon when Moos was the AD there. It took merchandising to a new level, enabling Nike to design a vast array of slightly varied jerseys, sweatshirts, hats, T-shirts, gloves and other sportswear for Oregon. Overnight, Oregon's apparel became a top seller at Foot Lockers and other retail outlets throughout the Pacific Northwest. Oregon's visibility soared, helped along by radically flashy uniforms that changed colors from week to week. Apparel sales became a lucrative revenue stream for the athletic department. And consumers became walking billboards for the university, which coincided with a rise in enrollment.

It's a sales and marketing strategy that Nike has spread throughout the country. Of the 125 top teams, Nike exclusively outfits 79 of them, including 9 schools in the SEC, 8 in the Big 12, 10 in the Pac-12 and 7 in the Big Ten. Nike's nearest competitor—Adidas—outfits just 29 teams.

At WSU, Nike gifts the university more than $1 million worth of shoes and apparel for the sports teams each year. In exchange for that, WSU agreed to exclusively outfit all coaches and players in Nike gear from head to toe. The agreement forbids coaches and players to wear any other brands. Nor are they allowed to "spat"—wear anything that covers the Nike swoosh on athletic wear.

With the apparel deal in place, Moos and Van Horne spent months rebranding WSU's uniforms and apparel. The goal was to roll out the new look in time for the start of the conference's new television deal.

On May 4, 2011, the Pac-12's commissioner, Larry Scott, held a news conference in Phoenix and announced a new twelve-year television contract with ESPN and Fox worth $3 billion. It marked the largest TV contract in the history of college sports. Thanks to the Pac-12's newly adopted equal revenue-sharing plan, every school in the conference stood to receive between $15 million and $20 million in television revenue starting with the 2012 season. Overnight, schools like WSU, Oregon State, Cal and Utah were flush with an unprecedented cash flow.

But these schools also had some scheduling work to do. Under the new deal, ESPN was insisting on each Pac-12 school playing nine conference games. There was room in the schedule for three nonconference games. But looking ahead to the 2012 season—the year the new TV contract would take effect—WSU had just two nonconference games on its schedule. Moos needed to find a third opponent. Many other schools were in the same situation.

Moos called ESPN's scheduling guru, Dave Brown. They knew each other well from Moos's Oregon days. Brown had helped orchestrate the Oklahoma–Oregon home-and-home series. Moos wanted his help this time setting up a home-and-home series for WSU with BYU.

Brown liked the idea. BYU had just gone independent and was trying to fill out its schedule. It needed opponents. Brown also thought the matchup was a good draw for ESPN—a Pac-12 school against a major independent with a national fan base. Brown said he'd approach BYU's AD, Tom Holmoe.

Before becoming AD at BYU, Holmoe was the head coach at Cal when Moos was AD at Oregon. Holmoe liked Moos. More important, he trusted him. When Brown proposed the home-and-home series with WSU, Holmoe said BYU was in. The two sides agreed that WSU would play at BYU in 2012 and BYU would go to Pullman in 2013.

———

Elson Floyd liked what he was seeing. With the new television contract in place and the Pac-12 Network set to launch, he met with Moos before the start of the 2011 season to discuss capital improvements. Floyd agreed to bring a proposal to the board of regents for an $80 million addition to and renovation of Martin Stadium. It would include a new press box, luxury suites, loge boxes and a club level with amenities for fans with premium seating. That was phase one. Phase two would be construction of an eighty-thousand-square-foot football operations building. (This at a time when the state legislature was dramatically cutting funding to the university.)

The good news was that Floyd felt there was a very good chance that the regents would approve the plan. The bad news was that new luxury boxes and premium seating would be nearly impossible to sell if the football team didn't start winning more games. Floyd didn't say it, but Moos knew what he was getting at: it was time to look at replacing the head coach.

Paul Wulff had been head coach at WSU for three years. Between 2008 and 2010 his overall record was 5-32. In the conference he was 2-25. The team had yet to show improvement under his leadership. But Moos wasn't ready to pull the trigger. Wulff had played at WSU as a lineman. He'd been loyal to the program. And he kept stressing that it takes more than a couple years to turn around a losing program. The Cougars were about to embark on year four under Wulff. Moos decided that the 2011 season was make-or-break for Wulff.

14 THE INVESTIGATORS

Big-game hunting

The national headquarters of the governing body of inter-collegiate athletics sits on the southwest edge of down-town Indianapolis. It's an impressive-looking place tucked off a redbrick path with more than a little Ivy League mixed with artistic distressed-copper columns. The surrounding White River State Park is a soothing mélange of walking paths, man-made canals and culture trails. There's even a slow-food garden.

If only life were so peaceful *inside* the National Collegiate Athletic Association.

From 2010 to 2012, leaders of the thousand-member organization, which traces its roots back to 1906, had been under pressure as never before. President Mark Emmert candidly described the NCAA as a "very weird organization," ten times the size of the United Nations, with twice as many voting members as Congress, and no one felt more pressure to reform the weird, unwieldy, increasingly divided group than he did, facing daunting challenges on seemingly every front.

The first major blow arrived in the October 2011 issue of *The Atlantic* in the form of a blistering expose by Pulitzer Prize–winning civil rights historian Taylor Branch. His article "The Shame of College Sports" denounced "the noble principles" on which he said the NCAA justified its existence—amateurism and the student-athlete—as "cynical hoaxes," while making a powerful argument that college athletes should be paid. After Branch's piece, influential *New York Times* op-ed columnist Joe Nocera began methodically hammering the NCAA over its treatment of select student-athletes, portraying the NCAA as an uncaring "cartel" similar to Big Tobacco. Major college athletic directors across the country openly—if anonymously—complained about being squeezed out of the decision-making process by what they saw as an increasingly imperial president.

Then there was that little matter of the fourteen-year, $10.8 billion television contract the private, nonprofit tax-exempt organization had signed with CBS and Turner Sports for the rights to televise what was, essentially, three weeks of March Madness. The NCAA was expected to generate nearly $800 million in 2012, mostly from media rights payments, 95 percent, which it said got funneled back to members' schools. Didn't matter. Bottom line, for better or worse, college athletics seemed all about the money.

In the scandal race, football had grabbed the lead: there was academic fraud at North Carolina; a booster gone rogue at Miami; an extra-benefits mess at USC; players trading game-used jerseys and other memorabilia to a suspected drug dealer for free tattoos at Ohio State. Legal land mines were present as well. In federal court the NCAA faced a potentially game-changing, bank-breaking lawsuit filed by former UCLA basketball star Ed O'Bannon—joined by the legendary likes of Oscar Robertson and Bill Russell—over the alleged exploitation of player likeness and images for enormous commercial profit.

"I don't recall a time where there has been less optimism about how the NCAA operates," Josephine Potuto, the former chairwoman of the NCAA's Committee on Infractions and a law professor at the University of Nebraska, told the New York Times in February 2012. "Whether that's on merit, or a confluence of events hitting at the same time, the fact is there's an overwhelming feeling that everything is wrong."

Ironic, given that since becoming president in October 2010 Emmert had pushed the glacial-paced organization to get things right—or at least move into the twenty-first century.

"I consider him an incredible change agent, the right man for the right time," said IMG's Ben Sutton. "I do consider him an activist."

In an August 2011 retreat in Indianapolis with more than fifty college presidents, Emmert had laid out his three-pronged activist attack: improve the academic performance of athletes; crack down on the outlaw programs; and simplify an archaic, complex rule book that had laws about whether there could be cream cheese on a bagel and the exact number of texts a coach could send during certain times of the year. In sum, Emmert wanted all that silliness replaced with a contemporary "values-based" approach to legislation and enforcement. He wanted a modern-day NCAA—an association that balanced the booming commercial and academic sides of college sports.

In a January 2012 speech at the NCAA's annual convention in Indianapolis, the former University of Washington president and chancellor at LSU went public with his plan. Emmert spoke of fundamental "story lines" that had served to shape public opinion and sparked the need for major reform: an association "powerless and unwilling to make change"; the term "student-athlete" "described as an oxymoron used with absolute derision . . . not even capable of getting educations"; the perception that all college presidents and administrators cared about was money. And, oh yeah, everybody cheats.

"The summary of all these story lines is essentially there are no ethics, no integrity in collegiate sports and the whole system is broken," said Emmert. "[And] here's some really bad news. There is some truth to those criticisms. We are at a curious fork in the road," he told more than thirty-four hundred attendees. "And we have to decide: Are we going to . . . make changes that we have to make, even ones that are hard to make but bring the collegiate model up to date in the 21st century, consistent with our values as academic enterprises. Or are we going to wave the white flag, throw in the towel, and say, 'Look, it's too much. Let's just pretend this is all about playing the games. It's all about driving the most attention we can to football and men's basketball. Take the money and run.'

"I know where all of you stand on that issue. You know where I stand on that issue. What we have to do is work together to make sure we act on those values. That we let the world know which fork we have chosen in the road."

In late October 2012 the NCAA Division I Board of Directors granted the first of Emmert's wishes. It approved sweeping changes to the enforcement model and staff.

The new approach went into effect on August 1, 2013, and expanded the level of violations from a two-tier system to four. It drew a hard line for head coaches who break rules in hopes of a multimillion-dollar BCS or salary payoff. The new penalty structure ranged from a severe breach of conduct (seriously undermine or threaten the collegiate model or provide a substantial or extensive competitive or recruiting edge) to incidental issues (isolated minor infractions and negligible, if any, advantage). Smart stuff.

More important, the *threat* of losing bowl revenue or scholarships had a new enforcement friend. If the money pouring into the sport was rising like Hurricane Sandy, well, so would the punishment for those caught cheating. Now if a program—no matter who committed the crime—was found guilty of buying players or some equally egregious misdeed, the head coach could be suspended for up to a full season. Programs could be fined as much as 5 percent of their total budgets. In the case of big-time football, that number could reach $5 million or more.

In addition, the Committee on Infractions was expanded from ten to twenty-four working members to facilitate the faster handling of cases. To that end, the NCAA had beefed up its enforcement staff by nearly 50 percent since 2010—from forty-one investigators to a record fifty-nine by the spring of 2013. More than 70 percent of the investigators had law degrees. Many arrived with law enforcement backgrounds.

This was good, because they had their work cut out for them.

Much like the cat-and-mouse game played in the world of performance-enhancing drugs, the cheaters in college football were always on the lookout for ways to stay one step ahead of the posse. Player payoffs and academic fraud had moved into the darker corners of the system. The days of depositing checks or providing equally traceable car loans or no-show jobs had long since been replaced by more creative payment methods. The big money moved almost invisibly now, impossible to trace, unless somebody screwed up or somebody started talking. According to sources, it moved in and out of personal debit or ATM cards or through the passing of chips easily cashed at a local casino. The payments were always in cash. Even the six-figure sums needed to close on a kid, collected from "friends" of the program and funneled to an assistant coach or another bagman to be delivered to a designated "uncle" or "adviser" three or four times removed from the recruit, were paid in cash.

But Emmert didn't care how it was done. He wanted it stopped or at least slowed down. He could be a blunt, caustic, sometimes sarcastic man. Like it or not (and at times he didn't much like it), he was the face of college sports, big-time college sports. He was tired of wasting time chasing penny-ante crime and sending penny-ante messages in a world of $100 million football budgets. He wanted to remove what he called "the risk-reward" calculus that tempted coaches to break the rules because they rarely paid the price.

Forget it. The gloves were coming off.

————

In May 2012 three members from the NCAA's football enforcement group settled around a large second-floor conference table at the association's headquarters in Indianapolis. In one seat was assistant director of enforcement Chance Miller, a University of Tennessee graduate whose résumé included a law degree and defending civil litigation cases for the fire, police and transportation departments in New York City. To Miller's right was assistant director Brynna Barnhart, thirty-one, a former basketball and softball player at Knox College in Illinois. After law school Barnhart had done defense work for large insurance and electrical companies. Also seated at the table was Rachel Newman Baker. An ex-investigator and former director of agent, gambling and amateurism issues, Newman Baker was now managing director of the seven-person football group.

In keeping with Emmert's "risk-reward" mandate, the enforcement group had shifted its focus to developing larger, "more meaningful" cases. The staff's approach had changed as well—more aggressive and innovative in the pursuit of violations and closing cases. In Emmert's war on corruption, the enforcement group had become the tip of the spear.

"We're trying to get smarter because you've got to expose one of those [big cases] to have it start resonating with people," said Newman Baker. "So if we get smarter in how we're doing our business, which is what I think we're doing . . . the penalties make it not worth the risk."

As part of its approach, NCAA investigators no longer waited for a blockbuster case to drop into their lap. No longer were they just following the leads of enterprising reporters or following up with renegade boosters or coaches with a story to tell. More and more they were doing their big-game hunting. On their own. Developing sources. Tracking down leads. Ear to the ground.

"I think we're doing business differently," said Newman Baker. "And we're trying to get a better handle on what's going on in the real world. By doing the outreach, by developing the relationships with sources, we're trying to not just base policy, or legislation or cases based upon what we *think*, but what we *know* is going on."

Lo and behold—and the sound you heard was certain college presidents, athletic directors, coaches, student-athletes and defense lawyers falling out of their chairs—NCAA investigators were actually becoming people persons.

"In this job that component is extremely critical," said Newman Baker. "Especially as we talk about football, out in the world with head coaches, assistant coaches, agents, trainers, prospects, their families. You need somebody that knows how to interact with people and can develop relationships."

"It's being able to sit down and put a face with a name," said the twenty-nine-year-old Miller, who had been hired by Newman Baker in February 2009. "When an agent hears NCAA, they only think bad things. So, it's going out and showing them, hey, we're human beings. We're personable. And acting as a resource for them."

High on the list of the NCAA problems was identifying and eliminating so-called third parties from the recruiting and eligibility process. They could be boosters. They could be street agents. They could be handlers. Increasingly, they were "runners" working on behalf of player agents. The arrival of financial advisers or marketing representatives looking to cash in on player contracts had only upped the corruptive stakes. The latest dodge had become under-the-table marketing "guarantees" or signing "bonuses" paid to players while they were still in school. Some of those guarantees or bonuses reached six figures.

For much of the last three years Miller had been digging into the agent underground in hopes of making a score. He started cold-calling agents.

"You could hear a pin drop on the other end when I said, 'Hi, this is Chance Miller from the NCAA,'" he said.

When the person on the other end finally found his voice, the first words were invariably "What did I do?"

Miller explained he was just trying to better understand the culture, the trends. Barnhart, meanwhile, attended all-star games and the Senior Bowl with her eyes open and mouth shut. The NCAA had investigators on the recruiting trail as well.

"I think everything comes back to third parties," she said. "Money comes back to third parties. Recruiting comes back to third parties. I think everything we're seeing as issues has a nexus to third parties—be it agents, financial advisers, the uncle who is getting involved, the local town guy who takes advantage of a kid's family situation. I really do think everything we see boils down to it."

———

Nowhere was the third-party problem more present than in the shadowy world of 7-on-7, the hybrid spring and summer touch football passing extravaganza that had flipped the college recruiting game upside down the last five years.

The basic rules of 7-on-7, or 7v7, made for a fun, fast, wide-open, often fiercely intense athletic contest:

Maximum twenty-four members per team.
Forty-yard field.
Twenty minutes' running time until the final two minutes of
    the game.
Fifteen yards for a first down.

No more than four seconds to throw the ball (timed to the tenth of a second).

Six points for a touchdown. One- or two-point conversions.

Two points for a defensive stop. Three for an interception.

The only players on the teams were quarterbacks, running backs, wide receivers, linebackers and defensive backs. For those in the booming talent evaluation and ranking business it offered a bird's-eye view of size, agility, arm strength and speed, the essence of prime-time college football.

Because of its structure, 7-on-7 had blossomed across the country since 2007, teams springing up like wildflowers in talent-rich Florida, Texas and California and every high school football hothouse in between. By 2013 there were an estimated two hundred teams nationwide. On any given weekend there were dozens of tryouts, shoot-outs, camps, combines or tournaments built around the game.

On the final weekend of June 2012 some of the very best 7-on-7 teams in the country had arrived in Bradenton, Florida, to compete in IMG's Football National Championships held at the IMG Academy. The two-day event took place on six beautifully groomed grass fields on the back side of the academy's 450-acre campus. Signs posted on the pebbled path leading to the competition made clear the organizer's intentions: NO AGENTS, BOOSTERS, OR FBS COACHES BEYOND THIS POINT.

At 8:00 a.m. on Saturday several hundred high school athletes, about 90 percent African-American, hung out in the brewing summer heat or under the Under Armour and Gatorade sponsor tents. Many of the players wore dark green skintight Spider-Man–like jerseys that showed off bodies sculpted by weights. Thumping house music played. There was even a tented Players Lounge. Hotel accommodations and some meals had been provided. The look and feel was of a special event.

At 9:00 a.m., Chris Weinke, IMG's director of football and a former Heisman Trophy–winning quarterback at Florida State, laid out the ground rules for coaches. The start of play was just a few minutes away.

"I want the guys to have fun, I want you to have fun, but I want to do it the right way," said Weinke. "I know it gets competitive. I understand emotions getting a little out of hand. But respect each other."

Twenty-five teams from as far away as California, Indiana, Michigan and Tennessee had qualified to play. The top-ranked travel team was Cam Newton's All-Stars out of Georgia, followed by Team Tampa and South Florida Express Elite. A small army of writers working for scouting and recruiting

Web sites and services devoted to the assessment of teenage talent were out in force—Rivals, Scout, 247sports.com, MaxPreps, Elite, ESPN.com, *USA Today*—along with hugely popular team sites like Warchant.com and BamaOnLine.com. They represented arguably the biggest—and, in many ways, most troubling—change in the high school recruiting game in the last five years: the explosive growth of the player evaluation business.

Some of the players, like five-star linebacker Jaylon Smith of the AWP Sports Performance team out of Fort Wayne, Indiana, had already committed to schools. In the case of the six-foot-three, 225-pound Smith it was Notre Dame. For the majority of other players, however, like athletic Jacob Mays and quicksilver wide receiver Jared Murphy, it was a golden opportunity to strut their stuff on a grand stage.

Mays, for one, caught eyes right away. He had one of those sculpted high school bodies that seemed impossible a decade ago—six feet two, two hundred pounds—with huge hands and the ability to find a seam. Tucked away in a losing season at a small high school in Georgia, he had received scant national attention. But then Mays made Newton's all-star team. Coaches on the sideline watching his first IMG game could barely believe their eyes.

"This kid is the real deal; he's a *football* player," said one.

In many ways the 2012 IMG championship was a bit like Mays—an Off-Broadway actor getting a chance to shine on the Great White Way. Several times over the course of the weekend an IMG executive talked about the ten-thousand-seat, multipurpose stadium set to be built nearby. In the fall of 2013, IMG Academy would break new ground by fielding a high school football team. IMG was betting big on high school football and doubling down on 7-on-7. In five years the hope was seventy-five teams would participate in its national championship. The title game would be played—under the lights—inside the new stadium in prime time on cable television.

"We saw an opportunity," said Odis Lloyd, at the time the vice president of business development for IMG and a former starter at safety for Arkansas.

Lloyd, now the co-owner of VTO Sports, a premier high school combine and college prep company based in Charlotte, North Carolina, believed that with such opportunity came responsibility. On that very day, in fact, IMG had announced the formation of the National 7v7 Football Association. The hope was to create sanctioned events governed by more consistent rules and regulations and structure, especially in terms of player safety, and a coaches' code of conduct. It was a big reason Renee Gomila, the NCAA enforcement staff's point person in Florida, was on the grounds keeping a close eye on things. In a private moment inside one of the management trailers, Gomila and Lloyd had tossed around ways to control the chaos without killing a wonderful showcase for kids. The key, they agreed, was bringing "stakeholders," like the NCAA, the National Federation of State High School Associations and high school coaches, parents and sponsors into the decision-making process.

"We felt if we could get them [the stakeholders] in one place, we could get some sort of system around it," said Lloyd. "We're never going to be able to stop handlers, aunts, uncles, we're not going to stop that. But everybody knows if you come to this event, it's not about that for us. It's not the Wild, Wild West."

Throughout the weekend there were repeated references to that exact phrase—"Wild, Wild West"—but perhaps the most apt metaphor was the corrupt culture long associated with Amateur Athletic Union (AAU) summer league basketball. Back in the early 1990s, thanks to a massive influx of shoe company money, the AAU summer recruiting scene had turned into a cesspool of problems: under-the-table payoffs, street agents, "coaches" with nothing more than a tight connection to a star player selling him to the highest bidder. The world of 7-on-7 wasn't at that level—at least not yet—but all the elements were unquestionably in place, including sponsor money, enormous pressure to win at the college level, a worrisome cast of characters and a troubling lack of transparency. And the lack of control and the seamy influences seemed to be growing by the day. By the summer of 2012—with a national football playoff on the way—an entirely new level of anxiety had set in.

Jamie Newberg, a writer for Scout.com, summarized that feeling when he said, "It's getting completely out of hand."

———

In the lobby of the Courtyard Marriott by the Sarasota airport, Brett Goetz sipped water and spoke in machine-gun bursts. It was nearly 10:00 on Saturday night. All around the lobby were members of his two South Florida Express teams—Elite and Pro—drained from five hours of pool play earlier that day. They had gone undefeated in five games but paid a price. One player was at the hospital being checked for a concussion; three others were nursing injuries. Dinner was about to arrive, and when it did, in the form of chicken wings and fries, about forty high school kids attacked like locusts, forcing Goetz into action.

BACK UP!

BACK UP!

BACK UP!

I SAID, BACK UP!!

BACK UP!!

Nobody moved. Not a single soul. Three hundred and seventy-five wings and several small mountains of fries packed onto serving trays evaporated in seconds. Goetz didn't eat. Instead, he stepped back and left every last piece for his players, coaches and a guest. It felt like one of those old *White Shadow* episodes. A perfect example of why so much of South Florida's frontline talent lined up each and every February to try out for Goetz's teams, in the process making the forty-one-year-old investment adviser one of the most powerful, respected and—to a point—outspoken figures in the world of 7-on-7. Goetz had been hip-deep in the cesspool for going on five years.

"There's so much shit I'd love to tell you because it makes me sick, so much shit that I see," he said. "I read the message boards. I go on message boards and see, oh, Brett Goetz is a street agent. Anybody can hide behind a keyboard. It bothers me because I do really great things with really great people to help these kids."

He had grown up in the Philly area, a die-hard sports junkie with a mind for names and numbers. He spent two years at Temple University before transferring to the University of Florida. Later, after he got into the financial services business, Goetz became involved in charity work and youth sports programs funded by the North Shore–Nor-Isle Optimist Club down in Miami Beach.

"Extremely rewarding," he said.

As often happens, one event for kids in need led to another. In 2001, Goetz proposed the idea of a weekend youth football camp, the forerunner to a league he wanted to start. The city fathers of Miami Beach were less than impressed. Forget it, they said, nobody's going to come.

"Two hundred kids showed up," Goetz said. "I started the program, ran it, funded it through the [Optimist] club."

The football league eventually ran for about six years on city fields—with the city's blessing. "It became more than football to me," said Goetz. "We helped so many kids." Toward the end, Goetz said he picked up a kid and, as he so often did, drove him to practice. The tenth grader told Goetz he dreamed of playing college football one day.

"I'll call some schools," Goetz told him. "I'll make it happen."

So he called Duke. Out of the blue. He looked up the name of the linebacker coach at Ohio State. Called him, too. Got the coach on the phone.

"Hey, I got a great kid for you," Goetz said.

The old names-and-numbers guy, who could list the starting five of Arkansas's 1992 national championship basketball team off the top of his head, started poring over recruiting Web sites and scouting services looking for the names of college recruiters. He got them on the phone. Talked up his player.

A Duke assistant finally looked at some film and a combine report Goetz had sent on the kid from Dr. Michael M. Krop High School in North Miami Beach who one day dreamed of playing college football. He offered a scholarship.

"Now," said Goetz, "I start calling the big boys."

Notre Dame, Ohio State, Florida. Writers from Rivals, Scout, ESPN and MaxPreps reached out for information, to swap stories. Goetz began to build a network of writers and recruiters. Then, in 2008, Ohio State offered a scholarship to the Dr. Krop kid with a dream. His name was Etienne Sabino. He would go on to become a starting linebacker and defensive star at Ohio State.

"It was unbelievable," said Goetz. "I said, 'I can make this thing happen for kids.'"

But in a world of ego and influence, of loud winners and sore losers, something else happened as well, the same sad story line so often heard in summer league hoops.

"I start hearing, when a coach didn't get a kid, 'Oh, Brett pushes kids to Ohio State.' I heard everything in the world."

Goetz was making a name for himself. In 2008, somebody from Scout .com asked if he wanted to bring an all-star team to a 7-on-7 tournament in Tampa. Goetz checked around. Invited thirty kids to come try out. Forty showed up. He took twenty-four. Then he rolled out what turned out to be a superstar South Florida Express team. Geno Smith, who went on to star for West Virginia and was drafted by the New York Jets, was Goetz's quarterback. His team finished second. Afterward, several of his South Florida kids received scholarship offers to schools like Florida and the University of South Florida. Coaches and parents and recruiting writers began to take notice.

In 2009, Goetz said more than a hundred kids showed up at his tryout. The next year the number doubled. The Miami Beach boys and a few good friends were still funding the team, with Goetz kicking in the rest out of his own pocket. In 2010 the South Florida Express won a national championship in Tuscaloosa, Alabama. By the time the 2011 tryout rolled around, 250 kids were waiting at Hallandale High School.

Goetz quickly lost control of his own tryout. Guys he had never seen in his life were all of a sudden walking around in the middle of drills eyeballing the talent and asking for phone numbers. The 7-on-7 meat market had officially opened.

"I never saw so many shady fucking people in my life," Goetz said. "I was sick about it. My name was tied to this. I see people involved in the process I didn't like the way they looked. It really hit me hard in the fact I didn't realize this was the monster I created."

By February 2013 the number of prospective kids wanting to play for the South Florida Express had jumped to three hundred. By now, the drain of making a living and raising a family had pushed Goetz out of the day-to-day operations of his teams. He still raised the funds—about $25,000 for fees and travel that year—but deeded full-time coaching and managing responsibilities to former NFL stars Sam Madison and Patrick Surtain, ex–All-Pro cornerbacks for the Miami Dolphins.

"It's a great showcase, it really is," said Goetz of 7-on-7. "The kids get better, they compete, and it gets them off the streets. It gets them looks by schools." He let out a long, deep sigh. "I think it's a great *concept*, I really do."

If there was one individual at the IMG event who raised the most questions, it was unquestionably Jimmy D. Smith.

The thirty-one-year-old coach of the Louisiana-based Bootleggers didn't help himself in the first-impression department. He was late to the coaches' meeting. And while some coaches mouthed off to referees and questioned calls as the stakes rose, Smith appeared to be the only coach who openly bad-mouthed his own players.

On Sunday morning the Bootleggers added to the head shaking when they barely avoided a forfeit in an elimination game against Cam Newton's All-Stars by showing up five minutes into the ten-minute grace period. They quickly found themselves down 15–0. But then a team chock-full of Division I talent got loose, and their long, languid Louisiana athleticism took over. A series of explosive plays put them up by nine, 24–15, with about three minutes left to play.

"We're on *fire* right now," Smith yelled to his team.

Thanks to a timely interception, the All-Stars roared back to tie the game up, 26 all, and then won it, 28–26, with a big two-point defensive stop with just seconds to go.

"Mistakes killed us," Smith told his team in a haphazard postgame huddle. "We were the best team out here. Every loss we had, we gave it to them.

Stay in touch with each other. If you need help with anything, let me know. Love you on three."

He didn't bother to stick around for the team picture.

A few minutes later Smith plopped down in the shade of a VIP-media hospitality tent. He wore a wrinkled gray polo shirt and matching shorts. He said he had grown up playing high school sports in New Orleans before finding some entry-level player evaluation and data entry work with Max Emfinger, a former Dallas Cowboys scout and the first person to establish a national ranking system for high school football players back in 1980.

Between 2009 and 2011, Smith said he worked part-time for the Dallas area–based New Level Athletics, founded by former University of New Hampshire all-American and 7-on-7 power broker Baron Flenory, and wrote scouting reports on North Florida/South Georgia kids for Fort Lauderdale–based Elite Scouting Services, owned by Charles Fishbein.

During that three-year period both New Level and Elite would come under the watchful eye of NCAA investigators attempting to get a handle on the fast-moving world of 7-on-7 and rapidly expanding outposts of player evaluations, rankings and combines. Investigators eventually homed in on Will Lyles, a Houston-based talent evaluator who worked for both New Level and Elite. Of particular interest to the NCAA were Lyles's dealings with then University of Oregon head coach Chip Kelly, now the head coach of the Philadelphia Eagles, and the $25,000 fee Oregon had paid in 2010 to a fledgling company started by Lyles, Complete Scouting Services, for recruiting profiles written, it turned out, in invisible ink.

Lyles eventually told *Yahoo! Sports,* which broke the story, that Oregon paid him not as a traditional scout but rather for his influence with top Texas recruits and his ability to navigate prospects through the signing and eligibility process.

In March 2011, Fox Sports labeled Lyles "the most dangerous" street agent in college football. Lyles would deny any wrongdoing and call such charges "unequivocally false."

"When I started working at Elite, Will had just got there," said Smith when asked about his connection to Lyles, New Level and Elite. "He was supposed to be running the Louisiana and Texas database. And my first time getting on the Web site and checking our database, we [Elite] have nothing on Texas. But yet we advertise and bill people for it.

"I knew there was a lot I didn't know," Smith added. "Here I am working for one company, New Level, that was getting hammered all over the Internet. And then they've got the Will Lyles thing going on with Elite. I was working for both companies at the same time. Every investigator came at me right away, thinking I may be the common link."

———

Smith said he had met with at least four NCAA investigators probing New Level, Elite and Lyles. And while Smith said he willingly provided certain information—texts, phone records, checking account—he said he stopped short of spilling the whole story. But he did inform Fishbein, the owner of Elite, that the NCAA bloodhounds were sniffing around.

Smith originally said Fishbein fired him on the spot. Later he said they had "parted ways." In an interview Fishbein said Smith's departure was by "mutual" agreement. He knew Smith had worked for Flenory at New Level Athletics and now he was talking with the NCAA.

"I said to him, 'Who are you? And why are they asking you these questions?'" said Fishbein. "'Are you working for the NCAA? Are you some kind of double agent? What's your deal?' I didn't know whether he was clean or dirty."

———

In April 2013, the University of Oregon released 515 pages of documents relative to the NCAA's recruiting investigation. Both the school and the NCAA agreed "major" recruiting infractions had occurred tied to the football team's improper use of Elite, New Level and Lyles's Complete Scouting Services. In particular, the NCAA cited the fact that Lyles, whom it called a "talent scout," had provided oral reports for his $25,000 fee rather than written quarterly reports as required. In June 2013, the NCAA Committee on Infractions placed Oregon's football team on three years' probation and levied a number of penalties, including the disassociation of Lyles from the program. Due in large measure to its cooperation in the investigation, the school avoided major scholarship reductions and a postseason bowl ban.

———

By 2009, Jimmy Smith had gotten serious about the Bootleggers. Asked how he funded the team's travel during that period, Smith mentioned an LSU fan site he owned and work he was doing for a University of Miami Web site. (No record of Smith owning an LSU site could be found; he was listed as recruiting operations director for a Miami-affiliated site called Southeast Insider.)

"I'm kind of a one-man show," he said. "Putting it together city by city."

His motivation, he said, was to help the kids. The Bootleggers were also "self-funded," Smith said, by parents chipping in for gas and hotels. Smith admitted that from time to time recruiters asked for special access to his players or pressed for "unofficial" visits to their schools. In return, they had offered some incentives—"small stuff, expenses for travel"—or the opportunity to work a coaching camp. Smith said he turned them all down.

"If you take money or something like that," he said, "it's almost like word spreads who will play the game and who won't."

Smith said it took about twelve hours to drive from New Orleans to the IMG National Championships in Bradenton. He had fourteen kids in the van, about two-thirds already with Division I scholarship offers, several from LSU. Still, Smith said, at least six schools had asked him to drop by during the trip.

"It just means they want to give the kids an unofficial visit on campus," Smith said. "We will meet with coaches, give them a tour. Kind of like they went from their high school."

NCAA rules allow for "unofficial" visits to college campuses as long as the "non-scholastic" coach received no compensation from the school. NCAA investigators and other sources said illegal unofficial visits—springing out of the 7-on-7 scene—had morphed into a huge problem. More and more schools were paying or otherwise rewarding "coaches," street agents, outside "third parties," even writers and owners of scouting services, to ferry kids to campus for a closer look. The scenario was the same as in summer league basketball: identify the top kids, find out who had the best access to those kids, then make your play.

As for Jimmy D. Smith, on September 27, 2012, the NOLA Media Group, which operated the *Times-Picayune* in New Orleans and its attendant NOLA.com Web site, announced that "James Smith" had been hired as a full-time employee as part of a new initiative to bolster prep and college coverage across the state. Given potential journalistic conflict-of-interest issues, Smith was asked if he planned to continue to coach the Bootleggers or be associated with other 7-on-7 teams. He said he no longer would.

Just a few weeks after that conversation, on the weekend of April 13, 2013, the Bootleggers came south to compete in a top 7-on-7 event in Tallahassee, Florida, where they reached the semifinals before falling to the eventual champions. One of the players on the Bootleggers was the sophomore Jacques Patrick, at six feet two inches and 210 pounds one of the most coveted high school running backs in the country. Patrick had more than forty offers from elite schools, such as Alabama, Florida, FSU and Ohio State, already on the table. According to his Twitter feed, he had been driven to Tallahassee from his home in Orlando to play on Sunday. He didn't say who was driving, but a source with knowledge of the situation pointed to a writer from the University of Miami–centric recruiting Web site, CaneInsider, with ties to New Level Athletics.

To make things even more interesting, the offensive coordinator on the Bootlegger team, according to several eyewitnesses at the event, was none other than—you got it—Jimmy D. Smith. And, oh, as Patrick made clear on his Twitter account, he would be dropping in at Florida State on Sunday for a "short" unofficial visit.

To complete the circle, on Tuesday night, April 16, Smith posted a story about the Tallahassee tournament on his NOLA.com recruiting blog. Three of the first four paragraphs in the story highlighted the Bootleggers, praising their performance. Smith went on to cite individual standouts. Third on his list was Jacques Patrick, who Smith said had dominated at wide receiver. "Has a chance to be the top prospect in the Sunshine State for the 2015 recruiting cycle," he wrote. "There's a lot of good things to say about the rising star."

Rising star. Rising stakes. The sweet smell of cash. The cesspool deepens and darkens.

The System evolves.

———

If Mark Emmert was looking for a sledgehammer to pound home his "cheaters will not profit" message—and he most certainly was—he found it in the form of former University of Miami booster and convicted Ponzi schemer Nevin Shapiro.

In February 2011, Shapiro contacted the NCAA enforcement staff with a story straight out of *Lifestyles of the Rich and Shameless*. The gist of it was this: Between 2002 and 2010 he had personally provided millions of dollars in "extra benefits" to at least seventy-two former Hurricane football and basketball players. At least $170,000 in cash. Hookups with prostitutes. Endless champagne-soaked nights partying on his multimillion-dollar yacht or in South Beach clubs. All with the knowledge or direct participation, said Shapiro, of at least seven Miami coaches. In other words, about a decade's worth of rock star partying with a big-bucks booster as the host. It made the SMU cars and cash scandal seem quaint by comparison.

Five months earlier, in September 2010, Shapiro had pleaded guilty to one count of securities fraud and one count of money laundering for his role in constructing a $930 million Ponzi scheme. Investors who believed they were buying into a grocery-distribution business were left holding an empty bag. (In June 2011, Shapiro was sentenced to twenty years in prison for securities fraud and money laundering.)

A team of NCAA investigators went to work, interviewing Shapiro and digging through boxes of documents. Ameen Najjar, a director of enforcement, supervised the investigation. Najjar had joined the enforcement staff in 2004 after a career as a police officer and later as legal counsel to the Indianapolis Police Department.

As the investigation pressed forward, certain "third parties" identified by Shapiro as aiding and abetting the corruption at Miami either refused to cooperate or suffered an acute case of amnesia when confronted by the NCAA. Shapiro's former bodyguard was one. Six months in, a potential game-changing case was beginning to stall out.

Emmert was not happy. And he was even less so when, in August, the *Yahoo! Sports* investigative reporter Charles Robinson delivered another blockbuster, publicly pulling the curtain back on a decade's worth of Miami vice, based on hundreds of hours of jailhouse interviews with Shapiro.

The pressure on Najjar to produce increased. In late September 2011, Shapiro's bankruptcy attorney, Maria Elena Perez, had an idea how to jump-start the investigation. She suggested using the bankruptcy proceedings in Shapiro's case as a means to leverage sworn testimony from at least half a dozen key—uncooperative—third-party witnesses. Unlike the NCAA, Shapiro's attorneys had subpoena power in the bankruptcy case—they could compel the witnesses to come in and give depositions. Why not use that power to question people about the alleged NCAA violations?

Najjar, the former Indy police officer, e-mailed the idea to Julie Roe Lach, the NCAA's vice president of enforcement, and Tom Hosty, managing director of enforcement. According to an external review later conducted by a prominent New York–based law firm, Hosty found the idea "most intriguing . . . this could be a creative solution for bigger break-throughs on evidence."

Lach forwarded Najjar's e-mail to Jim Isch, the chief operating officer of the NCAA, requesting approval for funding. Isch told her to proceed. He later explained he was only authorizing an expenditure of money and not—as the second-highest-ranking officer in the association—sanctioning a backdoor approach. The plan was passed to the NCAA's in-house legal staff for review.

What came back was not what Najjar wanted to hear: Forget it. Under no circumstances, he was told, could the staff hire Perez to take depositions on the association's behalf. In an e-mail to Najjar, a deputy general counsel for the NCAA wrote, "Any information obtained through such a manner for use in the NCAA process would be subject to significant scrutiny." Moreover, it would likely circumvent the legal limits of the NCAA's authority to compel people to testify. The legal counsel shared her opinion with both Lach and Hosty.

So what did Najjar do? According to the independent review, four days later, at 4:34 p.m. on October 25, 2011, he sent Perez this text: "I ran into a problem with our legal dept concerning retaining you but there is a way around it. I will call you tomorrow morning."

Think about that text for a second and the message it sent. A high-ranking enforcement officer charged with upholding NCAA bylaws was proposing "a way around" the very bedrock principles of honesty and fair play he was hired to uphold.

For Najjar, the "way around" meant not to formally "retain" Perez but only to *reimburse* her for legal expenses. Perez took it to mean the NCAA could not officially "retain" her but would pay her "costs and fees," including billable hours for depositions. Either way, the die was cast.

The external review later found Najjar never checked back with the legal staff to approve his way around the roadblock or informed Lach. Instead, he marched forward with Perez, telling Perez that "everything was approved."

It would be August 2012—nearly two years into the investigation—before the NCAA discovered what Najjar had done. And not from Najjar, who was reportedly fired three months earlier. Rather from an invoice submitted by Perez for $57,115 for billable hours between October 2011 and July 2012. By then, depositions of two alleged eyewitnesses to Shapiro's largesse, a former Miami equipment manager and Shapiro's ex-partner, had taken place. Uh-oh.

In mid-January 2013, the NCAA notified Miami that Najjar had gone rogue; a week later Emmert offered an unprecedented mea culpa to the media.

"This is obviously a shocking affair," he said in a conference call with reporters. "It's stunning that this has transpired."

So stunning that a month earlier the well-respected Lach had been fired by Emmert, even though the external review found she "never *knowingly* took any steps that were inconsistent with legal advice" and took "many steps" to ensure the proper legal procedures were taken. In her defense, the review cited her "daunting workload."

In a statement issued to *Outside the Lines* in April 2013, Lach took responsibility for what was nothing less than an unconscionable breach in ethics: "One misstep should not unravel the good work that's already been done, and more importantly, remains to be done by a committed and ethical enforcement staff."

In March 2013, Miami took the unprecedented step of seeking to have its entire case before the Committee on Infractions thrown out prior to a hearing in June. Columnists called Emmert's leadership into question. And called for his head.

"I'm very concerned about it," he said of the public's confidence in his organization.

Inside NCAA headquarters, the enforcement staff was reeling. Morale was bottoming out fast—full of tension and distrust. The firing of Lach had touched off a fresh wave of anxiety, leaving at least one staff member in tears. Then Dave Didion walked out the door. Didion had been a respected, integral part of enforcement for more than twenty years. Now he was resigning for "personal" reasons to take a job as associate athletic director in charge of compliance at Auburn. Soon after, Chance Miller and Rachel Newman Baker left the NCAA for jobs elsewhere.

Adding to the confusion and frustration was a brewing disconnect between Emmert and the enforcement staff, sources said. Here he was, still pushing his reform agenda in public, while inside investigators were being told it was best to "lie low" for a while in hopes that the erosion of trust at the heart of the Miami case would heal over. Meanwhile, the 7-on-7 world was only getting bigger and a national football playoff was looming. If cheaters wanted to prosper, they could not have picked a more opportune time.

No two ways about it—the monumental screwup in the Miami case had come at the worst possible time for the big-game hunters at the NCAA.

15 THE SYSTEM AT WORK

Ohio State and the consequences of $3.07

The black-and-white photograph is of a young African-American basketball player sitting on a bench. His head is down with a towel over it. You have to look close to see the caption. It reads: "Images are sometimes deceiving. This isn't a picture about defeat, it is about dedication and being tired."

Larry James had put the picture in a prime spot—eye level, as you exit his office—because he wanted to remember its subtle message, one he delivered in speeches to civic groups and scholarship winners all over town. *What they call you is one thing, but what you answer to is so much more important.*

In May 2012, James was sixty-one years old and, from the look of things, a young and highly successful sixty-one. He was a partner in a prestigious downtown Columbus law firm, a trustee of the Kenyon College board, a community leader and a country mile from his dirt-poor southern roots. The oldest of seven children from five fathers, James was raised on welfare by his single mom. His sport was basketball. By the time the family moved north to Elyria, Ohio, young Larry had got himself some game. But Ohio in the early 1960s, not long after *Brown v. Board of Education*, wasn't all that different from Alabama in the 1950s. But as he liked to say: *It's not where you start in life, it's where you finish.*

So, head down, he kept dribbling. Kept working. The first in his family to graduate from college, he later earned a law degree from Cleveland-Marshall in 1977. Thirty-five years later he was general counsel to the national Fraternal Order of Police and to USA Track & Field's board of directors. Earlier that May, James and his wife, Donna, had been honored as Humanitarians of the Year by the Greater Columbus chapter of the American Red Cross.

Three weeks after that award luncheon James was thumbing through files in the first-floor conference room of his firm's elegant South Front Street office. Dark wood walls were filled with arresting African-American art. Photographs depicting "colored only" take-out joints and white-only pools gave a sense of history to the halls. For his part, James was immaculately dressed in a blue-and-pink-striped shirt and matching tie accented with stylish horn-rimmed glasses. A visitor was on hand to talk about his role as lead counsel for Ohio State University and the sixteen football players he ended up representing on appeal to the NCAA. His assistant slipped in with an important file. "Oh, yes, yep, yep, I think we got it," James said. The legal juices had begun to flow. It had been a long, hard fight against a system at work.

"You start out with the lack of due process, a lack of notice of what it is you're accused of doing," he said. "A lack of adequate preparation. A lack of any rules to govern the process or procedure. So it just lends itself to abuse."

James, of course, was talking about what critics argue is the NCAA's often heartless, capricious enforcement process. James's specialty was administrative appeals, civil rights, labor/employment contracts and business and professional ethics, so he was up for a fight. Truth be told, he saw something of his own struggles in the Ohio State athletes.

James had originally been hired to represent the five OSU football players—Terrelle Pryor, Mike Adams, Daniel "Boom" Herron, DeVier Posey and Solomon Thomas—caught up in "tattoo-gate." Eventually there would be eleven more players. Some were part of allegations involving overpayments by longtime booster Robert "Bobby D." DiGeronimo from his Cleveland-based companies. Others had been caught up in the aftermath of a scathing *SI* cover story.

James quickly found himself "spinning plates," frantically trying to meet his clients, gain their trust, gather information and make sense of the far-flung charges—memorabilia sales, free tattoos, the questionable use and sale of automobiles, extra benefits, cash payments, even a questionable round of golf.

He quickly cleared nine players suspected of selling their Big Ten championship and Rose Bowl rings, game pants, helmets, jerseys and Fiesta Bowl watches to tattoo parlor owner and suspected drug dealer Eddie Rife and others. The players still had their gear. Pictures were taken and placed into an annotated binder and delivered to OSU and the NCAA. Done deal.

At the same time the NCAA was poking into wide receiver Posey's bank records, wondering where some deposits had come from. "They [the NCAA] were saying you're selling something, you're selling photographs, jerseys," said James. So he and other lawyers in his firm put together a spreadsheet detailing the source of the deposits. They obtained an affidavit outlining the family's relationship with a friend who had provided some of the money, Jeffrey Xavier, explaining his relationship. Then James dug even deeper to prove Posey's innocence.

"I created a family tree," said James. "Went down each deposit, where it came from. They didn't find anything beyond the tattoos. I put to bed the memorabilia. The car situation goes to bed. I stop that investigation. The golf? Posey played nine holes. Put to bed. I take care of the money. That's put to bed. I put everything to bed."

Everything, that is, except the allegations involving DiGeronimo's overpayment of a total of $1,605 to four players for manual labor at his construction company and car wash between 2009 and 2011. The first player interviews took place in the spring and summer of 2011. They turned out to be textbook NCAA. Its interviews. Its rules.

"If you've got a day's notice, you've found heaven," said James. "Lawyers can't do anything. We can't talk. We can't ask questions. We can't speak. So all you can do is try and dress rehearse these kids and try to prepare them for the process."

A tape recorder was out. Forms allowing investigators access to bank records, phone records, family records, girlfriends and so on were signed. Refuse and you ran the risk of losing the one thing that mattered most— your eligibility.

"I grew up in the Jim Crow South," said James. "There is nothing you can throw at me I haven't heard. This process is sheer terror for the athletes. I was just so frustrated I couldn't do anything."

Under the NCAA's system of justice there is no discovery, no legal obligation to share any information. It's a one-way street. In this case, one built around hours of questions to eighteen- to twenty-year-old kids pressed to remember specific times and dates one or two years earlier. The object for NCAA investigators: to uncover "inconsistencies" in testimony. Trapdoors—and sometimes trap questions—that, over the years, have tripped up countless athletes and universities trying to cover up the truth. Here is an example of a typical "inconsistency" exchange between NCAA investigator Chance Miller and OSU running back Daniel Herron.

MILLER: During that summer how many days would you work at the car wash?
HERRON: Three days. Three to four days. We had about a full week off, so I [and another player worked] as much as I could.
MILLER: So, you said three or four days?

HERRON: Uh-huh.

MILLER: And how long each day would you work there?

HERRON: A couple of hours.

MILLER: When you say a couple of hours, could you be more specific? Like what time would you arrive?

HERRON: I go around 9:00 and leave around 2:00 or 3:00.

MILLER: Would you have any breaks in between 9:00 to 2:00?

HERRON: I would grab something to eat, that's pretty much it.

MILLER: Were you given like an hour or thirty-minute lunch break?

HERRON: I would just tell the guy I was going to grab something to eat real quick and I'll be right back. There was a Burger King right across the street, I just run over there real quick, grab something and come right back.

MILLER: And did you keep track of your hours that you worked?

HERRON: I really, myself, I didn't—this guy did.

MILLER: You guess the guy at the car wash kept track of them.

HERRON: Yeah, yeah. I got there, I told [them] I was leaving, and he wrote everything down.

––––––

"Let's assume they've interviewed you one time, two times, three times, four times," said James. "Some of these kids were interviewed four times. They say, 'Okay, what did you do on February 8, 2010? Did you go to work that day? Well, we have here you went to work. What time did you leave Columbus?' 'I don't know, eight or nine.'

"One kid said I worked two hours, another said four hours, another, six hours. Two of the kids worked side by side; they say they don't remember. And they [the NCAA] get pissed. And [with] the egos and they [the kids] want to reach across the table and beat the crap out of them. Not just because 'I don't believe you.' It's 'I think you're lying.' 'Look, you've got one chance if you want to play.'"

What really upset James was this kind of cheap gamesmanship—the shell game NCAA investigators tend to play. Before he left for the USA Track & Field finals in Eugene, Oregon, James said he wrote a letter notifying the NCAA he would be out of town for a few days. He asked that his clients, several of whom he had yet to interview, be left alone during this brief period. Just as he was boarding the plane out west, James said he received a call from Miller. Interviews with Melvin Fellows and Marcus Hall were set for 9:00 a.m. the next day.

You can't do that, said James.

We're doing it, said Miller.

"I hadn't talked to either one of these kids. I couldn't get to them," said James. "So I got on the phone, the three-hour time difference, and they're the ones who started the inconsistencies because they were upset."

James repeatedly argued the players never knew their precise hourly wage or filled out time cards. They were performing yard work and hauling material and washing cars. They had no reason to believe their wages were being miscalculated or overpaid. In short, they were doing what thousands of athletes have done before—do the work, take the money and don't ask a lot of questions.

In the end this is what the NCAA alleged were the "overpayment" violations:

Melvin Fellows—63 hours worked at $15 per hour, 19.5 not worked, overpayment of $292.50.

Marcus Hall—51 hours worked, 15.5 not worked, overpayment of $232.50.

Daniel Herron—84.5 hours worked, 19.5 not worked, overpayment of $292.50.

DeVier Posey—21.5 hours worked, 48.5 hours not worked, overpayment of $727.50.

For Fellows and Hall, the NCAA said, the overpayment charges were based on "inconsistencies between the student-athletes" and figures in a letter DiGeronimo's company had sent to James.

As for Herron and Posey: "The staff and institution analyzed cell phone records to determine the dates and times [student-athletes] were not at the employment site and compared that information to the hours provided in DiGeronimo's letter to estimate the number of hours the student-athletes likely worked each day."

It's important to note that in the space of two paragraphs outlining its charges against the four football players, the NCAA used the word "estimate(s)" twice, along with "likely," "around" and "near."

James didn't need a map to know where this road ended. So, quietly, he reached out to DiGeronimo through Posey's mother. For his own reasons DiGeronimo didn't trust the NCAA. After initially saying yes to an interview, he refused to cooperate. But he told James he'd have someone go back through the books. In addition, James had his people pull bank records and research cell tower technology.

The final week of September, James sent Miller and Ohio State's director of compliance, Doug Archie, at least three long memorandums filled with new information outlined in painstaking detail: time cards had been found with specific hours, jobs, days and locations worked. As it turned out, even as a casual hire Posey had qualified for union wages and payment for drive time on certain days because he was working on a union job site. James also produced bank records showing Posey in the area of Independence, Ohio, the location of DiGeronimo's construction company, on the times and days Posey said he was working.

Finally, in a truly inspired bit of legal legwork, an associate at the law firm went online and checked the Federal Communications Commission (FCC) Web site. The NCAA had said only calls "originating" in Independence, Ohio, were considered to support Posey's hours.

On the FCC Web site the James gang discovered there were approximately 250 active cell phone towers and antennas within a ten-mile radius of Independence Excavating and Valley Laser Car Wash, Posey's two places of employment, located about a mile from each other. According to an FCC map, there were cell towers or antennas within the same ten-mile radius in five neighboring communities and ten additional Verizon towers and antennas nearby in Cleveland.

In September 30 and October 5 memos to Miller and Archie, James laid out his cell phone/tower evidence: he noted a Verizon customer service representative had said while customers are generally connected through a tower or antenna owned by Verizon, if the closest tower is experiencing high volume or traffic, the call will be routed through a different phone tower or antenna leased by Verizon.

Bottom line, the customer's "origination" entry in phone records may read two different locations within minutes, even though the customer is standing in the exact same spot. In other words, James said, Posey could have placed a call from Independence Excavating, and the call was transmitted through a cell tower indicating Cleveland, Garfield Heights, Bedford, Parma or other nearby neighborhoods.

To make his point, James provided cell records from a forty-seven-minute period between 9:19 and 10:06 a.m. on March 23, 2011. According to those records, Posey's "origination" entry bounced from Independence to Cleveland three times and, in one four-minute period between 9:40 and 9:44 a.m., from Cleveland to Independence.

"The current interpretation of Mr. Posey's cell phone records has wholly failed to take undisputed facts into account," James wrote to Miller and Archie.

The union wages. The cell phone explanation. Posey was innocent, James said. In fact, he had been overpaid not by $727.50 but by just $3.07.

Three dollars and seven cents. Total.

In the memo to Miller and Archie, James wrote, "The preponderance of evidence in support of Mr. Posey is difficult to refute. One would have to turn a deaf ear and a blind eye to reject the compelling evidence as presented."

Which was exactly what, James said, Ohio State and the NCAA did.

"At the end of the day it didn't matter," he said. "They ignored it all. After we had done everything to prove, to establish, to verify and check the hours, they said no. You're just like, 'Wow.'

"They decided they just weren't going to believe anything 'cause of the inconsistency of the testimony and the inability to talk to anybody from Independence [Excavating] irrespective of the documentation."

In October 2011, Herron, Hall and Fellows received a one-game suspension. Posey was slapped with five. Five more games on top of the five he had just served for the memorabilia scam. His entire senior season was suddenly reduced to two games.

"Posey's withholding condition is based on his own actions and responsibility for the violation," said the NCAA spokeswoman Stacey Osburn at the time.

"I'm sick about it," James told the *Columbus Dispatch* after the second five-game suspension. "I have lost so much sleep over this, because I've never had something that has been so with me and so troubling, because there just aren't any rules when it comes to due process and the NCAA."

Seven months later in the dead quiet of a conference room James was still chewed up. It's as if the NCAA punished Posey for fighting back, he said. Sending a message to others, as it has so many times in the past: *Buck the system and you will pay a price.*

In the end, James was so jaded—so suspicious of the system—he wasn't even sure all his memos found their way to the NCAA. He cited an October 11 memo to OSU's Archie breaking down all of Posey's hours in support of the $3.07 figure.

"They were calling me a liar, and I was calling them [the NCAA] a liar. On the appeal, the appeal review can only review what Ohio State submitted. The NCAA appeals only got what Ohio State wanted to submit. They couldn't consider anything else."

Crabbe, Brown & James was paid in excess of $142,000 to defend Ohio

State and its student-athletes. Money, it was easy to see—at least on this day—meant little or nothing to James. He took the case because he believed he would win. And like that athlete in the photograph by his office door, he sweated, head down, on a personal crusade to beat the system. But for all his dedication, this time the picture was of defeat.

"It's a nightmare. That simple," James said quietly. "In every way you can imagine."

———

Gene Smith's date with the NCAA began at 11:36 a.m. eastern standard time on October 14, 2011. Again it was investigators Chance Miller and Tim Nevius asking the questions. To begin, Smith was asked to provide a brief bio. He said he had officially started at Ohio State on Tax Day, April 15, 2005, after serving as athletic director at Arizona State. At Ohio State he supervised the nation's largest intercollegiate athletic program—thirty-six sports involving more than a thousand student-athletes. A former defensive end at Notre Dame in the 1970s, Smith was the first African-American president of the national association of athletic directors and a member of several elite NCAA committees.

Smith told the NCAA he first heard Bobby DiGeronimo's name about six months into the new job, in the fall of 2005. Normally, in his first year he "didn't make many decisions." He preferred to keep his "ear to the ground" and "eyes open" and learn. The rumbles on DiGeronimo, as far as he could tell, were that head coach Jim Tressel had started to clean up a pregame locker room crowded with friends of the program and that DiGeronimo was one of those swept out.

"There were a lot of hangers-on during the previous coach's time frame," said Smith. "Jim was trying to clean that up."

So was Smith.

"My mantra was and my style was to deal with those people head-on in a conversation eye to eye, and say, 'Hey, look, I mean, you're a booster, you get the rules, read the rules, stay away from our program.'"

DiGeronimo had been a loyal supporter of OSU athletics for more than thirty years. Seven of his eight children had attended Ohio State. Over the years he and his family had donated about $100,000 to the athletic department. He was a self-made millionaire many times over and either owned or had access, through his family, to twenty-four season tickets.

To his many admirers Bobby D. was a man of uncommon good. The kind of guy who handed a bag of chocolate-covered almonds to his favorite restaurant hostess as a way of saying thanks, who slipped the valet guy $20 for parking his Escalade twenty feet away and who said "God bless" at the end of almost every call and text. The kind of guy who regularly drove down to Columbus to drop off pizza and pasta for the basketball and football coaches working insane hours and gummy bears for players in need of a sugary fix.

DiGeronimo's friendship with OSU football and basketball coaches ran as far back as Earle Bruce and Eldon Miller, but he really drew close to the program during the thirteen seasons (1988–2000) John Cooper was the head football coach. He and Cooper became the best of friends. Cooper allowed Bobby D. to watch practice and games from the field and to hear his pregame speeches in the locker room before games. Once a year Cooper invited him to travel on the road with the team.

DiGeronimo enjoyed a similar relationship with Ted Ginn Sr., the highly respected high school football and track coach at Glenville High in Cleveland and founder of the prestigious Ginn Academy for high school boys. Ginn is the father of former OSU star Ted Ginn Jr. With Ginn Sr.'s help Bobby D. had reached out to Buckeye quarterback Troy Smith in 2006 and invited him to attend the upcoming Cornerstone of Hope gala. The charity had been co-founded shortly after DiGeronimo's three-year-old grandson, Bobby, had suddenly died of bacterial meningitis in 2000. Smith knew Bobby and agreed to come and brought a number of his teammates with him. When Ohio State found out the players had appeared at the gala without permission from the school, it filed a self-report with the NCAA that resulted in a minor secondary violation.

On April 20, 2006, Ohio State compliance director Heather Lyke wrote an e-mail to Gene Smith detailing five compliance issues she wanted the athletic director to discuss with DiGeronimo. In short, they were:

1. tickets—may not request or receive complimentary tickets from our student-athletes for any reason;
2. employment of student-athletes—make sure student-athlete registers with compliance office and he completes and returns all monitoring documents;
3. occasional meals—may not have occasional meals with our student-athletes;
4. fraternizing with our student-athletes—"Bobby's attempt to develop close personal relationships with our student-athletes is concerning";

5. probation—the fact we are on probation should elevate our concerns.

———

After discussing the memo with Lyke in his office, Smith told the NCAA he immediately called DiGeronimo.

"So I called him right there on the spot," Smith said. "He wasn't there. Left a message. And I told Heather, well, I'll just go up there and see him, 'cause I go to Cleveland quite a bit. And I went up, did not get a chance to go see him. I came back. He actually had returned my call. I called him back. And we talked. And I shared with him that, you know, I understand you have a, a habit of delivering pizzas to our football, basketball staff. You can no longer do that. You have to discontinue that practice. I understand you have some relationship with our student-athletes periodically. You have to discontinue any contact with our student-athletes. And I said, 'Bobby, you're a booster. Every year, you get booster education. You need to pay attention to these materials and follow the guidelines.' And I was very firm with my message. And he said, 'I understand.' And we ended up having chitchat about Cleveland after that. And so the conversation kind of shifted. And I really didn't hear his name again until our case."

At this point Miller asked Smith if that conversation took place before or after he received Lyke's e-mail. A pretty simple question involving time and place, much like the questions asked of the Ohio State football players caught up in the scandal.

"I can't remember, Chance," he said. "I can't remember the sequence."

During the course of a forty-nine-minute interview Smith would say the words "I can't remember," "I don't remember," "I don't recall" or "I can't recall" no fewer than twenty times.

Then, in the case of that first phone call to Bobby D., Smith said, wait, he could remember when he called. Sort of.

"But I did get an e-mail from her that had messages. In fact, she brought it, it had to be before because she brought it with, with her to the meeting 'cause she gave me a document, and I believe it was the document that had, I don't know, five or six things she wanted me to share with him. And, and I did not share those exact things with him."

That's because Smith said he didn't have Lyke's e-mail "in front of me."

"I was going from memory," he said.

Smith admitted he never specifically mentioned any of Lyke's bullet points to DiGeronimo—tickets, student-athlete employment, the occasional meals, the gala, the fraternizing, probation. Not one.

Still, he recalled, he was "very firm." His tone and demeanor were "pretty strong."

"I said, 'You need to stay away from our student-athletes and not engage with our student-athletes.'"

And then Smith said he never saw or heard from Bobby D. for almost five years.

———

It was listed in the Cornerstone of Hope's Ninth Annual Benefit Gala program as live auction item number 1005.

> Two (2) season tickets for OSU's 2012 home football games. See them all in the 'Shoe. Live the excitement of Buckeye football! O-H-I-O. Watch OSU beat Miami (Ohio), Central Florida, California, UAB, Nebraska, Purdue, Illinois and Michigan!
>   Value: Priceless.

The Disney on Ice package had already come and gone in spirited bidding in the ballroom at the Embassy Suites in Independence, Ohio. Tickets to Kenny Chesney and Tim McGraw's Brothers of the Sun Tour and the autographed Muhammad Ali boxing gloves had raised thousands more. Now auction paddles popped into the air chasing the OSU seats. A thousand. Two thousand. Twenty-five hundred. Three thousand. Thirty-five hundred . . . sold!

A guest from out of town turned to the man of the hour and whispered, "Those are your season tickets."

"Yes," said Bobby D. "They are."

Or were.

———

Five months earlier, on September 21, 2011, Robert DiGeronimo had been banned from Ohio State athletics for ten years for providing $2,405 in "extra benefits" to a total of nine football players between 2009 and 2011. He was notified of his "immediate disassociation" in a letter from athletic director Smith. Smith cited DiGeronimo's refusal to meet with NCAA and university officials in the "tattoo-gate" investigation; that DiGeronimo had "deliberately" not complied with NCAA rules covering money and extra benefits. Furthermore, six days earlier, DiGeronimo had been quoted in the Cleveland *Plain Dealer* saying, "Quite honestly, if there's no tattoo-gate, this thing [the NCAA investigation] doesn't come out." Smith admonished DiGeronimo for publicly implying he intentionally broke NCAA rules.

"The University is outraged and disappointed with this conduct," wrote Smith.

During his interview, NCAA investigator Chance Miller had asked the AD if he had ever been invited to a Cornerstone of Hope event.

"Never, never even—never actually heard the term Cornerstone of Hope until our case," Smith said.

Pity. The ninth annual gala was something to see. A sold-out, well-heeled crowd of nearly seven hundred had packed the place in support of a charity dedicated to love and loss. "Walking the journey of grief," the co-founder Christi Tripodi described it.

Tripodi's personal journey had begun on Mother's Day 2000. Her three-year-old son had been running a high fever and had taken a turn for the worse. Tripodi and her husband, Mark, rushed their son to the emergency room at a local children's hospital. They figured a couple of hours and he would be back home in bed. Mom and Dad didn't come home until the next night. When they did, their son wasn't with them. He had died from an infection caused by bacterial meningitis. Little Bobby.

"I'll never forget when they came back and Mark, my son-in-law, had unhooked his son, held his boy," the child's grandfather said in the fall of 2012. Bobby D. took a deep breath. "And now you've got to understand, for the next six months Christi couldn't get out of bed."

Seven brothers and sisters essentially moved into Christi and Mark's tiny house, staying night after night, never letting their sister out of their sight.

"Life was not the same for us anymore," said Bobby D.

And then, one day, a father heard a sound he had not heard in eighteen months. "I heard her laugh," he said. "And I said, 'Thank you, Jesus.' Because I didn't know if I was ever going to hear her laugh again."

Almost two years later Christi called her dad and said, "We have to own a place."

"What do you mean?"

"A place where people can get help. Will you be on the board?"

Bobby D. figured his daughter was just talking. Two weeks later there was a board meeting. Bobby D. thought, Hmm, they're serious.

"How will this be funded?" he asked his daughter.

A party center, she said.

No way, said her dad.

But word got out about the idea. Dino Lucarelli, the longtime director of public relations and alumni relations for the Cleveland Browns, called. Bobby D., you've helped a lot of people over the years, Dino said. You want to cash in some chips?

Yeah, said Bobby, I do.

In 2003, Cornerstone of Hope found space in a building DiGeronimo owned. It stayed in that space until a new place was built. The first real headquarters grew out of the converted old house on Brecksville Road in Independence where Sam and Mary DiGeronimo had raised their seven kids.

Bobby cashed in a lot of chips. Construction buddies, a big mechanical contractor, electricians, plumbers, the union guys, all anted up, donating about $600,000 in time and material. DiGeronimo personally put in $400,000 of his own money. And there it was: a rambling, warm, welcoming "Home for the Grieving." Bright, airy rooms upstairs for art therapy right next to a padded room where kids could untangle their emotions and let off steam; private counseling offices; a prayer garden. And the Mary DiGeronimo Chapel right as you walked in. Bobby D.'s mother's wedding dress preserved with honor in a back corner where parents and friends sat and prayed.

"Saint Mary," said Bobby D., "for putting up with Sam."

———

Former Buckeyes star running back Robert Smith served as the master of ceremonies for the 2012 gala. A college football analyst on ESPN, Smith left Ohio State as one of the Buckeyes' all-time greats and went on to set the Minnesota Vikings' career rushing record with more than sixty-eight hundred yards before Adrian Peterson eclipsed it in 2012. The room was loaded with men who had proudly worn the scarlet and gray: another great running back, Beanie Wells; quarterback Troy Smith; wide receiver Ted Ginn Jr.; and linebacker Tom Cousineau, another certified legend, still cool as can be, rockin' an Elvis Costello look.

At DiGeronimo's table sat another proud Buckeye. Jim Conroy was a successful Cleveland attorney who toiled on the offensive line on the 1968 national championship team under Woody Hayes. He and his wife had recently lost their twenty-seven-year-old son to suicide. Cornerstone had helped them deal with unimaginable grief.

"Everybody in this room loves Bobby," he said.

Two chairs away Troy Smith sat down and quietly started talking to

DiGeronimo. Bobby D. just listened. In person, he bore more than a passing resemblance to the actor James Caan. He had on a black velvet jacket, creased pants, a striped shirt and a muted tie. His shoes sparkled. His dark, slicked-back hair defied Father Time.

You could tell by the look on Smith's face that he was in need of some kind of help. Bobby D. had done a lot of listening and a world of good for Ohio State athletes over the years. "Bobby, can you help?" they asked. And he did. Not because he had to. Because, he said, it was the right thing to do.

"Now, you lose a grandson, it's about giving back even more," he said. "Now you want to do more."

Before the dinner began, a steady stream of well-wishers had stopped by the table for a handshake, a hug, a "How ya doing?"

"Thank you, thank you for coming, for your support," said Bobby D.

DiGeronimo's ban seemed to add a sense of urgency to the auction. When the night was over, the 2012 benefit netted a record $350,000—nearly half of Cornerstone of Hope's annual budget.

———

At a press conference dealing with additional charges against the school relative to employment and gala violations, Gene Smith made clear exactly who this "rogue" booster was, as if everyone in the state of Ohio didn't already know. Smith mentioned DiGeronimo's name at least three times when talking about the school's banning him from the athletic program for ten years. In large part, he explained, due to DiGeronimo's decision not to cooperate with the school or the investigation.

"We realized that wasn't going to happen," said Smith, "so we ultimately disassociated."

In his press conference Smith took great pains to point out that the failures at OSU were not institutional but rather "failures of individual athletes, a previous coach and a booster."

"So it's not a systemic failure of compliance," he said. "I'm optimistic and I'm confident that we will not have those charges."

Longtime observers of college sports saw Smith's presser for what it was: a systematic attempt to turn Bobby D. into the designated fall guy; to toss him on the altar of the powerful NCAA Committee on Infractions to avoid the dreaded "lack of institutional control" charge; to protect a cash-cow football program and the Ohio State brand at all costs. Thirty-five years of faithful support jettisoned almost overnight, a month *before* the NCAA released its official report.

As a college star, Robert Smith had seen a previous model of the system at work. He had openly tangled with the athletic department and head coach, John Cooper, for not allowing him to spend more time on academics in order to pursue a career in medicine. He knew full well what had happened to Bobby D., and he didn't like it one bit. That's why Smith welcomed the crowd with an impassioned speech praising a man who, few knew, had helped Smith during a particularly difficult period. They continued to speak every couple of weeks.

"I love you like a father," Smith said, looking directly at Bobby D. "You did more than my father did for me, more than any father could."

Nine months later.

The downtown tour had started north on Ninth Street just as Progressive Field, home of the Indians, came into view. "That's our building there," said DiGeronimo from behind the wheel of his Escalade. Early-evening traffic was light. The SUV rolled past the PNC Center, Superior Square, the old Medical Mutual building and the Justice Center. Independence Excavating had dug the holes for every single one of those jobs. Several more landmark buildings were proudly pointed out—the Quicken Loans Arena, the Rock & Roll Hall of Fame, the Science Center, the casino. Buildings imploded, dirt dug, removed, reused or sold; it was a commodity, like corn or wheat. Big jobs. DiGeronimo looped around the biggest job, Browns Stadium. Demolition, excavation, plus a ton of site work.

"Forty million dollars," said Bobby D.

Dirt had been in the DiGeronimo family for more than sixty years. Ever since Bobby's wild, ball-busting dad had arrived from Italy at about sixteen, worked in a factory, then opened a small general contracting business around 1950. The family operation was now spread across six privately held businesses—excavation, asbestos abatement, car wash, light materials division, a recycling center in Florida and communications. It employed more than a thousand people, four hundred with Independence Excavating alone. Over the last twenty years the DiGeronimos had helped reshape downtown Cleveland, rebuild it from below the ground up. The kids ran things now. Nine boys, some on the business side, others involved in field work or project management, and Bobby's daughter Lisa, who was in charge of human resources. Nieces and nephews all over the place. At sixty-five, Bobby was construction director emeritus, the big boss who stopped by every morning for coffee with the guys, checked out the jobs downtown and made a call or two when needed. The DiGeronimo Companies had grossed more than $200 million in 2012.

"We've been very lucky, very blessed," said Bobby D.

DiGeronimo's association with Ohio State athletics, his entry into the world of boosters, began back in the late 1970s when the head basketball coach, Eldon Miller, heard about him through the Columbus construction grapevine and called him up.

"Would you employ one of our players?" he asked.

"Absolutely," said Bobby D.

According to the university, from about 1988 until 2011 DiGeronimo had donated approximately $72,000 to Ohio State athletics—an average of about $3,000 a year—and purchased a number of season tickets for both basketball and football. One year, in honor of John Cooper's famed "Silver Bullet" defense, somebody asked Bobby D. if he could come up with sixty silver chains and bullets to give to the kids as keepsakes. Sure, he said.

"They would always ask when they needed something," said Bobby D. "Not that I was keeping score."

A day with Bobby D. began on a slate-gray Saturday in November 2012 in what looked to be a lodge but was actually the DiGeronimo home. It was three days before the presidential election. President Obama was making one last swing through the crucial battleground state. Daughter Christi and her husband, Mark, lived down and around a wooded lane near one edge of the forty-three-acre family compound. Brother Vic was in back with a stunning Italian job that would have fit in nicely next to George Clooney's place on Lake Como.

At Bobby D.'s house, where the clocks chimed, talk turned to Jim Tressel. DiGeronimo wasted no time.

"He's been a phony since I've known him in the eighties. He's always been that way," he said. "When someone says to me, 'Jim Tressel, he's a great guy,' if he's someone I know, I say, 'You know what? I know a different Jim Tressel. You don't know the Jim Tressel I know.'"

In the early days of The Senator's term in Columbus, all was good with Bobby D. His personal pizza and pasta delivery service to the coaches and players made regular runs between Cleveland and Columbus. The Buckeyes went undefeated (14-0) in 2002, and Tressel gave Bobby a championship ring, a classy show of thanks.

As it always does, the national title in 2002 altered the football universe at Ohio State; expectations and outside scrutiny increased. Then came the messy matter of Maurice Clarett. The program needed even tighter controls. Tressel cracked down on access. Gene Smith arrived from Arizona State. By the fall of 2005 the joke was you needed a CIA badge to get into practice; media and other access to players was restricted. On game day all non–Ohio State personnel had to be out of the locker room six minutes before the team took the field. The program was cleaning up its act. But DiGeronimo laughed at the notion that somehow he had been swept out the door.

"That's all BS," he said. "First off, I [had] field passes where it says I have access to the locker room. If I was pushed out of the locker room, I would have never come back. I'm on the field in 2006.

"One of the most baffling things to me was when he said he caught me hiding in the locker room with another guy [before a game]. If I was hiding in the locker in 2001, why did you still have me on the field in 2006? It doesn't make any sense."

In fact, in May 2005, Tressel sent DiGeronimo a note pointing out how hard the staff was working to be in "absolute compliance" with NCAA rules. In the note Tressel praised DiGeronimo as "one of the greatest friends to Ohio State Athletics." He closed with this line: "Thanks, Bobby! You are the best!"

But by the spring of 2007, Tressel no longer had any use for Bobby D. To this day DiGeronimo said he had no idea what triggered it. The first inkling of trouble came in April at Ted Ginn Jr.'s pro-day workout at the Woody Hayes indoor practice facility, which DiGeronimo had raised $100,000 to help build.

A month before, DiGeronimo had walked right in with Cooper for the Buckeyes' pro day. Not this time.

"Bobby, you can't go in there," said an OSU assistant coach.

"Okay," said DiGeronimo. "Is there a problem?"

"Coach doesn't want you in there."

DiGeronimo's phone rang. It was Ted Ginn Sr., Glenville High's head football coach. He had set up the workout at the facility for his son.

"I can't get in there," DiGeronimo told Ginn.

"What are you talking about?"

Bobby D. explained.

"Wait a minute," said Ginn.

As DiGeronimo and his son Kevin finally, thanks to Ginn senior's intervention, made their way in, Tressel came into view. DiGeronimo said Tressel saw him and walked the other way.

They stayed forty-five minutes and left.

Two months later at a Fellowship of Christian Athletes function, Tressel walked up to former Browns head coach Sam Rutigliano. DiGeronimo was at the table as well, but Tressel didn't say a word to Bobby D.

"Invisible," he said.

Two more months passed. This time the Cavs were in the NBA Finals. DiGeronimo had a grand suite in the Quicken Loans Arena. Tressel was in the arena walking around with NFL legend Jim Brown when the head coach saw DiGeronimo and stuck out his hand.

"Bobby D., how you doing?" Tressel said, according to DiGeronimo.

"Hi, Coach," said Bobby D. and walked right by.

"Now you're in Cleveland, you're on my turf, you're *my* friend," he said. "From that time on there was no sense of me being around a phony."

DiGeronimo stopped going to games. "Maybe two football games in the last four years," he said.

———

As the afternoon wore on, the conversation shifted to Gene Smith. DiGeronimo was told that in forty pages of transcript he went from a man Smith barely knew to a "hanger on" to a "bad actor" who "at the end of the day operated outside of the system and went stealth."

DiGeronimo's eyes were closed, his dark head of hair leaning back against the couch.

"Wow. Bad actor," he whispered. "Gene Smith is saying that?

"You know, it's funny," DiGeronimo said as he opened his eyes. "I'm reading this book called *Surrender,* and [it says] if you don't do this and that . . . you're going to hell. And you can't hate anybody. You got to pray for the people. You know what? I never hated Gene Smith. I don't respect him. You have to pray for people you don't like. So you know what, I said a prayer for him."

DiGeronimo categorically denied receiving any warnings from Smith to stay away from student-athletes or the program.

"Never," said DiGeronimo. "Never called me. Never called me one time. Never.

"Never any meeting. Never any voice mail. Everything he says is a lie. Everything."

DiGeronimo said he had seen or talked to Smith just twice in his life—the last time in the summer or fall of 2011 when Smith asked him to cooperate in the NCAA tattoo/memorabilia mess. The first time, he said, was a twenty-second encounter in 2006 after a lunch with former head football coach Cooper in Columbus.

"You know what he should have said, 'Hey, Bobby, you know what? I need to talk to you because I'm hearing some stuff'? He said nothing. By '06 he should have known who I was, heard the name. He should have said, 'Some things are bothering me. Can we talk?' I would have said, 'Sure, Gene, tell me what's the problem.' But he never did that."

DiGeronimo was reminded that Smith told the NCAA he spoke with DiGeronimo "at least four times" after Ohio State had been informed of what the NCAA called "supplemental violations" and that Smith told the NCAA he had hit Bobby D. "pretty hard on [cooperating], particularly the last three calls."

"One time," Bobby D. said. "He asked me if I would meet with the NCAA, and I said yes. That's it."

Internal Ohio State documents revealed that between at least 2002 and 2008 Independence Excavating had filled out and returned to Bob Tucker, OSU's director of football operations, the proper forms for employing student-athletes. DiGeronimo claimed he had also returned—but not copied—the same student-athlete employee paperwork to Tucker or his assistant Larry Romanoff through 2010. (The authors of this book made a Freedom of Information Act request to Ohio State for all student-athlete employment forms for the years 2009–11. Multiple word searches of the heavily redacted records for either "Bobby DiGeronimo" or "Independence Excavating" failed to find a single mention.)

"They won't give [the work forms] to you," said DiGeronimo, "because they don't want to incriminate themselves any more, because I filled [the proper paperwork] out. They're lying. They knew what I was doing. The point is . . . if I was really on their radar, wouldn't you say, 'Hey, Bobby, you have four or five kids working, what are they doing?'

"Here's the thing," he said. "The kids worked two weeks out of the year. We'd given them a hand check instead of putting them on the payroll. If it was two months, it's a different story. When the kids say, 'We didn't know what we were making,' it was true. I don't know, you might be making $12 [an hour], might be making $15. But there is a time card being put in by the superintendent on the job, but they don't know that. So they get a check, and most of them pay forty hours at $15 per hour or thirty-two hours at $15 per hour."

A request was made to the Ohio State athletic department to interview Smith about DiGeronimo and charges raised about the authenticity of

Smith's statements to the NCAA. Through a senior associate athletic director at Ohio State, Smith respectfully declined.

———

Over lunch, fourteen months after Ohio State banned him from the program for ten years, DiGeronimo said he had been willing to talk with the NCAA and defend the job program to the hilt, but when investigators declined to provide even a general idea of what they wanted to talk about, he walked away. He didn't trust them. "They were not looking for the truth so much as they were looking to nail Ohio State," he said. "Not that I was worried about Ohio State. I was worried about those kids.

"They don't care," he added, referring to the NCAA. "They have no heart. To do that to DeVier [Posey], his senior year, five [more] games. Give him one game. To do that, they have no heart and no mercy."

———

Later, back at his house, the Ohio State–Illinois game was on in the TV room. Against the backdrop of play-by-play, DiGeronimo talked about his love of sports, especially football, the physical side of the game, and how he excelled as a running back and defensive back at Independence High back in 1965. He talked about losing his older brother Don to colon cancer six years later at age thirty-four. How the other brothers—Vic, another late brother, Rich, Bobby and Tony—banded together and pursued Donnie's vision, hitting it big with the Justice Center job in 1972 and from there were on their way.

"I hope one day when the Lord judges me, he will say you were given a lot but you also gave a lot," said Bobby D. "We all want heaven someday."

———

The day after receiving the letter from Ohio State disassociating him from the program, DiGeronimo wrote one back. He said he understood the consequence of his actions and that he regretted doing the Cleveland *Plain Dealer* interview, in which he said that without the tattoo scandal the NCAA investigation would have never happened.

"As for myself," he wrote, "I will always hold my head high because my heart bleeds scarlet and gray. I know that these players are not compensated for their time spent giving back to OSU . . . I never did one thing for personal gain."

For good measure he attached a Mother Teresa prayer: "Do It Anyway." Two of the verses read as follows:

If you are kind, people may accuse you of selfish, ulterior motives. Be
   kind anyway.
If you are successful, you will win some unfaithful friends and some
   genuine enemies. Succeed anyway.

He copied two-time Heisman Trophy winner Archie Griffin, president and CEO of the alumni association, and head basketball coach Thad
Matta. In response, Smith fired off a letter to Mark Tripodi, executive director and co-founder of Cornerstone. It informed DiGeronimo's son-in-law
that "until further notice, Ohio State student-athletes are prohibited from
attending any activity associated" with the charity, volunteer or otherwise.
Smith ended by saying he was "very disappointed that Cornerstone of
Hope invited student-athletes" to attend the 2011 gala.

Now DiGeronimo was steaming. The AD had dragged his family into
the fight, his daughter's charity, the one he helped create after the loss of
his grandson. He contacted Smith's office repeatedly, he said, but nobody
returned his calls. He sent Smith a letter seething with emotion. "Cornerstone of Hope's mission of helping grieving families is more important than
sports," it read. "They do not deserve to be subjected to your department's
sanction in a blatant attempt to appease the NCAA. I hope your family
never requires the services . . . but their doors will remain open to you and
your family regardless of sanctions or disassociations . . . I certainly never
expected The Ohio State University to portray me as a rogue booster."

At this point in the game, Ohio State was running away from Illinois
early in the fourth quarter. More than 105,000 fans had filled the 'Shoe.
Did the booster break NCAA rules by slipping $200 in cash into the hands
of four players in 2011? Absolutely. DiGeronimo said he felt "indebted"
to them because they had driven three hours back and forth to help raise
hundreds of thousands of dollars.

"I was thankful," said Bobby D. "They didn't ask for anything. I just did
it, [to help] pay for their gas. 'Guys, if you want to stay over tonight, if you
drive back, get a meal.'"

Didn't matter. Providing players with money—no matter how noble
the cause—was a blatant violation of NCAA rules. The same with adding
a few extra hours a week to the paychecks of four football players during a
time the program generated tens of millions of dollars in profit every year.
To Bobby D., it seemed petty and uncaring.

"That's the way I look at it," he said. "And Ohio State, from that point
on, said, okay, we've got to find a villain and we got to say, hey, there's a

rogue booster here, Bobby D., and we didn't know all the stuff that was going on, and maybe we should have, but he was a bad, bad guy."

For nearly fifty years Bobby DiGeronimo had made an enormous profit in the dirt—digging it out, moving it around—only to be buried in it by his once beloved university.

"Yeah, maybe I shouldn't have done it," he said. "But I'm looking at these guys, and they have no character; they're phonies. If [they] want to use me as a sacrificial lamb, if that makes them feel better, I don't really care. It's not worth the time and effort to worry about it. Because . . . that's the way the system operates . . . I could care less right now because of the way I was treated. If I never see that campus again, it's not going to bother me."

The game ended. Ohio State had won 52–22 to improve to 10-0. DiGeronimo hardly noticed. His live-and-die days were over. Still, he felt awful about what happened to Posey. So, he said, he paid for him to travel to California to work out prior to the NFL draft and sent his mother and his girlfriend out west as well. Posey was later picked in the third round by the Houston Texans.

DiGeronimo Companies remained busy. It was involved in the massive Medical Mart convention center project and the construction of a bridge downtown and had recently expanded to Pittsburgh. What mattered most—faith and family and friends, his thirty-three grandchildren—was more important to Bobby D. than ever.

Just how important would become crystal clear at the tenth annual Cornerstone of Hope gala in 2013. The NFL and Browns legend Jim Brown attended the benefit, as did Robert Smith, again serving as master of ceremonies, along with Beanie Wells, Tom Cousineau and none other than Daniel "Boom" Herron. A record-setting $625,000 was raised.

16 THE ATHLETIC DIRECTOR

Part II, "It's going to be expensive"

E very athletic director has to have a trusted confidant, someone on staff capable of handling sensitive situations that arise
behind the scenes when running the most visible depart-
ment on campus. In Bill Moos's case, he turned to Mike Marlow, a gregari-
ous fellow who spent thirteen years toiling away in the athletic department
at Oregon. That's how Moos knew him. Marlow used to work for Moos in
Eugene. But Marlow was a graduate of WSU, and when Moos offered him
a job at his alma mater, he didn't hesitate.

When Marlow arrived in Pullman in August 2010, he was given
the same title he had at Oregon—senior associate athletic director—
and put in charge of marketing, fund-raising, tickets and dealing with
multimedia rights holders. But his most valuable asset to Moos was not
listed in his job description—the keeper of secrets. At the start of the
2011 season, Moos told Marlow something strictly confidential about
head football coach Paul Wulff: he had to win at least six games in
the 2011 season to keep his job. "This might not work out," Moos told
Marlow.

The make-or-break game came on October 22 against Oregon State.
The Cougars entered the contest 3-3. But their record was a little mislead-
ing. Two of their wins came against lowly nonconference opponents, Idaho
State and UNLV. WSU had been manhandled by San Diego State and overwhelmed by conference rivals Stanford and UCLA. The only semi-quality
win up to that point had come against Colorado.

Still, Oregon State was in even worse shape at 1-5. Playing at Seattle's
Safeco Field, WSU was heavily favored. Moos and Marlow settled into their
seats in the AD's suite high above the field. Despite the neutral site, WSU
had the abundance of fans. But Oregon State's fans had a lot more to cheer
about. The Beavers ran away with the game. As the final seconds ticked off

the clock, Oregon State led 44–21. WSU had fallen to 3-4. Worse, the team played with no emotion.

Angry, Moos turned to Marlow. "Let's go."

It was code that Marlow understood—*let's go find a coach.*

———

Turnover among head coaches in college football is at an all-time high. Between 2009 and 2010, forty-four head coaches at major programs were fired—thirteen more got the ax in 2013. A cottage industry has cropped up to handle the high demand for new coaches. Most athletic departments now outsource the selection process to search firms that track which coaches are trending.

But Moos had no intention of turning this decision over to a group of headhunters who spent their days crunching numbers on laptops. Nor was he going to assemble an internal search committee—too bureaucratic. He preferred a one-man committee consisting of himself. Ever since his days at Oregon, where head coach Mike Bellotti was constantly a candidate to jump to the NFL, Moos had maintained a short list of potential head coaches. From time to time, he'd cross off one name and add another. But he always had a list. And he kept it in his desk drawer.

The short list to replace Paul Wulff consisted of one name: Mike Leach.

Moos had only met Leach once. The two men talked over beers in a stadium parking lot before WSU's annual spring game seven months earlier. Leach was there to conduct a clinic at the invitation of Wulff's staff. Moos's interaction with Leach that day was limited. But he'd had his eye on Leach for a long time. He was one of the top names on Moos's short list at Oregon if Bellotti ever left.

The problem was that Moos had no clue whether Leach had any interest in the WSU job. It wasn't as if he could call and ask. Approaching Leach was tricky, especially in mid-season. If word got out that WSU made inquiries with a possible replacement, Wulff would instantly become a lame-duck coach, and Moos would have a controversy on his hands. The situation called for a go-between, someone with no ties to WSU who could act as Moos's pseudo agent. Moos turned to Mike Marlow to find that person.

———

Joe Giansante had served as an associate AD alongside Mike Marlow at Oregon. He'd also been a play-by-play announcer for the Oregon Sports

Network. A heavyset Italian with slicked-back black hair, Giansante had the gift of gab. He could strike up a conversation with anyone, anywhere. A journalist by training, he also had a reputation for being a bulldog, the kind of guy who would stay up all night poring over documents to ensure he didn't miss something.

Marlow and Giansante were close friends, and they'd been talking for months about the prospects of luring Mike Leach to Pullman. Giansante listened to Leach's show on Sirius Radio on a daily basis. "I was a big advocate of Mike Leach," Giansante said. "I told Mike Marlow that Leach was the perfect fit for WSU, given their position in the Pac-12 Conference." Immediately after the loss to Oregon State, Marlow told Giansante that the time had come to get serious about reeling in Leach. Giansante started gathering intelligence.

A week later, on October 29, WSU played Oregon in Eugene. The day before the game, Moos and Marlow ducked into El Torito restaurant for a prearranged, private dinner with Giansante. Over Mexican food and soft drinks, Giansante shared what he had come up with so far. For starters, it looked as if WSU might be in for some tough competition. At least four other schools appeared interested in Leach: Ole Miss, Kansas, Arizona State and UCLA.

But based on what Giansante had learned about Leach, he didn't see Ole Miss or UCLA as a good fit. Both programs were known for expecting their coaches to do a fair amount of schmoozing with high-end boosters at cocktail parties. Leach didn't own a suit and preferred to be alone in a film room analyzing game tape. Not a good fit.

Kansas, on the other hand, was a real contender. Leach was best friends with the AD there, and he knew the program well from his Big 12 days at Texas Tech. Arizona State was the wild card. Giansante hadn't gotten a good read on the situation there.

Moos had questions about Leach's departure from Tech. He was well aware that Leach had sued Texas Tech, ESPN and a PR firm tied to Craig James. But he wasn't clear on the facts of the case. Giansante had obtained a copy of Leach's wrongful termination suit against the university. He'd also read Leach's autobiography, which gave his take on the Tech situation. "If you read Mike's book, you'll get an accurate account of what happened," Giansante told Moos.

At that point, Giansante hadn't seen any of the depositions, talked directly to anyone involved in the matter or read Tech's response to Leach's legal claims. But he was pretty familiar with Leach's style. "There is no question that when he is coaching a football team, it is not a democracy," Giansante said. "Players don't get a vote. There are times when players are disgruntled. That happens on any team."

———

Moos wasn't too concerned about the lawsuits. Leach was the plaintiff in each case. It would have been much more worrisome if Leach had been the target of the suits. The bigger concern for Moos was the rumor that Leach was hard to get along with. That one had to be checked out.

Giansante said he'd do more digging.

Thirty minutes into the meal, Moos had heard enough. "Mike, would you excuse us for a few minutes?" he said.

Marlow stepped outside while Moos leaned forward at the table and lowered his voice. "Joe, I've got to have someone that can sell me to Mike Leach's agent."

Giansante nodded.

"And you know what I did at Oregon when I was AD," Moos continued.

Giansante nodded again.

"I gotta tell you this humbly," Moos said. "I need someone who can sell me because right now Washington State has got nothing."

A few minutes later the two men shook hands, agreeing that Giansante would come on board as a consultant to the athletic department and receive a onetime fee. For bookkeeping purposes, Giansante's consultancy would entail visiting Pullman and taking a thirty-thousand-foot view of the overall operation from media rights to marketing and advertising and recommend ways that the athletic department might improve things. But Giansante knew the deal: he was there to help reel in Leach.

The following day, Oregon beat WSU 43–28, marking the Cougars' fourth straight loss and dropping the team to 3-5.

———

Gary O'Hagan is no run-of-the-mill agent. He started IMG's coaching practice. His first client was John Wooden. Then he signed NFL coaches Steve Mariucci and Tom Coughlin. Mike Leach was the first college coach he landed. By 2011, O'Hagan represented more college coaches than any agent in America.

The son of a New York City detective, O'Hagan was a Wall Street trader before walking away to try his hand at negotiating multimillion-dollar deals for high-profile coaches. Smart, pushy and connected, O'Hagan knew all the players in the high-finance world of college football. He was at his home in Minnesota in the first week of November when he got a call from Joe Giansante, who introduced himself as a former associate AD at Oregon. "I'd love to talk to you about Mike Leach and his level of interest in getting back to coaching football," Giansante began.

O'Hagan had never heard of Giansante. He wanted his background.

Giansante rattled off the names of a few people he had worked with over the years. O'Hagan recognized most of them. Then Giansante said he was calling on behalf of Washington State. WSU, he said, was seriously considering a change at head coach and was looking at Mike Leach.

It was the first that O'Hagan had heard about WSU contemplating a change. He was immediately skeptical. Since Leach had lost his job at Tech two years earlier, O'Hagan had received at least a dozen similar inquiries. None of them had panned out. Moreover, O'Hagan didn't like working behind the back of a currently employed coach. He never liked it when a school worked to undermine one of his clients. So as long as Paul Wulff was the head coach at WSU, O'Hagan didn't want to say much.

Nonetheless, he wasn't opposed to listening. He reached for a pen and paper and took notes as Giansante made his opening overture.

Giansante began by talking about Moos, saying he was a coach's AD who had the full support of his president. At WSU there would be no interference from the president's office, regents or boosters. There was one more thing. Giansante had researched how Maryland had almost hired Leach, only to change its mind at the last minute. "They had gone through the entire process," Giansante said. "And then the president got cold feet and nixed it." Giansante wanted to assure O'Hagan that a similar thing wouldn't happen at WSU.

"WSU is not going to be afraid of some of the other things that some schools will be afraid of," Giansante told O'Hagan.

O'Hagan was intrigued.

Giansante then stressed that Moos knew how to build championship teams. He'd done it at Oregon. He'd also overseen Oregon's construction of the best facilities of any football program in the country. Plans were under way to expand and upgrade the stadium at Washington State, as well as to build a new state-of-the-art football operations facility. "There is an opportunity to be good here, and it absolutely can happen," Giansante told him.

O'Hagan marked that down as another plus.

There was one more thing Giansante wanted O'Hagan to know about Moos. WSU was his last stop. There would be no more jobs after this one. Moos wanted to go out with a winning legacy.

O'Hagan has a saying: "The only good pass is a pass that can be caught."

It's a sports euphemism for his philosophy about communication. In other words, for your message to get through to a stranger, you have to have the right pitch. It was clear to O'Hagan that Giansante had done his homework on Leach. After his experience at Texas Tech, the last thing Leach wanted was to go to another school where he'd be answering to multiple masters. Leach was looking for a situation where he could work closely with an AD who shared the same vision.

O'Hagan thanked Giansante for his call and said he would pass along the information to Leach.

———

By the fall of 2011, Mike and Sharon Leach had lived in Key West for nearly two years. They hadn't owned a car that entire time. They hadn't even bothered to get Florida driver's licenses. Leach had a license to go lobstering instead. They fished. They swam. They biked. They lived in bathing suits and cargo shorts. Island life suited them quite well.

Nonetheless, the Leaches were restless without a coaching job. Mike had found plenty of work to occupy his time. He had a radio gig. He'd also been active on the speaking circuit and putting on coaching clinics here and there. But he wanted back into coaching in a bad way. He'd interviewed at a number of places, and in 2010 he was a finalist for the Maryland job. But the circumstances surrounding his departure from Tech weren't helping matters.

In an attempt to clear his name and tell his story, Leach had gone as far as to write a memoir called *Swing Your Sword.* He was busy promoting it in the fall of 2011. O'Hagan was helping him line up appearances. Each night they'd check in. When Leach called O'Hagan one evening in early November, they went through the typical stuff: How did the event go? How many people showed up?

Then Leach asked if there was anything new on O'Hagan's front.

"You know, I got a really interesting call from a guy named Joe Giansante," he said.

"Who is he?"

"He's working with Washington State University. They may make a change at head coach."

"Okay."

"Anyway, he was really sharp. I was surprised."

Leach wanted to know what was so surprising about him. O'Hagan shared Giansante's comments about Bill Moos. "I really think he gets it, Mike."

Leach said to keep him posted.

The following morning, O'Hagan heard from Giansante again. "Did you talk to Mike?"

"Yes, I spoke to Mike."

Pleased, Giansante reiterated that Leach would enjoy working with Bill Moos.

O'Hagan didn't dispute that. But he preferred not to talk much further about the WSU situation until the season was over or it became clear that the job was truly available. Three years earlier, after Texas Tech knocked off No. 1–ranked Texas, Tennessee officials repeatedly called O'Hagan in an attempt to lure Leach out of Lubbock. When O'Hagan declined to have Leach fly to Tennessee for a job interview during the regular season, Tennessee came up with a creative plan to ensure that no one would know the two sides were talking. The officials offered to fly to Texas in a private plane and rendezvous in the middle of nowhere with Leach. O'Hagan said no way, and a couple weeks later Tennessee hired Lane Kiffin.

The one thing O'Hagan *was* willing to do with Giansante was tell him stories about his client. Giansante listened to as many as O'Hagan wanted to tell. The more he could learn about Leach, the better.

"He's not like most coaches," O'Hagan explained. "The people at Texas Tech took that personally. They felt snubbed at times. Mike wasn't doing that deliberately. He's from Cody, Wyoming. He's a football coach. He's not a hobnobber, and he's not an ass kisser."

———

Mike Marlow and Joe Giansante had a standing appointment to speak every weekday morning at 7:30. Giansante would be on the San Diego Freeway in his GMC Acadia. He referred to it as his mobile office. Marlow never did the call from his office, though. He always called on his cell phone from the parking lot next to the Sunset mini-mart in Pullman, a few minutes from campus. Marlow called it his "Leach spot."

Usually, the morning call would begin with Giansante saying, "Here's what I'm hearing," or "Here's something Bill needs to know." But on the morning of November 8, Marlow was the one with some news. Two days earlier Cal had pounded WSU 30–7. It was the team's fifth straight loss, dropping its record to 3-6. Only three games remained, against Arizona, Utah and Washington. WSU would have to win all of them for Wulff to hit the six-win mark. That was highly unlikely. But Moos was starting to look at other factors, too. He had asked one of his staff to compile a list of off-the-field problems involving the football team. The staffer came back with a list of players that was three pages long. Over the previous eighteen months, at least twenty-five WSU football players had been arrested or charged with offenses that carried possible jail time. Many of the offenses were misdemeanors—underage drinking, marijuana possession and theft. But there had been a few serious assaults, too. The point was none of this reflected well on the program or the institution.

The football players weren't pulling their weight in the classroom either. The NCAA had already yanked eight scholarships from the program a couple years earlier after a review revealed that the program had failed to meet academic standards.

It was time, Moos decided, to make a change.

"But," Moos had told Marlow, "I don't want to get a divorce until I know who my new wife is going to be."

Giansante asked Marlow what he wanted him to do.

Marlow told him that Moos wanted a face-to-face meeting with Leach as soon as possible—just the two of them. He was willing to travel to Dallas or Denver, any place where they could talk without being found out.

Over the next week, Giansante went back and forth with O'Hagan. Finally, they agreed on a meeting date: November 16. But Leach wanted to do it in Key West.

———

On November 12, WSU unexpectedly knocked off Arizona State 37–27 at home. It was far and away the team's best performance of the year. Bill Moos was on record saying that he supported Paul Wulff. Yet he was about to leave town in hopes of securing Wulff's replacement. In his mind, the victory over Arizona State didn't change things. Meanwhile, the clock was ticking. Giansante was hearing that Kansas was preparing to make Leach an offer. If Moos waited until the end of the season, Leach might be off the market. The situation called for stealth.

Normally, all of Moos's business-related travel was booked through the athletic department and paid for out of a travel budget. In this case, Moos booked his own trip to Key West and made sure to put the flight, hotel and rental car on his personal credit card. He even booked his flight out of Spokane to ensure he didn't run into athletic department personnel traveling in and out of Pullman. Other than his wife, his secretary and Marlow, no one knew where he was headed.

The day before Moos was scheduled to fly, Marlow burst into his office. "You gotta read the book," he said.

TOP In 2013–14, Alabama quarterback AJ McCarron will attempt to lead the Crimson Tide to its third national title in a row. *(Deanne Fitzmaurice)*

BOTTOM "Wow"—the first night game in University of Michigan football history against Notre Dame on September 10, 2011, drew a record crowd of 114,804. *(Michigan Photography)*

TOP Together, athletic director Dave Brandon (left) and head coach Brady Hoke have revitalized Michigan football. *(Michigan Photography)*

MIDDLE In the good old days, DFO Cleve Bryant (left) and Texas head coach Mack Brown communicated like an old married couple. *(Harry Cabluck/Associated Press)*

BOTTOM Towson University head coach Rob Ambrose and his Tigers put up a great fight before bowing on the road at LSU. *(Courtesy of Towson University)*

TOP BYU head coach Bronco Mendenhall has compiled a 74-29 record and led the Cougars to a bowl game in each of his eight seasons. Above, he celebrates in the locker room with his team after defeating Georgia Tech on October 27, 2012. (*Mark A. Philbrick*)

MIDDLE Kyle Van Noy was recruited by LSU, Oregon, Nebraska and UCLA. But after hearing Bronco Mendenhall speak at a Mormon church in Reno, Nevada, he chose to play for him at BYU. Van Noy chose not to enter the NFL draft in 2013 in order to complete his degree. He is projected to be a first-round selection in 2014. (*Deanne Fitzmaurice*)

BOTTOM Billionaire T. Boone Pickens (center) at the Oklahoma State–Texas game in Stillwater, Oklahoma, on September 29, 2012. Pickens has given $248 million to OSU, which is not only the largest donation for athletics but the largest single donation to an institution of higher education in American history. Oklahoma State's stadium is named after him. (*Jeff Benedict*)

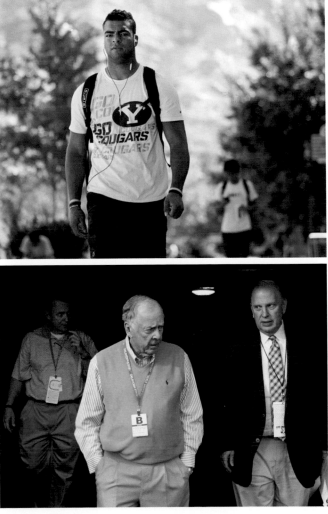

TOP Left to right: Former Cleveland Browns star Reggie Rucker and Hall of Famer Jim Brown joined Bobby DiGeronimo at the record-setting 2013 Cornerstone of Hope gala. *(Courtesy of Cornerstone of Hope)*

MIDDLE Washington State athletic director Bill Moos (right) hired Mike Leach three years after Texas Tech fired Leach over an incident involving wide receiver Adam James. *(Courtesy of Washington State Athletics)*

BOTTOM Mike Leach led Texas Tech to the No. 2 ranking in the country in 2008 and was named college football Coach of the Year. Below, he leads the Washington State Cougars in prayer prior to facing BYU on August 30, 2012. *(Deanne Fitzmaurice)*

TOP Quarterback Pete DiNovo of champion Team Tampa (Fla.) attempts a pass to teammate wide receiver Zach Benjamin in the 2012 IMG 7v7 National Championships. *(IMG Academy)*

MIDDLE Ezekiel "Ziggy" Ansah leaves the field after his final college game at the Poinsettia Bowl. *(Jeff Benedict)*

BOTTOM BYU's Ziggy Ansah (left) and Kyle Van Noy (right) converge on an opposing quarterback. In 2013, the Detroit Lions chose Ansah fifth overall in the NFL draft and Van Noy was named an all-American defensive player as a junior. *(Jaren Wilkey)*

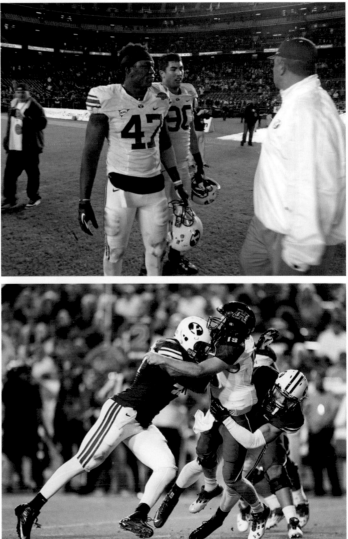

TOP It has become all too common to see college football players carted off the field with serious injuries. Roughly two hundred players sustained season-ending injuries during the 2012 season. This Georgia Tech player had to leave the game after being injured against BYU on October 27, 2012. *(Jeff Benedict)*

BOTTOM Ricky Seals-Jones surrounded by his parents, Buffy and Chester, before No. 4's final game for Sealy High School in Texas. *(Courtesy of the Seals-Jones family)*

TOP University of Utah recruit Alphonso Marsh and his mother Curley Rachal at home in Compton, California. Marsh escaped the lure of street gangs while in high school, but was shot multiple times while visiting home during his freshman year of college. *(Deanne Fitzmaurice)*

MIDDLE Dominguez High football coach Keith Donerson uses football to keep kids out of street gangs. In 2012, five of his players, including Alphonso Marsh, received scholarships to play Division I football. *(Deanne Fitzmaurice)*

BOTTOM Left to right: Reporter Tom Rinaldi, host Chris Fowler, producer Lee Fitting and analyst Desmond Howard doing some last-minute *GameDay* prep. *(ESPN Images)*

TOP Crimson Tide players getting a massive dose of the passion and pride that is Alabama—and SEC—football. *(Deanne Fitzmaurice)*

BOTTOM Nick Saban savoring, if only for a while, a glittering championship night in South Florida. *(Getty Images)*

"What book?"

Marlow handed him Leach's *Swing Your Sword*.

Moos flipped through the pages.

"You gotta read it before you interview him," Marlow said.

Moos called for his secretary and handed her the new iPad that Nike had given him. He asked her to download a digital version of Leach's book.

———

On the morning of November 16, Mike Leach slipped on a pair of sandals, some cargo shorts, a polo shirt and a baseball cap. Then he hopped on his bicycle, pedaled four miles to the Marriott Beachside Hotel, purchased a Styrofoam cup of coffee and headed for Bill Moos's suite.

The previous night, Moos had gotten word through Leach's agent that Leach preferred the meeting to be casual dress. But Moos had only packed a suit and tie. He ditched the tie and undid the top button on his white shirt. Then he had a fresh pot of coffee and a bucket of cold sodas delivered to his room for the 8:00 a.m. meeting. At 8:25, Leach knocked and Moos greeted him.

"Hello, Mike."

"Hi."

They shook hands.

"I got the word that casual was fine," Leach said.

"It is. You look fine. C'mon in."

"I'm sorry for being late," Leach said, trailing him into the room. "I rode my bike."

"You rode your bike?"

"Yeah, I don't own a car."

"How do you get around?"

"If Sharon and I and the kids go to a movie or something, we just saddle up and ride."

Moos laughed and offered him coffee. Mike held up his Styrofoam cup.

"Well, I've been reading your book," Moos said.

"Oh, yeah?"

"I'm from a small town in Washington, and I grew up watching *Gunsmoke*. So I love the part in the book where you talk about being a student at BYU and you got to your girlfriend's apartment. She's watching *M*A*S*H* and you turn the channel to *Gunsmoke*."

"Yeah, well, hell, I pretty much figured that Marshal Dillon could kick Hawkeye's ass any day, don't you?"

Moos cracked up. It was exactly the sort of thing Moos might say. A connection was instantly formed, and the two men spent the next thirty minutes discussing their favorite *Gunsmoke* episodes and swapping tales of growing up in the West. By the time they turned their attention to football, it was apparent that they spoke the same language.

Over the next two and a half hours they discussed Washington State football, Moos's administrative style and Leach's coaching style. At one point Moos brought up the fact that he was not happy with the number of off-the-field problems cropping up among football players. He asked Leach how he felt about a three-strikes-and-you're-out philosophy toward players who get in trouble.

"What do you think about one strike and you're out?" Leach said.

"Well, that's okay. You can be stricter than my rule. Just not more lenient."

Moos reiterated that he wanted to see a more disciplined approach overall. Leach shared his Three Queen Mothers rules—no stealing, no hitting women and no smoking pot. "It's probably going to take cutting a few guys to get the message through," Leach said.

They also discussed academics, and Leach said he was a stickler for performance in the classroom.

But most of the time was spent wading through all the changes under way in the Pac-12 and how those changes were enabling WSU to transform its stadium and practice facilities to be on par with the top teams in the conference. Moos pulled out renditions of the football stadium expansion. He talked about the massive football operations building that would follow—a new weight room, new locker room, new equipment room, new training rooms and tables, state-of-the-art meeting rooms and spacious coaches' offices.

Wrapping up, Moos made it clear that he wanted Leach to be the next coach at WSU. Leach liked everything he heard and said he was genuinely interested.

"If you come to Washington State," Moos said, "it's going to be you and me."

Elson Floyd had been trying to reach Bill Moos all morning. The board of regents was due to vote on the $80 million stadium expansion project in two days. He wanted to go over some last-minute details. Moos had caught a flight out of Key West. The minute he landed to catch a connecting flight, he returned Floyd's calls.

"Where are you, Bill?"

"I'm at the airport in Charlotte, North Carolina, dealing with our football situation," Moos said. "I feel confident we have the next coach."

"Who is it?"

"I've had a conversation with Mike Leach, and I think we can get him."

Floyd didn't know many coaches. But he'd certainly heard of Leach. Before he could respond, Moos began rattling off his credentials. "He's had ten winning seasons, ten straight bowl games," he said.

"You don't need to convince me," Floyd said. "If he's your guy, I support it."

"Well, it's going to be expensive."

"How much?"

Moos cleared his throat. "Elson, it's going to be $2 million."

Floyd paused. He was the highest-paid employee at the university, and his annual salary was $750,000. Moos was talking about paying more than twice that much to Leach. But four coaches in the Pac-12 earned $2.25 million or more per year. That was the going rate for a top coach.

"We'll make that work," Floyd said. "Let's go ahead."

Moos said he'd be back in touch as soon as he reached Pullman.

———

At a time when universities throughout the country were cutting jobs, reducing course offerings and raising tuition to keep pace with the rising costs of education, coaching salaries continued to skyrocket. At that time— November 2011—the average compensation for a Division I head football coach was $1.47 million annually, a jump of nearly 55 percent from six seasons earlier. The highest-paid coaches all earned well over $3 million annually.

1. Mack Brown, Texas: $5,193,500
2. Nick Saban, Alabama: $4,833,333
3. Bob Stoops, Oklahoma: $4,075,000
4. Urban Meyer, Ohio State: $4,000,000
5. Les Miles, LSU: $3,856,417
6. Kirk Ferentz, Iowa: $3,785,000
7. Bobby Petrino, Arkansas: $3,638,000
8. Gene Chizik, Auburn: $3,500,000
9. Brady Hoke, Michigan: $3,254,000
10. Will Muschamp, Florida: $3,221,000

"This market is crazy," Floyd explained. "I'm not sitting here justifying this stuff. I'm just saying that this is the world we have to play in."

Floyd knew the numbers. And he knew that in order for Washington State to compete in the Pac-12, it was going to have to put up the kind of money that other Pac-12 schools were shelling out for football coaches.

Nonetheless, the timing could not have been more awkward. Floyd and University of Washington president Michael Young had been pressing state lawmakers not to make further budget cuts to the state's two universities. Over the previous four years the state had reduced funding to WSU by 60 percent. At UW the cuts were even deeper—from $400 million to $200 million. To compensate, both schools were making painful decisions. WSU reduced its workforce by 12 percent, eliminating more than five hundred jobs. Some entire fields of study had been shuttered.

Against this backdrop, the highest-paid state employee in Washington the previous year was UW's head football coach, Steve Sarkisian. His gross annual pay was $1.98 million. If Leach ended up at WSU, he'd be the highest-paid employee in the state. Worse, WSU would still be on the hook for $600,000 to Paul Wulff for the remaining year on his contract.

Floyd was in a situation that many of his colleagues at other institutions had faced. "We all think this is absolutely absurd," Floyd explained. "We sign the checks because we have no other alternative. There is not a university president who said, 'Oh yes, that's the right thing to do.'"

As president, Floyd didn't need approval from the university's board of regents before authorizing Bill Moos to offer Leach a multimillion-dollar contract. But regents are the ones who hire and fire the president. Given the dire fiscal problems in the state, Floyd felt it was prudent not to surprise his board. He didn't want them reading about a deal this size in the newspaper. One by one he started calling his regents to give them a heads-up.

On November 19, WSU played its final home game of the season. It lost to Utah in overtime 30–27. Two days later demolition crews began tearing down one side of Martin Stadium to make way for the $80 million expansion that had been approved by the regents seventy-two hours earlier. The 2012 season was due to kick off nine months later. That left very little time to construct twenty-one luxury suites, forty-two loge boxes, twelve hundred club seats, a ten-thousand-square-foot club room for premium-seat patrons and a new press box.

Much of the construction costs would be paid for by the revenue coming from ESPN and Fox under the new Pac-12 television deal. But it fell to Moos to sell the suites and premium seating.

Outdoor club seats between the 0- and the 20-yard line—$1,700 annually
Outdoor club seats between the two 20-yard lines—$2,000 annually
Indoor club seats—$2,500 annually
Four-person loge boxes—$10,000 annually
Six-person loge boxes—$15,000 annually
Twelve-person suites—$30,000 annually
Eighteen-person suites—$40,000 annually
Twenty-four-person suites—$50,000 annually

Moos was banking on Mike Leach to sell out the first-class game-day amenities. If Leach came through, paying him $2 million a year would be a bargain. But Elson Floyd was having second thoughts. He'd been reading up on Leach's dismissal at Tech and the lawsuits that followed. He didn't like what he saw. Floyd asked Moos whether he had any concerns.

"Elson, I've read his book, and I've talked with him about those issues," Moos told him. "And I'm not concerned about it."

"Well, I need to do my own due diligence," Floyd said. "There are a couple of people I want to call."

Floyd had his staff research the lawsuit between Leach and Tech. Then he called the man who fired Leach, Tech's president, Guy Bailey. They were close friends. When Floyd was president at Missouri, he hired Bailey as chancellor of the Kansas City campus. He knew Bailey would give him the straight scoop on Leach and what went down at Tech.

After the two exchanged pleasantries, Floyd got to the purpose of the call. "It looks like we're going to hire Mike Leach," he told Bailey. "Tell me about his departure."

The two presidents had the sort of frank conversation that could only take place between trusted friends. Bailey began by giving Floyd some background. "There was a long context behind a lot of the difficulties at Tech," Bailey said. "Over time, a lack of trust built up. With lack of trust and lack of good communication, when the problem arose, rather than being resolved, it just blew up."

Trust and communication, Bailey told Floyd, were vital. "Just make sure your AD and coach get along," Bailey told him.

Floyd asked specifically about Leach as a coach.

"He will fill the stadium," Bailey said. "He's a great coach. If anybody can win in Pullman, Mike can."

––––––––

WSU finished the season on November 26 with a loss in Seattle to its rival University of Washington. On the short flight back to Pullman, Moos tapped Wulff on the shoulder and told him that he wanted to see him in his office the next day.

Wulff didn't think much of the request. It was custom to meet after the season to recap what happened and discuss what was ahead. Wulff shared his vision for the coming year. But Moos focused on the facts. The team finished 4-8. Morale was down. Attendance was shrinking. Yet construction was under way on an $80 million stadium expansion. It was imperative that those seats sell out. That wasn't going to happen if the team kept losing.

Wulff didn't like the vibe.

"Paul, I have to make a decision."

"Sounds like you already have."

––––––––

Later that day, Moos pulled out the template he used for coaching contracts at Oregon. Seated at his desk, he penciled out a simple offer to Leach: $2.25 million in annual base salary for five years, plus standard incentives and bonuses. Then he had his staff get it to Gary O'Hagan for review.

The following day O'Hagan sent word that the basic terms were acceptable. Moos agreed to send a one-page letter outlining the contractual terms. As soon as Leach signed it, Moos would announce the hire. The full contract would be executed after the fact.

With O'Hagan promising to get the letter of understanding to Leach, Moos went to see Elson Floyd. He wanted to give him the news in person.

"We got him," Moos told him.

A grin swept across Floyd's face, and he high-fived Moos.

Joe Giansante and Mike Marlow had reason to smile, too. Giansante was in his familiar place—stuck in traffic on the San Diego Freeway—when Marlow called. "We did it," he said. "We caught him."

The next morning—November 29, 2011—Moos held a press conference.

"At roughly ten o'clock this morning I dismissed Paul Wulff as our football coach at Washington State University," Moos began. "It was not an easy thing to do."

He kept his remarks brief, pinning the decision on fan apathy, a record low in terms of annual giving and the need to create enthusiasm around the university's recently announced commitment to invest $160 million in football facilities.

"We'll start the search for the successor immediately, later this afternoon, and hope to have somebody in that position in the next two or three weeks if at all possible," Moos told the press. Then he opened it up for questions. Hands shot up. The reporters wondered if Wulff deserved one more year.

"We're at a juncture where we've either gotta run with the big dogs or just admit that we're a doormat," Moos said. "I believe that we can be a contender for championships."

More hands. "Is it concerning to you with the large number of openings at big-name schools that you might not be able to attract a big-name coach?"

"May I say this? You're looking at the search committee," Moos said. "I've been through these before. I've got good contacts. My practice has always been to have a short list."

"Have you reached out to anybody on that list?"

"I've had discussions."

"Is it important to you . . . to bring somebody in that runs a similar system?"

"I'm not going to hire somebody that's going to run the Houston Veer. I believe that you fill the seats by having a flashy, high-octane offense that lights up the scoreboard."

———

The next day Moos announced that Mike Leach would be WSU's new football coach. Leach was at Disney World with Sharon and the kids when the news broke. A few days later Moos chartered a private jet to retrieve Leach and his family from Florida and deliver them to a press conference in Pullman. It looked more like a coronation. The fire marshal started turning students and alumni away after fifteen hundred people packed the ballroom at the student center. An overflow room with big-screen televisions was also packed. The marching band played and the cheerleaders chanted as Mike Leach and his family entered the room. Leach wore a gray suit and a crimson tie. After a raucous thirty-second standing ovation, he addressed the crowd.

"I know what you're thinking. And the answer to that is yes—this is exactly how I dress in Key West every day."

Laughter filled the room.

Leach kept his speech short but fielded lots of questions. "Do you have a five-year plan?" one reporter asked.

"My plan is to win one game a week," Leach said.

The place erupted. Moos sat on the dais, beaming. In his entire career he had never witnessed such enthusiasm over the hiring of a coach. Overnight, the mood in Pullman went from despondent to euphoric. The payoff was instant. Within ten days, all twenty-one luxury stadium suites, including the $50,000 units, were sold. Donations started pouring into the athletic department. More than three thousand people became new season ticket holders.

Elson Floyd was in his office, taking it all in, when a member of his staff in charge of payroll entered. "Dr. Floyd," she began. "We have a problem."

"What's the problem?"

"Our system can't handle $2.25 million. We don't know what to do."

Floyd wasn't sure what she meant.

She put it to him in simple terms. Washington State's payroll software was not adequate to process Coach Leach's salary.

Floyd laughed. The university, he assured her, would upgrade its payroll software. It was a sign that WSU had entered the realm of big-time college football.

17 THE WALK-ON

"I want to play football"

I t was the first week of August, days before the official start of the fall 2010 camp. All of BYU's scholarship players were already on campus for unofficial workouts. Bronco Mendenhall was in his office, making final preparations and going over depth charts.

At one point Mendenhall's secretary ducked her head in. His afternoon appointment had arrived, a potential walk-on named Ezekiel Ansah, an African student on BYU's track team who supposedly had serious speed. Mendenhall wasn't expecting much. Track athletes rarely panned out. Even at skill positions, football requires much more than just speed. Besides, the kid was from Ghana. They play soccer there, not football.

"Send him in," Mendenhall said.

When Ansah appeared in the door, Mendenhall's eyebrows shot up. This guy didn't look like a sprinter. He was six feet five inches and 250 pounds, and his shoulders filled the doorframe. He didn't appear to have an ounce of fat.

Mendenhall offered him a seat. "What can I do for you?" he asked.

"I want to play football," Ansah said in a deep but quiet voice.

"Have you ever played before?"

"No."

"Do you know how to play?"

"No."

Mendenhall nearly laughed.

"But I want to try out," Ansah continued.

Mendenhall cut him off. "I don't know anything about you," he told Ansah. "I don't know how you are living. I don't even know if you can make it through a workout."

In broken English, Ansah gave him his background in snippets. Sophomore. Statistics major. Excellent grades. Mormon. Played soccer in Africa.

Runs track at BYU. Pretty fast—clocked at 21.9 seconds in the two hundred, good enough to qualify for the NCAA outdoor championship.

"And I go by Ziggy," he said.

"Ziggy?" Mendenhall said.

"It's my nickname."

It was all a little much for Mendenhall to absorb.

"I promise I will work hard," Ansah said.

"If you are serious about this," Mendenhall said, "workouts start tomorrow morning. Our players get here at 5:45. We lift at 6:00."

Getting up early was the easy part. Despite his size, Ansah had never lifted weights and had to be taught how to use the equipment.

It got worse when uniforms were issued on the first day of camp. When the equipment manager handed him a set of shoulder pads, Ansah just gave him a blank stare. He'd never worn equipment in his life. Jordan Johnson, a freshman defensive back from Springfield, Massachusetts, was suiting up next to Ansah. "He was trying to shove the thigh pad in the knee pad slot," Johnson said. "He couldn't figure out how to put on his shoulder pads. It was hilarious. But nobody laughed at him. He was too big to laugh at."

Finally, Ansah tried on a helmet. He felt trapped, and his peripheral vision disappeared. In hopes of giving him encouragement, a couple guys smacked his helmet. "I told myself, this is going to be terrible," Ansah said. "I didn't know how I was going to run. The helmet felt so odd."

It was August 7, 2010—the first day of practice—when Ansah walked out of the locker room wearing cleats, shorts, a sleeveless T-shirt and a helmet. BYU associate athletic director Chad Lewis, a former BYU star who went on to play in the NFL, was on the edge of the field, chatting with a few starters, when Ansah approached.

"Hey, who is *this* guy?" Lewis asked.

"His name is Ziggy," one of the players said. "He's a track guy. Real fast. He's gonna give it a try."

"Bro, I know you guys have been playing football all your life," Lewis said. "But he's already better than you."

The players thought Lewis was being sarcastic. He wasn't.

But when Lewis asked around camp, no one seemed to know how Ansah ended up at BYU or what led him to try out for the team. Even Mendenhall didn't seem to know.

Ken Frei spent six days a week walking the dusty roads of Ghana's capital city, Accra, in search of people interested in learning about Mormonism. On his off days the twenty-year-old BYU sophomore from Idaho Falls played pickup basketball with fellow missionaries at a private K–12 school called Golden Sunbeam. It had one of the few courts in the city, and the headmaster—a Mormon—allowed the missionaries to play there.

Ansah, then eighteen, worked at the school as a teaching assistant. One afternoon in December 2007, he was hanging around the basketball court. Frei invited him to join in a game of two on two. A five-foot-nine former high school point guard, Frei matched up against the big local. Though he gave up nine inches and nearly a hundred pounds, Frei wasn't concerned; Ghanaians aren't known for their hoops prowess.

As if to prove the point, Ansah got the ball and flung up a wild shot that slammed off the glass. Frei expected as much, but he did not anticipate what happened next; Ansah elevated, snatched the rebound and threw down a two-handed dunk, his elbows nearly hitting the rim. Frei was speechless. Ansah grinned. "LeBron James is my favorite," he said, before adding, "One day I hope to play in the league."

Frei and Ansah bonded over their love of basketball, and Frei learned about Ansah's life. The youngest of five children, Ansah had been raised in a crowded, working-class neighborhood of Accra. His father, Edward, was a sales manager for a petroleum company, and his mother, Elizabeth, was a nurse.

Ansah's teenage years revolved around school, sports and religion. To stay in shape for track and soccer, he ran two to three miles through the busy streets each morning before school. At night he'd spend hours on a basketball court with his older brother practicing "LeBron" moves. Like most Accra families, the Ansahs didn't have cable TV, but a friend did, and Ansah would go there whenever the Cavaliers were on.

Raised an Anglican, Ansah attended a charismatic church—an all-black congregation with a passionate minister, soulful music and a rollicking atmosphere. He was devout, and religion became a regular topic of conversation between Frei and Ansah, who was already familiar with Mormon beliefs from working at the school. The pair spent hours discussing the Book of Mormon, and within six weeks, despite strong opposition from family, Ansah asked Frei to baptize him.

A few months after Ansah converted, Frei completed his mission and returned to BYU, but not before giving his new friend some advice. "I told

Ziggy that if he was serious about playing basketball, he should come to BYU and try out for the team," Frei said.

Ansah went to the headmaster at Golden Sunbeam, who had put two sons through BYU. With the headmaster's help, Ansah gained admission. A couple weeks before the start of the fall semester in 2008, Frei received an unexpected call: Ansah had just landed in Utah, and he needed a roommate.

Utah was a huge adjustment. Ansah had never seen snow, shopping malls or fast-food restaurants. When he wanted chicken back home, he'd go buy a live one at the local market, bring it home to slaughter, then cook it. Nobody pulled chicken from a freezer and popped it in a microwave. But the biggest change was being around so many white people. "At first I couldn't handle it," Ansah said. "Whenever I'd see a black person, I'd say hi to them, because it might be the only black person I'd see that day."

But that fall, Frei took Ansah to a BYU football game. It was the first time the Ghanaian had ever seen American football. "I didn't know what was going on," Ansah said. "I was cheering when everyone else was cheering, but I didn't know why." He also thought the game was way too violent. "It was intense—everybody hitting each other," he said. "I said to my roommates, 'I don't think I ever want to do that.'"

Instead, he tried walking on the basketball team. Despite his thirty-nine-inch vertical, ferocious dunks and study of LeBron, he got cut. The next fall he tried again. He got cut again. But he had made the track team and was tearing up the intramural basketball league on campus, which is where a few football players spotted him and insisted he try out for football. Frei kept saying the same thing. So did the track coach. Finally, Ansah got up the courage to go see Mendenhall.

———

Kyle Van Noy hadn't been formally introduced to Ansah. He'd seen him in the locker room and heard people referring to him as Ziggy. But on the first day of full contact in fall camp, Van Noy was in no mood for pleasantries. He was looking to make an impression. At one point Ansah was sprinting down the field, oblivious to what was happening around him. Van Noy tattooed him. Ansah went airborne. When he hit the ground, he rolled like an SUV that had been hit by a semi.

"I was just running," Ansah said. "I didn't see it coming. Kyle hit me—oh my goodness—I fell on the ground and rolled a few times."

Chad Lewis wasn't surprised. Van Noy was like an assassin. He was taking guys out all over the field. It was obvious he was a special player. Ansah, on the other hand, looked raw. It was obvious he had not grown up with the game. He didn't know how to move on the field, how to initiate contact and create leverage.

"He was not lowering down and gearing up to hit someone," Lewis said. "He was just running. That allowed him to hit opponents with a speed that they were not prepared for. But he also wasn't naturally protecting himself the way football players do. So he was taking blows to his body that most guys would never be able to endure."

Ansah was also getting worked into the ground by the coaches. He didn't know how to hit a blocking dummy or drive a sled. He had no idea how to use his hands. Even basic drills were over his head.

Nor was he used to the physical demands. "He couldn't make it through ten minutes of practice without taking a knee or lying down," Mendenhall said. "The workouts were just too hard. He was so mentally weak, and the culture was so different. It was ludicrous to think he'd ever see the field. He couldn't even get through the drills."

Mendenhall kept waiting for Ansah to turn in his gear. "But he kept showing up," Mendenhall said. "I was just like, 'What are you doing? There's no chance.'"

On the last day of fall camp, Ansah was still around. Mendenhall faced a decision. Under NCAA rules, Division I football programs are allowed a maximum of 105 roster spots. But schools are not allowed to offer more than 85 scholarships. That creates an opening for up to 20 walk-ons per team. Even though walk-ons pay their own tuition and are often relegated to the practice squad, those are coveted positions. Mendenhall decided to add Ansah to the roster.

———

In late October, BYU was preparing to play Wyoming. While going over practice film, Mendenhall and his staff noticed something odd on the kick returns. On every kickoff, Ziggy Ansah was barreling downfield, taking out blockers left and right. "He's not only knocking them down," said Mendenhall. "He's ten yards in front of anyone else on our team."

"Yeah, he's ten yards ahead of everybody," someone chimed in.

"Is everyone else tired?" one coach asked.

It was clear that wasn't the case. Special teams players—even the ones on the practice squad—have the biggest motors. They go all out every play. Ziggy was consistently beating the most intense players on the roster.

"We gotta try him in a game," one coach said.

Mendenhall wasn't convinced. Practice is one thing. Games are another. Until two months earlier, Ansah had never touched a football. The idea of putting him on the field in a Division I game so soon seemed premature.

"It's a huge leap," Mendenhall said. "He doesn't know what he's doing."

But that Saturday BYU was up 16–10 at the half. Mendenhall decided to conduct an experiment. On the opening kickoff of the second half, Ziggy Ansah trotted onto a football field in a game situation for the first time in his life. "It was scary," Ansah said. "I was trying to remember what I had been told, but it wasn't easy, especially with a lot of people yelling."

His instructions had been pretty simple. "We put him right in the middle of the field and said, 'Whoever catches the ball, run right to that guy,'" Mendenhall recalled.

When the ball was kicked, Ansah raced downfield, taking out two Wyoming players. But he didn't get near the return man. Convinced he had failed, he dropped his head and jogged back to the sideline. His teammates mobbed him. "Zig-gy, Zig-gy!" they shouted, slapping his helmet and butt.

"What?" Ansah said.

"You just blew up two guys," players yelled.

Ansah shrugged.

After that, Ansah started to see more time on special teams.

But at the end of the season, Mendenhall told him there would not be a scholarship for him the following fall. He was welcome to remain on the team as a walk-on.

––––––

BYU opened the 2011 season on the road against its SEC foe Ole Miss. ESPN did the game. BYU's offense had been stymied all day. With five minutes to play, Ole Miss had the ball and the lead, 13–7. Facing third and long, quarterback Zack Stoudt went into the shotgun. On the snap, Van Noy blew past the tackle and closed on Stoudt, swatting the ball loose while sacking him. Players converged on the loose ball. Van Noy popped to his feet, scooped up the ball and scampered into the end zone, tying the game. The Ole Miss crowd was silenced. With the extra point, BYU won 14–13.

Although just a sophomore, Van Noy had already established himself as the best all-around player on BYU's defense. After the Ole Miss game, Mendenhall had news for him. He was getting a new roommate: Ziggy Ansah. From that moment forward, every time BYU traveled, Van Noy and Ansah would share a hotel room.

At the time, Ansah was racked with self-doubt. He was beginning to wonder if he'd ever figure out the game of football. Maybe he should not have tried out in the first place. Maybe he should quit. The whole culture was so foreign to him. It just seemed as if he'd never fit in.

On one level, Van Noy could relate. "Because of the things I've done and the experiences I've had, I've been pretty down in the dumps," Van Noy said. "But because of those experiences I was capable of saying, 'Hey, you're not alone.' Coming to BYU made me realize it is okay to ask for help."

Pairing the team's best player with its most inexperienced one proved to be a stroke of genius. Van Noy and Ansah became best friends. In their beds at night they'd discuss their fears and dreams. And Van Noy started teaching Ansah the finer points of the game—how to hit, how to leverage his size and speed and how to condition himself to improve his endurance.

"Kyle is like a brother to me," Ansah said. "I love him. We watched a lot of film, and he taught me to stay low."

Midway through the 2011 season, Mendenhall and his staff posed another question about Ansah: "Can he rush the passer on third down?"

He certainly had the speed and size. But he had zero technique. In practice one day they tried another experiment. With Van Noy lined up on the strong side, they lined up Ansah on the weak side, outside the tackle. Once again they gave very simple instructions: "Go get the quarterback." He did just that, racing past the beefier tackle and recording a sack. The next time BYU was way up in a game, Ansah got to rush the passer on third down. Little by little, he was gaining confidence.

No one was happier for him than Van Noy. After the 2011 season, Ansah had one year of eligibility remaining. Following Van Noy's lead, he had lived in the weight room, bulking up to 270 pounds. He had even gotten faster, especially laterally. His importance to the team as a situational player on defense was increasing.

Mendenhall had seen enough. He offered Ansah a scholarship for his senior season in 2012.

"It's hard to even articulate how far this guy came," Mendenhall said. "He was so naïve, so raw, when he walked on. But he worked and worked. He's a statistics major. He'll do exactly what you tell him after you tell him one time. He doesn't know why he's doing it. But he'll do it."

18 SABAN'S WAY

The New Testament of college football

You better play the seam a little better, guys!" he barked. "Eight yards outside the seam!"

The voice was insistent and seemingly everywhere at once. On the Wednesday of a bye week in early October 2012 before a game against Missouri, at the final practice before a three-day break, Nick Saban was in his element. A minor misread by junior linebacker C. J. Mosley and Saban jumped his ass. Defensive lineman Damion Square made a mistake only Saban seemed able to see. "Ninety-two! You're doing the same thing every day! *Every day!*"

The Alabama practice stretched across three of the most pristine emerald-green fields that about $90 million in football revenue a year can buy. Rising nearby was a $9 million, thirty-seven-thousand-square-foot weight room and conditioning center complete with its own Performance Nutrition Bar, yet another of Saban's cutting-edge, damn-the-cost improvements, the result, actually, of input from his player leadership council that a few years before had brought up the quality of the training table food.

"He values our opinion," said Barrett Jones, a three-time all-American lineman.

Standing on the sidelines, NFL scouts from Houston and Tampa Bay watched as Saban, an old DB coach, went to work. He couldn't stand still. He grabbed a football, licked the first two fingers of his right hand and tossed a series of perfect spirals that landed in the outstretched arms of defensive backs who ran like gazelles. The pace was frenetic. A two-hour symphony of whistles and shouts emitted by a small army of assistants and staff.

"Blow the horn! Blow the horn! Ones and twos over here," yelled Saban.

First-team O against first-team D. Seven solid minutes of pad-popping intensity. Unlike most college football teams, the Tide practiced in pads four days a week with no shortage of contact. At midfield Saban paced like a lion. Ten feet one way, ten feet back. Up on his toes. Dissecting every drill. Coaching at Indy 500 speed.

"Let's go! Let's go! Let's go!"

At sixty-one, *this* is what got college football's greatest coach up at 6:15 every morning and drove him through a ruthlessly efficient schedule devoted to an approach that is a visionary blend of old-school football and New Age philosophy. Simply known as The Process.

In some quarters of college football The Process is seen as nothing less than the New Testament of coaching. It was spread by former Saban assistants to Michigan State (Mark Dantonio), Florida (Will Muschamp), Florida State (Jimbo Fisher), Colorado State (Jim McElwain) and other schools. The Saban Way is an increasingly popular answer for coaches seeking a fresh path to the top of the mountain. It is the result of a continuing forty-year journey: small, careful steps away from cheap motivational tools like playing-time incentives and intimidation and inexorably toward the higher power of *expectation* built around three major components—personal development, academic development and football development—Saban has been preaching like gospel for years. His multilayered system within the system is fueled by phrases and words like "internal excellence," "psychological disposition," "mental energy" and "accountability."

"You can talk about winning all you want," he said, "but really the goal is for our guys to go out there . . . and play with the best of their ability from an effort standpoint, from a toughness standpoint and from a discipline-to-execute standpoint."

Which from Saban's standpoint was what The Process was all about: creating a team of individuals striving to be the best at what they do.

"Successful, to me," he said, "is being all you can be at what you're trying to do. You have a trend that you're trying to develop with these habits so that people are doing the right things the right way at the right time so they have the best chance to be successful.

"You know you can put all that [winning] out of your mind if you just focus on being a relentless competitor, playing every play like it has a history and life of its own. Be the best player that you can be. That guarantees you the best result if you'll just do it that way."

———

Room 240 of the Mal M. Moore Athletic Facility at Alabama is home to the tight ends. Clean but cramped, the meeting room is outfitted with eleven industrial chairs, a large video monitor at the front of the room and white-boards along the side. It also happens to house the "office"—that is, two computers crammed onto a table stuck in a back corner—of twenty-two-year-old former Tide defensive back Wesley Neighbors.

In the fall of 2012, Neighbors was one of the youngest members on the largest and most expensive coaching staff in the country. For the 2011–12 season Alabama's football expenses totaled $36.9 million, according to NCAA data, $3.5 million more than second-place Auburn ($33.3 million) and $10 million more than third-place Texas ($25.9 million). In addition to listing nine assistant coaches, the 2012 Alabama Football Directory included an NFL front-office-like roster of thirty-five other staff members, such as directors of strength and conditioning, player personnel, football operations, player development, performance nutrition, rehab services, video operations and creative media as well as the more typical tasks of academic program adviser and assistant equipment manager.

All of which reflected what Alabama had now become—the NFL's thirty-third team.

On the staff page Neighbors was listed as a defensive analyst. His specialty was really breaking down special teams film and organizing day-to-day practice for the scout team. On the Tide coaching ladder he stood a rung or two above interns and student assistants. What made his job interesting to an outsider was his inside view of The Process at work.

"It goes top to bottom, but it also goes bottom to top," said Neighbors before practice one day. "The top of the totem pole works on the big details. The farther you go down, the finer the details get. The smaller the details get. And I would work on the smaller, finer details. That's kind of how I see my job."

It was two in the afternoon. Neighbors was wearing an Alabama football T-shirt, gray shorts and a two-day growth on his face. He looked as though he hadn't slept in a week.

The fact was that Saban didn't sleep all that much either, especially during the season. His mind, he said, was too busy dissecting the hours and days ahead. But you'd never know it from the look of him. Even up close, he bristled with the energy of a lightweight boxer training before a title fight, appearing nowhere near his actual age. What was powering his internal engine?

"No question," said his longtime defensive coordinator Kirby Smart. "He's driven to be the greatest coach in the game."

His days began in earnest no later than 7:15 a.m. in a cavernous wood-paneled corner office decorated in warm earth tones. By the time he arrived, he would be well into his early-morning routine: up at 6:15, watching the Weather Channel until 6:40—not 6:45, 6:40. He would eat two Little Debbie cookies in three small bites each and drink his first two cups of coffee of the day. Between 12:00 and 1:00 almost every afternoon, from the middle of February until the first of June, Saban would play an intense game of four-on-four basketball with selected members of his staff. The rules never changed: three games to eleven; baskets counted one point, three-pointers one and a half points (Saban rules). The opposing squad had come to be known around the football office as the Washington Generals, a nod to the longtime designated patsies of the Harlem Globetrotters. "We don't get too many calls," said Jeff Purinton, associate athletics director for football communications, who regularly drew the duty of guarding Saban. The coach, true to form, was known to become rather, shall we say, *exercised* when a teammate failed to block out or call out a screen.

Afterward, lunchtime. The same meal every day: iceberg lettuce salad topped with turkey and cherry tomatoes. The usual dressing, light Dijon mustard on the side, which has been said by close observers to actually change from time to time.

In a world where little things could make a big difference, Saban's microscopic approach to success stood alone. "He is very detail orientated," said Smart, who had worked alongside Saban since 2006 and was a regular in the noon hoops games. "I mean, he wants every second of practice organized, every walk-through rep. He wants to plan for it. He wants it on paper, and he wants you to execute it."

In the big picture Saban saw himself as the CEO of what he repeatedly referred to as "the organization." His style was similar to that of a chief executive officer—polite but fast moving, his fifteen-hour days during the season meticulously organized to strip away what he liked to call "the clutter" in his life. To wit, with the click of a garage-door-like remote Saban could automatically close his office door, saving precious steps and time; his master calendar was plotted out at least eighteen months in advance; meetings with academic advisers and coaches all but eliminated small talk in favor of a quiet, direct "What do we got?"

"You function better when you're in a routine. Most people do," Saban said during an interview with *60 Minutes* in the fall of 2012. "Maybe it's the obsessive-compulsive personality we all have to some degree, but I always function better in a routine. So when things go a certain way, I feel like I'm going to be more productive because I know what's going to happen next. I can stay more organized in my time management of doing things a certain way all the time and trying to duplicate that on a day-to-day and week-to-week basis."

But contrary to his intense, grind-it-out image, Saban always maintained a life away from football, particularly from about the middle of February until training camp opened the first week in August. His favorite methods of relaxation were golf (with practice, he played to about a 10 handicap), spending time on the water in his boat and reading. He was also not afraid to break out a deck of cards and challenge you to a hybrid game of gin.

––––––

Over the years Saban's departure from the Miami Dolphins and hiring by Alabama in January 2007 have been the subject of more than a bit of mystery and outrage by die-hard Fins fans. How was former Alabama athletic director Mal Moore able to spirit Saban and his wife, Terry, out of South Florida and on a private plane to Tuscaloosa? Especially after Saban had repeatedly denied the rumors, going so far as to say on December 21, 2006, "I guess I have to say it: I'm not going to be the Alabama coach."

And one might add: with good reason. At the time Alabama was in a sorry state. Mired near the bottom of the SEC pack, it was coming off five years of NCAA probation for recruiting violations. The Mike Shula era turned out to be long on hope and short on results, especially at the end.

It was late in the 2006 season, Shula's fourth and final year, when Moore said he began contemplating another head coaching change. When he finally pulled the trigger on November 27, after a fifth consecutive loss to Auburn in the Iron Bowl, he made clear one of his top priorities was hiring a man who had won a championship.

"I couldn't be trying anyone out," he said.

Moore, who died from a lung condition in late March 2013 at the age of seventy-three, was one of those athletic directors cut from a different cloth. Tall and courtly, he came from a more genteel and less cutthroat time in college football. He was anything but a CEO for hire; cut Moore open and he would have bled crimson and white. His 'Bama bloodlines stretched back nearly fifty years. He had first walked on campus in 1958 as a scholarship quarterback on Bear Bryant's first team. In the ensuing years Moore was part of ten national championships in football as a player, coach and athletic director. He returned to Alabama in 1990 as an offensive coordinator under Gene Stallings before moving into athletic administration in 1994. By the time he took over as athletic director five years later, the Tide had turned, and his beloved program was living in its gilded past. "Their side of the campus used to be an eyesore, including Bryant-Denny Stadium," said IMG's Ben Sutton, a longtime friend of Moore's.

During his tenure Moore turned Alabama into a shining star of the SEC, pumping more than $200 million into facilities improvements. His efforts helped produce conference championships in no fewer than eight sports, including baseball, women's golf, softball and gymnastics. Yet Moore knew full well on which side his financial bread was buttered; more than ever, he needed a rock star football coach, someone capable of winning games and reenergizing the fan and donor base.

In Moore's mind he had three candidates to replace Shula: South Carolina's coach Steve Spurrier, West Virginia's red-hot Rich Rodriguez and . . . Saban.

Moore said he first offered Spurrier the head job in December 2006 when they were both in New York City for a Hall of Fame dinner. "It was intriguing, that's the word he used, 'intriguing,'" Moore recalled. "But he said, 'Mal, I'm just too dug in at South Carolina.'"

But Spurrier had another candidate in mind. "He told me, 'You should go hard for Saban,'" said Moore.

Moore found this ironic. A few months earlier, midway through a second season with the Dolphins, Saban had sent word through Jimmy Sexton, his powerful agent, he was leaning toward leaving the NFL. Saban's first year of marriage in Miami had ended on a happy note: the Dolphins had reeled off six straight wins to finish the season 9-7. But his second year had dissolved into a difficult grind—a 1-6 start precipitated by problems at quarterback and players grumbling about the intensity of practice and what they saw as Saban's dictatorial style of coaching. Actually, the Sabans weren't all that happy either. Both Nick and Terry discovered they missed campus life and the spirit of the college game. Saban told a friend in Miami he felt as if he were going to work at a factory every day; he missed the camaraderie of college coaching and realized he felt much more comfortable building young men than fighting the habits of professional athletes.

So Moore set about trying to convince Saban to make Tuscaloosa his new home. He told Sexton, with whom he often spoke, he was prepared to make his client the highest-paid coach in the Southeastern Conference. "Well, you can stop right there," Moore said Sexton told him. "We need to be talking about the country, not the conference."

Moore made it clear he "absolutely never spoke with" Saban during the 2006 NFL season as he knew the coach was committed to focusing on the Dolphins. But that didn't stop Moore from working on a deal sheet with Sexton. They laid out a prospective salary, bonuses, access to private airplanes and all the rest. Then Sexton suddenly stopped returning his calls. So Moore shifted to Plan B and heated up conversations with Rodriguez, who had expressed a strong interest in the job. Talk to my agent, said Rodriguez. Again, another deal sheet was constructed. Then Sexton called back. Moore told him he was about to hire Rodriguez. It was the last thing Sexton wanted to hear. The NFL season still had a month to go; Saban needed more time. Time Moore frankly didn't have. Alabama's president, Dr. Robert E. Witt, had been quietly urging Moore to make a choice.

So on Thursday, December 7, 2006, Moore made one: He reached an agreement with Rodriguez, a rising star with back-to-back Big East titles under his belt. The reported offer was $12 million over six years, $700,000 a year more than his pay at West Virginia.

As Moore told it, he and Rodriguez sealed the deal with what Moore called a "blood oath" not to utter a word of what had transpired. By mid-afternoon on December 7 the paperwork had made its way to the Alabama administrative building for vetting by university lawyers. Then, said Moore, within two hours, around 5:00 p.m., news broke on ESPN that Alabama had reached an agreement to hire Rodriguez. Moore was anything but pleased with that piece of news.

The next day Rodriguez publicly denied any agreement had been reached, saying he had declined an offer. "This is my school, my alma mater, my dream," he said of West Virginia.

In Moore's mind it didn't matter what Rodriguez said. He knew. An oath had been broken.

"I never spoke to Rodriguez again," he said.

The clock continued to tick. Alabama was set to play in the Independence Bowl in Shreveport, Louisiana, on December 28. Miami's season ended three days later with a loss in Indianapolis to drop the Dolphins' final record to 6-10. Moore made his move. Instead of flying home with the team after the bowl game, he drove to Tuscaloosa to avoid the press and hopped on a friend's Gulfstream for a one-way recruiting mission to South Florida.

Upon landing, he reached Saban by phone. Terry joined them on the call.

The former Terry Constable had first met her husband in middle school science camp; she was in seventh grade at one middle school on the uptown side of the tracks and he was in eighth near the other side. As Saban liked to tell it—with one of his wry smiles—the woman affectionately known around Alabama as Ms. Terry "didn't know what a first down was when we first started dating, and there's no doubt in my mind she thinks she should be the head coach at Alabama right now. No doubt. And she is a hell of an assistant, even though she thinks she's the head coach, which, when she's around, I always make her think that."

But in many ways Terry Saban was the head coach—certainly of access to their home and her husband's off-field charity work. She was also the unquestioned force behind the Sabans' commitment to charity, particularly Nick's Kids Fund, which had distributed some $2.5 million to more than seventy-five Alabama charities. Said Saban, "I would say she's probably as big a part of the program as anyone in terms of her time, her commitment and all the things she does to serve the people in a very positive way that is helpful for us to be successful, not only in football, but in the community and what we can do to serve other people."

Moore spoke with husband and wife for about thirty minutes. Saban was struggling, clearly caught up in the persuasive powers of Dolphins' billionaire owner Wayne Huizenga whose business empire contained Waste Management, Blockbuster Video and AutoNation. "Nick told me he [Huizenga] knows how to close a deal," recalled Moore. "He said, 'I tell him I want out, and he talks me back in.'" But the call ended on an upbeat note. Saban told Moore he would call him the next day at noon.

Noon came and went. Ninety more minutes passed. Still no call. Moore checked out of his hotel and readied to return to Tuscaloosa. He called Sexton one last time.

"Hang in there," said the agent.

So Moore hung. He checked into another hotel closer to Saban's home, just in case. Saban called back. He told Moore to meet him at his home that night. He gave Moore the pass code to get inside the gated community.

That night, just as Moore was pulling in front of Saban's house, his phone rang. It was Paul Bryant Jr., Bear's only son and a member of the Alabama Board of Trustees.

"How you doing?" asked Bryant.

"I'm right out front of Saban's house," Moore whispered.

Nobody had to tell Bryant about the timing of his call. "I'm just afraid you were going to have a heart attack," he told Moore before hopping off the phone.

Once Moore was inside the house, he and Terry talked. Terry brought Moore coffee. They had never met. The conversation ranged from Huizenga to her husband's frustration with his job. Then the phone rang. It was Saban, still struggling over what to do.

"I called Terry and I said, 'I don't think I'm going to talk to him [Mal] tonight,'" he said. "She said, 'Oh, Mal's already here. We've been talking for an hour.' That was the first step in the right direction."

The next big step came when Saban finally arrived at home.

"If I made a pitch, it began with the way I see it you don't have a choice but to come to Alabama," said Moore. "If you get beat with the Dolphins, they're going to blame you. And if you don't and we win at Alabama, you're going to wish you were at Alabama."

Saban excused himself and went to another room to make a call. At that point, Moore recalled, Terry Saban grabbed his right arm and shook it hard with both hands. "We've got to get him on that plane!" she said.

Moore let out a big laugh. "I knew right then I was in a helluva lot better shape than I thought I was," he said.

Saban returned to say he had a meeting the next morning with Huizenga. He wanted Moore to return to the gated community and wait down the street for a call. The next morning Moore found himself waiting under an oak tree as television trucks gathered just outside the gate and helicopters circled the sky above.

Somewhere between 10:30 and 11:00 a.m. his phone rang. It was Saban. We're coming with you, the coach said. Give me until two o'clock.

Saban later said he never directly told Huizenga he was leaving, but Huizenga finally said, "Nick, if that's what you want, I want you to do it."

Moore headed back to his hotel to pack. The television trucks stayed put. The helicopters circled. By 2:00 p.m. he was back under the old oak tree. His phone rang once more. Moore told Saban they needed to get moving. Did he want to take two cars? No, said Saban. Back your car into our garage; the luggage is ready.

So that's what Moore's driver did, only to find the Sabans, their daughter and one of her friends waiting. Somehow the driver stuffed the luggage into the trunk, the Sabans and friend piling into the back. Off they went. Reporters followed. Helicopters chased. On the way to the airport Moore made two calls, one to the owner of the Gulfstream, the other to a name synonymous with Alabama football. He handed the phone to Saban.

"Congratulations, Coach," said Joe Willie Namath.

Half a dozen camera crews were waiting when Moore's car pulled up to the private plane entrance at Fort Lauderdale Airport. As the Sabans scrambled inside the jet, Moore reached into his pocket and pulled out a few hundred dollars. He handed them to his driver, his lone companion for three frantic days. By accident a $10 bill fluttered away. One of the airport workers picked it up and handed it back to Moore, shaking his hand.

"Great job, Coach Moore," he said. "I'm from Anniston, Alabama!"

Seven years later Moore let out another long laugh at the pure pleasure he derived from the oddity of that moment.

"I really could have hugged that man's neck," he said.

Inside the plane Moore popped his head into the cockpit. The pilot of the plane was the brother-in-law of Richard Todd, a former Crimson Tide quarterback. Welcome to the small world of the SEC.

Then Moore uttered a line that should live forever in Alabama football lore.

"I told him if I didn't come back on this plane with Nick Saban, he might as well have flown my ass straight to Cuba!!"

But there he was, one of the brightest minds in the game, sitting with his back to the cockpit. As the wheels rolled up, Moore said his new coach eased back in his chair and closed his eyes, finally allowing his emotions to unwind.

"Well, Mal," said Saban after he opened his eyes. "I guess you think I'm a helluva coach."

Yes, Moore said. Certainly. You're an outstanding coach.

Saban looked Moore straight in the eye. "You need to understand one thing," he said. "I'm not worth a damn without players."

"Thank God you understand *that*," thought Moore.

In a tribute to Moore shortly after he passed away, Saban told *ADAY*, the official game-day program of Alabama football, that his happiest moment with his friend came when Moore was honored as the nation's top athletic director in 2012.

Saban said Moore had tears in his eyes when he told Saban he had changed Moore's life by accepting the Alabama job.

"No, Mal, you changed my life," Saban said. "I'm a better coach. I'm a better person. I'm a better teacher for the lessons I've learned in partnership with you."

Pain is relative

The discussion around significant injuries in football hit a fever pitch during the 2012 season. The pressure to improve player safety reached a new level when President Obama weighed in.

"I'm a big football fan, but I have to tell you if I had a son, I'd have to think long and hard before I let him play football," Obama said in a January 2013 interview with the *New Republic*. "And I think that those of us who love the sport are going to have to wrestle with the fact that it will probably change gradually to try to reduce some of the violence. In some cases, that may make it a little bit less exciting, but it will be a whole lot better for the players, and those of us who are fans maybe won't have to examine our consciences quite as much."

This time, the conversation wasn't strictly about the NFL and the well-documented cases on long-term injuries and concussions. Instead, the president made it clear that college football players may well have the most to lose.

"I tend to be more worried about college players than NFL players in the sense that the NFL players have a union, they're grown men, they can make some of these decisions on their own, and most of them are well-compensated for the violence they do to their bodies," Obama said. "You read some of these stories about college players who undergo some of these same problems with concussions and so forth and then have nothing to fall back on. That's something that I'd like to see the NCAA think about."

———

The president's concerns were supported just two months later. A March 2013 study from researchers at the Cleveland Clinic found that college football players are likely to experience significant and long-term brain damage from hits to the head even when they do not suffer a concussion.

Blood samples, brain scans and cognitive tests were given to sixty-seven college football players before and after games during the 2011 season. The forty players thought to have absorbed the most serious hits showed spiked levels of an antibody that has been linked to long-term brain damage. The study, which was published in *PLOS ONE*, came after the NCAA had provided a $400,000 grant to the National Sport Concussion Outcomes Study Consortium.

But in some cases, the BCS still controlled when and where the message about head injuries could be released. Prior to the 2013 BCS championship game, Ramogi Huma, president of the National College Players Association, attempted to hold a news conference to talk about head injuries, but the Marriott, where the press conference was scheduled, caved under pressure from the BCS, according to the *Birmingham News*.

"The contracts were all ready to have a room [*sic*], but before they executed the contract, they checked with the BCS and Marriott pulled the plug," Huma told the *News* in January 2013. "We needed to inject the conversation of the health of these football players. The BCS has tried to actively silence us on this. That was pretty disturbing."

Significant injuries are nothing new to college football, but the aftermath and long-term effects continue to be felt long after players take their last snaps. During the course of the 2012 season, the authors and researchers for this book sent out individual surveys to 283 living starters from thirteen BCS title-winning teams between 1998 and 2011. Of the 283 living starters from those teams, 34, or 12 percent, responded to our inquiries. The players were interviewed about significant injuries they suffered during their college playing days and whether they continue to suffer from them. They were also asked if they graduated from college, how many hours per week were dedicated to football-related activities, and whether they were influenced to choose a major.

Of the thirty-four players interviewed for this book, nineteen (56 percent) said they suffered a debilitating injury of some sort as a result of their college football playing days. They described a wide array of injuries that continued to affect them to this day. For example:

- Miami defensive tackle Matt Walters from the 'Canes 2001 national title team suffered a third-degree separation in his shoulder, a broken clavicle and an injury in his pelvis that restricted him from getting out of bed in the morning. (He still hasn't fully recovered.)
- Donnie Nickey, Ohio State's free safety during its 2002 title run,

suffered multiple concussions and still has arthritis in his knees and back.

- Darrion Scott, one of Nickey's defensive teammates on that Buckeyes squad, had three shoulder surgeries during his career in Columbus.
- Matt Mauck, who was under center for LSU's 2003 national championship team, suffered a Lisfranc injury while in Baton Rouge that still causes him problems today.
- Justin Vincent, Mauck's backfield mate on that LSU team, still gets excruciating headaches, causing him to become light-headed from time to time.
- As a starting tight end for USC's 2004 BCS title team, Alex Holmes would go on to have a litany of injuries, including a broken back and separations of both shoulders.
- Florida guard Jim Tartt from the Gators' 2006 title team had shoulder surgery every spring he was in Gainesville and no longer has cartilage in one of his shoulders.

Even before the creation of the BCS, injuries were commonplace among perennial powers. In July 1996, Florida State center Jarad Moon knew something was wrong moments after he snapped the ball during his first practice. Defensive lineman Andre Wadsworth slashed through Moon's double-team. Fullback Drew O'Daniel saw Wadsworth coming and cut left to have leverage in the collision. But Wadsworth came at him low and O'Daniel's cleat dug deep into the grass, forcing the fullback's body to spin while his foot remained planted, tearing his MCL, LCL and ACL. O'Daniel never played football again.

It was an unforgettable lesson to Moon on just how fragile a college football player's career can be. In his senior year Moon was reminded of that lesson again. In a game he was hit so hard that he went airborne. When he landed on his tailbone, Moon's hips and back twisted, causing his L4 and L5 disks to bulge. Like a soldier, he was trained to endure the pain and play through the injury. But the pain was unbearable. He couldn't even bend over, so he approached the team doctor while the game was still in progress and asked for something to dull the pain. He was not examined or X-rayed. The team doctor prescribed Cataflam, an anti-inflammatory drug, and sent Moon back onto the field. From that moment on, Moon said, he couldn't play without the painkilling drug.

Despite the lingering neck injuries, Moon made it to the NFL. In 2001, he signed a three-year contract as an undrafted free agent for just under $1 million with the Carolina Panthers. Despite an increased dependence on Cataflam, the rigors of the NFL proved too much. That summer, Moon left the Panthers before playing a down in the NFL. Moon was finally finished with football. But, as his chiropractor would say, football was not finished with him.

Today Moon feels every one of those college injuries. There's chronic weakness in his left shoulder, tightness in his neck, his back locks up at least once a year. He still can't bring himself to call it pain, though; he simply sees what he feels as "annoyances," because pain, well, pain is a relative thing.

———

Athletic training staffs from Seattle to Syracuse were busy in 2012. According to data collected from injury and media reports, there were at least 282 season-ending injuries among the eight BCS conferences and independents between January 1, 2012, and January 7, 2013, the day of the BCS championship game.

SEASON-ENDING INJURIES BY CONFERENCE IN THE
  2012–13 SEASON
ACC: 31
Big East: 22
Big Ten: 38
Big 12: 31
Conference USA: 24
Independents: 15
Mountain West: 31
Pac-12: 44
SEC: 46

Of the 282 season-ending injuries, 190, or 68 percent, were lower-body injuries. The 2012 data come as the most recently released NCAA figures, which tracked injuries between 2004–5 and 2008–9, found that 50 percent of all football injuries, both season ending and not season ending, were lower-body injuries. The 93 knee injuries alone made up almost one-third of the season-ending injuries in 2012.

TOP FIVE SEASON-ENDING INJURIES IN 2012
  1. Knee, 93
  2. Shoulder, 31
  3. ACL, 29

4. Leg, 27
5. Ankle, 19

Even with nearly three hundred season-ending injuries in 2012, there were undoubtedly far more, given the reluctance to release such information. For instance, conferences such as the Pac-12 do not mandate their members file NFL-style injury reports that list player injuries in various categories such as "probable," "doubtful" and "out." In the Pac-12, at least five programs—Oregon, Stanford, USC, Washington and Washington State—declined specific comment on injuries, sparking considerable controversy throughout the conference in 2012. (This happened while California became the first state to mandate financial protections for student-athletes at Cal, Stanford, UCLA and USC who suffer career-ending injuries.)

"It's just a competitive disadvantage for us when other teams don't and we do, so that's going to be the road we take," said Washington's head coach, Steve Sarkisian, in September 2012, referring to his decision not to report or comment on injuries.

Overall, while the SEC accounted for half of the teams in the final top ten poll, the conference also suffered the most season-ending injuries in 2012—with forty-six. (Alabama would lead the conference with six season-ending injuries in 2012.) The positions with the most season-ending injuries in college football's premier conference came at running back and offensive line, reflecting the SEC's physical, ground-and-pound schemes. On average, SEC teams lost at least one running back or offensive lineman in 2012. The Pac-12 was just off the pace with forty-four season-ending injuries, with injuries to defensive linemen and defensive backs leading the way.

Some programs in particular were challenged by losses of big-time talent at various points of the season. TCU running back Waymon James went down with a left knee injury in the second game of the season, a significant blow to the Horned Frogs' attack. Texas's standout defensive end Jackson Jeffcoat ruptured his right pectoral muscle during the Red River Rivalry against Oklahoma in October 2012. Tailback Fitz Toussaint of Michigan needed surgery after he took a serious hit to his left leg against Iowa in November 2012.

Arguably, the most significant discovery of the 2012 data could be called the October Surprise. It indicated—in a significant way—that if teams can physically survive their October slate of games, the odds of having a player go down with a season-ending injury are lowered considerably. Just 20 percent of reported season-ending injuries in 2012 came after October. But in October alone, there were ninety-eight season-ending injuries. That works out to 35 percent of all season-ending injuries for 2012.

MONTH-BY-MONTH INJURY BREAKDOWN IN 2012
August: 67
September: 62
October: 98
November: 48
December: 7

Jim Thornton is the president of the National Athletic Trainers' Association and the head athletic trainer at Clarion University in Pennsylvania. He said that the sharp uptick in October injuries was likely the result of fatigue and teams not adjusting their conditioning programs as the season wore on.

"Football is a taxing sport that is a great sport, but by October you have to realize that they have been through spring conditioning, summer conditioning, camp and a season that has hitting, collisions, et cetera, associated with it and they get tired," Thornton said. "Subsequent to all this, the conditioning they get sometimes is not focused on what will prevent these injuries; rather, it is focused only on overall strength and getting 'big.'"

He added, "There has to be a paradigm shift that is specific to prevention and performance enhancement rather than just throwing weights around. The programs that are not focusing on these concepts are most likely the ones that have a higher incidence of injuries."

Among the eight BCS conferences and the independents, Maryland suffered the most season-ending injuries in 2012—ten. At one point the Terps lost all four of their quarterbacks to season-ending injuries, forcing them to use a freshman linebacker under center to finish out the season.

CONFERENCE LEADERS FOR MOST SEASON-ENDING
    INJURIES IN 2012
ACC: Maryland, 10
Big East: Pittsburgh, 6
Big Ten: Wisconsin, 7
Big 12: Oklahoma, 8
Conference USA: Rice, 8
Independents: BYU and Notre Dame, 5
Mountain West: Hawaii, 8

Pac-12: Arizona, 7
SEC: Alabama, 6

The most peculiar case of injuries may well belong to Rice. Starting off 2-6, the Owls reeled off four straight wins to finish 6-6 and become bowl eligible for the first time since 1961. To cap it off, the Owls won their bowl game against Air Force.

"We research every injury to our players," said Dave Bailiff, the Owls head coach. "Our medical staff, strength coaches and our coaching staff look at it, and we try to do our due diligence to determine if there was some way to avoid the same thing happening in the future. We've not had a rash of one specific kind of injury, and some of the injuries that have hit us hard in the past have come on noncontact drills.

"We do our best to keep every player as physically prepared to play as possible, but injuries are always going to be a by-product of this game."

———

Lying on his back at Williams-Brice Stadium last October, Marcus Lattimore wanted—and needed—to know his fate from the South Carolina trainers. He had to hear it for himself.

"I asked them right there, 'Am I done?'" the South Carolina running back recalled. "And they told me, 'Yeah, you're done.'"

Lattimore knew the feeling. He had torn the ACL in his left knee the year before reemerging as one of college football's premier running backs. His thirty-eight career rushing touchdowns topped the all-time list at South Carolina. The junior had also reestablished himself as the No. 1 running back on most scouts' big boards heading into the 2013 NFL draft.

But now it was all in jeopardy.

On October 27, 2012, No. 13 South Carolina held a 21–14 second-quarter lead over its SEC East rival Tennessee. Lattimore, who ran for nearly six yards a carry against the Volunteers, led the Gamecocks offense, highlighted by a twenty-eight-yard touchdown run in the second quarter. The performance had been a return to form for Lattimore, who had accounted for just forty-eight yards on sixteen carries in consecutive losses to LSU and Florida.

He had burst onto the national scene in 2010, earning National Freshman of the Year honors after running for 1,197 yards and seventeen touchdowns, helping turn the Gamecocks into a force in the SEC and nationally pushing South Carolina to a No. 2 ranking before back-to-back losses to LSU and Florida.

With 4:55 left in the first half against Tennessee, the Gamecocks were at their own twenty-five-yard line, facing second and ten. South Carolina had called a power running play to the left.

"It's one of my favorite plays, actually," said Lattimore.

As the play unfolded, Lattimore missed an open lane to the inside, so he bounced it outside. Tennessee defensive back Eric Gordon hit Lattimore with his helmet on the inside of Lattimore's right knee. Lattimore went down as if he'd been shot.

"Guy came out of nowhere," Lattimore said. "It kind of felt like it was a dream because of how it happened. I didn't even really feel it happen."

Lying on the turf, Lattimore caught a glimpse of his right knee—then went into shock. "I had never seen anything like it," he later said. In that netherworld, he said, he thought about his future, about whether or not he should even move. He remembered placing his hands over his face.

"All I could do was pray," Lattimore said. "Pray that everything was going to be okay."

The 80,250 fans inside Williams-Brice Stadium suddenly fell silent.

"Oh no," said ESPN analyst Brian Griese.

By now five trainers and three teammates had surrounded Lattimore on the field. It was clear the knee was at the very least dislocated. Behind a human curtain, the trainers told him to stay calm. The knee was popped back in place, Lattimore experiencing a feral, almost apocalyptic kind of pain. About five minutes passed. With a towel on his head and tears streaming down his face, Lattimore was ever so carefully helped to his feet and onto the cart. The entire stadium stood and applauded. Both South Carolina and Tennessee cleared their sidelines as players from both sides gathered around Lattimore. The ultimate show of respect.

Right before the cart eased off the field, South Carolina tight end Rory Anderson hugged his teammate and kissed the white Gatorade towel over Lattimore's head. The home crowd gave Lattimore one last roar as he exited a college football field for the final time.

Towel on his head, faced buried in his hands, Lattimore cried his way into the tunnel, where his mother, Yolanda Smith, was waiting. They cried together as Marcus's father looked on.

"It's over," said Marcus. His NFL dream, it seemed, had died.

In his postgame press conference following South Carolina's 38–35 win, Steve Spurrier chose his words carefully. There was no need to belabor the horror of what had occurred. He lauded Lattimore as the most popular player in team history. He called the injury "severe."

The subsequent medical exam confirmed everyone's fears: Lattimore had torn the right ACL, detached both the MCL and the PCL and dislocated his knee.

The outpouring of support for Lattimore was immediate and overwhelming. Lattimore received letters from as far away as California and Hawaii. Two days after the game Governor Nikki Haley of South Carolina, a fierce Clemson fan, declared Lattimore's twenty-first birthday, October 29, 2012, to be Marcus Lattimore Day. "[My husband] and I ask every South Carolinian to join our family as we lift up in prayer Marcus Lattimore and his mother Yolanda Smith during this challenging time," the Republican governor said. "He has been more than just a Carolina football player—he is a great role model for our state."

———

As soon as he saw the hit on Lattimore, Dr. James Andrews figured the injury would be significant. The go-to surgeon for knee, arm and shoulder injuries, Andrews knew Lattimore's ligaments had almost certainly been torn and the knee dislocated. On November 2, 2012, Andrews, a South Carolina team consultant, operated on Lattimore. He was joined by the esteemed physicians Jeffrey Guy and Lyle Cain. In the operating room the doctors found—just as Andrews suspected—that Lattimore's ligaments were torn. The good news was there was no nerve damage. After reattaching the MCL and the PCL, the group repaired Lattimore's ACL with a patella tendon. Given the explosive damage, the surgery went better than expected.

Meanwhile, Lattimore had been thinking. Hard. After he had suffered the torn ACL in his left knee in an October 2011 game against Mississippi State, Lattimore and his family had taken out a $1.7 million insurance policy, the number based on what round in the NFL draft Lattimore figured to be selected. The policy cost the family between $5,000 and $15,000. They could claim the $1.7 million if Marcus could not play football again. Following the horrific scene against Tennessee, cashing in on the insurance policy had become a real possibility. Doctors put Lattimore's initial timetable for recovery between twelve and fifteen months, meaning there was a good chance he would not play a single down in 2013.

With his future in doubt, Lattimore knew one thing for sure: his dream could not wait. On December 12, 2012, a little more than a month after the surgery, he declared for the NFL draft.

"The main thing I was thinking about was, what if it happened again and I came back to college?" he said. "I was thinking that I'd rather not get hurt at all, but if it was to happen again or anything was to happen again, I'd rather it happen at the next level."

Even when a running back has two good knees coming out of college, predicting his long-term health is risky business; it's far and away the most disposable position in sports, with an average NFL life span of about two and a half years. In parts of three seasons at South Carolina the junior running back had already racked up 629 plays from scrimmage (accounting for 3,444 yards) and two torn ACLs. His body had been battered. His NFL future appeared anything but bright.

If Lattimore was looking for hope—and he most certainly was—he found it in the story of former University of Miami running back Willis McGahee. On January 3, 2003, McGahee took a screen pass in the fourth quarter of the BCS National Championship game when Ohio State safety Will Allen leaned his shoulder into McGahee's left knee. Right before that hit, like Lattimore, McGahee was considered the top running back on NFL draft boards. After the hit he was staring at a torn ACL, PCL and MCL. Faced with a similar decision on insurance, McGahee decided not to cash in the $2.5 million insurance policy. Instead, he declared for the NFL draft and, against all odds, worked his way back into the first round despite missing the entire 2003 season. Nine NFL seasons later, McGahee had more than eight thousand yards rushing and sixty-eight total touchdowns.

In his darkest hours Lattimore reached out to McGahee.

"He mainly told me to just keep family close right now," said Lattimore. "That was the main thing he drilled in my head, because there's going to be times that you're going to be real down and you'll need somebody there. He just said, 'Keep that same focus that you've had before this happened, because this happened for a reason, and this situation will set you up for success in the future.' That has stuck with me, and it's going to stick with me. He believed it, and look what happened to him."

Two days after declaring for the NFL draft, Lattimore moved to Pensacola, Florida, to start an intensive rehab program with Dr. Andrews's staff at the Andrews Institute for Orthopaedics and Sports Medicine. During the course of the rehab, Lattimore worked with Stephen LaPlante, who specializes in rehabilitation of cartilage injuries, ACL rehabilitation and return-to-field drills following knee injury. LaPlante also developed the protocol for the institute's Athletic Performance Division's Bridge Program to ensure the correct rehabilitation techniques following ACL surgery.

In Florida, Lattimore found himself living a life far removed from college. He was for all intents and purposes a pro now. Up by 8:00, at rehab by 10:00, working with LaPlante from 10:00 to 11:45. After a break, he would return at 2:00 p.m. and continue the rehab protocol—heavy on single-leg workouts—until late afternoon. In January, he started jogging in the pool to help build up strength in the right ACL. Soon, Washington Redskins quarterback Robert Griffin III, recovering from ACL and LCL damage, joined Lattimore in the pool, cheering on the running back during daily sessions. Lattimore said that the single-leg squats he was doing less than ten weeks after surgery stunned his therapist and his agent, Pat Dye Jr.

"If anyone saw that injury, and I saw it, I happened to be watching the game live, it's amazing he is where he is," said Dye.

Physical recovery was one thing, climbing the emotional mountains something else entirely. By the end of March 2013 the South Carolina star had yet to talk with Gordon.

"In about five years, I'll reach out to him," Lattimore said.

"There have been bad days," he added. "On those bad days, the one thing I think about and the one thing my girlfriend always tells me is, 'Somebody has it worse than you do. Somewhere in the world, someone has it worse. Someone doesn't even have legs right now. Somebody can't even walk right now.'

"That puts it all into perspective. I'm down here by myself, down here living on my own. It's rough. But with my faith in God and knowing everything is going to be okay in trusting his plans and not my plan, I know these dark days will pass."

In the weeks leading up to the draft, it became clear NFL teams had high interest in Lattimore. Before the draft Dye said he would have been shocked if the running back wasn't picked somewhere in the middle rounds. There was hope Lattimore could get on the field in 2013.

"It's going to take a special effort," Dr. Andrews told NFL.com. "Mother Nature's got to help us. The good Lord's got to help us. This kid's future is good regardless of what happens, because of his character."

The San Francisco 49ers selected Lattimore in the fourth round with the 131st pick. As a Niner, he would join former University of Miami star Frank Gore, who overcame two serious knee injuries to excel in the NFL. On the surface, the faith and will of an extraordinary athlete had been rewarded with a perfect place to continue his comeback.

The Ricky Seals-Jones sweepstakes

In what would turn out to be the final day of his son's high school football career, Chester Jones stood at the end of his driveway with a stack of recruiting letters in his hand.

It was an early November Friday in 2012 in Sealy, Texas, a working-class, countrified city of six thousand about fifty miles west of Houston. Sealy High's annual backyard brawl with its archrival Bellville Brahmas was just three hours away, and Jones, a tall, outgoing bull of a man, was feeling a bit anxious, particularly about the bum right ankle that had kept his son pretty much sidelined the last few weeks.

Back in the mid-1970s, Chester Jones was an all-state center in basketball who earned a football scholarship to Prairie View A&M before a torn hamstring cut his college career at tight end short. After graduating, he took to the roads, making a living hauling manhole covers for sixteen years. Now he worked with a friend in the insulation and air-conditioning business, which kept him closer to home.

In his hand now was the daily dose of sugar: fourteen sweet-talking letters in all, eleven from Texas A&M alone, and from the look of things the comely coeds up in College Station had cornered the market on lipstick-colored love letters. The other three letters were postmarked Baton Rouge, home of LSU. The mailings were but the latest entries in the Ricky Seals-Jones sweepstakes, the all-out battle to sign arguably the most talented high school athlete in the country.

By any measure, Seals-Jones would be some kind of catch. At seventeen he stood six feet five, weighed 225 pounds and carried the lean, strong look of a budding all-pro. His hands were huge, the size of a catcher's mitt. And he ran with a long, gifted grace. He played all over the field—quarterback, wide receiver, safety. He led the state in scoring in basketball as a junior, averaging thirty-two points per game. For added measure he had a nice little nasty streak.

Every major recruiting site in the nation was salivating over his size, speed and pure athleticism. ESPN.com had him ranked as the No. 1 wide receiver and "athlete" in the country; Rivals.com listed him as the No. 2 athlete in talent-rich Texas. He was the personification of *student-athlete:* an honor roll student blessed with the kind of humble "yes, sir, no, sir" attitude and game-breaking talent that can cause coaches in the winning business—and with access to discretionary funds—to do whatever it takes to sign him.

The Joneses' rambling redbrick home is set on four family acres about a mile down an aging asphalt road. Chester liked conducting tours of the living room and of the Life of Little Ricky, pointing with pride at pictures of his son in oversized peewee football gear looking like a "peanut head" and in Little League taking a major-league-worthy home-run trot ("See, no smile on his face").

Chester said he noticed that seriousness and promise early and nurtured it. His older sons were good athletes: one, Chester junior, from a first marriage, played quarterback at nearby Blinn College, while the other, Jamal, was a walk-on wide receiver at the University of Houston. But Ricky was different. Chester could see it in the look on his boy's face before summer baseball games and in the way he quarterbacked his undefeated Pop Warner team to a championship down the road in Katy, where some serious ball was played. Father and son worked out as one, Ricky tagging along as his dad ran that old asphalt road and that hill out back. And when age took its toll and Dad slowed down, Ricky kept going. Kept working. By the time Ricky arrived at Sealy High, Coach Jimmie Mitchell knew he would never see a second on the freshmen or JV team. He started him at safety in ninth grade.

"I pushed him. I pushed him to the limit," Chester said. "I told him you've got to grind, you can't quit. I want Ricky to make it. I want to see him play on Sunday. I want to live to see that day."

His wife, Buffy, on the other hand, had different priorities. And who could argue with her, given what happened to her brother—Ricky's namesake—after he won the hundred-meter dash at a regional track meet at nearby Blinn. A day so full of joy and promise ended in a late-night car accident on Highway 36, just ten miles from home. Ricky Seals had fallen asleep at the wheel coming home from his girlfriend's house. He was dead at seventeen.

That was what Chester was remembering as he stood silently at the mantel, pointing to a fresh-faced teenager wearing uniform No. 9, with RICKY SEALS 1973–1990 inscribed underneath.

He pointed to another photograph: a Christmas card in a place of honor. "That's Eric right there," he said.

Eric, as in Hall of Fame running back Eric Dickerson, the pride of Sealy, Texas. Owner of the NFL's single-season rushing record, Dickerson was one-half of SMU's prolific Pony Express backfield from 1979 to 1983 at the center of a $60,000 cars/cash/boosters-run-wild recruiting scandal that resulted in the school's football program being shut down by the NCAA's first and only use of the death penalty. Dickerson was now acting as an unofficial recruiting adviser to his first cousin. When those sweet talkers came calling, ED was there to translate.

And if the dining room table—the one covered in an avalanche of mail—offered any indication, Seals-Jones was in need of some sage advice. Stacks and stacks of letters sat neatly organized by school, more than fifty colleges in all. Nebraska, UCLA, Miami, Iowa, Oregon, Tennessee, Texas Tech, Missouri, Michigan, Notre Dame, Arizona, Houston, Baylor, Oklahoma State.

The three tallest stacks belonged to Texas, Texas A&M and LSU. Seals-Jones had verbally committed to the Longhorns in February 2012, only to rock the recruiting world four months later by de-committing. Now, in November, the field had been narrowed to two favorites—A&M and LSU—with Oregon and Baylor looming on the outside. The college football world was left waiting to find out which school would win the sweepstakes and, it turned out, the price some were willing to pay to come out on top.

———

On the first Sunday in September 2012, Ricky, Buffy and Chester sat down for lunch at Tony's, a busy down-home diner not far from their house, to talk about the foreign army of recruiters who had invaded their life.

"Been a lot of stuff happening around here lately, a lot of stuff," said Chester at one point, shaking his head.

"It's been hectic," added Ricky. "The rankings come out and you're No. 1 and everyone is congratulating you. Even my [football] friends, they say, 'We know you're No. 1, but we're going to try and beat you out and get it.' You got to keep that in the back of your mind, but you still got to enjoy it. It's a once-in-a-lifetime opportunity. You just got to go with it."

One seat over, his mother simply nodded. A pretty, petite woman, she worked for the school district as a part-time bus driver and administrator, up every weekday by 5:00 a.m. She was deeply invested in not just her son's life but also those of many others his age. Her concern was clear: Ricky was not just her youngest child, the last to leave, but also a visual, daily reminder of what happened to her brother. She called Ricky several times a day. She wanted to know where he had been, the people he was hanging with and where he was going.

He might be out of sight, but he was never out of Buffy's mind.

She had pulled Jamal out of Houston when his grades fell below her expectations. Ricky would be an honor student—that's all there was to it. In a bedroom filled with trophies and awards, with size 15 Jordans and school caps lined up like cadets, perfect attendance certificates and a kindergarten diploma were among the awards most prominently displayed.

By Ricky's sophomore year everyone from local fans to Division I recruiters knew he was going to be special. He broke out nationally his junior year, when he was district MVP and college football coaches started showing up at his *basketball* games. One afternoon he got called out of class and down to the office. The principal and a counselor were waiting when he arrived.

"Now I'm thinking I left trash on the floor or something," Ricky said.

Not quite. It was LSU's head coach, Les Miles, who had guided the Tigers to the 2007 national title, stopping by to say hi, all smiles and charm as he and Ricky walked the halls together. One girl was so awed by the sight that, as Ricky put it, "she about passed out." Coach Miles casually offered that he'd love to have Ricky come down and see how he liked the campus. Seals-Jones giggled remembering the moment. "He's a smooth talker," he said of Miles. "He's just so smooth when he talks."

The same week a Baylor assistant coach dropped by. Then TCU's head coach, Gary Patterson, arrived carrying a box. A sudden crack of sunlight shone down like magic as Patterson opened it up to reveal a set of diamond-encrusted rings, including one from his team's undefeated Rose Bowl season in 2010–11.

"This is what happens when you come to TCU," he told Ricky. "We win championships."

By now Ricky couldn't go anywhere without hearing what he called the million-dollar question: *Have you decided where you want to go?* "I could go into Walmart and somebody comes up who I don't know: 'Have you decided where you want to go? I think you should go here.'"

He got to making a joke of it, playing a game with a bunch of his hotshot buddies from the national 7-on-7 circuit. They would tell reporters they were going to shock the world and commit to Bethune, as in Bethune-Cookman, the historically all-black school that plays in the Mid-Eastern

Athletic Conference. "And they were writing it down!" Ricky said. "We were laughing. One of us would make a big play, we were like, 'Beth-THUNE...,' reporters just writing it down. We were just messin' with them."

As the winter of 2012 wore on, fans and coaches searched for any sign of where Seals-Jones might be headed. One day Buffy wore a Texas shirt, and in no time the recruiting message boards were buzzing: *Seals-Jones leaning to Texas!* His parents learned the hard way what *they* said, what *they* wore, was news. Then, in February, after a Junior Day visit to Texas, where coaches implied they were handing out only a few select scholarships, Ricky made some news of his own. He verbally committed to Coach Mack Brown and his Longhorns.

"I felt like that was it, but I felt like I rushed it," Ricky said.

"I felt like he was being rushed, too," said Buffy.

The smart coaches—meaning just about everyone in the Seals-Jones sweepstakes—barely blinked; yeah, it was Texas and all, but "verbals," they knew, were little more than foreplay to National Signing Day in February. The letters, e-mails and texts—especially the texts—continued to pour in: USC, Clemson, Illinois, Oregon, Michigan, Mississippi State, Florida State, Oklahoma State, Alabama, Auburn . . . all talking about playing him at wide receiver, but mostly just talking and talking. And talking . . .

"The recruiters, they didn't care what time it was," said Ricky. "They just kept calling. I would wake up, and I'd have ten missed calls. It was, like, two in the morning, and I'm like, 'Dude, don't y'all sleep?'"

Meanwhile, his cousin Eric, the Hall of Fame running back, weighed in, cautioning his cousin to be patient. They want you. Take your time. Make sure where you want to go. Advice that hit Ricky like a linebacker when in early June 2012 he attended the UT football camp in Austin and took stock of some of the Longhorn recruits, worried they weren't up to their four- and five-star billing. Within two days he called Texas and told them he was de-committing.

"They didn't want to let me off the phone," said Ricky. "The whole coaching staff got on the phone. They said there was no place like Texas. I just told them I just wanted to open up my options and look around."

The news spread like a Texas wildfire across recruiting sites and Twitter. Longhorn fans did not take kindly to the fact that Seals-Jones was suddenly playing the field. Soon Ricky noticed strange cars driving slowly past the house.

"You live in the country; you kinda know the cars," said Ricky.

The cars were one thing, the death threats something else. Four or five showed up on his Twitter feed, one warning him if he didn't come to his senses, his family was going to miss him.

"I just shook it off," Ricky said.

His parents certainly didn't after he finally confessed to the threats a month later at a Nike event in Oregon.

"I said, 'What?'" recalled Chester.

"That just shook me up," said Buffy.

———

By the summer of 2012, Seals-Jones was blowing up on the invite-only showcase circuit. He was selected as the top wide receiver at the Rivals100 Five-Star Challenge 7-on-7 in Atlanta and named the MVP at a Next Level camp in Houston. He was abusing some of the top-rated cornerbacks in the country with highlight-reel plays that were exploding on the Internet.

In mid-June the entire family took a trip to College Station for an unofficial visit to A&M. The arrival of pass-happy coach Kevin Sumlin in December 2011, the school's impressive facilities and the Aggies' move to the SEC had electrified an already formidable fan base. In addition, Sumlin was proving he could recruit with the big boys. At A&M the Jones family was escorted to a room where a pristine Aggies jersey bearing Ricky's high school number, 4, was laid out on a table, along with a helmet, socks and gloves. The unmistakable message: It's all yours. Then an assistant coach showed a video of an A&M wide receiver running with the ball and getting caught from behind that—magically—morphed into shots of Seals-Jones running downfield untouched for a touchdown.

"Man, they were selling that stuff," recalled Chester.

Coincidentally, two days later the family had a meeting set in Austin with Texas basketball coach Rick Barnes. The Longhorns had been floating the notion of allowing Seals-Jones to play two sports, something he talked openly of wanting to try. When Mack Brown found out that Seals-Jones was on campus, he flew into action, canceling a trip to a coaching clinic in San Angelo, and set up a meeting in a Texas-sized conference room in the football offices. There, around a big burnt-orange table, Brown, Barnes and several assistant football coaches and school officials made their pitch.

Said Chester, "They wanted him to commit again."

"I'm talking about the whole coaching staff in there," said Ricky.

"Man, they went from pleading the third to the fifth," Chester recalled. "Mack. Everybody. They said, 'Whatever you decide to do, Texas is going to beat this, beat that, everybody is going to take care of you.' They're going to do this here, this there. A job when you graduate. [They'll take care of] people in your life."

Chester remembered one assistant coach kept asking, *What's it going to take? What do we need to do?*

––––––––––

It was an hour before the Sealy-Bellville brawl, and the stands were filling up fast. Sealy's record stood at 6-3, and to make the Class 3A playoffs, the Tigers needed to win the game by at least nine points. It had been a roller-coaster season for Sealy and for Seals-Jones, who began the year scoring five touchdowns in a 62–6 win over Houston Milby before suffering a major setback one week later against Houston's powerful St. Pius X, in a game nationally televised on ESPNU.

The special Thursday night telecast had opened with ESPN analyst Tom Luginbill singing the praises of Seals-Jones and with Sumlin making a dramatic entrance via helicopter onto St. Pius X's Parsley Field. A graphic listed Seals-Jones's top choices: Texas, A&M, LSU, Baylor, Oklahoma and TCU, with Oregon and USC in the mix. But Luginbill said he believed Seals-Jones was still "75 percent" committed to Texas. The truth was nobody knew. Not even the kid behind center, who on his very first carry glided for nine yards and moments later, on a QB draw, hit a crease and sped seventy-one yards for a 7–0 lead.

By late in the third quarter Seals-Jones had accounted for 213 yards rushing on just twelve carries. He had run for two more touchdowns (sixty-one and four yards). Still, the Tigers trailed the Panthers 31–21 when Seals-Jones, making a tackle from his safety position at the end of a St. Pius running back's thirty-one-yard gain, fell awkwardly. "I knew he was hurt when he came down," said Chester. The fall caused Ricky's left kneecap to pop out of its socket.

Strapped into an air cast, Seals-Jones was carted off the field on a stretcher and taken to a local hospital, where a doctor reset the knee. The family didn't get home until 5:00 a.m. Chester watched the replay over and over on local news and ESPN until he couldn't stand it anymore. But a new day brought encouraging news: no structural damage to the knee and a recovery time of three to four weeks.

Ricky was "freaked out" by the injury, but fortunately for him his cousin Eric came to town the following week. Dickerson helped calm Ricky down. He told him the injury had come at the best possible time, early in the season. "Don't go back until you're well, all the way right," he said. "If they want you, they know what you can do. High school doesn't matter."

Sure enough, the phone never stopped ringing, and texts kept flying in at all hours of the day and night. Ricky received so many scholarship offers that it was hard to keep track. Florida State one day, Baylor the next. Texas was still after Ricky, and according to Chester, Longhorns' assistant coach Oscar Giles pushed too hard during a phone conversation.

GILES: Well, Ricky made any kind of decision yet?
CHESTER: Decision on what?
GILES: He made any kind of decision on what he's going to do?
CHESTER: Man, we're just trying to get Ricky well.

At this point Chester said another assistant coach came on the line with an ultimatum: if Ricky doesn't commit, Texas is going to stop recruiting him.

To which Chester said he replied: "Well, you gotta do what you gotta do. We gotta do what we gotta do." Then he hung up the phone.

Two days later OrangeBloods.com, a UT fan Web site, reported the team was no longer recruiting Seals-Jones.

"Boy, that deal there, we don't know what happened," Chester said. He said Giles tried to contact him again through Ricky's high school coach and also tried reaching out to Ricky directly. But Chester Jones is a proud man. He told his son not to return any calls from anyone at Texas. In Chester's mind the Longhorns had gone all in at the wrong time with a bad hand. They were out of the game.

———

On Senior Night at Sealy High, the cheers rang out loudest when Seals-Jones walked onto the field arm in arm with his mom and dad.

A few minutes later, sitting with other family members and friends near the twenty-five-yard line behind the Sealy bench, Chester was asked if he was nervous.

"Little bit," he said.

On paper Bellville was no pushover, although in the first drive the Brahmas offered little in the way of resistance. The Tigers took less than three minutes to open up a 7–0 lead with Ricky switching between wide receiver and quarterback, content, it seemed, to act as a decoy or to hand off to the hard-charging running back Kris Brown.

The next possession gave a glimpse of No. 4's skill set. He easily hauled in an over-the-shoulder catch and raced fifty yards down the sideline. He followed that little act by nearly making a phenomenal one-handed catch of an overthrown alley-oop pass in the corner of the end zone. A short field goal gave the Tigers a 10–0 lead.

But with about four minutes left in the second quarter, frustration was building in the Jones section of the stands. Seals-Jones had seen only two more balls thrown in his direction. At the end of the half, Bellville was leading 13–10. Ricky's decoy role continued well into the second half, and Sealy fell behind 27–10. Perhaps Sealy's head coach, Jimmie Mitchell, was trying to protect his star's bum ankle, but Chester could barely contain himself.

"I don't know what y'all coaches are doing," he said out loud, not for the first time, to a chorus of agreement.

With Bellville driving for a put-away score, Seals-Jones picked off a pass at his own ten and electrified the crowd with a weaving runback to midfield. He did so with the gliding stride of Dickerson, the effortless shift into a third and fourth gear. It seemed to jolt his coaches into action. Seals-Jones was now where he should have been all night, in the shotgun, behind center, giving the defense fits. But there was only 6:54 left to play. Seals-Jones had been handed the near-hopeless task of trying to pull this game—and the season—out of the fire.

It took less than thirty seconds for him to produce another highlight: a shifting, dodging scramble leading to a twenty-yard strike into the end zone. The score was now 27–17.

"They can't tackle him!" yelled Chester. "Been waiting for them to do this all night!"

The Tiger crowd was in an uproar—the rivalry *on*—when Sealy recovered the onside kick. With 5:50 to go, it was fourth and ten from the Bellville twenty-nine, the game on the line. Seals-Jones completed a pass to his best friend, Brown, a playmaker who dived headlong for a first down. The line judge rushed in and spotted the ball a half yard behind what looked to be Brown's forward progress.

"That's a *bad* spot, Ref!" yelled Chester. "That's a bad spot!

"*C'mon! Ref!*"

Bellville took over on downs, and by the time Sealy got the ball back, there were only about three minutes left. It was clear the ankle was a problem for Seals-Jones—he couldn't explode—but he gave no quarter. He scrambled for six, then twelve, then again from one side of the field to the other before firing a bullet that was caught at the ten-yard line. The clock ticked down. The final offensive play of Seals-Jones's high school career ended with an interception in the end zone.

When the game was over, Seals-Jones was the first Sealy player to cross the field and shake hands. It was the kind of unscripted act that speaks volumes about upbringing and character.

Several Tigers were in tears as they walked off the field embracing parents and friends. Later, outside the locker room, his own eyes puffy and rimmed in red, Seals-Jones whispered to his dad, "We could have won, we could have won."

A visitor suggested that his quarterback could have done a better job getting the ball into his hands when Ricky was playing wide receiver. Here, many a high school star of Seals-Jones's stature would have agreed and called out a teammate, but the quiet seventeen-year-old again offered a class in class.

"He's just a sophomore," he said. "He'll get better."

Seals-Jones turned to find his mother, decked out in a sparkly white No. 4 jersey. They shared a long, emotional hug. All week she'd been tending to her son's injured ankle, favoring old-fashioned remedies like rubbing alcohol to reduce the grapefruit-sized swelling.

With the towel around his neck her boy wiped away more tears.

"It sucks—it hurts," he said. "It hurts to be a senior and lose against your rival. It just hurts."

———

Chester Jones always told his son if you put God first, family second and yourself third, you'll be fine. In virtually every conversation over the course of many months, he has never failed to point with pride to something his son has done.

"If he doesn't play another down, I'll be proud of him," Chester said more than once.

The way the system works, it was during that crazy summer of 2012 that Chester Jones found his own priorities—his belief in faith and family—put to a test.

Paying players under the table in college football goes back to the days of leather helmets. The only things that have really changed are the methods and the amounts. And forget agents or financial or marketing advisers for the moment. That's another dirty pile of laundry. Just stick with the big-time schools. Within that world the $100 postgame booster handshake still exists. But the delivery system for the serious money—the up-front down payment, always in cash—has changed over time, becoming far more discreet and difficult for NCAA investigators to trace, like those involving the use of ATM cards with individual PIN codes and predetermined monthly withdrawal limits set up by a booster. Offers are rarely written and often passed on to relatives by intermediaries to better provide "plausible deniability" to coaches with the most to lose.

The modern touchstone for the value The System had put on a top recruit was the $180,000 Cam Newton's father allegedly solicited from Mississippi State in November 2009 just prior to his son leading Blinn to the national junior college championship. The NCAA investigated and, over the course of fifty Newton-related interviews, found that while it was clear Newton's father had sought payments, no evidence existed that such payments were made. Or that his son was aware he was being shopped.

At the time, the mega-programs were generating in the neighborhood of $70 million per year—not the $80 million to $100 million they were in 2012. For that reason, it was difficult to extrapolate the Newton numbers into 2012 dollars.

Until now.

According to a source with direct knowledge of the conversation, in late June 2012, Chester Jones said "people" representing a perennial top twenty program had approached him with an offer:

- $300,000 in cash
- use of a luxury suite during the football season
- eight season tickets
- $1,000 a month for Ricky and $500 a month for the family

"He was trying to process it, to be honest with you," the source said. "He was in conflict. Not about taking the money. Conflict from the standpoint of disbelief over the offer."

In the living room of the family home the offer was repeated back to Chester Jones. A digital tape recorder was running. The specific school was named.

"Nah, they didn't offer nothing to Ricky," Jones said. "No, never. They never offered us a dime. It never did get to that . . .

"We don't want to hurt Ricky. We do something wrong . . . sooner or later you got to pay for it. I don't want to do anything to hurt Ricky like that Cam Newton deal. That's the thing—it ain't about me, it ain't about Buffy. It's about Ricky. I don't want to hurt Ricky."

The next morning Jones sat down to breakfast at Tony's diner. Inside the front door a veteran from the local VFW Post 5601 was pinning red poppies on the collar of those kind enough to slip a dollar or two into his cookie jar.

Chester Jones said he finally got to bed about 1:30 in the morning after sharing cake with some of the reporters from recruiting Web sites he'd come to know and like and sitting up talking with Buffy.

"I must have got a hundred phone calls last night," he said above the breakfast clatter.

The subject of the alleged offer of money, tickets and use of a luxury suite if his son would commit to a certain school was raised once again. The tape recorder was on the table.

"Man, we ain't ever talked to [the school] about nothing like that," he repeated once more. "They never did go at us like that. I had other schools tell you that stuff, other schools just came up and said, 'What will it take?' What kind of number would it take for Ricky to change his mind when he had committed to Texas?

"I'm not the one. Somebody else would always talk. I did not want to meet the people. [People] come back and tell me what they said. Some of the other coaches, AAU [basketball] coaches that I knew, they would talk to the guys, 'cause Ricky played basketball for them, and the college coaches would get to them guys, and they'd come back and tell me, you know, them guys, they want Ricky.

"They'd catch me sitting at a game [and say], 'I got to holler at you, Jones. That boy of yours, man, a lot of these coaches, man, they want that boy, and they are willing to do whatever.'"

What is the definition of "whatever"? Was the number accurate? Three hundred thousand dollars?

It was at that point Chester Jones opened a window into just how valuable some very special high school football players are to multimillion-dollar football programs dependent on their talent.

"Oh, it was higher than that," he said of the $300,000 figure. "It was a lot higher than that. Some of the guys, I know, one said"—he names a school in the ACC, another in the SEC—"they'll double whatever someone else offers. Six hundred. Seven hundred. You know, Ricky wasn't going to go to [that SEC school], so why would I get into that? I used to laugh, and they said, 'You're playing around and we're serious.'"

Jones was reminded of the obvious: $600,000 or $700,000 is a boatload of money.

"Man, those people don't care," he replied. "You know, where if some-one offers you seven, one guy said we'll offer double whatever they offer you to change [your] mind. That kind of stuff."

It was put to Jones that what it boiled down to was this: Did he want to sell his son to the highest bidder?

"No, I don't want that," he said. "The thing about it, you've still got to look yourself in the mirror and see yourself. And say why? I mean, we're doing okay. We're not rich. But we're doing okay. And, ah, you know, my dad always told me an honest dollar is better than a fast dollar.

"What a lot of people don't understand is it's not up to me. I know Ricky. When he goes somewhere to play football, that's why he's going to do it. You know what I told him? 'You already got $200,000—they gave that to you. In a scholarship.'"

A month later, on the day before Christmas, Chester Jones—a man of faith and family before all else—would offer one final reason as to why he said no.

"God will punish me, punish me through Ricky. He will not bless Ricky for our faults," he said. "I know what the consequences were going to be."

———

With the football season now over, Chester could see the pressure building on his son, taking a toll. Ricky had been playing it cool and cagey up to that point—wearing gloves that were maroon, an A&M color, for his final two high school games and a purple shirt and tie (a nod to LSU) when he accepted his invitation to the Army All-American Bowl in San Antonio. Quietly, Chester did some fishing, but Ricky wasn't biting.

"I ask him sometimes, 'Ricky, what do you think? LSU or A&M?'" Chester said in November 2012. "He told me, 'Dad, [if] I tell you, the whole world is going to know.'"

Though Ricky had yet to make official visits to A&M and LSU, his unofficial visits had underscored how much each school coveted him. Students at the LSU–'Bama game in Baton Rouge suddenly chanted "R-S-J! R-S-J!" when Ricky walked by on the field before the game, play-fully hauling him into the stands for some serious Death Valley love. The reception was even wilder at A&M. In the locker room following the dis-mantling of Missouri, half a dozen A&M players came up to Seals-Jones and said they wanted to show him around College Station (not surpris-ingly, Buffy put the kibosh on that, telling them, "Oh no, not this time"). Then quarterback Johnny Manziel and Seals-Jones huddled alone for a few minutes. Johnny let Ricky know just how much he looked forward to throwing to him the following season. "I saw your highlights; I know what you can do," said Manziel. "You're a big target, and when I'm moving, I see you out there, I'm throwing the ball to you." They promised to stay in touch.

In early December, Seals-Jones told his dad he wanted to change his cell phone number; the calls and texts never seemed to stop. Florida, Nebraska, Missouri and LSU were pushing right to the end. Two LSU assistants made two in-home visits, and A&M's recruiting coordinator, Clarence McKinney, visited as well, strengthening the bond he'd built with the family, particularly Buffy. By the first Thursday of the last month of 2012, Ricky had had it. He called his father on the phone and told him he was ready to commit. On Sunday night he finally told him where.

"My mind's made, Dad," he said of his decision. "That's what I want to do."

On Friday of that same week Manziel sat surrounded by cameras and microphones in the O'Neill Room on the fourth floor of the Marriott Marquis in New York City. The redshirt freshman was on the verge of winning the Heisman Trophy thanks, in large part, to his Houdini-like performance in the Aggies' upset of then–No. 1 Alabama in Tuscaloosa. The following night at the Downtown Athletic Club he would accept the award. On Monday morning, at exactly 9:45, Seals-Jones would call Kevin Sumlin at A&M. The phone rang four times before Sumlin picked up.

"Coach, it's Ricky. I'm calling to let you know I'm going to be an Aggie next year."

"That's good," answered Sumlin. "Like I told you, you're going to be something special. Next year maybe you and me will be going to New York."

At 10:00 a.m. in the Tiger Room at Sealy High, Seals-Jones sat down before the cameras and reporters and pulled an A&M cap out of his jacket and onto his head, verbally committing to the Aggies. On February 6, 2013, he made it official, signing a National Letter of Intent.

For better or worse the Ricky Seals-Jones sweepstakes was finally over.

21 THE COACH

Part III, "The starting lineup is voluntary, too"

Coaching changes most often occur in December, right after the regular season ends and just as the recruiting season hits its white-hot period leading up to National Signing Day in early February. New coaches must hire a staff and instantly go on the road in an effort to shore up commitments from high school seniors. The schedule leaves no time for things like finding a place to live, obtaining a new driver's license or registering vehicles. Those details inevitably fall to a coach's wife.

Mike and Sharon Leach arrived with their two teenage children in Pullman in December 2011. They spent their first two months living out of a Holiday Inn. After Sharon got the kids enrolled in new schools, she went house hunting. Mike immediately left town with his new staff in search of new recruits. His most important target was Tyler Bruggman, a six-foot-two pro-style quarterback at Brophy College Prep high school in Phoenix. The top recruiting services all listed Bruggman as a four-star quarterback, as opposed to a five-star. But Leach didn't pay much attention to the ratings services, especially when it came to quarterbacks. That position, more than any other, influenced the success or failure of a team. So Leach spent more time evaluating high school quarterbacks than anything else, studying them on paper and on film. There was no one he wanted more than Bruggman.

But other schools wanted him too. He had offers from plenty of programs that traditionally throw the ball a lot—Houston, BYU, Purdue and Washington among them. A dozen schools in all had offered. Before Leach arrived at WSU, Bruggman had narrowed his choices down to Arizona State, Michigan State and Arkansas. Then his high school coach got a call from Leach in late December. That was enough to change Bruggman's entire approach.

"I had watched Coach Leach at Tech," Bruggman said. "I knew he was a great coach, especially for quarterbacks. The opportunity to play for him would be an honor."

Suddenly Washington State was in the running for Bruggman's services.

———

On February 9, 2012, Leach had a couple of hours before a team workout, so Sharon drove him to a restaurant for dinner. It was a rare moment alone. But during the drive, Leach spent most of his time talking by phone with teenage boys. Every college football wife comes to realize that her husband will spend far more time talking to teenage boys than to her. It's called recruiting, and it never stops.

Leach's cell phone buzzed the minute he sat in the passenger's seat. It was an offensive lineman, a kid who had yet to commit to WSU.

"I think you ought to come here for the same reason I came here," Leach told him. "We are going to lead the nation in passing, in offense. The most cherished skill a lineman does is pass protect."

The kid asked about facilities.

"We are building a brand-new football complex," Leach said. "Our weight room will be thirteen thousand square feet. What's really exciting here is they have a tradition of going to the Rose Bowl. We have a chance to get this thing back on track. As a head coach I've been to ten straight bowl games, and I plan on going to one this year, too. We need guys like you to help us usher that in. You are the type of guy we need to build a future with around here."

By the time Leach finished his fourth call, Sharon had pulled up to an out-of-the-way Mexican restaurant. They found a quiet table in the back. The discussion quickly turned to the kids, the new house, the new car, insurance and the movers. He ate while she updated him. She ate while he asked follow-up questions. Then they paid the bill. On the way out, the owner stopped Mike. "Good luck, Coach," he said.

"Thank you."

"If there is ever anything I can do for you, let me know," the owner said.

"I appreciate that. Do you guys cater?"

While they chatted, three cute college-age girls entered the restaurant. They immediately recognized Leach and approached. "Can we get a photo with you?" one of them asked.

As Leach posed, his wife stood off in the distance, unnoticed. "His time is not his own," she said. "I have to share him with everybody."

Moments later they were back in the car, and he was back on his cell phone, returning a missed call that had come in during dinner.

"Yeah, this is Mike Leach."

The kid on the other end started talking fast.

"Well, I'm not sure who I'm calling," Leach interrupted. "Somebody called me from this number. Who's this?"

It was a high school senior from Los Angeles. He hoped to walk on the team at WSU. He had watched the *60 Minutes* segment on Leach at Texas Tech. "I'd like to play for you," the kid said.

"You say you are from Compton?" Leach said.

"Yes," the kid said.

"I'm going to have you talk to Dave Emerick," Leach said. "I can't say for sure we'll have a spot for you. I can't say we won't either. We might."

Sharon dropped off Mike at his office. He immediately went on Rivals .com to look up the kid who had just called him. Then he texted a link of the kid's scouting profile to his director of football operations, Dave Emerick, along with a message: "Research this kid."

Moments later, assistant coach Jim Mastro entered the office. The stout forty-six-year-old running backs coach had been at UCLA the previous season. Before that he had spent eleven seasons at Nevada. When Mastro was a college running back at Cal Poly in 1987, Leach was one of his coaches. He jumped at the chance to join Leach's staff at WSU.

Mastro was prepping for that night's team workout, something Leach called Midnight Maneuvers—an intense physical-conditioning session held from 10:00 p.m. to midnight. NCAA rules prohibit official workouts for football players during the eight-week period from January 1 through the start of spring practice in late February. Every BCS program gets around this rule by holding what are called "voluntary" workouts. What made Leach's approach unusual was the timing of these so-called voluntary sessions—late at night.

"Everywhere I've ever coached," Mastro said, "no one does this. People do conditioning at six in the morning. Leach's philosophy is that no one is ever in the fourth quarter of a game at six in the morning. The fourth quarter happens late at night."

————

At five minutes to ten, Leach pulled a new Nike sweatshirt over his head and entered the indoor practice facility. A dozen stations were set up— one with tiny orange cones; one with hula hoops; one with medicine balls; and another with two-by-fours. Roughly 125 players wearing shorts and

T-shirts were at the center of the field house, stretching. Scaffolding had been erected at the far end of the facility. Fifty feet up, Nick Galbraith, a skinny nineteen-year-old accounting major, looked down on the players. Weeks earlier one of Leach's graduate assistants had approached Galbraith on campus and asked him if he had any good music. Galbraith, an aspiring college football coach, said he did. So Leach hired him to perform a very important function—select hip music to motivate football players to go all out during Midnight Maneuvers sessions.

Galbraith connected his iPod to huge speakers positioned throughout the facility. He had his playlist cued up. All he needed was for Leach to give him the signal.

At precisely 10:00 p.m., Leach blew his whistle. "Everybody, up."

Players and coaches surrounded him at center field.

"We're gonna have the music on tonight," Leach said. "That doesn't mean you can dick off. But you need to enjoy what you are doing to be really good at it. You should thrive on the energy. Nothing better than being on the road and sticking it up the other guy's ass."

An assistant looked up at Galbraith and nodded. Angus Young's guitar solo at the start of AC/DC's "Thunderstruck" began pulsing through the field house as the team broke the huddle and ran to their stations.

I was caught
In the middle of a railroad track (Thunder).
I looked around
And I knew there was no turning back (Thunder).

"Let's go!" a coach shouted. A group of defensive linemen got on all fours, their hands on two-by-fours. On the whistle, they pushed the boards along the AstroTurf at top speed from one end of the station to the other, then back again. Nearby, linebackers sprinted in and out of cones while their position coach shouted at them to go faster. Offensive linemen dropped for push-ups, bounced up for jumping jacks, dropped back down for rolls. The place had the look and feel of boot camp at West Point with one exception: deafening music.

No one noticed when two campus police officers entered the facility and approached an assistant coach closest to the exit. The music was so loud that it violated a campus noise ordinance. The assistant coach motioned to Galbraith to take the volume down a couple decibels. He did, but barely. By then players were sweating to 50 Cent.

Meanwhile, Leach moved from station to station with a clipboard, grading players on effort: great, average, below average. He wrote "great" next to offensive lineman John Fullington, a six-foot-five, three-hundred-pound junior who was running wind sprints. "He's the hardest-working guy in the bunch," Leach said as Fullington burst across the finish line, cursing himself for not being faster.

"I love guys like that," Leach said. "He's never satisfied."

After all the players had been through every station, they huddled at the center of the field house, hands on their knees, heads down, gasping for air. Most of them were shirtless by then, sweat beads running over the tattoos that colored their biceps. Leach congratulated them on their effort.

"These workouts are voluntary," Leach said. "But here's the thing. The starting lineup is voluntary, too. If you think you are going to dick off and do some half-ass bullshit, the starting lineup is voluntary, too."

Players returned his gaze with a hard stare. None of them had ever participated in team workouts so intense, so late at night. But there were more new things in the works.

"Now, we're going to get some boxing equipment in here," Leach continued.

Players looked at each other with confused expressions.

"We want you to start learning to use your hands and improve your hand speed," Leach said. "You know why dinosaurs have small hands?"

A few guys turned their heads from side to side. Coaches smirked.

"Because they never used them," Leach said. "So they got real small and shriveled up."

Everyone laughed.

"We don't want that to happen to any of you," Leach said. "I want you using your hands and being violent with your hands. So we're bringing in boxing gear."

Players nodded in approval.

"Now, some of you are lazy," Leach continued. "Let's face it. If we had a hundred nuns here, a few of them would be lazy. So if in the back of your mind you know you're lazy and you're thinking you don't want to do the conditioning, also what you need to have in your mind is that if you don't do the conditioning, you're fucking him." He pointed to a player.

"And you're fucking him," he said, pointing to another player. "And him and him and him and me."

The players stopped laughing.

"Any questions?" Leach said.

There were none.

Midnight Maneuvers were over. At 11:45 p.m. the players left the field house. Lineman John Fullington stayed behind to remove the athletic wrap from his ankles and wrists. "I love the atmosphere," he said. "I love Coach Leach's style."

Leach returned to his office and studied film until 1:00 a.m.

———

The following morning, one of Leach's graduate assistants picked him up at 9:45 and took him by Safeway for his morning fix—a tall cup of coffee. They were on campus by 10:15. The first item on the schedule was a meeting with Chris Cook, the director of academic support. Leach and his entire staff took their seats around a giant conference table in the football office. Cook passed out copies of his "Football Eligibility Report," a breakdown of every football player's academic profile. Players of concern were highlighted.

Leafing through pages, coaches sipped coffee while Cook walked them through steps being taken to keep players at a 2.0 GPA—increased study hall sessions, increased tutoring sessions and enhanced monitoring protocols. The report suggested very few academic problems. GPAs were up, and absences were down.

"If a guy misses a class or a tutoring session, we want to hammer him that day," Leach said. "If we are pretty punitive on the front end, it will help us."

Cook nodded. "We understand that you want to amp up the checking system," he said.

"The other thing is if a player is below a 2.0, he is moving back in the dorm," Leach said. "You need to let the players know."

The list of players with academic problems was short, raising doubts among the coaches. "If you don't see a player on the list, you don't need to be concerned," Cook said.

Skeptical, Leach looked up at Cook. "Either these guys are the greatest choir class ever—and if they are, we need to make them meaner—or they are missing more classes and we're not catching it," he said.

Cook reported an incident involving a player who had been chewing tobacco in study hall. When the study hall monitor told him to stop, the player refused, arguing that if he had to be there for two hours, he was going to do what he wanted.

"In terms of squeezing somebody's balls," Leach said, "I don't care how many snaps he took or if he's an all-American. I want to make sure we are all on the same page philosophically."

"These guys need to know that academics trumps 7-on-7," another coach added.

At 11:20 the academic support meeting ended, and Leach went into a battery of breakout sessions with individual position coaches. By 3:00 p.m., the five quarterbacks showed up for a film session. They took their seats around a conference table. Leach put in the instructional video for quarterbacks that he had made at Kentucky. It featured NFL quarterback Tim Couch teaching techniques. The film had barely begun when Leach hit pause, stood up and illustrated the precise position he wanted his quarterbacks in when throwing a pass.

"Get your hips around so you are aimed at the target," Leach said.

He twisted his hips, showing what he meant.

The next sequence featured Couch doing a two-step drop and throwing quick strikes. Leach repeatedly hit rewind to show the same steps. "The ball needs to make it from the center's ass to the receiver's hands as fast as possible," Leach told them. "You are just the middleman."

The session lasted an hour. Leach had been on the job for close to two months. He still had no idea who his starting quarterback would be in the fall.

———

Construction workers in hard hats and orange vests stood atop scaffolding, directing a crane operator as he set a giant steel girder between two crossbeams. Sparks flew as ironworkers welded the girder in place. On the ground below, the drums on cement trucks churned, and carpenters shored up forms designed to hold new concrete. The start of the 2012 football season was less than five months away, and the push was on to complete the $80 million stadium expansion in time.

Next door, the sound of cleats click-clacking on pavement echoed off the athletics building as football players exited the locker room and trotted toward the practice field. It was 2:15 on a Tuesday afternoon in early April. Sunlight blanketed the brand-new artificial turf. A few linemen were already on the blocking dummies. The quarterbacks were tossing lightly on the side.

Under NCAA rules, football programs are permitted to hold formal practices in the spring. Leach stepped onto the field wearing a black sweatshirt, red baseball cap, sunglasses, khaki shorts and running shoes. He stopped to watch the receivers, a young, unproven group. The one exception was Marquess Wilson, a six-foot-four, 185-pound junior receiver. Wilson was a genuine NFL prospect. He was only the second wide receiver in WSU history to have multiple thousand-yard seasons. But he was the only one to accomplish that in his freshman and sophomore seasons.

One look at Wilson and it was obvious that he was head and shoulders above the rest. He was bigger and faster, with Velcro hands and a nose for the end zone. He could flat out elevate and snatch just about anything thrown in his vicinity.

"Pump the arms," Leach shouted at Wilson as he ran a route. "Pump the arms. It gives the illusion of speed. As you slow down, the defense thinks you are speeding up. It's an optical illusion. It works every time."

Wilson nodded.

"Marquess can be really good," Leach said, one of his assistants standing beside him. "The kid has real potential. He just needs to be tougher. He's got to see the physical part of things."

As far as Leach was concerned, the entire roster needed to increase its toughness. Thirty minutes into practice he blew his whistle. "Bull in the ring," he shouted. "Bull in the ring."

The drill is as old as the game itself and a favorite among players at top programs throughout the country. Hooting and hollering, players formed a circle in the center of the field. Defensive line coach Joe Salave'a, a six-foot-three, 350-pound Polynesian wearing shorts and his trademark muscle shirt, took charge of the drill. A ten-year NFL veteran, Salave'a is an intimidating hulk of a man with no neck; his arms rival the size of some players' thighs. He stepped to the center of the ring, and Leach called the names of two players: receiver Marquess Wilson and a linebacker. They stepped into the ring and faced each other. On the whistle, they plowed into each other at full torque.

"Go right through that mothafucka," Salave'a thundered. "Right through the bitch."

After the initial collision, the linebacker drove Wilson to the turf.

"It ain't a fuckin' church," Salave'a shouted. "Get your asses up. Let's go."

Leach called off the next two names. A running back and a defensive player stepped into the ring. On the whistle their helmets collided, and the shorter running back drove his opponent backward.

"Hell, yeah," Salave'a yelled. "Hell, yeah."

Both players pumped their legs, grunting and hammering away at each other, as the rest of the team shouted at them.

"Let's go mothafucka," Salave'a yelled, pounding his hands together. "Go. Get him! Run through the mothafucka."

The players forming the ring fed off the energy, shouting and egging each other on.

After fifteen minutes, Leach blew the whistle—time for the next drill.

———

Tyler Bruggman had notified Leach that he planned to attend a couple days of spring practice in Pullman. He was leaning heavily toward committing to WSU. But he wanted a firsthand look at Leach's methods. His parents, intimately involved in their son's recruiting process, flew up with him from Phoenix. "Quarterbacks have to commit early," Bruggman said. "I wanted to see Washington State before I made my decision."

Leach invited him to sit in on a quarterbacks meeting. Bruggman stood in the back of the conference room while Leach and the quarterbacks huddled around a conference table, going over film from the previous day's practice. The first sequence was a series of plays in the red zone.

"Here's one thing," Leach said, freezing the video. "When we get down here and start moving the ball, there can't be this hoping that we're gonna score. It has to be *Now we're gonna score.* And it has to start with you guys. You are the ones doing the talking. It can't be *Maybe we're going to score.* No. We're scoring!"

He fast-forwarded to the next play. Two receivers ran seven-yard patterns, side by side, forcing an outside linebacker to cover both players. But neither receiver bothered blocking the backer. "If we want this piece of real estate," Leach said, highlighting the outside linebacker, "and we pay double the value"—he highlighted the two receivers in the area—"somebody has to block."

Leach's passing game hinges on creating open passing lanes, a point he kept stressing to his quarterbacks. "The most important thing is space," Leach said. "Space and personnel. You have to utilize your personnel and figure out where you have space. The defense may try and fill the space. But if you have a combination of routes and there is integrity to the routes, when they try to fill up one space, they will give up another space. So you want routes that attack a variety of spaces—high, low, right, left. As you go through the priorities of the play, it will take you to the right route."

The quarterbacks nodded. One of them asked to see the previous play one more time.

Leach went through a few more sequences until coming to a play where two receivers in the middle of the field hadn't bothered to block because the play was going away from them. "Are you shittin' me?" Leach said, freezing the video on a safety running across the middle of the field. "You can knock the hell out of this guy," he continued. "Wouldn't it be kind of nice to find out what their No. 2 safety is like? Let's find out if he's any good."

The quarterbacks smiled.

On the next sequence, Leach froze the film on a simple eight-yard crossing pattern that left one receiver wide open. "There's more space than it's possible for them to cover," he said.

The quarterbacks pointed at the screen, focusing on the wide-open lane.

"Just make routine plays," Leach said. "Not super plays. Routine plays. Besides the eight yards we get, now they are unraveled in terms of the pass rush lanes. It all comes unraveled."

By the end of the film session it was easy to see the fatigue factor setting in among many of the players. "That's why we have highly conditioned athletes as opposed to the Swedish bikini team," Leach said.

The guys laughed. Leach shut off the film.

Bruggman had never seen a film session like that. He wished he could put on pads and play for Leach right away. "I always knew he was a great coach," Bruggman said. "But I was surprised at how funny he was. I didn't realize what his personality was like. He is very funny."

Leach gave the quarterbacks a parting story.

"When I was in law school, I hated the Dodgers," Leach told them. "But I lived fifteen minutes from Dodger Stadium and I like baseball. So I went and watched them and rooted for the other team. That's when the Dodgers were rolling and going deep into the playoffs and winning the World Series. There was game after game that the Dodgers won that they should not have won. But they won because they were the Dodgers and good things happened at the end of the game. They just expected to win. They had this whole expectation thing. That's what has to happen with us. One of the quickest places for our team to get that way is for you to talk to them as a quarterback. 'We're gonna win this.'"

After the visit Bruggman talked to his parents. He told them he was leaning heavily toward WSU. They thought that was wise.

22 CRIME AND PUNISHMENT

The SEC leads the nation

Samuel Jurgens had a sunny disposition. The twenty-year-old history major loved being a student at Alabama. He especially revered 'Bama football. A month after the Crimson Tide won its third national title in four years by manhandling Notre Dame, Jurgens left a friend's dorm and headed toward home on the other end of the Tuscaloosa campus. It was just past midnight on February 11, 2013. Walking swiftly, Jurgens had on headphones and a backpack over his jacket when he came upon an African-American man wearing a red beanie and a navy-blue jacket. As Jurgens passed him on the sidewalk, he noticed the guy was saying something. He quickly removed his headphones.

"Hey, do you have a lighter?" the man asked.

"I don't smoke. I'm sorry." Jurgens put his headphones back on and resumed walking. After a few more strides, out of the corner of his eye he saw a second man approaching from an adjacent parking lot. He was big and burly and was wearing a raincoat and jeans. Again, Jurgens removed his headphones.

"Do you have a lighter?" the larger man asked.

Jurgens thought the situation was odd. "Sorry," he said. "I don't smoke."

He put his headphones back on and took a few more steps, unaware that a third man had come up behind him. The next thing Jurgens knew he was on the ground, fading in and out of consciousness, unsure how long he'd been there. His lip was split open. His left eye was swollen shut, and the entire left side of his face was numb, bruised and enlarged. He'd been struck with such force that he was knocked unconscious. Then he was kicked in the back and chest. But he had also sustained a concussion and had no memory of the attack when he came to on the sidewalk. All he knew was that his jacket and headphones were drenched in blood. The men were gone. So were his glasses and his backpack containing his Apple MacBook Pro.

Dazed and struggling to see, Jurgens used his cell phone to call his friend. "Something bad has happened to me," he told him.

Moments later, his friend found him and led him back inside the dorm. The police were called, and Jurgens, still confused and disoriented, was taken to the ER.

An hour later, another Alabama student—Caleb Paul, a civil and construction engineering major—encountered the same trio along Seventh Avenue, near the UA Energy, Mineral and Material Science Research Building. Two of the men looked on from a dark-colored SUV while one of them approached Paul and asked him for a light. Then Paul was punched in the head and face and knocked to the ground before his wallet was stolen.

The University of Alabama police promptly issued an advisory reporting two robberies. Physical descriptions of the suspects were posted on the campus police Web site.

By 5:00 on Monday, Sam Jurgens had finally been released from the hospital. His parents had driven from Birmingham to retrieve him. They took him back home to rest and recover. But hours after they arrived back in Birmingham, Jurgens received a call from the University of Alabama police. They informed him that the suspects were in custody and would be held overnight in the local jail. The police wanted Jurgens to return to Tuscaloosa right away to sign an affidavit. Jurgens's parents wanted him to spend a few days in bed before traveling.

"Is this that big of a priority?" Jurgens asked the police.

"Normally, no. But in this case, yes," an officer told him. "This is a high-priority case."

Jurgens asked if the assailants were on the FBI Most Wanted list or something of that nature.

"No," an officer told him. "They are football players."

The three men who had attacked Jurgens and Paul the previous night were on Alabama's championship team:

D. J. Pettway, twenty, a six-foot-three, 270-pound redshirt freshman
Tyler Hayes, eighteen, a six-foot-two, 210-pound linebacker
Eddie Williams, twenty, a six-foot-three, 200-pound safety

All three were booked on two counts of robbery and jailed.

Williams, it turned out, was already in trouble. The day before the robberies he had gotten into a dispute with a BP gas attendant, who reported that Williams had become erratic and was "threatening that he had something that he had something in the trunk of his vehicle." The Tuscaloosa police later stopped Williams in a Honda Accord and frisked him. He had a gun on him and was charged with carrying a concealed weapon without a license and released on bond.

A fourth player, twenty-year-old running back Brent Calloway, had no role in the robberies. But he was charged for knowingly using a stolen debit card taken from Caleb Paul's wallet. Calloway had previously been arrested during his freshman year when police discovered marijuana stuffed in his sock after they had stopped him for driving without his lights. That case was disposed through a plea agreement.

———

Nick Saban was relaxing with his wife at their new beach home near Naples, Florida, when his phone rang. It was his director of football operations, Joe Pannunzio. Days earlier, Alabama's recruiting class had just been rated tops in the country. Saban was finally taking a moment to get away from football and exhale. But Pannunzio made it clear that this wasn't that moment. He briefed Saban on the situation back in Tuscaloosa.

The arrests called for a quick response. Saban decided to start by indefinitely suspending all four players until he had more information.

By morning all four players had been released on bail. Later that day, Saban issued a prepared statement. "Their actions do not reflect the spirit and character that we want our organization to reflect," he said. "It's obviously very disappointing and unacceptable what happened."

Meanwhile, Hayes and Williams promptly confessed to the robberies, and Calloway confessed to knowingly using a stolen debit card.

But back in Naples, Saban was fuming. He had little patience for players who failed to appreciate the privilege of playing college football at Alabama and the responsibility that it entails. Lawlessness went against everything he tried to instill in his team. Worse, this wasn't the first time he had faced this issue at Alabama. When he took over the program in 2007, the team had a rash of off-the-field problems and disciplinary issues. In his first fourteen months on the job, eight players were arrested, including five for disorderly conduct. A total of thirty games were missed due to player suspensions.

Since that rocky period, Saban's team had gone nearly five years without any serious off-the-field issues. But suddenly he faced the situation again. Only this time Alabama was the reigning national champion, making the spotlight much brighter. After a brief respite in Naples, he returned to Tuscaloosa and spoke to the players, their parents and members of the university about the situation. "People were asking me, 'What are you going to do to help these guys?'" Saban said. "Others were looking at me and saying, 'What are you going to do to punish these guys?'"

Ultimately, Saban called a team meeting and conveyed a direct message. "I told my team, I can't help you when you do something criminal," Saban said.

After a two-week internal review by the university's judicial affairs committee, the four players had their scholarships revoked, and Saban permanently removed them from the team. At that point, the court process was just getting started, and none of the players had been convicted of anything. But as far as Saban was concerned, they had violated team rules, and that was sufficient to remove them from the program.

"I've had players get out of what they did," Saban said. "But I know they did it, and I still kicked them off the team. With me, it's not whether you're guilty or not guilty."

While unfortunate, the robberies provided an opportunity for Saban to send an important message to his team. "No matter how pretty the garden," Saban said, "pruning is part of making things healthier. Sometimes you have to have problems to make people understand."

But Sam Jurgens and his family might not ever understand. The Jurgenses had family roots in Tuscaloosa stretching back five generations to 1840. Their ties to the university were deep. And Sam and his father had bonded by rooting for Alabama football. "Football in the South is like a civil religion," Jurgens said. "A lot of people are very passionate about it and value it in ways not much different than religious congregations."

The beating Jurgens took at the hands of Alabama football players certainly caused him to reconsider how much of an Alabama football fan he'd be in the future. But more troubling was the fact that he never heard one word of apology or concern from anyone associated with the program. "The university has been very supportive and reimbursed me for all of my losses and expenses," Jurgens said. "But members of the football team sent me to the hospital and robbed me. But I've had no one from the football team—not a coach or anything—approach me."

In the second week of April 2013—two months after the incident—Jurgens approached Alabama's dean of student affairs and expressed a desire to speak to Coach Saban about his ordeal. "I still identify myself as an Alabama football fan," Jurgens said. "I had so much fun with my father with it over the years. But no one should have to go through what I went through."

Despite his ordeal, Jurgens said the athletic department informed him that no one from the football coaching staff would meet with him.

The arrests of four Alabama players after the 2012 season were indicative of a general problem that every BCS program confronts these days—student-athletes running afoul of the law. Research conducted for this book found that 197 players on BCS teams were arrested in 2012. That's an average of 16 arrests per month. The SEC had the most arrests with 42, followed by 37 in the Big 12. Arkansas and Missouri led the nation in player arrests; both programs saw 8 players arrested in 2012.

Fewer than 25 percent of the 197 players who ran afoul of the law in 2012 were kicked off their respective teams. But virtually every player who was arrested more than once was dismissed or suspended. There was only one exception—Florida State's star running back James Wilder Jr. Despite being arrested three times in 2012, he was not held out of any games. His first arrest occurred in February outside his girlfriend's apartment. Police were there to arrest her. But Wilder intervened and was charged with battery against a police officer—a felony. Florida State's head coach, Jimbo Fisher, indefinitely suspended him. But in early April, Wilder pleaded no contest to a misdemeanor—resisting an officer without violence. He was put on six months' probation and required to take anger management classes. The same day that Wilder entered his plea, Fisher reinstated him to the team, enabling him to play in the spring game.

"The punishment for misdemeanor offenses for student-athletes at Florida State rests with the head coach," said Rob Wilson, associate athletic director for communications at FSU. "However, no student-athlete can represent the university until any jail time related to a misdemeanor is completed. A felony offense means immediate suspension for any FSU student-athlete. So Mr. Wilder's punishment has been and is in the hands of the football coach at this time."

Over the summer, however, Wilder spent eleven days in jail after pleading no contest to violating his probation. His arrest was triggered when he registered a 0.01 blood-alcohol level while taking a court-mandated Breathalyzer test. Prosecutors had also accused him of failing to complete his anger management courses. Again, Wilder was indefinitely suspended from the team. But upon his release from jail he was reinstated to the team, clearing the way for him to play in all the team's games during the 2012 season. He rushed for eleven touchdowns. Then, after the Orange Bowl, he was arrested a third time—this time for failure to appear. In January 2013 he pleaded no contest to driving without a license.

———

Individual criminal acts by student-athletes are one thing. But the way institutions respond to allegations against student-athletes can sometimes be even more disturbing.

On August 31, 2010, Lizzy Seeberg, a nineteen-year-old freshman at St. Mary's College in Notre Dame, Indiana, went with a girlfriend to hang out with a couple guys they had met the previous night. Both men were Notre Dame students; one of them was a starter on the football team. The two couples ended up in the football player's dorm, where they had a couple beers. At one point, Seeberg was alone with the football player in his room. The following day she met with a rape counselor, a sexual assault nurse and the Notre Dame campus police and reported that while they were alone, the football player had torn her shirt off and sucked and groped her breasts before trying to forcibly remove her pants. In the midst of the encounter the player was distracted by a text message from his friend. The two of them had been texting back and forth throughout the evening, including during the brief interlude while Seeberg was in the football player's room. But after the latest text, the student-athlete backed off, and Seeberg was able to leave without further incident.

Two days after reporting all of this to the authorities, Seeberg received an ominous text message from the accused player's friend: "Don't do anything you would regret. Messing with notre dame football is a bad idea."

Scared, Seeberg immediately forwarded the text to the Notre Dame police. Under Indiana law, harassment is a crime when "a person who, with intent to harass, annoy, or alarm another person but with no intent of legitimate communication . . . uses a computer network or other form of communication."

On the morning of September 10, Seeberg met again with her counselor and expressed embarrassment over the sexual assault. She also reported feeling vulnerable and anxious over the prospect of pressing charges. After providing reassurances, the counselor nonetheless asked Seeberg to return to the office that afternoon for a follow-up session. But Seeberg never made it back. That afternoon she was found dead in her dorm room. She had taken a lethal dose of medication prescribed for depression and anxiety.

By that time, ten days had passed since the alleged assault, and Notre Dame police still had not talked to the accused player. Nor had the authorities requested the text messages between the student-athlete and his friend on the night in question. And no action had been taken over the threatening text message sent to Seeberg. Concerned about the quality and integrity of the investigation, her father, Tom Seeberg, wrote to Father Tom Doyle, Notre Dame's vice president for student affairs. Seeberg also met directly with Notre Dame police.

But his requests for a thorough, transparent investigation fell on deaf ears. Frustrated, Seeberg retained former U.S. attorney Zachary Fardon. A decorated Chicago prosecutor, Fardon conducted his own investigation. He e-mailed a letter to Father Doyle detailing evidence that Fardon felt Notre Dame had overlooked, such as communications between the student-athlete and his friend that suggested the sexual encounter with Seeberg was part of a premeditated plan.

Doyle, however, declined to read the letter.

"When I opened your attachment," Doyle wrote back, "I could see immediately that significant portions of your letter contained information about the case. When I recognized this I stopped reading."

Doyle also declined to forward the letter to Father John Jenkins, the president of Notre Dame. "Reading your letters could impair his objectivity as protector of process and potential court of appeal."

Fardon fired back: "Father, I respectfully suggest that concern over not wanting to know the specific facts so that you and Father Jenkins can remain objective is misplaced. It is past time for the University to show leadership here. And it is precisely because you are in decision making positions that you should have access to all of the facts."

In the end, no charges were filed. Notre Dame police forwarded the results of their investigation to the St. Joseph County prosecutor, Michael Dvorak, for review. He declined to file sexual battery charges, insisting that since Ms. Seeberg was no longer alive to testify, her police statement would be inadmissible as hearsay. "Only Ms. Seeberg and the student-athlete were present during the alleged battery," Dvorak said. "Conflicts exist between the witnesses' accounts of the events given to the police."

Dvorak also declined to prosecute the player's friend for harassment. "The content of the text messages sent does not rise to the level of a criminal act as defined by Indiana's Harassment statute," Dvorak said. "The student subjectively believed Ms. Seeberg's complaint was false and therefore he had a legitimate purpose for his text messages."

Devastated, the Seeberg family nonetheless appealed again to Notre Dame in hopes of having their daughter's complaint adjudicated through the university's internal judicial process. But they were told that they did not have standing to pursue a case. The accused player, meanwhile, played through the season. It got to the point where Tom Seeberg could not watch Notre Dame games on television.

"We just wanted a disciplinary proceeding," Seeberg said. "We wanted an investigation of the truth."

Meanwhile, when Notre Dame officials suspected that linebacker Manti Te'o might have been the victim of an online prank, the university hired private investigators and moved heaven and earth to get to the bottom of the so-called hoax.

———

The see-no-evil standard set in South Bend paled in comparison to the widespread institutional cover-up at Penn State. In June 2012, former Nittany Lions defensive coordinator Jerry Sandusky was convicted of forty-five counts of serial sexual abuse of ten young boys dating back to the late 1990s. He was sentenced to no less than thirty years in prison. But the most infuriating aspects of Sandusky's case were the actions—or, worse, inactions—taken by legendary Penn State coach Joe Paterno and top officials at the school to bury decades of abuse.

When news of the Sandusky scandal broke in November 2011, Paterno was viewed as a paragon of virtue across the sporting landscape, nothing less than the conscience of college football. The author of the so-called Grand Experiment, Paterno preached that a powerhouse football program could be built on the cornerstones of athletics and academics. He had a record of success to prove it. His teams maintained a 90 percent graduation rate while winning two national titles and racking up 409 wins, giving Paterno the most wins among Division I coaches. And during his forty-six years of coaching Penn State, the university had no major NCAA violations, undoubtedly another record.

But success begets power. At Penn State, Joe Pa wielded extraordinary power. For much of his reign Paterno proved a benevolent king: over the years he donated more than $4 million to the university and raised millions for scholarships and charity. A nine-hundred-pound, larger-than-life bronze statue was erected in his honor—a shrine to an "Educator, Coach and Humanitarian," as the words on the bronze base read. Beaver Stadium was repeatedly enlarged (by more than 60,000 seats to 106,000-plus) to hold the growing masses worshipping at the Church of Blue and White; an economic-medical-industrial complex grew as the school did, bigger and stronger, feeding a sense of power and secrecy around the praiseworthy coach and his team.

During an eight-month investigation commissioned by the historically weak-kneed Penn State Board of Trustees, a legal team headed by former FBI director Louis Freeh interviewed more than 430 people and reviewed 3.5 million pieces of electronic data and documents. Freeh's 270-plus-page report singled out the Penn State culture for permitting a "serial sexual predator" to operate at will on campus. Freeh cited what he called "the callous and shocking disregard" for the safety and welfare of Sandusky's child victims by the most senior leaders at Penn State, including Paterno.

For those inclined to believe top school officials were involved in a cover-up—a charge an independent investigation commissioned by the Paterno family claimed was just not true—the most damning evidence proved to be a critical series of internal e-mails from 1998 through 2001. The e-mails implicated PSU president Graham Spanier, senior vice president Gary Schultz and athletic director Tim Curley in what Freeh called "an active agreement to conceal" Sandusky's sexual abuse from the authorities, the board and the public.

Why?

"The brand of Penn State, including the university, including the reputation of coaches, including the ability to do fund-raising, it's got huge implications," said Freeh. "In other words, there are a lot of consequences that go with bad publicity."

The Sandusky sex abuse scandal resulted in the severest penalty ever issued by the NCAA: five years' probation, no postseason bowl games for four years, the loss of at least forty scholarships and a record $60 million fine.

———

Reports of college football players in trouble with the law are nothing new. As far back as the late 1980s the Oklahoma Sooners generated national headlines when the FBI busted their star quarterback, Charles Thompson, for selling cocaine to an undercover narcotics agent in Norman. On February 27, 1989, Thompson appeared on the cover of *Sports Illustrated* in an orange jumpsuit and handcuffs next to the headline HOW BARRY SWITZER'S SOONERS TERRORIZED THEIR CAMPUS. Thompson's arrest came on the heels of three Sooners being charged with gang-raping a woman in a campus dorm and another player being arrested for shooting a student-athlete in another dorm. At the same time, the team's best linebacker, Brian Bosworth, said the team regularly used cocaine and fired off guns in the dorm. Thompson ended up pleading guilty to conspiracy to distribute cocaine and served time. Switzer resigned.

Since then, one program after another has endured scandals involving lawlessness. But there had not been a comprehensive examination of college football and crime until 2010, when *Sports Illustrated* and CBS News jointly spent six months performing criminal background checks on all 2,837 players who were on the rosters of *SI*'s preseason top twenty-five as of September 1, 2010. The checks—performed through state and local courts and law enforcement agencies—revealed that 204 players had criminal records resulting in 277 incidents. Nearly 40 percent of the alleged incidents were serious offenses, including 56 violent crimes (assault and battery, domestic violence, sexual assault and robbery). The report, "Criminal Records in College Football," also ranked the teams based on the number of players with records. On one end of the spectrum, TCU had no players with a record and Stanford had only one. At the other extreme, Pittsburgh topped the list with twenty-two players (nearly one in four) who had records. Most teams in the top twenty-five at the start of the 2010 season averaged between five and nine players with criminal records.

But one of the most important aspects of the *SI*–CBS News investigation was the focus on high school recruits. One logical explanation for the uptick in student-athlete arrests is that more football recruits are arriving on campus these days with prior arrest records. Most states do not permit public access to juvenile arrest records. But Florida does. And an analysis by *SI*-CBS News of the 318 athletes on the top twenty-five teams in 2010 from Florida found that 22 had been arrested at least once before turning eighteen. If that rate were extrapolated to the entire pool of players in the *SI*-CBS News study, it would suggest that approximately 8 scholarship athletes per team have arrest records before setting foot on a college campus.

Without a doubt, some—perhaps most—of these players deserved a second chance. But when juvenile arrests entail crimes of violence—sexual assault, assault and battery, armed robbery—or offenses involving illegal drugs or the use of firearms, there are obvious risks associated with offering these individuals football scholarships. The danger, of course, is a repeat offense on a college campus, which could endanger students and subject a university to adverse publicity, not to mention the possibility of lawsuits. On the other hand, there are situations where football is the only thing between a young man going to college and a young man ending up on the street.

Another potential trip wire for recruiters these days is the proliferation of street gangs. A 2011 study funded by the Justice Department found that nearly 70 percent of campus police chiefs and athletic directors who responded believed gang members were participating in athletics at their schools or another institution. "This is the first study that systematically looks at gang membership among Division I athletes," said Scott Decker, director of the School of Criminology and Criminal Justice at Arizona State and the co-author of the study. "I think the most surprising thing was how aware police chiefs were of both the crimes that college athletes are involved in, but also the high level of gang membership among individuals recruited to play Division I athletics."

Decker and his counterpart Geoffrey Alpert, a criminal justice professor at South Carolina, surveyed 120 BCS conference schools and 10 other universities with Division I basketball programs. "What it said to me is that gang membership in Division I athletics is a significant problem," Decker said. "It is an issue we need to pay attention to because these young men and women bring a set of relationships with them, bring a set of past practices with them, that if left unattended could pose real problems and liabilities for universities."

Perhaps no region of the United States better illustrates the dangerous nexus of street gangs and college football recruiting than the "South L.A. strip," a stretch of gang-ravaged cities south of downtown Los Angeles that runs from Inglewood at the northern tip to Long Beach at the bottom. Compton, the birthplace of the Bloods and the Crips, is right in the center. The city of ninety-six thousand was called the murder capital of the United States in the 1990s. These days Compton is home to thirty-four active street gangs—often several on the same block—and more than a thousand gang members. It is also a hotbed for college football recruiting.

Keith Donerson has been coaching football at Compton's Dominguez High for more than twenty-five years. Heading into the 2011 high school football season, he had five seniors on his roster who were being heavily recruited by BCS programs. All of them lived in neighborhoods plagued by gang violence.

"We try to let the kids know you have to pick a side," Donerson said. "You're either going to play football, or you're going to be a gangster."

Donerson, whose shaved head and steely gaze give him the appearance of a marine sergeant, spends about 60 percent of his time mentoring and 40 percent teaching Xs and Os. "Football decisions are minor," Donerson said. "But a decision to go to a party is not minor. Not for these kids."

One of the best high school football players in greater Los Angeles was murdered in Compton on May 24, 2009. Dannie Farber, an all-city wide receiver, was eating with his girlfriend at a fast-food restaurant when a member of the Tragniew Park Compton Crips gunned him down. Farber had no gang ties and didn't know the shooter.

"A lot of kids in this neighborhood are gifted athletes," said Sergeant Brandon Dean, a supervisor in the L.A. County sheriff's office assigned to the gang unit in Compton. "Unfortunately, some get involved in a gang and commit crimes. Others get involved in the sense that they are mistaken as gang members and ultimately get shot and killed as a result."

That's what law enforcement officials believed happened to Farber. His senseless death shocked the city. USC's head coach at the time, Pete Carroll, spoke at his funeral. Stevie Wonder sang.

Every high school football player at Dominguez knows the Dannie Farber story. He played for rival Narbonne High. In an attempt to minimize his players' exposure to gang violence, Keith Donerson uses football as a substitute for family. "A lot of kids around here are raised by grandparents," he said. "The father is in jail or dead. The mother is preoccupied. So the kid is on the street."

Gangs typically fill the void left by broken homes. But at Dominguez, football offers an alternative. "We try to create a family-type atmosphere," Donerson said. "We do a lot of things together. We lift weights, we run, we condition, and we go to camps. We spend a lot of time together."

At the start of the 2011 season, Donerson sat down with four of his best players—offensive tackle Lacy Westbrook, linebacker Lavell Sanders and cornerbacks Brandon Beaver and Alphonso Marsh—to discuss the unique pressures of living in Compton. None of them had ever belonged to a gang, but all of them had witnessed gang violence.

"We all have friends who gangbang," said Sanders, the leader of the group. "Football is a big outlet. It separates you. You easily could make the wrong decision and be in the streets. But thank God for our fathers that they kept us going in the right path."

All four players limited their time to school and football. They almost never went out. "Basically, from Thursday to Saturday night I don't go anywhere unless it's to a USC game or church," said Sanders. "The rest of the time I'm either at practice or working out or staying inside."

"I'm afraid of going out," added Brandon Beaver. "I was at a party and shots were fired. People were running everywhere. I don't go out anymore."

Donerson's players didn't have tattoos either. Beaver explained, "All of my friends have tattoos all over their neck and face," he said. "They are in jail. They smoke. It's easy to be like everyone else. Being different is hard."

Three of the four players—Beaver, Westbrook and Sanders—came from two-parent homes. Cornerback Alphonso Marsh was the exception. He was fatherless. "Coach Donerson is a father figure," said Marsh. "If it wasn't for Coach, I wouldn't have stayed with football. And if not for football, I'd be on the street, gangbangin', or I'd be in jail. I owe a lot to him."

The comment got Donerson choked up. "Basically, it boils down to family," Donerson said, placing his hands on his players' shoulders as they sat side by side in the weight room. "I teach these boys that a man provides for his family. He's a friend. He stands up when he's wrong. A real man takes responsibility for himself."

All four players would eventually end up with college football scholarships in 2012. But the story of Alphonso Marsh's recruiting process was an odyssey that reveals just how much is at stake when a prestigious institution of higher learning decides to offer a football scholarship to a boy from a faraway, dangerous place.

Curley Rachal was born and raised in Compton. Her parents—part Indian and part Haitian—were from Louisiana and spoke Creole. They named her Curley after the black curly hair she had at birth.

Wiry thin with a soft, meek voice, Curley had four children of her own. Alphonso was the baby in the bunch. His father abandoned him when Alphonso was five. He kept his father's last name—Marsh—but his mother became the apple of his eye. "Him and me are like paper and glue," Rachal said. "We are always with each other."

From the time Marsh was little, Rachal hoped and prayed her baby would make it out of Compton alive and have the opportunity to get a college degree. But paying for college was something she couldn't fathom. Rachal has been disabled for years. She raised her Alphonso on a fixed income. By the time he was twelve, she had started thinking her dream could come true when Marsh began displaying unusual athletic abilities. By then she had amended her dream to hoping he'd grow up to be a pro athlete.

But the pull of street gangs threatened to put all those dreams at risk. Then, one day, Rachal met Keith Donerson. First he talked Marsh into playing high school football. Then he started driving him home after practices and picking him up on game days. It was like having the father that Alphonso never had.

In the summer between Alphonso's junior and senior years of high school, Donerson drove him to a Nike 7-on-7 camp in Las Vegas. He also paid the expenses. "Camps help kids get recruited," Donerson said. "And I like my kids to get an offer right away, preferably from a Pac-12 school. So I pitch in a little bit."

After the 7-on-7 event Marsh's ranking on the scouting Web sites shot up, and offers started flowing in. Within days after the camp ended, Donerson got calls from Arizona, Washington, Boise State and New Mexico about Marsh. One of those schools called Marsh directly on his cell phone, offering him a scholarship. A couple schools sent coaches to Dominguez to communicate their interest in Marsh directly to Donerson.

By the start of his senior season in September 2011, Marsh was ready to commit. Donerson discouraged him.

"A four-year commitment is like a marriage," Donerson said. "It might look good. It might smell good. But it might not *be* good. It's better to figure that out before getting the phone call in the middle of his freshman year because he didn't get used to that type of environment."

———

One day midway through the fall of 2011, Utah's defensive coach Chad Kauha'aha'a (pronounced cow-ha-a-ha-a) showed up at Dominguez. Coach Chad, as his players and fellow coaches referred to him, had seen film on Marsh. His primary interest, however, was Marsh's best friend and fellow cornerback, Brandon Beaver. But when Coach Chad encountered Marsh in Donerson's office, he was surprised at his size—six feet two inches and 183 pounds, with an unusually long wingspan.

"That's when Utah really came in on Alphonso," Donerson said. "Sometimes you like a kid on film, and then you actually see him and you are like, 'Oh, he's a lot bigger than I thought he was.'"

Before long, Utah head coach Kyle Whittingham made a home visit and met Curley Rachal. The crowded living room of her one-story home showed signs of a cousin, niece and nephew who lived there with Alphonso and his mother—pacifiers on the end table, a makeshift coatrack lined with children's clothes in the corner, a boom box and a circular fan to circulate the hot air. "He grew up in some very humble circumstances," Whittingham said. "It was a credit to him that he was in a position to further his education. We place a lot of pride on character with the kids we bring into our program. Alphonso is a good kid. We thought he was a good fit for us."

Rachal felt honored to have Whittingham in her home. But she was a little overwhelmed. "I didn't know too much about the process," Rachal said.

As was often the case, Rachal's biggest concern boiled down to finances. "I'm on a set income, and I don't have the money for his college," Rachal said. "I was worried about how the scholarship would work and when it would start."

Whittingham and his staff put all of her fears to rest. Alphonso's scholarship, they explained, would kick in when Marsh enrolled in school. It would cover all of his expenses—tuition, books and food. He'd even have medical insurance. She had nothing to worry about. Everything would be taken care of.

A relationship of trust was formed. Rachal was at ease, which put her son at ease. He agreed to make an official visit to Salt Lake City.

———

On Friday morning, January 13, 2012, a black Lincoln Town Car pulled up in front of Alphonso Marsh's home. It immediately drew attention; limos weren't the norm in Marsh's neighborhood. Kids on bicycles stopped to stare. Men walking past the liquor store next door whispered and pointed.

Marsh had been waiting on his front step with his bag. After a kiss for luck from his mother, he said good-bye and headed past the onlookers to the curb. Air travel scared him. He had never flown prior to the recruiting process. This marked just his second flight.

A burly limo driver wearing a cap and a black suit over a white shirt took his bag and put it in the trunk. Then he opened the rear door. Marsh waved good-bye to his mother one last time before ducking into the backseat. As the car drove away, he slipped on his headphones, pulled up his iTunes and selected the rapper Curren$y for the ride to Long Beach Airport.

His teammate Brandon Beaver met him at the gate. Despite already narrowing his choices down to Nebraska and Washington, Beaver had accepted Utah's invitation for an official visit. A couple hours later he and Marsh touched down in Utah. There was snow on the ground. Neither of them had ever seen snow before.

Coach Chad picked them up. After taking them out for breakfast, he brought them to campus, where they met up with eight other recruits and toured the football facilities. They tried on jerseys in the locker room, checked out the Under Armour gear and met with different coaches. The feeling of camaraderie had a big impression on Marsh. At one point the coaches took all the recruits tubing in Park City.

Before he flew back to Compton, Marsh had made up his mind: he was going to Utah.

But four days after he returned from Salt Lake City, some unexpected visitors showed up at Coach Donerson's office: Washington State's head coach, Mike Leach, and five of his assistants. Leach had barely hired his staff, and they were on a whirlwind recruiting swing through Southern California.

Leach asked Donerson about his two corners, Beaver and Marsh.

Beaver's mind was made up, Donerson told him. He was going to Washington. Marsh, he said, was leaning heavily toward Utah.

Leach wanted to meet both kids.

Donerson pulled them out of class.

Marsh was caught off guard by the number of coaches from WSU. He didn't know which one was the head coach until Leach introduced himself and made his pitch: defensive backs at WSU will practice every day against the best receivers. He stressed one in particular—Marquess Wilson.

"I really didn't know that much about Leach," Marsh said. "But he had a little vibe. I liked what he said."

The next day Marsh was on a plane to Pullman for an official visit. There was even more snow there than he had encountered in Utah. When he landed, he met Marquess Wilson, who was assigned to be his host for the weekend. Wilson showed him around campus, talked up the new facilities that were under construction and even brought Marsh to watch WSU's basketball team beat Cal 77–75 in a barn burner.

Marsh liked Wilson a lot. The idea of sticking a guy like him in practice every day had some appeal. He liked that WSU was a Nike school. And he especially liked Leach. By the time he left Pullman, he was confused. "I was lost over what I should do," Marsh said. "Where should I go?"

Back in Compton, Marsh talked to the people he trusted, starting with his best friend, Beaver, who had already made up his own mind. Nebraska pulled out all the stops to get him, even arranging for him to have a one-on-one with the legendary coach Tom Osborne when Beaver made his official visit to Lincoln. But Osborne might as well have been Ozzy Osbourne. Beaver had never heard of the man who walked on water in Lincoln. More important, as much as he loved the electric atmosphere in Lincoln's Memorial Stadium, he didn't think he'd be comfortable on such a rural campus. "Too many cornfields," he said. He chose UW because it had an urban campus. Seattle wasn't exactly L.A., but it felt much more like home than Nebraska.

Marsh took all that in. But Salt Lake City and Pullman both seemed foreign and distant to him. So he talked to another friend, Delshawn McClellon, a wide receiver from Long Beach. They were close, and McClellon, also a high school senior, had committed to Utah. That had Marsh leaning toward the Utes.

Then he asked Donerson for advice. The choice between Utah and WSU put Donerson in a tough spot. He liked both programs and both coaches a great deal. Plus, he wanted to maintain good relations with both programs in hopes that they'd continue to recruit his kids in the future. But he pointed out that WSU would have a powerhouse passing game under Leach, which meant lots of reps for DBs. That had Marsh leaning back toward WSU.

The truth was that he really wanted to go to school in the L.A. area. "I wanted to stay home," Marsh said. "Through the whole recruiting process I thought, 'I don't want to do this. I'm not ready.'"

At the same time, he recognized what was at stake. "There is not many people that I grew up around that actually make it to a four-year university," Marsh said. "To say that I got a scholarship to a four-year university makes my mom really happy."

On the eve of National Signing Day, Marsh talked to his mother about the big decision. "If you have games in Utah, sometimes I can travel out there," she told him. "In Washington, I wouldn't be able to go because I'd have to fly. And I've never been on an airplane in my life."

That sealed it. Marsh called Whittingham. "I'm coming to Utah," he told him.

———

The moment Alphonso Marsh and Brandon Beaver graduated from high school, they got ready to leave for college. "The colleges like to get these guys on campus as soon as possible," Donerson said. "That gives them a head start on college classes, and it gets them out of Compton right away. There is nothing here for them but trouble."

On June 19, Marsh and Beaver got together to say good-bye. They posed for pictures. And they talked about the fact that Utah and Washington were scheduled to play each other in 2012. Then they made a pact.

"Ball out," Beaver said. "We're gonna do our thing."

"We're not on the same team no more," Marsh said. "It's going to be different."

"But we're gonna make it to where we want to make it," Beaver said.

"We're always on the same team," Marsh said. "No matter what."

"No matter what."

Saying good-bye to his mother was even harder.

Rachal faced her son. "Keep your grades up," she told him. "And stay out of trouble."

"Okay, Mom," he said.

"Be careful," she said. "I love you."

"I love you, too, Mom," he said.

They embraced. "I'm very happy," she whispered. "Very happy. Very happy."

Then they both cried. It was the first time since he was a toddler that Marsh had shed a tear.

As he walked off, Rachal melted. "My baby is leaving home," she thought. "He's all grown up."

The drive to Utah took two days. Marsh traveled with his friend Delshawn McClellon. Along the way, Marsh thought about turning back. The "stranger in a strange land" second thoughts were something Whittingham had seen many times before. "The reality hits a recruit in the face when it is time to tell your mom good-bye," Whittingham said. "A recruit is starting a new life at that point."

Marsh did what many high school seniors do in his situation: kept his mind on his dream of reaching the NFL. To get there, he had to go through college football. They arrived in Salt Lake City on June 21, a hot summer day. An assistant coach took them to the apartment they'd be sharing for the summer. It was clean, spacious and empty. One cupboard had packages of the all-American college staple—Top Ramen noodles—inside. The refrigerator had some energy drinks.

The coach left them to unpack, a process that took Marsh all of five minutes. He had brought one duffel bag containing his clothing. Other than that, he had a cell phone in one pocket and $200 cash in another pocket. That was it.

A couple days later he sprawled out on some perfectly manicured grass beneath a cluster of leafy trees. The sky was blue. The air was warm. The campus was quiet. "It's so nice here," he said. "It's so different. It's joyful. I can walk around without looking over my shoulder."

Whittingham wasn't surprised. "We get that same story from a lot of kids that have grown up in some rough places," he said. "Being up here is a breath of fresh air. It's a chance to be at ease."

That same week, Marsh enrolled in summer classes—College Prep and Writing 110. He worked out with his new teammates every day—mainly weight lifting. The food was great; he ate with the team four times a day. Everything was clicking.

Then his appendix burst. Suddenly he couldn't participate in workouts. Alone, he started thinking about home. Then he got word that one of his best friends had been gunned down. That marked the fifth friend he had lost to gun violence in Compton. He went to a tattoo shop in Salt Lake City and got COMPTON tattooed on his forearm.

Early in the 2012 season, the situation at home prompted Marsh to head back to Compton. He left without telling his coaches. When he returned, Whittingham sat him down. "Alphonso," he told him, "that's not how it works here. You don't just arbitrarily decide you are going home for x amount of days and not tell anybody."

On October 12, Utah traveled to Los Angeles to play UCLA. This time Marsh got permission to leave the team and deal with some personal matters. By that point he was contemplating withdrawing from Utah. Keith Donerson made a point to talk with Marsh that weekend.

"There is nothing here for you if you come back home," he told Marsh. "At least there you have a place to stay. You have meals. And you are getting an education."

Utah lost to UCLA 21–14 that weekend. When the team flew back to Salt Lake City, Marsh remained behind in Compton.

The following week Utah released him from his scholarship. "We just mutually agreed that he would go home and take care of things," Whittingham said. "I firmly believe if he hadn't had the appendicitis, he probably could have gotten through it all. When everyone else was doing two-a-days, he wasn't involved. He had a lot of time to think and get homesick."

Marsh ended up enrolling at West Los Angeles College. But after one game he was in a car accident and separated his shoulder. No more football.

Then, in late December, Marsh was shot multiple times. One bullet lodged in his abdomen. He ended up spending Christmas in the hospital.

"Hit twice but one still inside," he tweeted on January 7, 2013. "Doctor tomorrow for X-rays then last bullet out of my body."

Two months later his mother passed away. More than ever, Marsh thought long and hard about his life and now fervently wished to return to Utah. The odds were low, but he did reach out to Whittingham. There was a hope he might come back—a small one—but a hope nonetheless.

23 THE GAME

"I hate losing more than anything"

Students shuffled between class buildings as sunlight blanketed the cottonwood trees at the center of BYU's campus. It was a little after 11:00 on August 29, 2012, the day before BYU's season opener at home against Washington State. Kyle Van Noy was standing in the quad, facing a female photographer from a national magazine. A backpack strapped over his shoulders and earbuds around his neck, he had on a white Cougars T-shirt, black cargo shorts and a pair of white-and-blue Nikes.

"Do you want me to smile?" he said.

"If you are feeling happy, smile," the photographer told him.

A grin swept his face.

Click. Click. Click.

Van Noy had plenty of reasons to smile. He was on the preseason watch list for the Lombardi Award, which recognizes the top lineman or linebacker in the nation. Mel Kiper's Big Board had him listed as the No. 2 junior linebacker in the country behind Georgia's Jarvis Jones. Agents were burning up his cell phone, positioning themselves, telling him he'd go in the early rounds if he declared for the NFL draft at the end of the season. The latest thing was a flurry of text messages from friends, saying they saw him on the new giant billboards BYU had put up along the I-15 corridor from Salt Lake City to Orem.

It was surreal. Three years after arriving in Provo on probation, he had literally become the face of the university in its new marketing campaign: Y TRADITION: FOUR DECADES OF WINNING.

Van Noy's on-field success was the result of his new off-the-field routine. Up at 7:00 every morning and in bed by 11:15 every night, he filled his days with classes and tutoring sessions, team meetings, practices and countless hours of weight training. He even met regularly with a BYU dance instructor to optimize his lateral movement and flexibility.

His schedule left him no time for parties, girlfriends or anything else that might distract him from his goal—playing on Sundays.

"Back in the day I used to be focused on girls and all these distractions that got me in trouble," Van Noy said. "Now I'm just focused on football. It only lasts for a little part of life. I'm trying to take full advantage of it."

That meant remaining in Provo year-round. "Guys that make plays are here summers, working out as a team," he said. "These are unofficial but official workouts. I only see my parents a couple times a year. I would get to go home more if I was in the NFL."

In the previous calendar year, Van Noy spent just four days in Reno, over an abbreviated Christmas break. During that visit he caught up with his old high school friends one evening. When it got late, Van Noy said he was heading home to go to bed.

"The party is just starting," said one of his friends.

"Not for me. I have to get up early and start my day."

"Who *are* you?" said the friend.

"Yeah, what's up with that?" another said.

Van Noy smiled. "You guys have no idea what I do now."

That was the last time he saw them.

His new best friend was a Provo police officer, Cody Harris, a married man with three small children. Van Noy met Harris playing pickup basketball. Something clicked. As a result, when Van Noy needed a place to hang out, he went to Harris's home to have dinner, watch television and play with the kids. They thought Van Noy was their adopted big brother.

The photo session was wrapping up. "Just a few more shots," the photographer said.

Students had begun congregating. "Kyle, good luck tomorrow night," one of them said.

He nodded and smiled.

"Go get 'em, Kyle," another said. "We're with ya."

Then he headed for a meeting. It was time to turn his sights to Washington State. "I'm looking forward to playing against Mike Leach's offense," he said to a reporter. "They throw the ball a lot. But I think we'll shut them down."

———

The front page of *USA Today*'s sports section featured a big picture of Mike Leach above a bold headline: THE NEW SHERIFF. The story reported that since Leach's hire all luxury suites at the new stadium in Pullman had been sold and season ticket sales and donations to WSU athletics were at all-time highs. Expectations were big as Leach boarded the team bus outside the Provo Marriott and a police escort led the way on the five-minute ride to LaVell Edwards Stadium. ESPN had rescheduled the game to its prime-time slot on Thursday night.

Inside the stadium gates, vendors fired up popcorn machines and rotisseries with fried dough, pretzels and cotton candy. Members of BYU's marching band milled around. Leach ducked into a stadium tunnel for a quick pregame interview with ESPN's sideline reporter. The players filed into the visiting locker room. Two big tables greeted them, one stocked with boxes of bananas and energy bars, the other holding two giant Powerade sports drink coolers bearing the NCAA logo. Game jerseys hung neatly in front of each locker—Tuel, Wilson, Long, Fullington.

For the next ninety minutes the players stuck to a carefully scripted schedule that included stretching, on-field warm-ups and walk-throughs. At 7:56 the players left the field for final pregame preparations. Leach paced around the locker room, a cup of coffee in hand. Rap music blared as players, already sweating, sat on stools in front of their lockers. Leach made his way around the locker room, patting players on the shoulders, shaking hands.

"All right, bring it up," Leach yelled. "Get in here. Everybody, up."

The music went off. Players huddled around him.

"All right," he said. "Now take a knee."

Players dropped to one knee.

"Grab the guy next to you," Leach said. "Lord's Prayer."

The players held hands and bowed their heads.

"Our Father who art in heaven," Leach began. The players repeated his words. At the end of the prayer, everybody stood.

"Okay, now listen," Leach said. "Here's what's important. You've got to make sure you do your job for sixty minutes. Make sure you make the routine plays for sixty minutes. Make sure you play the next down for sixty minutes."

The players clapped and screamed.

"All right," Leach yelled. "Break it down."

The players clapped and yelled louder as they huddled even tighter.

"Let's go," one of the captains shouted. "Let's go."

"One, two, three, win!"

———

Over the summer Bronco Mendenhall had finally awarded Ziggy Ansah a scholarship. Two years of slogging away as a walk-on had paid off. He was promised a lot more playing time, too. On WSU's first possession of the game, Ansah watched from the sideline as quarterback Jeff Tuel methodically drove his team from its own twenty-yard line deep into BYU territory, completing passes for four, one, five, twenty, seven, thirteen and four yards. It was exactly the kind of drive Leach wanted. On second and six from BYU's eighteen-yard line, Mendenhall called Ansah's number.

On the snap, an offensive lineman grabbed Ansah's jersey, trying to drag him down. Tuel dumped a pass behind the line of scrimmage to a running back. Shedding a blocker, Ansah dropped the ball carrier for a five-yard loss, setting up third and eleven from the BYU twenty-three. Mendenhall declined the holding penalty drawn by Ansah. Tuel threw an interception on the next play. Minutes later BYU scored to go up 7–0.

BYU added two more touchdowns and a field goal in the second quarter while WSU could only muster a couple field goals. Down 24–6 at the half, Leach tried to rally his team. "Everybody, up," Leach said as the players crowded around him in the locker room. "Now I want you to listen to me. Players and coaches, listen. Here's what needs to happen. First of all, think about why you came to Washington State. The reason you came to Washington State was to pull the fuckin' trigger, to play hard and to get excited about making plays.

"Here's the problem with the first half. We go out there frantic. We're a combination of frantic—trying to do too much. We're timid—you're afraid to make mistakes. We already know you're going to make mistakes! But the biggest mistake is hesitating. Do not fucking hesitate. You didn't sign up to play college football to hesitate."

Washington State nearly ran the second-half kickoff back for a touchdown. The return man was dragged down at BYU's thirty-five-yard line. But on the first play from scrimmage, Van Noy beat his man and sacked Jeff Tuel for a big loss. WSU drew a penalty on the next play, setting it back further. Then Van Noy beat his man again, forcing Tuel to throw under duress. His pass was picked off and returned all the way to WSU's nine-yard line. Minutes later BYU kicked a field goal to go up 27–6.

WSU never recovered. Van Noy ended up with four solo tackles, two sacks, one pass breakup and three hurries. WSU ran the ball sixteen times for a total of minus five yards. Leach's offense reached the red zone just one time the entire night. The final score was 30–6.

Leach removed his headset and stood in silence on the sideline as his team and assistant coaches headed to the locker room. It wasn't supposed to begin this way.

Two weeks later, BYU traveled forty-five minutes north to face Utah. It marked the eighty-eighth time the two teams had squared off in a rivalry known throughout college football as the "Holy War," a reference to the vastly different cultures represented by two schools where the majority of students were Mormons. But the rivalry had taken on a nastier, personal tone since the 2005 season, when Bronco Mendenhall and Kyle Whittingham were named head coaches at the two schools within days of each other. In head-to-head competition, Whittingham had beaten Mendenhall four out of seven times in what *Sports Illustrated*'s Stewart Mandel called the best coaching rivalry of the decade.

There were parallels to the heated rivalry between Notre Dame and Miami in the 1980s, when Notre Dame fans printed infamous T-shirts that said, "Catholics vs. Convicts," helping fuel a pregame brawl and finger-pointing between the teams' head coaches, Lou Holtz and Jimmy Johnson. Things got so ugly that Notre Dame fans complained of being spit on and having beer poured on them by Hurricane fans at the Orange Bowl. The longtime Notre Dame beat writer Tim Prister described the atmosphere at the Orange Bowl as "nastiness" and "evilness," adding, "It was the most vile, vicious venue for a college football game that I've ever been in. They weren't there just to see Miami win. They wanted blood from Notre Dame."

Things were headed that way in Utah, especially after a dramatic BYU comeback in 2007, highlighted by a dramatic fourth-and-eighteen catch by future NFL receiver Austin Collie. "Obviously, when you're doing what's right on and off the field, I think the Lord steps in and plays a part in it," Collie said afterward. "Magic happens."

Two years later BYU won 26–23 in overtime, thanks to a touchdown pass by Max Hall. "I don't like Utah," Hall said after the game. "In fact, I hate them. I hate everything about them. I hate their program. I hate their fans. I hate everything. So, it feels good to send those guys home." Hall apologized the next day but insisted that his "family was spit on, had beer dumped on them and were physically assaulted on several occasions" at Rice-Eccles Stadium a year earlier.

Van Noy wasn't around back then. But as BYU's brightest star, he endured the wrath of Utah fans as he and his teammates entered Rice-Eccles Stadium in street clothes to make their way toward the visiting locker room on September 15, 2012. The Rolling Stones' "Sympathy for the Devil" was playing on the stadium's sound system. A guy waving a Utah flag leaned over a railing separating the bleachers from the field to greet the Cougars. "Welcome to hell, boys," he said.

"You assholes," another shouted.

His earbuds in, Van Noy didn't hear any of it. That night he had one of the best games of his college career, chasing Utah's quarterback all over the field. "Fuck you, Van Noy," one boisterous Utah fan yelled from behind BYU's bench after Van Noy threw Utah's quarterback to the ground, registering his fourth sack.

While Van Noy shone, Utah built a seventeen-point lead going into the fourth quarter. But with under thirty seconds to play, BYU had cut the lead to three and was nearly in position to kick a game-tying field goal. Then, with time running out, quarterback Riley Nelson's third-down pass was deflected and fell incomplete as time expired. Utah fans rushed the field, taunting BYU players. The scene on the field quickly became chaos. But Bronco Mendenhall protested that one second remained on the clock when Nelson's pass hit the turf. After officials reviewed the play, they restored one second to the game clock while boos and expletives rained down from the stands. Thousands of fans had to be cleared from the field so BYU could attempt a fifty-one-yard field goal. The kick was blocked. By the time a BYU player recovered the ball and was tackled behind the line of scrimmage, Utah fans had rushed the field again. This time Utah players joined fans as they rushed toward BYU's side of the field, finger-pointing and celebrating. But there were penalty flags, and Utah was assessed a fifteen-yard unsportsmanlike conduct because the fans had run onto the field during the play. As the penalty was announced, BYU fans returned the favor, pointing and ridiculing Utah players and fans.

Calm amid the swirl, Van Noy stood on the sideline, helmet tucked under his arm, silently looking on as security cleared Utah fans from the field a second time and officials marked off the penalty. Then BYU lined up again to attempt a game-tying field goal, this time from thirty-six yards out. The kick hit the upright. Utah held on 24–21. Fans rushed the field a third time. Police had to step between as Mendenhall went toe-to-toe with a heckler as the Cougars tried to get off the field.

"I hate losing," Van Noy said, standing in the back of the end zone as Utah fans celebrated all around him. "I hate losing more than anything. I hate losing at tic-tac-toe. So words can't describe how I feel right now. But win or lose, I'm grateful to be part of this university. I'm grateful to be alive. That's all that matters. Not many people in the world get to know what it's like, playing the game of football."

Later, a BYU official led Van Noy to the postgame press conference.

"Talk about that finish," a local reporter said. "Was that as crazy as anything you've been a part of?"

"In my life?" Van Noy said, flashing a smile. "No."

"On the field?" the reporter said.

"Yes."

———

Through the first three games of the 2012 season, Bronco Mendenhall used Ziggy Ansah as a situational player, mainly as a defensive end or an outside linebacker in passing situations. In every case, his instructions were simple—get the quarterback. But in week four, everything changed. Early in the game at Boise State, noseguard Eathyn Manumaleuna, the Cougars' best defensive lineman, sustained a season-ending injury.

When the Broncos recovered a fumble on BYU's one-yard line with 8:19 remaining in the third quarter, Mendenhall sent Ziggy in to play noseguard. Boise State had no scouting report on No. 47 as a noseguard; Ziggy had never played the position. He introduced himself immediately. On first and goal Ansah exploded out of his stance and met running back D. J. Harper just as he took the handoff, stuffing him for a one-yard loss. On second and goal Harper got the call again, and again Ansah beat his man, dropping Harper a yard behind the line. Van Noy made a tackle behind the line of scrimmage on the next play. The Cougars ended up taking over on downs.

That goal-line stand erased any questions BYU coaches had about Ziggy's ability to stop the run. Ansah ended up with a career-high eight tackles. The next week against Utah State he started, recording two sacks and two quarterback hurries. From then on Mendenhall started him in every game. Playing every down, he became a nightmare for opposing offensive coordinators. After just four starts he led the team in tackles for a loss, and he was tied for twenty-fifth in the nation with tackles behind the line of scrimmage. NFL scouts who were watching Van Noy started noticing Ansah. After Ansah had another monster game against Georgia Tech on October 27 in Atlanta, *Sports Illustrated*'s NFL draft expert predicted Ansah could be a first-round pick.

By that point, NFL scouts were showing up at BYU practices. They were already very familiar with Van Noy. They were pleased to discover that Van Noy and Ansah were roommates. "Another thing he has going for him is that his roommate is Kyle Van Noy," one NFL scout said. "He's living with the other best player on the team. They are best friends. We see that as a good thing. When you're checking the boxes for what he has going for him, that's another plus."

Mendenhall was floored. "If anyone knew where he started, I can't even articulate the jump he's made," he said. "This is a guy who literally didn't know how to put on his pads. Now he's projected as a first-round draft pick. We've had more NFL personnel in our facility this year than in my previous eight years put together. This is a guy I never took seriously."

Part IV, The letter

On November 1, 2012, President Elson Floyd and the Washington State University Board of Trustees received a disturbing letter via e-mail. It came from the parent of a football player who had recently left the team. "As stewards of WSU you have a responsibility to make sure the athletes are not getting mistreated by their coaches," the letter began. "I feel that Coach Mike Leach and his staff are out of control."

The parent named eighteen scholarship players in addition to his son who had left the program since Leach arrived. Player abuse, the parent insisted, was behind the departures. The letter specifically cited "Midnight Maneuvers," punishing players for missing off-season "voluntary" workouts and forcing players to do drills that were more demanding than those required in military boot camps. In one instance, the letter alleged, offensive linemen were forced to do drills in a sandpit after performing poorly in a game that WSU had lost. "Players were made to hold 45-pound plates over their heads while coaches sprayed water in their faces with water hoses," the parent wrote, adding that Coach Leach had instructed players not to talk to their parents or the administration if they had concerns about the way the program was being run. "I would expect WSU to investigate these allegations which I know to be true," the parent continued. "WSU has an obligation to protect these young men."

Floyd was uneasy. The letter was a scathing indictment of the football coaches. Granted, the claims had come from a parent whose son had no chance of seeing any playing time and ultimately quit the team. Floyd learned that context from athletic director Bill Moos. Still, if only half of his accusations were true, WSU had a problem on its hands. Worse, the letter dredged up reminders of Leach's infamous departure from Texas Tech. The situation could not be ignored.

But Floyd had no interest in micromanaging the football program. Nor did he want to undermine his athletic director. Moos had hired Leach. If legitimate questions arose about Leach's fitness for the job—and the claim that players had been hosed while being forced to carry forty-five-pound plates through a sandpit certainly raised a red flag—Moos was the one who needed to get to the bottom of the situation.

Yet the letter had been addressed directly to Floyd and his board. Some trustees were uncomfortable. The board's chairman, Scott Carson, had plenty of experience dealing with crises. He had previously been the executive vice president of the Boeing Company, as well as the president and CEO of Boeing Commercial Airplanes. A letter from a student-athlete's parent alleging abuse had to be taken seriously. In talks with Floyd, Carson recommended a series of steps.

First, the letter required a response from the athletic director.

Second, the letter should be referred to the appropriate board committee for further review and possible action.

Third, the AD needed to brief the board on the situation within the football program.

Floyd passed all of this on to Moos.

When Bill Moos read the parent's complaint letter, he looked at the situation through the lens of a football coach as well as an athletic director. From that perspective, he knew it was not out of the ordinary to hear complaints from parents—including complaints about their sons' treatment. Unlike those running the university, Moos had played big-time college football. He knew the sort of discipline and hard-nosed approach required to compete. It is, after all, football, not the glee club. Oregon, USC and UCLA were pushing their players to the brink. If WSU hoped to compete with those teams, players had to be pushed just as hard.

Moos was also pretty familiar with the eighteen players who had already left the program since Leach arrived. Five of them were kicked off the team for breaking the law. "The pot smokers and thieves aren't going to make it in Leach's program," Moos said. "Two of those guys that he cut were linebackers that were NFL caliber."

The fact that Leach had cut two of his best players for breaking the law was a good sign as far as Moos was concerned. A couple other players were let go due to substandard academic performance. Others quit or were let go due to the stepped-up conditioning and high expectations. All of this, as far as Moos was concerned, was simply part of the process of rebuilding the program. "Anytime you are in transition, you have defections," he said.

Before speaking with Floyd, Moos called Leach into his office to discuss the letter. Leach was very familiar with the player whose father wrote it. The abuse claims, he said, were ridiculous. But he wasn't necessarily surprised that the student-athlete's father had complained. Not every student-athlete is cut out for the rigors of Division I college football.

At the same time, Leach preferred to deal with the situation right away. His team was 2-6 and had dropped five straight in the Pac-12. He was trying to get the team ready to play Utah, one of the few teams on WSU's schedule that was struggling. WSU was scheduled to fly to Salt Lake City the following day. He had a lot to do to get ready.

"You want me to call him right now?" Leach asked.

Moos liked the idea.

Leach called his former player's father on the spot. Stunned, the parent spoke his piece. Leach listened and then did the same. After the call, Moos reassured Leach and told him to focus on Utah.

Marquess Wilson was not happy. Two weeks earlier he left the Cal game after taking a hard hit in the end zone. The following week he lost his starting position to a freshman. When Leach announced the starting lineups for the Utah game, Wilson was once again relegated to second string. He still ended up leading the team in receptions and yardage. But Washington State lost to Utah 49–6. WSU's only score came on the game's final play, a meaningless five-yard touchdown pass. The loss dropped WSU to 2-7, guaranteeing a losing season and snuffing out any last hope of getting a bowl invitation.

Leach was pissed. Losing was one thing. But playing without heart was another. Above all, Leach valued effort. He didn't see much of that in Salt Lake City.

"Our effort today was pitiful," Leach said in his postgame press conference. "Square one is a good effort and our effort was horrible."

The Utah game was by far the worst loss of the season. WSU had been beaten badly in every facet of the game, especially along the line of scrimmage. The defensive line got pushed around all day. The offensive line gave up six sacks. A reporter asked Leach about the lack of protection for his quarterback.

"A part of it is effort, and some of it borders on cowardice," Leach said. "It was one of the most heartless efforts up front I've ever seen. And our D-line wasn't any better."

Typically, reporters get postgame interviews with a couple of players after hearing from the coach. But Leach was in no mood for protocols. He sent out the entire offensive line and defensive line. Battered, humiliated and feeling out of place, the linemen looked blankly at a bank of reporters who were equally unsure about what to say. Finally, questions trickled out.

Defensive end Logan Mayes stepped up. "Everybody on this team works hard," he said. "We just couldn't get it done at the end of the day. There's no lack of want-to on this team. Sometimes you want something really bad and you don't get it. We're all going to go back and work our asses off this week and find a way to get it done."

Senior Travis Long, the team's best defensive player and its hardest worker, suddenly bolted out of the press conference. He appeared to have tears in his eyes.

The whole scene was surreal. "In four decades of covering the conference, I've never seen anything like it," wrote the *Seattle Times*'s veteran sports columnist Bud Withers.

———

The atmosphere on the plane ride back from Salt Lake City resembled that of a funeral home. It was late at night by the time the team touched down in Pullman. Leach told his staff not to go home. He wanted to talk to them at the football office.

Tired and in a foul mood, the coaches trudged into a meeting room. Leach vented. The assistants vented. The season had reached a low point. With just three games to go, there was nothing left to play for but pride. But the team had clearly lost its confidence. There was disagreement over how to restore it. The next day was a Sunday, typically a light practice day. The coaching staff decided to scrap practice and put the team through conditioning drills.

The following afternoon, the players were divided into groups and sent to one of four conditioning stations. Marquess Wilson was in the group that started in the sandpit, where players were required to sprint, roll and do bear crawls on hands and feet through forty yards of sand. Wilson didn't see the point. About fifteen minutes into the session, he walked off the field. He didn't say a word to the coaches. He had had enough.

Wilson was the best receiver in the school's history. Yet from the moment Leach arrived, it seemed as if he had been openly critical of Wilson's effort, suggesting he needed to toughen up and become more of a leader. Wilson didn't appreciate it. He didn't take well to some of the physical demands either, stuff like making receivers run twenty-five hundred yards per practice. Even NFL teams don't do that. Plus, he had lost his starting position—a move the coaches hoped would send a message to the star player that he needed to pick up his effort.

After Sunday's practice, Leach discovered that Wilson hadn't just walked off the practice field. He had cleaned out his locker. The next morning the school announced that its star player had been indefinitely suspended for violating team rules.

Hours later, Wilson's stepfather in California called Moos. He recognized the gravity of the situation and wanted to resolve it. He asked Moos what he could do to help.

"You tell him to come see me," Moos said.

The next day Wilson showed up at Moos's office.

"You got all this talent," Moos told him. "But you need to be a leader on this ball club."

Wilson appeared nervous but sincere.

"What I suggest you do is take a deep breath," Moos said. "Go through the weekend. Watch us play UCLA. You'll have a hollow feeling. Trust me. You'll have a hollow feeling. Then come see me after the game. And if you're committed to being on this team, I'll go to bat for you."

In addition to trying to quell the Wilson dustup, Moos had to prepare to brief the board of trustees in response to the letter from the disgruntled parent. Meanwhile, public criticism against Leach mounted. "Argh, matey! Remember all that excitement that came with the hiring of Mike Leach?" a *Seattle Weekly* blogger wrote. "Turns out the Leach Era in Pullman is already a disaster, and getting uglier and more embarrassing every day. This morning comes news that star WSU receiver Marquess Wilson left last night's practice in a tiff and . . . quit the team. If the school had any sense AD Bill Moos would make Leach walk the plank this morning. Somewhere Paul Wulff looks pretty good right now."

National writers were calling out Leach, too. "Back in the preseason I was among the many delusional media types that thought Mike Leach would sweep into Pullman and lead Washington State to its first bowl berth in nine years," wrote *Sports Illustrated*'s Stewart Mandel. "As it turns out, the 2-7 Cougars will not be bowling, and Leach has had one of the worst debut seasons of any newly hired coach in the country. It's not just that Wazzu is 0-6 in the Pac-12; it's that the Pirate is compounding things with some of his comments and actions." Mandel called Leach's actions following the Utah game "a Bob Knight–esque exercise in verbal bullying."

Leach ignored the criticism. "I'm not real conscious of it," he said. "People want change and accountability around here. Then you do it and they don't want it."

In Leach's view, the team had reacted very positively to the loss to Utah and Wilson's departure. Team unity had cemented, and the players were practicing with a renewed sense of commitment and determination. That was especially true among the receivers. "There are a bunch of receivers playing really well right now," Leach said shortly after Wilson left. "They viewed Marquess as the alpha receiver. They thought they had to be like him to be a good receiver. Now that he is gone, they are stepping up. We lost some talent. But we gained in terms of other guys starting to play harder. And walking off a team is the football version of treason."

One person who was particularly sensitive to all the controversy swirling around Leach was Bill Moos. With UCLA scheduled to arrive in Pullman in a couple days for a Saturday afternoon game, Moos showed up in Leach's office unannounced. Leach was at his desk, prepping for the Bruins. Moos handed him a *Los Angeles Times* story dated December 26, 1993. One of his staff members had found it on the Internet. The headline was RING OF FIRE: IN HIS FOURTH SEASON, BADGER COACH BARRY ALVAREZ PROVIDES THE SPARK THAT HAS IGNITED WISCONSIN'S LONG-DORMANT HOPES FOR THE ROSE BOWL.

"Read this," Moos told him. "In Alvarez's first year at Wisconsin, he had fifty-two players leave the program when they learned what was going to be expected of them."

Leach thanked him and read the piece. In Alvarez's first season at Wisconsin, in 1990, the team went 1-10. The only team it beat was Ball State. "From my first day with the team, when I talked about commitment, I knew we were in trouble," Alvarez told the *Los Angeles Times*. "They weren't ready to make the commitment. One by one, they knocked on the door."

The Rose Bowl was pretty far from Alvarez's mind back then. "I kept telling myself to be patient," he said. In 1991 and 1992, Wisconsin went 5-6. Then, in 1993, the Badgers went 9-1-1 and landed in the Rose Bowl, where they defeated UCLA and finished the year ranked ninth in the nation.

Leach put down the Alvarez article. He knew one thing: Bill Moos had his back. That was something he never felt at Tech.

———

Kickoff was about an hour away. UCLA and WSU players were warming up on the field. ESPN cameramen were in position. Despite the twenty-degree temperature, students were already filling the seats behind WSU's bench. Leach was pacing, watching his quarterbacks try to get warm.

Moos was taking it all in from his skybox. UCLA was 7-2 and heavily favored. But Moos had an odd feeling as he looked down on the field: WSU was going to give the Bruins a run for their money.

Then one of his staff members entered the suite with some news: Marquess Wilson had just released a letter to the media. Moos read it.

Dear Cougar Nation:

It is with a heavy heart that I announce my decision to forgo playing football for Washington State University. I realize the school is saying that I am suspended for violating team policies and may return next week, but this is a lie. This is an attempt by the athletic department to cover up what is really happening in the locker room.

It has been a privilege to be a Cougar, to perform on your field and wear the Crimson and Gray. I would like to thank Washington State University for giving me the opportunity to do what I love most, to play football and receive a quality education for the past three years. I'm grateful to the athletic department for the coaching, care and encouragement I have received prior to this season.

This was going to be our year. My teammates and I were aspiring to be the winning team you deserve. Unfortunately for all, the new coaching staff has destroyed that endeavor. I believe coaches have a chance to mold players, to shape men, to create greatness. However, the new regime of coaches has preferred to belittle, intimidate, and humiliate us. This approach has obviously not been successful, and has put a dark shadow on this program.

My teammates and I have endured this treatment all season long. It is not "tough love." It is abuse. This abuse cannot be allowed to continue. I feel it is my duty to stand up and shed light on this situation by sacrificing my dreams, my education and my pride. I resign from this team. I am deeply sorry to those I am letting down. I am not a quitter. I was raised by my family, and many previous coaches to exhibit dedication and embrace sacrifice, but there comes a time when one has to draw a line in the sand.

Lastly, I thank my fellow teammates, those who also have left the program this year, and those we are leaving behind. I hope our departure will bring awareness to the physical, emotional and verbal

abuse being allowed in the locker room and on the field. I pray for
healing and recovery for all those who have been hurt by this treatment.

Moos stopped reading. "Judas priest!" he said.

Claims of abuse from a disgruntled fourth-string player's father through a confidential e-mail were one thing. An open letter to the media from the team's biggest star was another thing altogether. Moos knew what this meant: the shit was about to hit the fan.

It already had. He had barely finished reading Wilson's letter when he got a text from ESPN's sideline reporter. She wanted his reaction to Wilson's claims. Then his phone vibrated. The call was coming from an AP reporter. Moos ignored them both, turning instead to his assistant. "We've gotta get word to Mike," he said. "Find Super Dave. Have him meet me in my office."

———

As director of football operations, Dave Emerick was crazy busy on game days. He walked around with a clipboard containing a minute-by-minute breakdown of where players and coaches were supposed to be. When he wasn't directing traffic, Emerick was usually one step behind Leach, ready to respond to any last-minute situations that arose. That's where he was when an associate athletic director told him to report to Moos's office at once.

When Emerick reached the AD's office, Moos was handwriting an official statement for the media. He briefed Emerick on the Wilson situation.

Used to the storms that always seemed to be circling Leach, Emerick just raised his eyebrows. It took a lot to rattle him.

"You gotta let Mike know," Moos told Emerick. "This is a nationally televised game. Sideline reporters will grab him. I don't want him to be blindsided."

Emerick reached Leach just before he left the field to return to the locker room for final pregame preparations. Leach was stoic when he heard that Wilson had quit and accused him of abuse. "Yeah, well . . ." Leach said, his voice trailing off. There was a game to coach. Minutes later he was standing in the locker room, surrounded by players. "Everybody, up," he said.

———

By the time the game started, the headline on ESPN.com read "Marquess Wilson Targets Coach." The story led with excerpts from Wilson's letter. It also contained a portion of Moos's statement in response: "I believe I join many Cougars in wishing Marquess well in his future endeavors. We have procedures in place that were developed to monitor student-athlete welfare in all of our sports programs. We will continue to follow those procedures and modify them as needed."

Between ESPN and AP, the story was everywhere. Less than two hours after Wilson released his letter, it was being tweeted and shared on social media Web sites.

––––––

Elson Floyd often entertained in his private box at home games. For the UCLA game he was hosting Pac-12 commissioner Larry Scott. It was Scott's first visit to Pullman since Leach had been hired and the new stadium renovations had been completed. Floyd was showing Scott around the president's suite when he got the call from Moos informing him about Wilson. The minute he hung up, Floyd excused himself from Scott and stepped into his private conference room in the corner of the suite.

While Scott took in the game, Floyd read the online stories about Wilson's departure. He also read Moos's official statement. It was clear WSU had a full-fledged PR disaster on its hands. He sat there, trying to figure out what to do.

"There were three things in my decision-making process," Floyd said. "One is the allegation surrounding Mike's departure from Texas Tech. I am acutely aware of that circumstance. I did my due diligence around it. But I was still aware of the public perception of his departure from Tech. Second, I have this allegation from a parent involving his son in the program. Third, I have this issue involving Marquess."

There was one other factor. Moos had already issued a formal statement to the media. He hadn't run it by Floyd. Nor was he required to. But in this case Floyd wished he had been given a chance to review it. "When I read it, it seemed a bit dismissive and defensive," Floyd said.

He placed another call to Moos, who defended his statement. Moos also pledged to conduct an internal review of Wilson's claims. As soon as the game was over, he planned to drop everything and turn his full attention to interviewing players and coaches.

Floyd didn't discourage Moos. But he also knew Moos was very close to Leach and the football program. Floyd, on the other hand, had purposely kept his distance, never traveling with the team or attending practices. "Part of the whole vexing issue with university presidents and athletic programs is that university presidents get too close to the program," Floyd said. "They lose their objectivity. We have to manage athletics like we do everything else at the institution. There is a balance between supporting a college coach and his team without all this engagement."

Sitting alone in his conference room, Floyd had a gut instinct that an internal review conducted by the athletic department wasn't going to be sufficient. Not this time, anyway. Wilson's letter had cast a national spotlight on WSU. The university's response would be closely scrutinized. "I wanted to be objective," Floyd said. "But I had the potential of a huge PR issue on my hands involving a highly paid football coach at WSU. I had to get ahead of it because if I did not it was going to overtake the institution and me."

When Floyd emerged from his conference room at halftime, UCLA was crushing WSU 37–7. The game was shaping up to be an even bigger disaster than the previous week's loss to Utah. That was the least of Floyd's concerns. He invited Scott into the conference room for a private discussion.

Behind closed doors, Floyd briefed him on the situation. Scott immediately grasped the implications. Floyd then went out on a limb: he asked Scott to conduct an investigation into Wilson's claims.

"I have a lot of confidence in my AD," Floyd said. "I had no concerns about that. But in the spirit of transparency, I have to have some independent review that will confirm or deny the allegations. I have to bring the issue to closure. I also have to bring the Texas Tech issue to closure. That was the subliminal issue here."

Scott wanted to help. But he had a concern. The Pac-12 had never conducted the kind of external review of a program that Floyd was requesting. There was no precedent for the conference investigating one of the conference coaches. Scott wasn't sure the conference had the manpower or the know-how to do what Floyd wanted: a full-fledged, transparent probe of the allegations by Wilson and the parent who had written a letter the week before.

Floyd assured Scott that the conference would be given unfettered access to players, coaches and the athletic department. There would be complete cooperation on the part of the university. "Clearly, in a post–Penn State environment I have to take these issues very seriously," Floyd said. "The issue shifts to how is a president going to deal with it."

Scott promised that the Pac-12 would conduct an investigation. It might require outside help. But it would get done.

By the time Floyd and Scott emerged from the conference room, the mood in the president's suite had changed dramatically. VIPs were shouting and clapping. WSU was making an improbable comeback. Down by thirty at the half, Leach's team played with a renewed sense of urgency. The Cougars ended up scoring twenty-nine second-half points. Even Floyd got swept up in the electricity that had filled the stadium. With 1:36 remaining in the game, UCLA clung to a 44–36 lead.

A few suites down, Bill Moos watched as UCLA ran out the clock, escaping with the win. But Moos was ecstatic. The first half and the second half were like two different games. WSU had roared back. It was proof that the players believed in Leach and his system. The only thing that bugged him was the fact that the team's effort was sure to be completely overshadowed by Wilson's letter.

He was right. After the game, Floyd got an e-mail from Ryan Durkan, a member of WSU's board of regents. One of the top land-use lawyers in the Pacific Northwest, Durkan was already concerned about the letter from the parent when she saw the news about Wilson's letter. She addressed her e-mail to Floyd and the chairman of WSU's board of trustees, Scott Carson. "Elson and Scott, it seems that now the allegations have risen to the level of physical abuse, that we have an issue on which the Board should be briefed. With the vote on the football ops center coming up at the next meeting, we risk looking ill informed if we don't address the allegations. We are not in a position to judge the merits, but after the training we had on the Penn State situation, it seems that we at least have a duty to ask questions. Your thoughts are most welcome. Ryan."

Floyd e-mailed her, saying he'd call her. He planned to tell her about the Pac-12 investigation.

Scott Carson had just gotten off a plane in Seattle when he heard the news about Wilson and saw Durkan's e-mail. He sent a note back to her and Floyd. "I do believe we have an obligation to understand what in the world is going on," Carson said. He wanted to talk to Floyd on Sunday.

———

Wilson's claims drowned out WSU's impressive comeback. The postgame press conference made it pretty clear that Leach's off-the-field problems had eclipsed the game. The situation had reached a point where it threatened to compromise Leach's impressive recruiting class. It was bad enough that WSU had fallen to 2-8. But all the noise about abuse wasn't going to resonate well with parents—particularly mothers—of high school players leaning toward WSU.

Frustrated, Moos was still awake at 11:33 on the night of the game when his cell phone buzzed, alerting him that an e-mail had just come in. It was from Marquess Wilson. "Mr. Moos this is Marquess . . . With that letter I wasn't trying to accuse the coaches of hitting players or anything. I was just trying to put it in different terms and now everything is getting misinterpreted and I didn't like that at all . . . I simply was trying to get my story across and get my name cleared instead of having it say I'm suspended for breaking team violations . . . That could mean like I did drugs or something . . . I was never trying to harm the university or the program with it."

Moos read it again. It was hard not to be incredulous. But Moos also felt an instant sense of relief. Wilson had essentially validated what Moos had believed all along: that players were not being abused; they were being pushed to become better. And for whatever reason, Wilson wasn't on board. So he bolted.

Moos told Leach. His reaction was anticlimactic. He didn't think the original complaint was a big deal. The fact that Wilson recanted hours later wasn't a big deal either. One thing that Leach had learned a long time ago is that when you are coaching a hundred-plus kids—most of whom aren't old enough to drink legally—issues are going to flare up. It's best to keep a level head and keep moving forward.

It was after midnight by the time Moos forwarded Wilson's e-mail to Floyd with a simple note: "Elson, sent to me at 11:33. Unfortunate as our guys gave a valiant effort and deserved to be the lead story. Bill."

Floyd didn't see Moos's note until Sunday morning, around 8:00. It did little to change his mind about doing an outside investigation. He e-mailed Moos: "Well, the damage is done now. I must repair it and move on. ESF."

Over the next couple days, Floyd received some push back on his plan to have the Pac-12 conduct an investigation. What was the point? Wilson had recanted. Besides, Moos was still doing his internal review. And there were all kinds of risks associated with having outsiders poking around the football program. It was impossible to predict what they might find and where those findings might lead.

But that was exactly why Floyd felt compelled to go forward. "Why do this review if Marquess recanted?" Floyd said. "Well, it was because I had another complaint that no one knew about. [The letter from the parent.] So Marquess's recant wasn't sufficient."

Richard Evrard is a partner at Bond Schoeneck & King, a law firm out of Overland Park, Kansas. Before joining the firm in 1992, Evrard was an attorney for the NCAA, where he worked on enforcement and was the director of legislative services. After leaving the NCAA, he represented institutions accused of NCAA infractions. His expertise caused the law firm to ultimately put him in charge of its Collegiate Sports Practice Group, which had represented Minnesota, Kansas, Ohio State and other universities through major scandals involving academic fraud, payments to players and recruiting violations.

When Larry Scott directed the Pac-12's general counsel, Woodie Dixon, to choose someone to conduct a review of WSU's football program on behalf of the conference, Dixon retained Evrard to develop an investigation outline, conduct interviews and draft a final report to be presented to the Pac-12 and the university. Specifically, Evrard and his team developed four areas of review:

1. Claims of physical, verbal and emotional abuse reported by Marquess Wilson.
2. Sandpit workouts and whether the coaching staff endangered the welfare of student-athletes by having them participate in conditioning/disciplinary workout sessions conducted in the pit.
3. Student-athlete injuries and whether football coaches were requiring injured players to participate in practices when institutional policy gave authority for that decision to the training and medical staffs.
4. Practice hours and whether the football program violated NCAA legislation limiting the amount of practice hours in which student-athletes can be required to participate.

All of these lines of inquiries were potential minefields that could expose the university to lawsuits and NCAA sanctions. No one understood that more than Evrard.

By way of background, Evrard's team started by looking into the events that touched off Marquess Wilson's departure from the team. The trouble began at halftime during the Utah game in Salt Lake City. WSU had played a miserable first half. Things came to a boiling point in the locker room when a defensive coach attempted to motivate players by using his hands to urge his players to be more physical. He emphasized his point by pushing some players on the breastplate sections of their shoulder pads while shouting four-letter words at them. At least one player got emotional and used equally strong language to shout back at the coach, a reaction that the coach said was exactly what he was looking for. That's what he wanted to see them do in the second half—respond with emotion.

Wilson wasn't one of the players being pushed in the locker room during halftime. But that incident, coupled with the coaching staff's decision to make players do sandpit drills on the day following the loss to Utah, is what brought him to a breaking point. But when asked by investigators whether he had been physically abused, Wilson insisted he had not. "I wasn't trying to accuse anybody of abuse," Wilson told investigators. "I mean, they never touched us. I wasn't trying to say that in my letter . . . I mean, that, there was no point where I was trying to say that they're abusing us."

The halftime incident at Utah wasn't deemed abusive. "Concerning the incident in the locker room at the Utah game, the evidence indicates that a coach was trying to motivate his players through the use of some emotionally charged language and physical acts," Evrard wrote. "Football is a physical game and it is not unusual for a coach in football to try and exhort his players to be more physical by getting physical with them."

Regarding verbal abuse, Wilson told investigators it was common for coaches to call him and his teammates "coward, pussy, bitch, all that." He added, "Where I was raised you don't let people call you that."

Evrard and his team interviewed twenty coaches, players, parents and athletic department leaders. Many of the interviews were conducted in person. Most of the players who were chosen were team leaders or played the same position as Wilson. All of the interviewed players confirmed that the language reported by Wilson was similar to what they heard from coaches. But none of them considered the language abusive.

"Most of the student-athletes indicated that they have heard that kind of language from coaches most of their lives and are not offended by it," Evrard noted, concluding that Leach's staff was merely using the universal language of football. Wilson simply got a bigger dose of it because he was a highly talented player who, according to his teammates, often failed to display maximum effort.

Investigators also asked about the use of a sandpit for conditioning and disciplining players. Leach said he believed the sandpit to be a great tool of cardiovascular conditioning that also helped reduce injuries to ankles and knee joints. He'd been a proponent of using a sandpit for conditioning football players long before arriving at WSU. And plenty of other programs used sandpits.

But Evrard wanted to know if the pit was used to discipline or punish players. One assistant athletic director who had witnessed sandpit sessions told investigators that the "discipline in the sand does get at time, uh, questionable." On one occasion, the assistant AD reported, he witnessed the strength and conditioning coach spraying student-athletes with a hose and instructed him to discontinue the practice. Bill Moos had also instructed the football staff to stop the use of water in the pit. Leach told investigators he was unaware of any incidents where the strength coach had sprayed athletes during workouts.

One by one, Evrard's team went through every allegation raised by the parent's letter and Wilson's letter. Investigators were on WSU's campus and in the football operations building, getting a close view of the inner workings of Leach's system. The coaching staff started to feel as if it were under siege. At one point, Moos met with Leach. "Hey, you just keep coaching this football team," Moos told him. "And coach it the way you always have. Don't be worrying about this. You just coach."

———

On the day after Thanksgiving, WSU played its final game of the season, a nationally televised contest against its archrival, Washington. WSU entered the game with an eight-game losing streak and a 2-9 record. The Huskies were 7-4. After three quarters, UW led 28–10. Fans started leaving. Then WSU stormed back, scoring eighteen unanswered points to force overtime. On the first possession of the extra frame, WSU kicked a field goal to win the game 31–28. Fans stormed the field. Leach and his players were mobbed. Moos practically knocked people down giving them high fives. And Floyd raised the Apple Cup trophy in a ceremony at midfield. "We kicked the Huskies out of the place," Floyd shouted over the public-address system, drawing cheers.

Leach did a bunch of interviews and told his team in the locker room how proud he was of their effort. Two hours had passed by the time he had finished talking to everyone who wanted his ear. It was late in the afternoon. He had just thirty minutes until he had to attend a recruiting dinner at a Pullman restaurant with all the high school players and parents who were in town. The season had just ended, and he was already turning his sights to the next season. It was close to midnight before he finally got home.

The next day *Yahoo! Sports* ran a story reporting that Leach had received a $25,000 bonus for winning the Apple Cup. To celebrate, *Yahoo! Sports* reported, Leach had gone to Valhalla Bar and Grill, the most famous student bar in Pullman, and spent $3,000 on drinks for fans. "That's what makes Leach one of college football's great and sometimes controversial characters," the story reported. "But letting the fans drink up on his Apple Cup bonus—Leach might be the only coach in America who would celebrate that way."

Leach had never gone anywhere near the Valhalla. But he didn't bother to refute the story. He didn't have the time.

On January 7, 2013, Pac-12 commissioner Larry Scott overnighted Rick Evrard's final report on the Washington State football program to Elson Floyd. The twenty-nine-page summary detailed foul language, intense workouts and emotional outbursts. But in the end, Evrard and his team determined that WSU's program was basically like any other major college football program. "All parties agreed that the coaching staff is tough, they demand discipline and they will not tolerate anything less than maximum effort when involved with their program," the report concluded. "Based on the totality of the information obtained and reviewed by the investigative team there does not appear to be any form of abuse in the football program."

Floyd read every word. Then he sent copies to his board of trustees and directed his staff to release copies to the media. By this time, Moos had completed his internal review, giving the program a clean bill of health. But Evrard's report gave the program an outside stamp of approval. It also satisfied Floyd's ultimate concern. "The reports put to bed the Tech issue and the Marquess issue at the same time," Floyd said. "It was Texas Tech that served as a shadow over everything else. Now that's over and I'm glad to have that chapter closed."

Nobody was more pleased than Bill Moos. He immediately got word to Leach. "I'm happy," Leach said. "But I'm not surprised."

Moos wasn't surprised either. Nor was he bitter. "I like to find lemonade in lemons," Moos said. "The Adam James thing was always going to be out there. I think it is good we went through this and nothing turned up. Next time we say, 'Hey, we've been down that road.' Mike didn't do anything except demand maximum effort and win football games."

One month later, Leach landed his prize recruit. Despite an aggressive last-minute push by Arizona State, quarterback Tyler Bruggman signed his letter of intent to attend WSU. "The majority of the selling point was Mike Leach," he said. "WSU is a great university and all. But from a student-athlete perspective, having a guy like Leach is huge. He is the reason I chose WSU. My parents are looking forward to handing me off to him for the next four years."

THE DRAFT PICK

To go pro or not to go pro

An official NFL sign on the San Diego Chargers' locker room wall read CONCUSSION: A MUST READ FOR NFL PLAYERS—LET'S TAKE BRAIN INJURIES OUT OF PLAY. It listed the facts and symptoms resulting from helmet-to-helmet contact, trauma that can alter the way the brain functions. Kyle Van Noy and Ziggy Ansah walked past the warning as they stepped into the dank, narrow tunnel that leads to the field at Qualcomm Stadium. It was December 20, 2012, and BYU was playing in the Poinsettia Bowl against San Diego State. Stretching side by side on the lush green sod, Van Noy and Ansah got their first look and feel of an NFL facility—gigantic, concrete and cold. It was exactly the kind of place where they would soon be making a living.

That realization sank in as they went through pregame warm-ups. Ansah's late-season surge had every NFL draft analyst calling him a sure-fire first-rounder. Van Noy, meanwhile, was among the nation's leaders in sacks, forced fumbles and unassisted tackles. The two of them had anchored BYU's defense, which was the third best overall in the nation. Despite a rock-solid defense, BYU's often-anemic offense resulted in the team finishing 7-5. Most of the criticism was directed at Mendenhall for his priorities. "There is his always-controversial contention that winning football games is only fifth on his priority list, behind spiritual development, academic achievement, character advancement and service," one *Deseret News* columnist lamented after the 2012 season. "Rest easy, Alabama."

Even former star players from the LaVell Edwards era went public with their criticism of Mendenhall's approach. "I'll say this much," wrote Vai Sikahema, "Tom Holmoe better get BYU into a conference quickly. There is no way ESPN can justify renewing its contract with BYU if this is what it's going to get."

But Mendenhall made no apologies for his brand of football. "This system is so contrary to what is normal," he said. "But I'm trying to build the most complete program."

Ansah and Van Noy were aware of all the criticism directed at their coach. But they dismissed it. "The reason I respect Bronco so much is because he cares about our well-being," Van Noy said. "Football is just a short thing. The things he teaches last a lifetime. That's why I play so hard for him."

———

Fifteen minutes before kickoff, Van Noy and Ansah sat on stools in front of their lockers. Their teammates did the same. Assistant coaches stood, their backs against the wall. The locker room was dead silent—no music, no talking. The only movement was the team trainer, going player to player, offering smelling salts. Everyone was waiting for Mendenhall, who was alone in his office. Finally, he emerged.

"Bring it up," he said.

Players circled him and took a knee.

"I just want to say how proud I am of you and how proud I am to be your coach," he said quietly. "It's such a privilege to represent what we represent. Leave nothing on the field today."

His pregame speech lasted all of thirty-nine seconds. He never mentioned the other team. He never raised his voice. He showed no emotion.

"Riley is going to lead us in prayer," Mendenhall said.

Quarterback Riley Nelson stood up. "Heavenly Father," he began, "we thank thee for the opportunity to be part of this brotherhood."

When Nelson said "amen," Mendenhall headed for the door. The team lined up single file behind him and walked out in silence.

BYU won the coin toss and elected to kick off. On the first possession, San Diego State's quarterback, Adam Dingwell, dropped to pass. Ansah applied pressure up the middle, forcing him to throw early. As soon as Dingwell released the ball, Ansah turned and sprinted downfield toward the intended receiver. The pass ricocheted off the receiver's shoulder pads and into Ansah's hands—his first interception.

"Ziggy! Ziggy! Ziggy!" fans chanted. The ESPN broadcasters immediately started talking about Ansah's rapid rise on NFL draft boards.

Later, Van Noy blocked a punt. Those two plays were the extent of the excitement for the first three quarters of the game. Both offenses were dismal. At the start of the fourth quarter, San Diego State led 6–3, and the Poinsettia Bowl was on track to go down as one of the most boring bowl games in the history of college football. Then BYU's Nelson threw a goal-line interception. San Diego State took over on its own three-yard line. As BYU's defense prepared to take the field, the linebackers coach screamed: "We need a turnover! We need a turnover!"

On San Diego State's first play, Van Noy blitzed from the outside as Dingwell dropped back to throw out of his own end zone. Blowing past his man, Van Noy left his feet and went lateral. Fully extended, he hit Dingwell just as he began to bring his arm forward, jarring the ball loose. From his knees, Van Noy scooped up the ball just as Ansah landed on top of him. Touchdown BYU.

Up 10–6, BYU kicked off. After another turnover, BYU went up 17–6. Then, with 6:29 remaining, Dingwell threw from the San Diego State nineteen-yard line. This time Van Noy had dropped into zone coverage. As Dingwell's pass went toward a receiver near the sideline on the thirty-five-yard line, Van Noy leaped and intercepted it. Cutting back across the field, he eluded would-be tacklers and scampered into the end zone. Touchdown BYU. The defense mobbed him in the end zone, and the chants rained down from the stands: "B-Y-U! B-Y-U! B-Y-U!"

In a span of nine minutes, Van Noy had scored more touchdowns than both offenses combined. Along with his fumble recovery and interception, he had registered one blocked punt, two sacks and nine unassisted tackles. As Van Noy came toward the sideline clutching the football, Mendenhall was waiting for him. They made eye contact. Mendenhall nodded, smiled and clenched his fist. Those three things were the ultimate form of compliment. Van Noy nodded and smiled back.

At the conclusion of the game, Van Noy ran to the first row of stadium seats to get a kiss from his mother and a hug from his father. Then he joined the team at midfield for the Poinsettia Bowl trophy ceremony. Van Noy was named the game's MVP. After his teammates retreated to the locker room, Van Noy went to a corner of the stadium occupied by BYU fans for a lengthy postgame television interview. As the interview ended, Van Noy waved to the fans. They began chanting, "One more year! One more year! One more year!"

Alone, he turned and walked across the end zone where he had scored both touchdowns, waving over his shoulder to the fans. "What a way to go out," he thought to himself, pausing beneath the goalpost to look out over the field and empty stadium. "I have done everything I need to do. I have played my last game at BYU."

Ziggy Ansah sat in silence at his locker, realizing how much he was going to miss BYU football. It was 9:00 p.m. His teammates had showered, dressed, said good-bye and headed for the team bus. Ansah was still in his grass-stained uniform. Even his high-top black cleats were still laced. He didn't want to say good-bye. He didn't want it to end.

Finally, Van Noy entered the locker room, trailed by Mendenhall. They had come from the postgame press conference. Ansah stood to greet them. Mendenhall embraced him.

"I love you," Mendenhall whispered.

"I love you, too," Ansah said.

Moments later, Ansah pulled off his gear and made his way to the showers, leaving Mendenhall and Van Noy alone in the locker room. They looked at each other and smiled. Then they wrapped their arms around each other. "I'm so proud of you, Kyle," Mendenhall said. "So proud."

"Thank you," Van Noy said.

———

On January 19, 2013, seventy-three underclassmen were approved for the NFL draft. That marked an all-time high. But Kyle Van Noy's name was not on the list. After the Poinsettia Bowl he went home with his parents to Reno to celebrate Christmas. But their conversations kept coming back to the question: Stay in college or go pro?

Three different agents had assured him that he would be drafted at the start of the second round. Overnight he'd go from a poor student-athlete to a wealthy professional. He'd fulfill his boyhood dream, too.

As good as it all sounded—and as certain as Van Noy felt—something kept nagging him. The turning point was a conversation with one of his closest confidants, Chicago Bears running back Harvey Unga. He and his wife maintained a home in Provo. In 2009, Unga became BYU's all-time leading rusher as a junior, amassing 3,455 yards in his first three seasons. But Unga withdrew from BYU prior to his senior year after violating the school's honor code. It was a decision he discussed at length with Van Noy.

"Harvey is like an older brother to me," Van Noy said. "He told me that I didn't want to have regrets about not finishing my senior year."

After talking with Unga, Van Noy told his parents he'd made up his mind. He wanted to finish what he started. That meant obtaining his degree. He also felt as if he had unfinished business on the football field.

The team, he felt, was on the verge of something big in 2013. He wanted to be part of it. But the main thing on his mind was his legacy.

"Especially with my past, staying will have an impact on a lot of younger people," Van Noy said. "There will be kids who say, 'If Kyle can graduate, then I can, too.'"

His parents took out an insurance policy in case Van Noy was injured during his senior year. Then Van Noy called Mendenhall. "I'm staying for my senior year," he told him. "I'm coming back."

―――――

All thirty-two NFL teams were present at the Senior Bowl in Mobile, Alabama, on January 26, 2013. All eyes were on Ezekiel Ansah. He had only started nine games in his college career. This was an opportunity to see him compete against the best offensive players in the nation. In the third quarter he left no doubt about his ability to get after the quarterback when he shed two blockers and tracked down Syracuse's Ryan Nassib, hammering him as he scrambled, forcing a fumble in the process.

But the play that solidified Ansah as a first-round pick came on a run play. The North handed the ball to Michigan speedster Denard Robinson on a reverse. Initially, Ansah had been fooled by the misdirection. Still, he planted his toe in the ground, changed direction and gave chase. Despite having no angle, he chased down Robinson with ease and threw him to the ground. It was a remarkable display of speed, strength and agility.

Three months later Ansah sat between his mother and Bronco Mendenhall backstage at Radio City Music Hall in New York City. At the lectern, NFL commissioner Roger Goodell turned the microphone over to Hall of Fame running back Barry Sanders.

"With the fifth pick of the 2013 NFL draft, the Detroit Lions select Ezekiel Ansah, defensive end, BYU."

The audience went wild.

Ansah stood and hugged his mother. Then he turned to Mendenhall, who gave him a bear hug and congratulated him.

"We have coming out of the greenroom a young man who just a couple years ago hadn't even played the sport," said a commentator from the NFL Network. "We have a fifth overall pick in this draft with four and a half career sacks."

"Please understand the magnitude of this story," chimed in another NFL Network commentator. "The reason he's playing football is that the BYU basketball team cut him twice. Then he went to the track team. He never came to football until 2010 as a walk-on. He's six feet five inches. He weighs 270 pounds. And he has frightening physical skills. Coming off the edge at the Senior Bowl, he dominated the Senior Bowl."

Ansah stepped to the stage wearing a Lions cap and his trademark lensless glasses. First Goodell hugged him, then Sanders did. Holding his new Lions jersey, Ziggy faced the crowd and smiled.

Twenty-four hours later he entered Ford Field in Detroit to chants of "Ziggy! Ziggy! Ziggy!" It was Draft Fan Fest, and the place was rocking.

"You can't explain this," Ansah said. "It feels warm. I feel the love. I'm ready to fall in love with this place."

The genius of ESPN

All right, let's see the open, let's walk through the open."

The clock inside the production truck read 9:48:40. Game time for ESPN's *College GameDay* was less than thirteen minutes away.

"Signs, fellas, we need signs," said the thirty-eight-year-old producer, Lee Fitting, long and lean with some age around his eyes.

Like magic, I WASH MY DIRTY CLOTHES WITH TIDE popped up on one of a dozen monitors in front of the director, Tom Lucas. SABAN WEARS CROCS. AJ MCCRYIN'.

"Clip those off," Lucas said.

"Signs, signs, everywhere signs," Fitting sang softly to himself.

He downed some coffee and set the Starbucks cup inside a roll of masking tape. Fitting was a senior coordinating producer at ESPN, in his ninth year at the helm of the gold standard of pregame shows. The challenge was keeping a show in its twenty-sixth season looking and feeling fresh and unscripted. "Organic," he called it.

"Hey, how about these guys get to the set one week on time!"

"These guys" were Chris Fowler, in his twenty-third consecutive year as anchor and host of *GameDay* and his twenty-sixth overall at the network; Heisman Trophy winner Desmond Howard; Kirk Herbstreit, the game's top analyst; and crazy-as-a-fox Lee Corso, known to the crew as "Coach" or "LC."

Fitting pressed a small button on a communication console, enabling him to speak directly into the ear of talent.

"LC, good morning," he said. "I need you to play to the crowd."

Fitting did not have to ask twice. Corso grabbed an Alabama helmet from the *GameDay* desk and raised it over his head. Well, that certainly woke up the early-morning crowd that had gathered in Atlanta's Centennial Olympic Park. Then, for good measure, Corso gave the same salute to the Georgia fans.

Since it first hit the road in 1993—No. 1 Florida State versus No. 2 Notre Dame in South Bend, on NBC no less—*GameDay* had rolled onto virtually every major campus in college football, some a dozen times or more. Austin, Tuscaloosa, Eugene, Ann Arbor, Knoxville, Gainesville, South Bend, Baton Rouge, Boise State, the Bayou Classic in Houston, a terrific trip to the Division III Amherst-Williams clash, the MEAC and the MAC. Only one spot remained on the crew's collective bucket list—The Grove at Ole Miss.

"Ah, sundresses and alcoholic beverages," Fitting said with a sigh.

Week in and week out the editorial and emotional tone of the two-hour show was set by what's known in the business as the "open"—a two-minute or so video montage at the very top of the broadcast. Fowler always wrote and narrated the open. Hell, he wrote the entire show. But the open was critical. *GameDay* set the tone for Saturday's biggest games, and the open set the tone for *GameDay*. Nobody took that responsibility more seriously than Fowler.

"Our audience is very rare," he said during a quiet moment on the *GameDay* bus. "We have to work really long and hard—that's where the late hours come in—to make the show 2 or 3 percent better [every week] because our audience is so informed.

"I think of myself as the conscience of the show," he said when asked about his role. "The show very clearly knows what it is. And I think too many shows forget what they are—or never figure it out. We are a pregame show. We are what the fan on the couch wants to talk about, hear about, two hours before kickoff. That's what we are. We are not a magazine show. We are not a show of record. We are not all things to all people. We are counting down to the [game] sites of the day."

On the first Saturday in December 2012—championship Saturday— the *GameDay* circus was in Atlanta, counting down to the SEC title game later that afternoon. By the time two jam-packed, fun-filled hours were over, *GameDay* had offered its audience three terrific features, snappy game highlights, a complete breakdown of the Alabama–Georgia game, high- octane opinions and signature nods to Michael Jordan, Ray Charles, Tupac and the Kardashians, all the while showcasing the best on-set chemistry of any pregame show on the planet.

"It's really like a team; you've got to check your egos at the door," said Corso. "You know, in television, some guys have big egos, and when they do, it hurts the team. I think ours are very much kept under control. We don't have egos. I think that's very important."

"None of it's contrived," Fitting said, relaxing on a hotel hallway couch after a two-hour Friday production meeting. "The guys on the set act the same way in the meeting. They act the same way on our Monday conference call. They act the same way when we go out to dinner. It's real, natural, chemistry."

The clock in the truck read 9:55:29. Four minutes and change to air.

Herbstreit had finally made an appearance on the bright orange Home Depot set it took six hours to construct. Fitting saw himself as the "orchestra leader" of the show. He loved the locker room banter, the chance to bust chops. On the fourteenth and final show of the regular season, Herbstreit had unwittingly provided the first opportunity of the day.

"Hey, Herbie! Nice of you to fuckin' join us! Every week! I've had it with you!"

The clock was ticking. The conductor wanted to see and hear the open one more time.

"Do it again," said Fitting. "Let's treat this as a real read."

———

Live sports programming is among the most deceptive of arts. Done right, it flowed like a superhighway on the screen, a rapidly moving sequence of what's called "traffic"—plays, replays, sideline reports, graphics and promos—unfolding before the viewer's eyes without the slightest stumble or interruption.

Pregame shows are even more difficult to produce than games because there's no particular pattern to the traffic; it's free-form television art. And without question in the last decade or so *GameDay* had grown into the highest form of that art. Bucking the cable TV trend that more is better—more stats, more graphics, more, more, *more* on the screen—under Fitting and Fowler, *GameDay* had stripped away the clutter and gone increasingly old-school. Less was more. Their goal: simple and clean. A show bursting with talent and opinion driven by the energy of its unique live audience and the passion and commitment of the man Fitting saw as the "quarterback" of the *GameDay* team.

"It starts with Fowler," he said. "He always says, 'We can't make the show the same as last week.'"

"In ten ... nine ... eight ...

"Roll X."

"Sound full, open Chris's mike."

"Have a good one, fellas," said Fitting. "Let's finish strong."

"Take music."

Setting the big picture of college football for that weekend, a "beauty" shot of the serene campus of undefeated and top-ranked Notre Dame filled the screen. Fowler's strong, expressive voice took it from there.

"All's calm and quiet at Notre Dame today . . . where prayers have been answered. Resilience rewarded. Perfection achieved . . ."

In Fowler's right hand was a blue index card the size of a paperback book. On the inside was the open. Every word was capitalized in thin black ink. Words Fowler wanted to emphasize had been underlined. It looked exactly like this:

THE DOGS DEFENSE IS WOOFING! TALKING UP THEIR
TALENT—<u>VOWING</u> TO BRING ENOUGH <u>SWAGGER</u> FOR
A <u>SIXTY MINUTE TUSSLE</u> W/THE <u>TIDE</u>. ARE WE <u>BUYING</u>
THEY CAN <u>BACK</u> IT UP?

Fowler had been up until 2:30 tightening the text and transferring the notes and wordplay he'd sketched out on his iPad during the week to his cards. He liked to work late for a couple of reasons: it assured the latest possible information, and what he wrote stayed fresh in his mind. At a point of his career when he could have easily just mailed it in, Fowler religiously called coaches and sources during the week while living online digging for the latest college football news. He also employed the son of a tennis partner, a Cal grad with an eye for what Fowler called "very different" information, to augment his own research and reporting. He loved his work and it showed. He was living in what he called the golden age of *GameDay*.

"This thing has taken a lot of twists and turns over the twenty-three years of doing it," he said on the bus. "There were the experimental years. The wild and woolly years, when we really didn't know what we were doing, it was growing so fast, and people were just sort of catching on. [Now] we are all very much middle-aged, mature. We know what we're doing. It's well-oiled in every facet of it. From the stage to the truck to the set."

"I've been around ESPN since '96, and nobody is as committed to the product as he is," said Fitting. "Strictly committed to serving the college football fan. And he will push back at me at times—push back at management at times. When I sit back and really think about what he's doing, it's always for the betterment of the show for the fan. Period."

"That's very nice," Fowler said after the compliment was relayed. "First of all, it starts from not just me, but everyone has a genuine passion for the sport. If this was a weekly *assignment* for somebody, they need to go someplace else. This is where all of us want to be on Saturday and no place else. For fourteen weeks we want to be at the biggest game. Talking about it. Setting the table. Analyzing what's going on that Saturday. It's a labor of love for all of us."

Fowler absolutely killed the open, knocked it out of the park, leading to the show's rowdy Comin' to Your Cit-taaay theme song by country stars Big & Rich.

"That a boy," said Fitting into Fowler's ear. "Hum that cheese."

Translation: In the baseball equivalent of his final start of the regular season, Fowler had brought his fastball.

"Chris brought his heater to the show today," Fitting said. "Chris Fowler, bringing that four-seam cheese."

Fitting had grown up on the North Shore of Long Island dreaming of becoming a sports announcer, the next Chris Berman. At James Madison University in Virginia, he entered a Dick Vitale soundalike contest. Now, as the "guys" were about to come on camera for the first time to discuss the story lines of the Alabama–Georgia game, he channeled his inner Dickie V.

"Don't let Herbie get going early, boys! He's like Adrian Peterson! He gets eight or nine early . . . don't give him too many carries early, he'll be calling for the rock all day!"

"Nine to Fowler."

"Stand by on camera, gentlemen . . . stand by, here we come."

Fowler welcomed the audience at home and thousands more cheering and chanting behind the set. "Great to be here in Centennial Park—Chris Fowler, Kirk Herbstreit, Desmond Howard and the Coach, Lee Corso."

Just one small problem: Howard's microphone had suddenly gone dead.

"We don't have Desmond's mike right now?" asked Fitting.

No, he was told. He pressed a button on his console.

"No opening comment from Dez," he told Fowler.

All fine and good except at the exact moment, just as Fitting's words were hitting Fowler's aural canal, the anchor had turned to his right, toward Howard, for the first comment of the day. No problem. As if by remote control Fowler glided left and looked toward Herbstreit.

"Good, everybody," said Fitting. "That's how you bob and weave. Always have a backup to the backup."

Not *GameDay*. In virtually every other pregame show the anchor copy was scripted and rolled from a teleprompter. After the open, Fowler's blue index cards contained little more than bullet points and plays on words. There was no teleprompter, no cue cards, no safety net on the *GameDay* set. The backup to the backup was Fowler.

To an experienced television eye he had the gift, the savant-like ability to process rapid streams of information spoken into his ear while moving seamlessly between elements—from highlights to graphics to commercial countdowns. Most important, he kept the *GameDay* train on track—no easy task given the personalities—never once giving a glimpse of the controlled chaos in the truck to the audience at home. In the world of network television you could count the number of other broadcasters with such skill on one hand: Bob Costas, the brothers Gumbel (Bryant and Greg) and Matt Lauer. That was about it.

"He does things on the spur of the moment that are unbelievable," said Corso. "You don't see them. He does so many things that keep us under control."

"Chris Fowler can do anything," Fitting said, and he wasn't blowing smoke. "He could host the Olympics. He could host a morning show. He could host the evening news. He's brilliant. Without a doubt there's never a situation on the show that I'm worried about. With Chris you don't have to put the ball on the tee. He can hit the ball when it's falling off the tee."

Now in his early fifties, Fowler had arrived at ESPN in 1986, a golden boy out of the University of Colorado with a bachelor of science in radio/television news, already with two years of production and on-air experience at KCNC, a big NBC affiliate out of Denver. He spent his first two years at ESPN as the host/reporter for *Scholastic Sports America*, a high school sports magazine show. In 1988, he moved to the college football sidelines. Since then, he had hosted ESPN's Final Four coverage for thirteen seasons, Grand Slam tennis (a favorite), Triple Crown coverage, the World Cup and its Heisman award show.

"I think the best compliment people can say is you make things *easy*," he said. "This isn't going to sound right, but if the quarterback knows what he's doing and he's been doing it a million years, he's not going to forget the snap count."

Sitting in a black leather chair at the back of the *GameDay* bus, his feet outstretched, Fowler said, "It's not different from playing quarterback. There were many years you can't check down to our third or fourth option because the pass rush was in your face. It's not all that different from this job. You see it. It's a very tough thing to adapt and learn. There are a lot of moving parts. In order to make it work, and feel organic, you have to have a presence of mind."

Like it or not, the acid test of a news or sports reporter comes during moments of crisis. (See Al Michaels, 1989 earthquake, World Series, San Francisco.) Fowler's biggest test arrived unexpectedly in November 2011 near the end of a short commercial break. Watching the wires, a news editor in the production truck noticed an Associated Press story out of New Haven, Connecticut. A rental truck carrying kegs of beer driven by a student had suddenly gone out of control and run into a tailgating crowd at the Harvard–Yale football game. A thirty-year-old woman had been killed, and three others had been injured.

Fitting heard the news and thought, "Holy shit, we've got to get this on the air right now."

"I get in Chris's ear and say, 'Breaking news, you're going to be on camera in a single shot, and here's the story.'"

"He likes to talk about that," said Fowler.

Fowler said as soon as he heard the words "Listen to me, this is important," he knew Fitting wasn't about to kill a TCU graphic. Fowler had grown up admiring the late, legendary ABC Sports broadcaster Jim McKay. "He was always able to say . . . the right thing," Fowler said. "You would just say, 'Wow, if I could just somehow hope to approach that ability and get it right more than wrong, that would be something I'd like to do.'"

GameDay was just back from the commercial break when Fitting got in Fowler's ear. "I may have given him a line or two," said Fitting. "As we come out of the break, he's saying the line or two, and I'm reading from the wire story into his ear, and he's just reciting it out. I swear to God, flawlessly."

Said Fowler, "You get that little adrenaline burst where you realize, shit, this is awful, this is important in a way that nothing else we're talking about today is important, and you better damn well listen and get it."

———

Nobody was more beloved by the *GameDay* crew—or in college football for that matter—than Corso. At seventy-seven, he was something of a cult figure among the college crowd, known for his signature "Not so fast, my friend" catchphrase and unpredictable predictions at the end of the show, when he donned the mascot's headgear of the team he picked to win. Kids young enough to be his great-grandchildren held up signs that either praised or berated what they saw as this crazy, lovable old coot. Classics like CORSO IS NOT WEARING PANTIES.

"As I told a guy," said Corso, "every week I make half of the fans really pissed at me, and over the years I've got the other half really mad at me. I've done that for twenty years. So you can imagine. But I found as long as you do it with humor and sincerity . . ."

Corso had stumbled upon the mascot idea—one of the most original acts in the history of sports TV—back in October 1996 at an Ohio State practice the day before a home game against Iowa. "Brutus the Buckeye walked by, and I said to Herbstreit, 'If you can get me that head, I'll put it on. I won't have to say a word. People will know I picked Ohio State.'"

Turned out, Herbie carried some sway at OSU. A former quarterback, he had captained the team his senior year. Arrangements were made.

"Man, the crowd went crazy," recalled Corso. "The truck went crazy. And ESPN went crazy. I thought, 'Maybe I should stick with this.'"

In the spring of 2009, Corso suffered a minor stroke. It slowed his speech and visibly altered the crucial on-air chemistry of the show. The fear was his *GameDay* days were over.

"To be honest, there was a tough couple of years there," said Fowler. "He knows it. He lived it. Part of it was his fear of locking up. And so did we. Herbie has been so great with Lee. Whenever he sort of trips up, it's not a smart-ass laugh, it's an affectionate laugh."

"I couldn't be Lee Corso in my biggest dream," Herbstreit had told an audience of more than five hundred people at the twelfth annual Jimmy Rane Foundation dinner in Pine Mountain, Georgia, seven months earlier as the special guest speaker at an event that raised hundreds of thousands of dollars for college scholarships. "I've really learned the entertainment aspect of television just watching and sitting next to Lee."

The 2012 season marked Herbstreit's seventeenth on *GameDay*. He was all of twenty-six when he auditioned in 1996. He had grown up listening to the Cincinnati Reds and Cris Collinsworth on WLW's burgeoning sports-talk show. "Everyone else was listening to Van Halen," Herbstreit said. "Nobody wanted to get in my car."

When Herbstreit graduated from OSU, he called a couple of local stations and made his pitch: former team captain and quarterback who loved sports-talk radio. One station bought in, and the next thing Herbstreit knew he had a job for twelve grand a year. No benefits. Nothing. Most people, he said, would have jumped at the pharmaceutical sales job he had been offered—the stability, 401(k) plan, company car and bonus. "But for me, I was coming off a scholarship check. For me $12,000, with three roommates, I was going to be *rich*. That sounded fine. Plus, I was going to be doing something I loved. I didn't have any idea where that choice would land me, other than I knew it was something I loved to do."

The local radio gig led to some sideline reporting for OSU and a chance on-field chat with Jack Arute, a total pro who roamed the college football sidelines for ABC Sports for years. It didn't take Arute long to size up the articulate ex-Buckeye with Abercrombie looks.

"You should do TV," he said.

So Herbie made an audition tape. He convinced Eddie George and Joey Galloway, the two biggest stars on the team, to be guests on a fictional show called "Buckeye Corner." For good measure, Herbstreit added a fake sideline report from the stadium and sent the package to ABC and ESPN.

"Never heard anything from ABC to this day," he said to laughter at the charity event. "But ESPN called me back. Said they were about to start a new network called ESPN2 and wanted me to come in for an audition."

Not long after, notes from the Alabama–Georgia game arrived, and Herbstreit set about doing what he had always done as the son of a coach. Preparing. Over-preparing. He stayed up until four in the morning making his "Board," a color-coded poster board listing the starting offensive and defensive teams and backups, with sizes, weights and numbers. He showed up in Bristol ready to knock people's socks off.

"I did a *GameDay* segment for three minutes," he said. "I said, 'What about the Georgia–Alabama game?' I've got my Board. Spent hours on it. I still have it. They put the game on the monitor. Jack Edwards was doing play-by-play. And he's looking at me like I'm from Mars. 'What are you doing with all this stuff?' I'm thinking we're going to do three hours. We did three plays. And that was it. I was done. Shook my hand. Thanked me. That was April. April, May, June, July, early August, I didn't get a letter. I didn't get a call, thanks for coming in. I didn't get anything. I had actually forgotten I even went to ESPN. I was in the Upper Peninsula fishing. My roommate said some guy named Mo Davenport from ESPN called you."

Herbstreit called Mo back.

"They want to offer you fifteen games as a sideline reporter working for ESPN2, see how you do," Davenport told him.

It was the start of the 1995 season. By the end of it Craig James had departed *GameDay*. A number of people auditioned for the coveted spot, including Herbstreit: "They literally told me you're not going to get the job, but it would be a really good experience for you to go through the process and see what you think."

The network brought in Corso and Fowler for the audition. The music started up. And Herbstreit freaked out. Somehow, someway, with Corso at his side, he got through it.

Two months later his agent called.

"By the way," he said, "you got the *College GameDay* job."

"I'll never forget sitting next to Lee," Herbstreit told a spellbound audience in Georgia. "I thought they had hired me to talk football. And I'm sitting there next to Lee, and I've got all this information in my head. And Lee's all about putting a hat on. Cover 2? Inverted safeties? Three technique? Who's got time for that stuff? Who cares? I just kind of watched him and learned that—he's like a Yoda when it comes to this, he really is; I think he's the greatest entertainer in sports television—I would just sit there and listen to him, and he wouldn't talk about *anything*. And if he were here, I'd tell him that. But he had a way of relating to the crowd. He was an entertainer."

Corso's single greatest accomplishment in broadcasting may well be the passing of that advice to generations of ESPN producers and on-air talent, especially ex-coaches starting out in the business.

"Entertainment," said Corso. "Our show is for entertainment. Football is just our vehicle."

"It took me five years to get the right chemistry," said Fitting. "This is one of the few shows in the business where all eighty to eighty-five people are hand selected. That should mean something. Nobody is *assigned to College GameDay*."

Before the 2012 season Fitting and Fowler had tweaked the on-air supporting cast. They brought in Scott Van Pelt, the hipster *SportsCenter* anchor and ESPN radio host who seemed to really connect with the players. The veteran *ESPN the Magazine* columnist Gene Wojciechowski came aboard as well, as did twenty-six-year-old Samantha Steele. "Wojo" added a different tone and style to features, while Steele's role was as a feature contributor and co-host of the 9:00 a.m. *GameDay* on ESPNU. They joined former Georgia all-American David Pollack, who packed a punch as an analyst, and reporter Tom Rinaldi, flat-out one of the best interviewers and storytellers in the business.

A long first segment had offered a tasty buffet of *GameDay* treats: Fowler took a rib shot at the BCS bowl format—"Fairness in the BCS is an occasional accident"—while Corso chipped in with a pithy comment about Bulldogs quarterback Aaron Murray being just 1-10 against ranked teams; Herbie said Georgia would try to force Alabama quarterback AJ McCarron to throw down the field, before Fowler picked up the ball and broke down the day's key games, including Wisconsin–Nebraska with a spot in the Rose Bowl on the line ("Good seats still available in Indy"), Oklahoma–TCU, Florida State–Georgia Tech and Collin Klein of Kansas State trying to move back into the Heisman race at home against Texas.

Then Fowler offered a poignant good-bye to the Western Athletic Conference, shutting its doors after fifty years, before offering a tip to his betting-minded audience. "Also today," he said, "the matchup that Las Vegas said is the highest-scoring total in recorded history—Baylor–Oklahoma State has a total of eighty-seven . . . maybe we'll pick that game later. A shoot-out. Maybe we'll pick the over-under later. Eighty-seven is a really, really high total, double what some games are."

The first commercial break lasted three and a half minutes. Along with Fitting and director Lucas, nine staffers were packed inside the cramped, airless production truck. There was a graphics operator, a producer, a co-producer, a technical director, an associate director, an operations producer, an operations assistant, a runner and a news editor. None looked over the age of thirty-five, most under thirty.

"Is [Notre Dame's head coach] Brian Kelly here?" Fitting asked.

"He's in the bus."

Fitting viewed Kelly as behind enemy lines. Cheerleaders for Alabama and Georgia stood outside the bus ready to provide a sweet southern welcome. But the orchestra leader had a different tune in mind.

"When Kelly walks off that bus, the cheerleaders shouldn't be cheering him; they're Alabama fans, they should be booing," he said.

A voice: "I'll get them going."

Lucas informed cameramen stationed outside the bus what the truck had in mind. "Tell the cheerleaders when Kelly gets off the bus, let's have some playful booing going on," he said.

The second segment of the show was really an extended highlights package that served up a nice stew of opinion. For Herbstreit that meant praising Northern Illinois's huge double-overtime win over Kent State but making clear the MAC team had no business anywhere near a BCS bowl game. As Fowler wrapped up the segment and headed to commercial, Lucas showed a shot of Notre Dame's Kelly stepping off the bright orange *GameDay* bus.

On cue the crowd began to boo.

Out of the commercial Kelly was seated on the set next to Fowler as the host set the table with this introduction: "And Brian Kelly has navigated the Irish back, one step from their first national title since 1988. Wrapped things up at USC. Down here in Atlanta, not on a scouting trip, right, just visiting. And you keep wondering why they kept chanting, 'A-C-C.'"

In the truck Fitting uttered a single word.

"Perfect."

Producer and director had rolled the dice. Now all the Irish head coach had to do was pay off the bet.

"I've been in this business a long time," Kelly said with a smile, "but as I was walking up, to get booed by the Georgia and Alabama cheerleaders, I thought it was a milestone."

Come to Papa . . .

Wojciechowski had just wrapped up a fabulous feature on the Georgia linebacker Jarvis Jones dealing with the death, at age fifteen, of his nineteen-year-old brother. An emotional tour de force, it included lines like "If there's a statute of limitations on grief, Jones hasn't reached it yet." Then Pollack, the former Georgia linebacker, stepped into the spotlight. Old No. 47 in the red and black, Fowler announced. "A stud," Fitting had said the day before. Right away, Pollack threw down against his former team. He challenged Bulldogs quarterback Murray to put on his big-boy pads against Alabama.

"Aaron Murray has got to step up," he said. "When you watch him on tape and you break him down, he's a very robotic quarterback. You can't be robotic.

"Aaron Murray has to pull the string today. He's got to get the ball in tight windows . . . He's a film junkie, he knows what he's supposed to do, but sometimes when things don't go right, he gets a little bit weirded out and sees ghosts in the pocket. Aaron Murray's got to go, 'I'm going to throw the football.' You've got to fit the ball into tight windows and pull it if you want to win against 'Bama."

Howard chimed in: "My only question about Aaron Murray, especially after watching him live and in person in the South Carolina game on the road, does he have that fire, that intangible you need to go out there and lead your team? Not just the physical skills, but mentally are you tough enough and strong enough to go up against this Alabama defense for four quarters?"

Howard looked at Pollack. "You were a three-time all-American at Georgia, correct?"

"Yeah."

"You had the fire in you to rush the passer and stop the run, you know what I'm saying?" continued Howard. "I haven't seen that from Aaron Murray yet, and that's what it's going to take."

"Good, Dez," Fitting said.

"Does he have the mental capacity to last four quarters against that type of [Alabama] pressure?"

"He can't be afraid to make a mistake," replied Pollack.

Herbstreit capped it off by going with a big-picture look.

"This is Atlanta," he said. "The SEC is going to be decided in the trenches. We can talk Aaron Murray all week long, but if his offensive line doesn't do a good job and help him out, he doesn't have any chance to execute. If they don't open up some running lanes, he doesn't have any chance."

It was going on 11:00 a.m. in the East. Minute by minute, more and more college football fans were waking up to their favorite pregame meal. The Centennial crowd had come alive, growing in size. It was time to talk football, SEC football, and the guys were bringing it—*GameDay* at its absolute analytical best. Fitting saw it and mentally racked back to Wojo's piece. Emmy submission, he thought.

"Mark this down," he barked. "Feature, analytical tape and good strong points from both guys. Don't fucking forget it either."

"Doing it right now, big boy," said producer Tom Engle.

The next segment featured another home run from Van Pelt as part of his "Bald Man on Campus" interview series. This time he was down in College Station probing the mind of Johnny Manziel.

"I'm watching you," he told Manziel, beginning a typical laid-back remark, "and I'm thinking, man, that No. 2, he's one confident dude."

Soon it was Rinaldi's turn, and he backed Van Pelt's revealing interview with a standout sit-down of his own, humanizing the notoriously reticent Saban with questions like "You've said pain instructs. What do you mean by that?" and "Who gives you your pregame speech?" The answers: Loss breeds focus and my wife.

In a production meeting on Friday afternoon Saban told the *GameDay* crew that as a motivational tool the night before he had shown his team a video clip from the 1989 NBA playoffs between the Chicago Bulls and the Detroit Pistons. Fitting latched right on to that tidbit. Bristol was called. A production assistant pulled game three from the digital archives and fed it down to Atlanta. Now, out of Rinaldi's piece, Fowler was buttoning the interview with the Saban video story.

"Eighty-nine playoffs," he began. "Jordan and the Bulls against the Pistons . . . and the clip he showed, Bulls down by one, nine seconds to go, and [Pistons head coach] Chuck Daly is miked at the time out, describing exactly what Chicago is going to do. Jordan is going to get the ball at the top of the key and dribble right . . . imploring Dennis Rodman not to let him go right . . . do not let him go right."

"Roll blue," director Lucas said to a tape operator.

"Then he plays the clip. And what happens? Jordan gets the ball. Top of the key. He goes *right*. Everybody in the world knows it." (On tape Jordan scores over Rodman.)

Fowler, back on camera.

"Saban and the Tide. They're like Jordan and the Bulls. You know what they're going to do. We do it. You just can't stop it. Predictable. But effective. His team seemed to like that analogy."

For almost any pregame show, that would have been the end of it. But not *GameDay* and certainly not Fowler. He had Georgia on his mind and a poetic point he wanted to make.

"Meanwhile, for Georgia, their rallying cry, they might want to go with one of Ray Charles's lines in the classic song, 'Georgia, the whole day through.'

"Georgia, the whole *game* through. Not half a game. Like last year. But all *sixty minutes*. That's what it will take today."

"That worked," said Fitting. "Awesome, nice. Chris, great job."

———

No matter how rich the video nuggets turned out to be, the Michael Jordan or Ray Charles references, the compelling features or on-set guests, the most *entertaining* part of the show was, hands down, the picks. Fowler was there now, starting with the former Heisman Trophy winner from Michigan.

"Mr. Howard," he said. "Who wins the SEC championship and goes on to Miami to take on Notre Dame in the BCS championship?"

"That's a very good question," said Dez, who, it was clear to Fitting, was soon taking far too long to answer.

"Let's go . . ."

"*C'mon!*"

"I got to go with the Tide," Howard quickly said.

Pollack was next. He showed a set of journalistic stones by picking against his alma mater.

"My heart obviously said Georgia," he said, "but my head said Alabama. I think they win the game."

One final commercial break. In the truck, Fitting dropped segments like the airlines cut costs. "Okay," he said. "J 2 through 6 is dead. Be ready to lose Oklahoma State–Baylor."

The day's guest picker was Matt Ryan, quarterback for the 11-1 hometown Falcons, who liked being called "Matty Ice."

"Boise State versus Nevada next," announced Fowler, a few picks in. "The Broncos can clinch a piece of conference title . . . San Diego State and Fresno State also have a piece . . ."

"Let's go, Chris," Fitting said into the anchor's ear. "No one cares."

"I got Boise State," said Ryan.

"*Great* pick," said Corso. "By a touchdown and a field goal. Nine points."

"Nine points?" said Herbstreit.

"Six minutes off," said associate director Brian Albon.

Ryan took Pitt over South Florida.

"Not so fast, Matty Ice," said Coach. "I'm going with South Florida in an upset. I'm from Florida."

Five minutes off.

Four minutes off.

Ryan was still picking games. Georgia Tech over Florida State.

"Let's go," Fitting told Fowler. "Let's go . . ."

Wisconsin–Nebraska. Oklahoma–TCU . . .

"Please hurry up, *please.*"

Finally, it was time for Texas–Kansas State. If K-State won, Bill Snyder's squad was headed to a BCS date in the Fiesta Bowl.

Herbstreit liked K-State at home behind Heisman Trophy hopeful Collin Klein.

So did Corso. Only it came out "Calvin Klein."

The truck broke up.

"It's all good," said Herbstreit.

Fowler lost it. He put his head in his hands. He nearly fell out of his chair.

"Look at Chris," said Fitting. "Calvin Klein."

Ninety off.

Fitting snapped back to the business at hand.

"Let's go!"

With about one minute left in the show, it was Herbstreit's moment to shine. His routine—the phone calls to coaches and keen film study—framed what proved to be the most prescient remarks of the morning.

"Georgia, I think the intensity will be there," he said. "I think they will hang around for three and a half quarters . . . [but] at the end of the day I think Alabama has been there and done that, and that's the difference. I like Alabama to win."

One minute off . . .

LC time . . . Pick it, Coach.

"I tried to get a live elephant!" he yelled, playing things up. "Ten thousand dollars! Not worth it! Then I said, 'How about a dog! UGA' [the Georgia bulldog mascot]? No way!"

Thirty off . . .

Twenty-eight . . .

Knowing what was coming next, Corso's cast mates and a roaring crowd egged Coach on. Like the skilled entertainer he was, he held back the punch line, letting the laughter and anticipation build.

Twelve . . . eleven . . . ten . . .

Then he yanked a floppy-eared elephant over his head and started to wave good-bye.

"Roll, Tide," said Corso from beneath the 'Bama hood.

Seven . . . six . . . five . . .

Herbstreit playfully tugged the mascot's floppy nose up and down.

Three . . . two . . . one . . .

GameDay.

"We're gone," said Fitting. He leaned back in his chair and clapped his hands. In the row of monitors in front of his face an outrageously organic, *entertaining* moment played out on the set.

"Great job, guys," he said. "Beautiful. Really, really good."

———

Ten days prior to the SEC championship game, ESPN had pulled off arguably the biggest deal in its thirty-three-year history. In the process it slammed the proverbial door on every last one of its college football competitors through 2026.

As any conference commissioner or athletic director will tell you, there is no greater force in the world of televised sport than the Worldwide Leader. In March 2013 the gross national product—forget international—coming out of Bristol, was staggering:

- eight domestic cable networks
- 98.5 million homes each for ESPN and ESPN2

- four thousand employees stretched across its eighty-seven-acre campus, including sixteen buildings, three studios and twenty-seven satellite dishes

Odds were, if you wanted to find men between the ages of eighteen and fifty-four during the day or night, they were watching some edition of *SportsCenter, Pardon the Interruption,* a studio show or one of those lab experiments that embraced debate. ESPN's subscriber fee for cable operators was in excess of $5.50 a month—more than double that of the next-best cable network. In 2012 the network reportedly earned more than $11 billion in revenue.

Nowhere was ESPN's ubiquitous investment in live-event programming more complete or controlling than college football. It had at least $10 billion tied up in long-term rights deals with the SEC, Pac-12, Big Ten, Big 12, ACC and Big East. It had $300 million more invested over twenty years in the Longhorn Network and hundreds of millions more in the new SEC Network. In 2012 it had aired some 450 regular- and postseason college football games across ABC, ESPN, ESPN2, ESPNU, ESPN Deportes and other platforms. On Kickoff Week alone it aired forty-three games. It televised thirty-three bowl games and owned seven outright.

But nothing ESPN had done in the past compared with the deal president John Skipper announced in November 2012. Beginning in the 2014–15 season, the network had acquired wide-ranging media rights to the new four-team college football playoff for twelve years. In addition, ESPN had secured similar rights to the Rose, Sugar and Orange Bowls.

Burke Magnus was ESPN's point man in negotiations with BCS executive director Bill Hancock. Magnus had steadily risen up ESPN's editorial and programming ranks to senior vice president, responsible for the strategic direction of college football, basketball and NCAA championships across various ESPN platforms.

In talks with Hancock and key conference commissioners, Magnus had placed a premium on exclusivity. Translation: ESPN wanted the whole postseason-playoff enchilada. "Not knowing how big it was going to be or ultimately how many games it was going to be, the premium on exclusivity on something like this was paramount," said Magnus in an interview shortly before the 2013 BCS championship game in Miami. "For us, it's way more than a three and a half television window for the games. It underpins the regular season from a sales and sponsorship perspective. It's the payoff for our investment in the regular season."

Network sports executives had drooled over the prospect of a television sports event second only to the Super Bowl. Fox made clear it wanted in; so, surprisingly, did Turner; NBC less so. CBS, given its multibillion-dollar commitment to college basketball, the NFL, the SEC and the PGA, sat this one out. At one point, Magnus said, the notion was floated of splitting the seven-game postseason bowl and playoff package.

"I knew that was really problematic for us," he said. "It completely undercuts the sales side."

So Magnus put the network's proverbial foot down. Hard. We want it all, he told Hancock. Eventually, industry sources said, ESPN put a huge number on the table, an estimated $610 million a year—$413 million for just the semifinals and the national championship game, an average of nearly $140 million *per game* for just three playoff games.

In June, at a meeting of the BCS Presidential Oversight Committee in Washington, D.C., ESPN's offer was put up to the twelve-person vote. Magnus felt optimistic. He had strong support from key conference commissioners. He was tired. Negotiations had lasted nine months. His phone rang. It was Hancock calling from the meeting. The decision was unanimous.

"It's done," he said.

GameDay was done as well. It was early afternoon, and Fowler was once again stretched out in the back corner of the bus.

"Calvin Klein," he said with a smile. "I don't know where that comes from."

Somebody said Corso wore Calvin Klein.

"I didn't know that," said Fowler. Pause. "I wish I didn't know that."

Sam Steele stopped by before heading out of town.

"Calvin Klein, that may have been one of the funniest things I . . ."

"It would have been worse if he said 'Colon,'" said Fowler. With a big smile Steele likened Corso to a crazy grandpa everybody loved. Fowler agreed.

"I think people kind of watch for those moments anyway," he said. "It just makes it more fun."

As the Oklahoma–TCU game was coming down to the wire, *GameDay*'s quarterback judged 2012 as one of his favorite seasons. "I think Coach had a real strong year," Fowler said. "He's improved back from the stroke every year. Desmond and David's work, the features, everyone has sort of shown up *energized*."

Corso walked in and plopped down in the black leather chair next to Fowler. The Jovan Belcher murder-suicide story was breaking. *SportsCenter* anchor Rece Davis cut in with an update. Corso kept his eye on the Oklahoma game; he had picked the Sooners to win. He was still worked up over Klein—Collin, not Calvin—and how the K-State quarterback had been shoved out of the Heisman race after throwing three picks in a devastating loss to Baylor on the road that ended a 10-0 run.

"The fact is he only threw three other picks for the season," said Corso.

"I understand that," replied Fowler, "but the belief is it was a pressure game and he lost. They were ranked No. 1, and he went into the toilet."

Corso was the first to admit he didn't do much preparation for *GameDay* because, he said, "I lived the preparation." Few of his viewers knew Corso had been a stud athlete in college, earning four varsity letters (baseball and football) at Louisville and Florida State, where he played quarterback, running back and defensive back for the Seminoles from 1953 to 1956. He owned FSU's all-time interception record before it was broken in 1980. The old coach loved to dissect teams from the sidelines, forming the essence of his picks, like his upset special of A&M over Alabama.

He took a look at Fowler. Calvin Klein. Collin Klein. After more than fifty years as a player, coach and broadcaster, Lee Corso had more than a little left on *his* fastball.

"Yeah," he said. "But you're not going to win many games when the other team scores fifty-two."

27 BUILT BY BAMA

In a class by itself

Seven years after the private plane touched down in Tusca-loosa and Nick Saban waded into an adoring crowd, he was nothing less than the game's most powerful coach, a certified deity in certain parts of the South. Saban was being paid like a CEO, earning more than $5 million in salary, fees, bonuses and other perks and payments in 2012. When asked if he was worth that much money, Saban offered one of his slightly strained smiles, laughed, then said, "Probably not. Probably not. But I think on the other side of that is you almost have to look at what return has there been on that investment. So, we're paying this guy a couple of million more than the last guy. But if we're making a lot more because of it, then I guess that's the value."

Just how valuable has Saint Nick been to Alabama since the 2007 season? Let us count some of the ways:

- Athletic department revenue had risen by more than one-third— from $90 million to $125 million in 2011–12.
- Football revenue had jumped from $52 million to $82 million in the same period.
- Bryant-Denny Stadium underwent a $65 million expansion and beautification in 2010, the same year Saban won his first national title in Tuscaloosa, increasing the capacity by nearly 10,000 seats (to 101,821) and including thirty-six new skyboxes and seventeen hundred club seats.
- Sales of multimedia and merchandising rights had skyrocketed to around $18 million a year, behind only Texas and ahead of the likes of Michigan, Georgia and Ohio State.

Said Ben Sutton, the president of IMG College, "Whatever they've paid Nick has honestly been returned twentyfold."

From his spot low on the totem pole, defensive analyst Wesley Neighbors rarely interacted with the man in charge. But he knew full well the weight of Saban's expectations.

"Here," said Neighbors, "detail is everything."

For Neighbors that meant working seven days a week during the football calendar and sixty-plus hours during the season. He broke down upcoming opponents' special teams video, thirty to thirty-five plays per game—every kickoff, kick return, punt, punt return, field goal and field goal defense—as many as seven or eight times each. His job was to identify and catalog tendencies and alignment, searching for the tiny details on which Saban game plans are constructed. "What's their strong point? But more importantly, where are their weaknesses?" Neighbors explained. "Do they use certain personnel for certain things? That's a big tendency. It's almost like *I Spy*. It's like trying to find that little small something that unlocks the key of what they do."

By Sunday afternoon he would draw up schemes and plays and then organize them into a computerized scouting report created with another defensive analyst whose job mirrored Neighbors's. That report was passed up the ladder to their immediate supervisor, special teams analyst John Wozniak. "The data has to be correct," said Neighbors.

Once he had reviewed and refined the report, Wozniak would send the computer program to his boss, special teams coach Bobby Williams. It was up to Williams to shape that material into a specific plan to be scrutinized by Saban. Throughout the organization every single member of Saban's staff was expected to operate in the exact same way. The Saban Way. Dig deep. Measure up. And even when you think you have . . .

"It's the best when you walk in and you think you're protected by the halo rule. I'm not going to get it today," said Scott Cochran, the director of strength and conditioning who started with Saban at LSU. "Nah, you're going to get it. As soon as you get comfortable . . ."

It all traced back to tiny Monongah, West Virginia, and a man known to everyone as Big Nick.

In 2013 only about a thousand people, mostly rural poor, lived in the former coal-mining town, site of the worst mining disaster in American history back in December 1907, when 362 miners died. Even by the standards of coal-mining country Nick Saban Sr. stood apart. He had a flinty edge and unmistakable appetite for perfection. He was a good-hearted man who founded a Pop Warner team for kids in the neighboring towns, but he was as hard and tough as they come.

Nicholas Lou Saban was named after his father and a cousin, Lou, the longtime pro and college coach. By the time young Nick was eleven, he was working at his dad's two businesses, Saban's Dairy Queen and Saban's Service Station, learning the *right* way to pump gas, clean a window, check the oil or wash a car.

"The biggest thing I learned . . . was how important it was to do things correctly," Saban said at a national championship press conference in January 2013. "There was a standard of excellence, of perfection. If we washed a car . . . I hated the navy blue and black cars because when you wiped them off the streaks were hard to get out, and if there were any streaks when he came, you had to do it over.

"[My father] was the same way as a [Pop Warner and American Legion] coach; attention to detail, discipline, doing what you're supposed to do, the way you're supposed to do it . . . I think that sort of perfectionist type of attitude my parents instilled sort of made you always strive to be all that you could be, and that's probably still the foundation of the program we have right now."

If The Process was born in the hills of West Virginia, it evolved on the football fields of Kent State, where Saban, despite his small size, earned a scholarship in the early 1970s as a hard-hitting defensive back and spent a year as a graduate assistant under head coach Don James, an early advocate of the personal, moral and academic development of players.

Assistant coaching positions at premier programs (Syracuse, West Virginia, Ohio State, Navy, Michigan State) followed, leading to Saban's first head coaching job, at the University of Toledo in 1990. His team went 9-2 that year and finished as co-champion of the Mid-American Conference. From there it was on to the Cleveland Browns and four seasons (1991 to 1994) as defensive coordinator under Bill Belichick.

"One of the best around, that's Nick," Belichick said in October 2005, during Saban's first year in Miami. "You know, it's funny. When you write those 'personal evaluations' of players, every once in a while you come across a player, 'Strengths: All. Weaknesses: None.'

"Strengths?" added Belichick. "He knows schemes. He knows personnel. He's a good motivator. He is very adaptable to change. He is excellent at evaluating players. Weaknesses? Uh, I didn't see any."

When Saban moved on to Michigan State in 1995—he spent five seasons in East Lansing before leaving for LSU—he brought along the message Belichick had posted throughout the Browns facility. Signs that reminded players to forget about what others were doing and focus on what they alone could control. The signs read DO YOUR JOB.

How many times had Neighbors heard that phrase?

"Too many," he said with a laugh. "Everyone is put to the standard that he [Saban] wants to maintain. You're never satisfied. He said that to the players. But he also said that to the coaches. Don't be satisfied. Don't be complacent. You always want to try and get better."

High achievers. That's what Barrett Jones liked to call them. The kind of kid—and that's really how they all start in college, as kids—capable of playing for a perfectionist like Saban and under the unremitting pressure the impassioned "Roll Tide" fans can produce. With all due respect to South Bend, Ann Arbor, Austin, Columbus, Eugene and every ESPN *GameDay* stop in between, nothing compared with the spotlight at Alabama. Not when Birmingham has been ESPN's No. 1 television market for college football for the last ten years; not when more than seventy-eight thousand showed up for the *spring* game; and not when Paul Finebaum, a sports-talk radio star, could turn his syndicated call-in show, once beamed out of Birmingham, into a multi-platform deal with ESPN and the new SEC Network.

No matter the look of the palace or the size of the budget, as Saban made clear to Moore during their flight to Tuscaloosa, the lifeblood of every college football program was the players. Every year at Alabama The Process began not with the recruitment of talent but with the *selection* of it.

Saban and his staff followed what defensive coordinator Kirby Smart called "the blueprint" for success. As detailed by Andy Staples in *Sports Illustrated*, that blueprint targeted high school athletes who fit certain character/attitude/intelligence criteria and position-specific height/weight/speed guidelines tailored to Alabama's offensive and defensive schemes. Cornerbacks, for example, should ideally be between six feet and six feet two inches and about 190 pounds and run a sub-4.5 forty-yard dash; linemen should stand no less than six feet two because, as Smart drily noted, "big people beat up little people."

One of Saban's pet peeves was the gross expansion of the entire recruiting game and the overload of information. The recruiting Web sites and four- and five-star rankings held reduced weight inside the program. "We have player descriptions, player profiles," added Smart. "Guys that don't necessarily fit that description, they may be a five-star guy, we're just not interested in [them] because that's just not what we're recruiting. Sure there are exceptions to the rule, but we don't want a team full of exceptions."

For all his old-school temperament, Saban was decidedly new-school when it came to communicating with recruits. He maximized social media, routinely carving out thirty minutes to Skype with athletes he believed fit the Alabama profile.

Coming out of his high school in Memphis, Barrett Jones heard from all the big schools and all the slick pitches from coaches at Florida, North Carolina and Tennessee. "Everyone told me we'd win championships if I came there," he said. But not Saban, after a lackluster 7-6 record his first year at Alabama. While others said it, he *showed it.*

"Coach Saban came with a detailed plan as to how he was going to do it," said Jones. "He had much more impact. He walked me step-by-step through the process. After my first meeting with him I was blown away. I was set to go. I committed soon after that."

Dee Milliner was one of those athletes who fit the selection process to a T. At six feet one and about 199 pounds, and with a vertical leap approaching forty inches, he was rated the No. 1 cornerback in the nation by Scout.com and was a *Parade* high school all-American. Everybody who was anybody wanted Milliner—USC, Florida State, Georgia, Oklahoma, Stanford, Auburn and Tennessee, to name but a few of the finalists. Then, one day, Saban showed up unannounced—at least to Milliner—in the football coach's office at Stanhope Elmore High in Millbrook, Alabama.

"It was kind of a shock to see Coach Saban," said Milliner.

Saban got right to the point.

"He didn't sugarcoat anything," recalled Milliner. "He didn't tell me, 'If you come here, you're going to play.' He said, 'Look, you're a great player. I want you. But I don't need you.' That's what I was looking for. That caught my attention right there. He didn't lie to me at all. He didn't tell me I was going to be a starter. I had to work for it."

For Milliner the work—The Process—began in the classroom, proving to Saban he could be on time and make good decisions. "He would tell us, 'If you're not doing it in the classroom, you're going to have a problem with me on the field,'" said Milliner. After the textbook came the playbook, and more tests, Saban again looking for consistency. "He starts trusting you," said Milliner.

Milliner would earn enough trust to start his last eleven games as a true freshman in 2010 and make some freshman all-American teams. He started six times his sophomore year. In 2012 he earned consensus first-team all-American honors and blossomed into one of the true stars and trusted leaders on the team before coming out early for the 2013 NFL draft.

"It was a long process," said Milliner, the ninth overall pick of the draft, selected by the New York Jets. "But it was worth it."

Damion Square knew full well the meaning of those words. He committed to Alabama in the spring of 2008, along with Jones, shortly after Saban's initial season, which saw the Tide lose four of its last five games. The six-foot-three, 286-pound Square was such a talent coming out of high school in Houston that he was ranked in the top forty nationally as a linebacker, defensive tackle and defensive end. He had stunned Smart and other coaches with his athleticism. Saban went to Houston and made his pitch. "Coach Saban said to me, 'You come here, we're going to win games,'" said Square. "'That's the way we recruit. We only recruit great ballplayers that want to play ball and that fit into my system.'"

Square accepted the challenge and chose Alabama over LSU. He was on his way to being a star when, as a redshirt freshman, he suffered a serious knee injury and was out for the year. But Saban and his staff loved his attitude and athleticism, and by the time his final season was starting at the Capstone, Square was as well. It was his face featured on the cover of the 2012 football media guide.

"He handles us like men," Square said in an emotional locker room following the BCS title-game win over Notre Dame. Square found that out firsthand during one particular leadership training session in which he had stood up to Saban, telling him, in essence, he didn't want to be a leader. All he wanted to do was his job.

Saban gave him a look. "That *is* your fucking job," he snarled.

"He holds us accountable for everything," said Square. "And that's the way I live my life now."

Sometimes lost in the holistic-sounding nature of The Process was this cold-blooded football fact: under Saban, the Crimson Tide had become the most physically dominant team in college football. Beyond big athletic linemen, the Tide consistently rolled out tackle-breaking backs, quicksilver corners, smashmouth linebackers, a quarterback who could think and throw and top-end athletes at every skill position. And then there was this: Alabama is unquestionably the best-conditioned team in the country.

To that end the program employed no fewer than four strength and conditioning coaches, led by Cochran, the 2011 Samson Strength & Conditioning Coach of the Year and a certified wild man known for his signature yell—*Yeah, Yeah, Yeah, YEAH!*—and infectious high-octane energy. "The days you *don't* feel like it, that's when I'm going to get the most out of you," he said. "And you might hate me at first, that's okay. But you're going to have to do this for your own kids and your own job one day—and I'm not going to be there! I'm not going to be sitting right there jumpin' your tail when you ain't ready to get up."

Watch the start of the fourth quarter of any Alabama game ever played and you'll see Cochran five or six steps onto the field in the center of a swarm of players, arms above his head and four fingers extended. He's not signaling the start of the final fifteen minutes of the game. No, those fingers and thumb symbolize something else entirely. "Commitment, discipline, effort, toughness, and the thumb is pride," said Cochran.

Those fingers also symbolized Alabama's Fourth Quarter off-season conditioning program, a not-so-secret weapon at the heart of the Tide's success.

"The longest hour of my life," said running back Eddie Lacy, describing the seemingly endless drills and sprints the previous spring and summer. "Seemed like five hours."

"Running, tears as you sweat," recalled Milliner.

"It will get you prepared, I tell you that," said starting left tackle Cyrus Kouandjio. "It will get you prepared for anything you have to counter during a game."

In its most basic form the Fourth Quarter program was no different from any other elite program. Spring and summer months devoted to drills and 110-yard sprints until you dropped. Saban used Fourth Quarter first at Michigan State, then later at LSU, where he hired Cochran, who at the time was an assistant strength coach for the NBA's New Orleans Hornets.

There was no magic to any single drill or sequence of sprints, said Cochran. The difference, he said, was—not surprisingly—in the details: how the players were coached; the pressure Saban put on his assistants to ensure *every* little thing—the placement of a foot in a mat drill, for example—was done *exactly* the way he wanted it. "Coach Saban has a command that each coach has to use for their drill," said Cochran. "Coach walks around, and if it's not the way he sees it, that coach is going to get coached up. So the players know they better get in line or their coach is going to get chewed."

Jones told the story about the importance of putting your hand *exactly* on the line for sprints. Not an inch over the line. Not an inch behind the line. On the line.

"If not, and Coach catches it, we start [the sprints] all over again," said Jones.

To watch the discipline and suffering firsthand is to see a methodical breakdown of ego and self. In March 2013 about 120 players attended a Monday afternoon conditioning session, every single player, from stars like quarterback AJ McCarron on down, identified by the last names taped to the backs of their T-shirts. In the middle of the indoor practice field stood, or actually, more accurately, raged Cochran, screaming in some foreign football language long on grunts and indecipherable roars. He took charge of about 60 players lined up in waves of 10 or 12, running them through an endless series of explosive, oxygen-sucking push-ups, jumps, hops and knee lifts, all conducted under the watchful eye of a platoon of trainers, managers and coaches.

"Right now! Right now!" he screamed.

Meanwhile, along the outer edges of the field two more groups of about 30 players experienced wave after wave of commitment-testing sprints: Line up. Sprint a hundred and ten yards down one sideline. Walk the back line of the end zone. Line up. Sprint a hundred and ten yards down the other sideline. Walk the end zone. Line up . . .

All the while Saban stalked the field like a hungry cat.

"I've said it a hundred times today and nobody sprints," he said to one group at one point, biting off each and every word. "So we'll just have to start all over."

So they did. More sprints. More drills. More taste of what it's like to be part of The Process.

In the locker room celebration after the national championship game, Square had paid tribute to Cochran and the bond the Fourth Quarter program had built. "We ran together like brothers. 'Coch' worked us like crazy. That's what jells you, man. You put in those hours with the guys. You're out there running those one-tens; that's what comes out in the fourth quarter. That's what we're thinking about when we're coming out of the locker room. That training. That winter training. Getting up at 6:30 in the morning and getting a workout in. Coming back at 4:00 and running. Those are brutal days. But they are all for this moment."

Yet in recent years the Built by Bama theme touted by the school's marketing gurus had come to mean the mind as much as—or even more than—the body. This was another reflection of Saban's gifts as a coach. Said defensive coordinator Smart, "To me that's where he has established himself as a coach ahead of the curve because of his ability, mentally, to create an advantage with his team. And he makes us realize as coaches it's not going to be about what we call, it's not going to be about what we rep, it's about the mind-set in [a player's] head that's going to make the difference in this game."

"I think it's huge," said Saban during his *60 Minutes* interview. "If you create a lot of anxiety because you're a worrier, you're not going to perform nearly as well . . . I think consistency in performance is what helps you to be successful. I think to get that consistency in performance in anything you do, the mental part is the key."

Saban was asked how many consultants or coaches he had who focus on the mental side.

"As many as will put up with me," he answered with a laugh. "'Cause, you know, I think that's where it all starts. How you think is very important to how you act, the result that you get."

Saban had at least half a dozen player development consultants on the payroll at any one time. Dr. Kevin Elko, a top motivational speaker, was one. Another was Trevor Moawad, the former director of performance and mental conditioning at IMG Academy in Florida now working with Athletes' Performance in Arizona.

"There's nobody even close to what Nick is doing," said Moawad in the summer of 2012.

Moawad estimated that he had spent twenty-five hours a year for the last seven years consulting for Saban, dealing primarily with issues like visualization training and mental toughness.

"Performance is not just about movement, speed and strength," he said. "Performance is about how you think, communicate and respond, all of these elements. And these elements can be taught."

In addition, Saban regularly brought in a string of speakers to address the team. Some would talk about overcoming adversity or addiction; others, the power of belief and conviction; still others would deal with relationships, stress, personal growth and expectations. Moawad said the most intense sessions occurred during August training camp and that part of Saban's genius was that he understood that no matter the skill set, he was inheriting vulnerable kids from various backgrounds. For those times when they made mistakes or poor decisions, as they invariably did, the safety net had to be strung as far and wide as possible.

———

Wes Neighbors knew full well the size of that net. He enrolled in Tuscaloosa as a third-generation member of certified Alabama football royalty. His grandfather Billy, who passed away after a heart attack in 2012, co-captained Bear Bryant's undefeated national championship team in 1961. A two-way star at guard and defensive line, he played eight seasons in the AFL and NFL with the Boston Patriots and the Miami Dolphins. In 2004 he was elected to the College Football Hall of Fame.

Wes Neighbors Sr. was next. A center, he played under Ray Perkins from 1983 to 1986 and was so good, like his father, he won the SEC's award for best lineman. Wes junior started playing the family game in the seventh grade and quickly fell in love. By the time he graduated from Huntsville High in Alabama, he was an honorable mention all-state safety and ranked in the top twenty-five safeties in the country by ESPN.com. Vanderbilt and Georgia Tech offered scholarships. Then the Tide came calling. "I mean, this is where I wanted to go," he said. "I've been going to games here since I was born."

Rocked by the intensity of practice and long, grueling days, Neighbors, like so many freshmen, hit the wall early. At Alabama the average football day began at 6:15 a.m. and didn't end until some fifteen hours later after a training table meal and two hours of tutoring and study hall. "I feel like I almost came in here blind because it is such a time commitment," said Neighbors. "It does become your life."

Neighbors admitted he had his "fair share of issues" his freshman and sophomore years—not the least of which was buying and drinking alcohol underage. "The program found out," he said. "I had to face the consequences." There was a sit-down in Saban's office where they talked about decision making and whether Neighbors was willing to hold himself accountable for his actions and attend individual and group sessions with counselors. He was.

"It helped me a lot," Neighbors said. "I wasn't representing the football team as best I could. Some people don't ever become aware. They don't realize they're representing their team and their university in a way that's unacceptable."

He redshirted as a freshman in 2008. In 2009 he didn't play a down, serving solely on the scout team at practice. But by the time Neighbors was a redshirt sophomore—his junior year academically—the six-foot-one, two-hundred-pound defensive back was starting on every special team. Then, just a few days before the first game of the 2010 season, he tore the meniscus in his left knee in practice. He missed the first game. He played the next week against Penn State but felt a mysterious pain in his right foot that doctors eventually traced to an old fracture. The pain grew worse as the season wore on and limited Neighbors's ability to cut. His role was reduced to straight-ahead kickoff coverage. At the end of the season he was medically released from the team. In March 2011 he found himself back in Saban's office for a different reason.

"We've always had a cordial relationship where I felt very comfortable talking to him about certain things," Neighbors said. "It was pretty open. I just asked if there was any way to stay and help. And he was, 'Of course, of course.'

"I knew I wanted to stay involved. Coach told me he thought I had great potential to be a coach someday. So I was allowed to come in as a student assistant."

Saban believed that if you invest—honestly and truthfully *invest*—in building a better person—whether it's Wes Neighbors or stars like McCarron and Amari Cooper—you end up with athletes who, in times of intense stress, embrace the moment rather than run from it. "The mental game can't win it for you, but it can lose it for you," said Moawad. "It's a 5 to 6 percent difference, and at this level that's big."

Saban seemed to understand better than any other coach of his generation the razor-thin difference 5 or 6 plays could make during a 135-play game. The Process was built for those defining plays—for times when trained leaders stepped forward and rallied the troops and an entire team displayed the ability to perform at its best.

Nowhere was that 5 percent factor more evident than in the 2012 SEC Championship game in Atlanta. The game was a spectacular sixty-minute slugfest between two jacked-up, athletically gifted teams. No. 2–ranked Alabama beat No. 3 Georgia 32–28. But only after the Bulldogs, led by quarterback Aaron Murray, playing the game of his SEC life, came up just five yards short with four seconds left on the clock.

With six and a half minutes left in the third quarter, 'Bama had found itself down 21–10 after a seventy-five-yard Georgia touchdown drive and a fifty-five-yard Bulldogs TD run off a blocked field goal. The hometown crowd in the Georgia Dome was in a frenzy. On the sidelines, Smart said later he wondered if the Tide had what it would take to come back in the Bulldogs' backyard. "I was questioning it," he admitted. "You're sitting there going, Well, here we go. This is another challenge to our competitive character. Are we going to be able to get the stops and get the scores necessary to bring it back?"

Lock in, lock out. Control what you can control. Play the play. Be the best you can be. You could almost hear all the mental mantras and collective suffering of the Fourth Quarter program at work. And sure enough, the Crimson Tide responded as one.

The offensive line just kept coming, stuffing the ball down the throat of a stout Georgia defense that had allowed only nineteen total points in its last three SEC games. Freshman tailback sensation T. J. Yeldon finished off a penalty-aided seventy-seven-yard, four-play drive with a ten-yard scamper for a score. The two-point conversion made it 21–18. 'Bama quickly got the ball back on downs, and this time it was Lacy and the line pounding away for the go-ahead touchdown. Score: 25–21 with 14:57 to go.

Georgia roared back with a TD of its own—28–25 now, 12:54 left in the game. Once more Alabama ditched the pass and doubled down on the run. Facing a make-or-break third and five with 4:01 left, Yeldon slammed through a hole and into a tackler, crashing forward for a crucial first down. Then, with the Bulldog safeties crowding the line of scrimmage, quarterback McCarron lofted a perfect pass to Cooper for forty-four yards and what turned out to be the game-winning score.

In the end, Alabama had rushed fifty-one times for a championship game record of 350 yards. Afterward, Saban spoke of having to restart his heart. He spoke of a team that would not be denied. With a shot at the national championship on the line, his team had been the best that it could be.

"The thing about the whole process is, The Process leads to success," said Neighbors. "You've just got to get people to see it. And once they see it, they start believing it. And once they believe, you have nowhere to go but [to] that success."

After reaching the pinnacle of such success—the merciless 42–14 demolition of Notre Dame in the BCS title game—a word unavoidably arose among players and the press. Saban swatted it away like a gnat. "I don't think words like 'dynasty' are really words I'm much interested in," he said. He would celebrate for twenty-four hours and not an hour more. The championship ring would join the others on his office coffee table for recruits to see.

"'Look what I got'—that's not my style," he said.

The national championship victory had touched off a wild on-field celebration. There were hugs and kisses and handshakes as a scene unique in sports unfolded like a thousand New Year's Eves in one. Suddenly there was Saban, surrounded by security, scanning the crowd until he found the person he was searching for—his wife, Ms. Terry. Hand in hand, they walked up the stairs onto the makeshift stage.

Addressing a roaring crowd, Saban spoke of what a great win it was for the "organization," admitting to ESPN's John Saunders that it was okay now for his players to talk about repeats because, well, they'd just repeated. Linebacker C. J. Mosley was next. Saban shifted off to the side. Head slightly down, he nibbled on a nail. One could only wonder what was going on inside his head. The slippery night of player partying to come? Future expectations?

Then someone handed him the gorgeous glass football, which twinkled in the metal halide lights. As he hoisted the trophy above his head, a small, contented smile crossed his face. "Sweet Home Alabama" poured out of the stadium speakers. The crowd chanted "Roll, Tide, Roll!" in perfect unison at just the right opening, as if those words were part of the song.

On this night, they were.

When the ceremony finally ended, Saban descended the stage into a barricaded area reserved for family and friends. There was only one more place to go. And his security team pushed toward it against a crush of television cameras and photographers. Finally, Saban made it—to the exit, near Section 156, right behind a goalpost. The cheers and screams grew even louder. Before he left the field, Saban stood for a moment—only a moment—and let the sound of worship wash over him. Then he was on the move again. But just before he disappeared into the tunnel and out of sight, Saban's right hand rose up, tentative at first, until a single index finger pointed straight to the sky. Saban's way of saying that until somebody proved it on the field, when it meant the most, there was but one team, one coach, one system, in big-time college football.

———

For one night, everything glorious about college football was on display. The vivid pageantry, collective excellence, communal celebration and fierce competition provided the grand spectacle only NCAA football played at its highest level can deliver. One could almost forget the unremitting pressure, the scandals haunting the sport—the bidding wars for top recruits; the booster payoffs; the horrific injuries; the academic cheating; the rising tide of criminal acts; the brute fact that the young men who sacrificed on the field were interchangeable pieces who received exactly none of the billions of dollars of revenue the game generated.

Almost.

ACKNOWLEDGMENTS

This book could not have been written without exceptional access to the individuals and programs profiled on these pages. We are indebted to them for their time, their hospitality and, most important, their trust. So we begin by thanking those who allowed us to see, hear and tell their stories:

Mike and Sharon Leach; Michael Crabtree; Graham Harrell; former Tennessee hostesses Lacey Earps and Charlotte Henry; Dave Brandon, Brady Hoke and Dave Ablauf at the University of Michigan; Don King in Austin, Texas; former BYU head coaches LaVell Edwards and Gary Crowton; detective Devon Jensen and prosecutor Donna Kelly in Provo, Utah; attorney Ted Liggett in Lubbock, Texas; Kent Hance and Guy Bailey at Texas Tech; Craig James; Rob and Jared Ambrose, Devin Crosby, Mike Waddell and David Nevins at Towson; Matt Doyle at Stanford; Zach Maurides from Duke; Cleve Bryant at Texas and his attorney Tom Nesbitt; Kyle Van Noy, Ezekiel "Ziggy" Ansah, Bronco Mendenhall and Tom Holmoe at BYU; T. Boone Pickens; Mike Holder at Oklahoma State; former Missouri tutors Teresa Braeckel and Lauren Gavin; prosecutor Andrea Hayes in Columbia, Missouri; Sarah, Donald and Derrick Washington; Bill Moos, Elson Floyd and Mike Marlow at Washington State University; Chance Miller, Brynna Barnhart and Rachel Newman Baker at the NCAA; Ohio State booster Bobby DiGeronimo; agent Gary O'Hagan; Joe Giansante; Nick Saban, the late Mal M. Moore and Jeff Purinton at Alabama; former Florida State lineman Jarad Moon; Marcus Lattimore and his agent Pat Dye Jr.; the entire Ricky Seals-Jones family; Alabama student Samuel Jurgens; Notre Dame alumnus Tom Seeberg; Coach Keith Donnerson and his players Alphonso Marsh, Brandon Beaver, Lacy Westbrook and Lavell Sanders at Dominguez High in Compton, California; LAPD's Brandon Dean; Kyle Whittingham at Utah; the entire Washington State coaching staff; and ESPN's John Skipper, Burke Magnus, Lee Fitting, Keri A. Potts and the entire team at *College GameDay*.

Behind the scenes there were many more who helped arrange and facilitate our reporting. We can't possibly name them all. But we are especially grateful to: Jay Rosser in T. Boone Pickens's office; Sally Geymuller and Monica Long at Oklahoma State University; Brett Pyne and Kenny Cox at BYU; Stacey Osburn and Erik Christianson at the NCAA; Travis Van Noy; Debbie Nankivell, Robert Giovannetti, Linda Ann Nelson, Gil Picciotto, Ginger Druffel, Debra Jo Dzuck and William Stevens at Washington State University; attorney Bill Marler; agents Todd Semersheim and Jonathan Butnick; court officials Diana Taylor and Bonnie Adkins in Columbia, Missouri; paralegal Eunice McMillan in Ted Liggett's law office in Lubbock, Texas; and George Pine, Ben Sutton, Sandy Montag, Kim Berard and Johnny Esfeller IV at IMG.

At *Sports Illustrated,* former editor in chief Terry McDonell and college football editor B. J. Schecter championed the feature stories we wrote on crime and gangs in college football. This book grew out of those projects. At CBS News, producer Josh Gaynor and associate producer Sarah Fitzpatrick collaborated with us on those stories. Gratitude to CBS News chairman Jeff Fager, CBS News president David Rhodes, former CBS News president Sean McManus and producer Craig Silver and his entire CBS Sports college football crew.

We also had a great team working with us in the trenches: reporters Timothy Bella, James Oldham and Michael McKnight; researchers J. J. Feinauer and Jeff Gasser; photographer Deanne Fitzmaurice; editor Craig Neff; fact-checker Alex Wolff; intern Hannah Waite, IT specialist Cameron Berry; and travel agent extraordinaire Mark Johnson.

Our agent Richard Pine at Inkwell Management was a visionary behind this book idea and a driving force to see it through to completion. We are grateful for his impossibly high standards and professional touch. We can't say enough about William Thomas, publisher and editor in chief at Doubleday. He was involved in every step of this project and provided exceptional guidance and a skillful editor's touch to the manuscript. His trusted assistant Coralie Hunter was indispensable. Publicist Todd Doughty and attorney Amelia Zalcman were valuable members of our team, too.

Deep and abiding thanks to the Flemings, Jonathan and Amy, two family members whose gracious offer to stay at their beautiful Cape Cod summer house on Wakeby Pond for seventeen quiet days and nights made all the writing difference in the world.

Finally, we pay tribute to our families. The book is dedicated to Lydia Benedict and Dede Keteyian for a reason. They put up with us and lived through every step of this two-year odyssey through big-time college football with us. We are two very lucky guys.

NOTES

Much of this book is based on firsthand observations. Between September 2011 and April 2013 we spent more than four hundred hours shadowing and interviewing coaches, athletic directors, student-athletes, boosters, high school recruits, directors of football operations, ESPN *GameDay* crew members, NCAA investigators and fans. We attended spring practices, off-season workouts, team meetings, fall camps and 7-on-7 tournaments. We also traveled with teams (by charter plane and bus) and were present on the sidelines or in the locker room before, during and after games. In addition, we traveled and attended games with boosters, fans, athletic directors, university presidents and television broadcasters. In all, we attended fourteen regular-season games, the SEC Championship game and two bowl games (including the national championship game) during the 2012–13 season.

Throughout all of our reporting we carried tape recorders. In many instances we also chronicled our travels with still photography or video. Virtually all of the descriptions and dialogue from chapters that take place between 2011 and 2013 come from what we or our designated reporters saw and heard firsthand.

For this book we also conducted more than five hundred interviews, including multiple interviews with key characters. Some of those were done with individuals we were shadowing or observing. But many more were conducted for chapters that cover incidents and events prior to September 2011. Almost all interviews were on the record, and many of them were tape-recorded. Some cases were also videotaped as part of a story on big-time college football that aired on *60 Minutes* in the fall of 2012. Most of the quotations in the book are from our observations or our interviews. When they're derived from a different source, we've done our best to cite it here. In instances where we reconstructed dialogue, we almost always attempted to interview both parties to the conversations. We also pulled quotations and dialogue from trial transcripts, grand jury transcripts, NCAA interviews, court depositions, affidavits, police reports and video-recorded press conferences, practices and games. The sources for quotations that did not come from our reporting—and were not public statements—are noted below.

Hundreds of people are identified by name in this book. We used pseudonyms in only four instances. The identities of a juvenile rape victim and a member of her family who was a witness for the prosecution were changed to protect their privacy in accordance with customary journalism standards consistent with the rape shield law. The other sexual assault victims who are identified by name in the book authorized us to do so. The names of a University of Texas football player and a stripper with whom he maintained a sexual relationship were withheld at their request because reporting their names would jeopardize their current employment.

With a couple exceptions, we did not use anonymous sources in this book.

Along the way, we had invaluable assistance from four reporters and one photojournalist who worked on the book. Timothy Bella, a former producer and investigative reporter for CBSNews.com in New York and now the lead digital producer/reporter for Al Jazeera America's *America Tonight,* did extensive statistical research, conducted forty-two interviews and helped write the chapter on injuries. J. J. Feinauer is Jeff Benedict's executive assistant. He developed and maintained a database that tracked player injuries, arrests and graduation rates. He also conducted twenty-five interviews and helped write the chapter on injuries. Jeff Gasser, a former research assistant to Jeff Benedict, did extensive reporting for the *Sports Illustrated* cover story on college football and crime. Gasser also compiled a September 2011 research report that helped form the basis of the authors' proposal for this work. James Oldham, a former reporter at the *Lantern,* the newspaper of record at Ohio State, conducted ten interviews and worked on one of the Ohio State chapters. Deanne Fitzmaurice is a Pulitzer Prize–winning photographer. She accompanied the authors while they shadowed players and coaches at Washington State, Alabama, BYU, Utah and Dominguez High in Compton, California.

In addition, *Sports Illustrated* executive editor B. J. Schecter oversaw the six-month investigation that led to the *SI* cover story on college football and crime, as well as the feature story on college football and gangs. Those two pieces were instrumental to the foundation of this book. Schecter, who also oversees college football for the magazine, had a direct hand in shaping the Ohio State chapters and providing input at various junctures of the project. Craig Neff, a former colleague of Armen Keteyian's at *Sports Illustrated* and now an assistant managing editor who has edited some of Jeff Benedict's pieces at the magazine, provided invaluable editing and editorial counsel on several chapters, including those involving Towson University, Ricky Seals-Jones and Alabama. It goes without saying that a book of this depth and scope is not possible without the groundwork laid by writers and reporters who cover college football on a regular basis. With that in mind we'd like to offer a heartfelt nod to, in particular, Andy Staples, Stewart Mandel and Pete Thamel of *Sports Illustrated,* Bruce Feldman of CBSSports.com, Dan Wetzel and Charles Robinson of *Yahoo! Sports,* Steve Wieberg at *USA Today* and Greg Bishop of the *New York Times.*

Finally, any mistakes are those of the authors and the authors alone.

PROLOGUE: Game on

The descriptions, conditions and play-by-play of the Notre Dame–Alabama game are based on firsthand observations by the authors and official game notes. The kind of stadium lights (halide) used was confirmed by the engineering department at Sun Life Stadium. The source of teams on probation for major violations came from the NCAA's database on such matters. The Auburn graduation rate and white-black disparity came from an abstract written by Rodney K. Smith, a distinguished professor at Thomas Jefferson School of Law in San Diego. The time demand figures were part of a GOALS study of approximately twenty thousand student-athletes conducted in the spring of 2010 and presented to the 2011 NCAA Convention. The October 2009 Knight Commission on Intercollegiate Athletics report ("College Sports 101") proved invaluable, as did *USA Today*'s extensive research and continued reporting on coaching salaries. The spending differential statistics between academics and athletics were the product of a 2010 research study conducted by the American Institutes for Research. Principal researcher Donna M. Desrochers was the author of the study.

The quotations attributed to Brent Musburger were taken directly from the ESPN broadcast.

1. THE COACH: Part I, Mike Leach after midnight

The portrayal of Mike Leach is based on extensive interviews with Mike and Sharon Leach. Some biographical information was also taken from his autobiography, *Swing Your Sword: Leading the Charge in Football and Life* (New York: Diversion Books, 2011); Michael Lewis's profile "Coach Leach Goes Deep, Very Deep," *New York Times Magazine,* December 4, 2005; and a *60 Minutes* segment on Leach that aired on January 4, 2009.

The characterization of BYU's offensive scheme in the early 1980s is based on interviews with LaVell Edwards and information provided by Steve Young, who quarterbacked the Cougars during Leach's senior year of college.

Texas Tech provided the graduation rates for its football players under Mike Leach via e-mail to the authors.

The game scenes from Texas Tech and the dialogue are based on interviews with Mike Leach, Michael Crabtree and Graham Harrell, as well as video footage of the Texas–Texas Tech game.

Additional information was gleaned from "Huskies Coaching Search: Texas Tech Coach Mike Leach Meets with UW," *Seattle Times,* December 3, 2008; and "Leach, Tech Reach Five-Year Agreement," ESPN.com, February 19, 2009.

2. THE CLOSER: The life of a college football hostess

The portrayal of Lacey Earps is based on interviews with her. Additional interviews were conducted with Earps's attorney, Alan Bean, and the Tennessee hostess Charlotte Henry. Henry's professional résumé provided additional biographical detail, including her grade point average. Some information about Orange Pride was obtained from the school Web site.

Tennessee recruits Bryce Brown, Brandon Willis and Corey Miller did not respond to requests for interviews. Nor did the hostess Dahra Johnson. Joyce Thompson from the NCAA declined to be interviewed, as did former Tennessee head coach Lane Kiffin, assistant coach David Reaves and Tennessee's director of student-athlete relations and lettermen, Condredge Holloway.

Quotations from the press conference introducing Kiffin as the new head coach at Tennessee were taken from a video recording. Similarly, quotations attributed to Kiffin accusing Urban Meyer of cheating were taken from a video recording of Kiffin's speech to boosters in Knoxville, Tennessee.

Text of the SEC's reprimand of Kiffin was taken from published reports.

We also relied on reporting from Pete Thamel, "N.C.A.A. Puts Tennessee's Recruiting Under Scrutiny," *New York Times,* December 8, 2009; columns (and a photograph) by Andy Staples at SI.com; and published reports in the *Knoxville News Sentinel* quoting Corey Miller's father.

The information on the arrest of Nu'Keese Richardson is based on arrest reports and footage from a security surveillance camera outside the convenience store where the incident occurred.

Quotations from the press conference where Kiffin announced his decision to leave Tennessee for USC were taken from a video recording.

Information from the NCAA investigation was taken in part from Infractions Report No. 342, published on November 16, 2012. Further information was obtained from conversations and e-mails between the authors and the NCAA.

3. THE BRAND: Going all in at Michigan

The portrayal of athletic director Dave Brandon is based on multiple interviews with Brandon both in Ann Arbor and on the road at the Cowboys Classic. Personal observations of his professional behavior came from home and road games and Michigan practices. Interviews that helped shape the portrait were conducted with David Ablauf, associate athletic director of public and media relations; Hunter Lochmann, chief marketing officer; Ben Sutton, president of IMG College; and Mike Vollmar, associate athletic director, now a senior associate athletic director in charge of football at Tennessee. Editor John Borton's article "Investing in the Future," *Wolverine,* September 2012, supplied key athletic department financial data that was double-checked with Brandon. Adam Rittenberg's work for ESPN.com was critical, especially his July 2011 interview with Brandon on branding.

The portrayal of head coach Brady Hoke was the product of interviews with Brandon, Vollmar and several Wolverine players, as well as Hoke, the latter as part of the fall 2012 *60 Minutes* report on college football. In addition, Hoke was observed at a practice, during film sessions and at games. A Grantland.com Q&A by Davy Rothbart (August 2012) was instrumental in bringing Hoke to life, as was Michael Rothstein's "Hokefication of Michigan," *WolverineNation,* June 2012; and Kellie Woodhouse's profile on AnnArbor.com.

The synopsis of the Rich Rodriguez era was drawn from *Three and Out* (New York: Farrar, Straus and Giroux, 2011), John U. Bacon's incisive book on that period, and a follow-up interview with Bacon at a coffee shop in Ann Arbor.

The Denard Robinson mini-profile was born out of an interview with Robinson and discussions with Bacon, Ablauf and other Michigan sources, as well as personal observation of Robinson in multiple game and off-field situations.

The description of the Cowboys Classic—the scene sets, practice, game and postgame— came from one of the authors' observations. Reporting by Mark Snyder of the *Detroit Free Press* and Angelique S. Chengelis of the *Detroit News* proved extremely valuable in filling in critical blanks during the U-M season. Snyder's March 2010 interview with Brandon played an important role, too.

4. BIG MAN ON CAMPUS: A pretty awesome asset

The portrayal of The Man was the result of multiple interviews as well as conversations with another individual with direct knowledge of his personal relationships.

Published reports and personal observations formed the basis for the description of the University of Texas football program, including its finances, and Darrell K. Royal's legendary status at the school. Descriptions of the efforts to honor Royal at the Iowa State game and the game summary came directly from reporting in the *Austin American-Statesman.* Information pertaining to Joe Jamail's professional career was readily available online and then double-checked personally with Jamail.

The portrait of Don King was the product of several phone conversations, King's personal Web site, and a leisurely afternoon by one of the authors with King and his colleagues at Big Daddy's sports bar in Austin.

5. THE VICTIM: "They had suffered enough. They lost their scholarships"

The following individuals were interviewed for this chapter: former BYU head coach Gary Crowton; current BYU head coach Bronco Mendenhall; BYU's athletic director, Tom Holmoe; Provo detective DeVon Jensen; prosecutor Donna Kelly; criminal defense attorney Greg Skordas; Karland Bennett; and a juror in the rape trial of two BYU football players.

We communicated with the victim through the prosecutor's office. But she declined our request for an interview. We have used the pseudonym Jane Brown to protect her identity. We also used a pseudonym—Kim Smith—for the victim's cousin.

The account of the gang rape was drawn from police reports, depositions, secret grand jury transcripts and trial transcripts. All four accused players gave statements to law enforcement. We had access to those statements. Additionally, Karland Bennett provided a lengthy interview to prosecutors. We obtained a transcript of that interview, as well as his testimony at trial.

Dialogue between the victim and the players is based on extensive interviews conducted during the criminal investigation, all of which were turned over to the authors. Statements attributed to Gary Crowton and assistant coach Mike Empey are taken from their depositions in the criminal case.

The medical evidence pertaining to the victim's injuries, as well as her medical history, comes from the grand jury proceedings. The authors were given access to transcripts from the entire grand jury proceeding.

In all, we reviewed roughly a thousand pages of court and police records from the rape case.

B. J. Mathis and Ibrahim Rashada declined to be interviewed. Karland Bennett was in prison while this book was being written.

The statistics on sexual assault among college athletes, as well as the arrest and conviction rates for athletes accused of sexual assault, were taken from the following studies, for which one of the authors of this book was a lead researcher, and publications, written or co-written by an author of this book: Jeff Benedict, *Public Heroes, Private Felons: Athletes and Crimes Against Women* (Boston: Northeastern University Press, 1997);

Jeff Benedict, *Athletes and Acquaintance Rape* (Thousand Oaks, Calif.: Sage Publications, 1998); Todd Crosset, Jeff Benedict and Mark McDonald, "Male Student-Athletes Reported for Sexual Assault: A Survey of Campus Police Departments and Judicial Affairs Offices," *Journal of Sports & Social Issues* 19, no. 2 (1995); Jeff Benedict and Alan Klein, "Arrest and Conviction Rates for Athletes Accused of Sexual Assault," *Sociology of Sport Journal* 14, no. 1 (1997).

Quotations from the press conference where Gary Crowton resigned were taken from a transcript of his remarks. Quotations from criminal defense attorney Jere Reneer and B. J. Mathis's grandmother following the verdict were obtained from published reports in the *Salt Lake Tribune* and the *Deseret News*.

The information about Karland Bennett's criminal record in Texas and his incarceration for murder was obtained through interviews with law enforcement and court officers in Dallas, as well as court and police records obtained through the police department in Richardson, Texas, and the courts in Dallas.

6. THE COACH: Part II, Terminated

The following individuals were interviewed for this chapter: Mike Leach, Sharon Leach, Ruffin McNeill, Craig James, Ted Liggett, Kent Hance, Guy Bailey, Victor Mellinger and one court official in Lubbock who asked not to be identified.

Texas Tech officials would not allow us to speak with trainers Mark "Buzz" Chisum and Steve Pincock. However, Tech did provide us with sworn affidavits from both trainers. The dialogue attributed to both men comes largely from their sworn affidavits, which we also relied on for some of the detailed descriptions of Adam James's concussion symptoms. Tech also provided us with affidavits from team physician Dr. Michael Phy.

Dialogue between Mike Leach and Kent Hance comes from interviews with both men, as well as their depositions. Dialogue between Craig James and Kent Hance comes from interviews with both men, along with their depositions. Dialogue between Craig James and his wife comes from our interview with Craig James.

Dialogue between Adam and Craig James—via text message and otherwise—comes from our interview with Craig James, as well as court records that included their phone records.

The description of the storage shed where Adam James was put comes from court filings and video footage of the interior and exterior from local TV affiliates.

The scene at the Belo Mansion & Pavilion comes from an interview with Kent Hance.

The description and dialogue from the meeting involving Mike Leach, Ted Liggett, Guy Bailey and Gerald Myers are based on interviews with Leach, Liggett and Bailey.

The description and dialogue from the meeting held in Judge Sowder's chambers are based on interviews with three individuals who were present.

Charlotte Bingham's actions and her report were taken from court filings. We obtained copies of Mike Leach's employment contract at Texas Tech; a letter sent to Mike Leach by Gerald Myers and Guy Bailey on December 28, 2009; and Leach's termination letter signed by Guy Bailey on December 30, 2009, as well as a transcript of Bingham's voice mail to Ted Liggett (provided by Liggett's law office).

The authors also had access to e-mails and text messages to and from Texas Tech trustees Larry Anders and Jerry Turner.

In all, we reviewed close to a thousand pages of court documents from *Mike Leach v. Texas Tech University,* filed in the Ninety-ninth District Court in Lubbock County, Texas.

Reporting on Mike Borich's degenerative brain disease was based on two reports issued by the Boston University School of Medicine available at http://www.bu.edu/cste/news/press-releases/october-22-2009/ and http://www.bu.edu/cste/case-studies/mike-borich/. Additional information about Borich's death was obtained from his obituary published in the *Deseret News* on February 11, 2009, at http://www.legacy.com/obituaries/deseretnews/.

We also relied on: Alan Schwarz, "Concussion Trauma Risk Seen in Amateur Athlete,"

New York Times, October 22, 2009; Joe Schad, "Leach Suspended After Player Complaint," ESPN.com, December 28, 2009; and "Statement from Texas Tech on Suspension of Football Coach Mike Leach," http://today.ttu.edu/2009/12/statement-from-texas-tech-on -suspension-of-football-coach-mike-leach/.

Descriptions of the reaction to Leach's firing were based on reports in the *Lubbock Avalanche-Journal,* http://lubbockonline.com/stories/123009/upd_541069858.shtml.

7. THE SACRIFICIAL LAMB: Towson University plays with the big boys

The portrait of Towson University football and its "business trip" to play LSU on Saturday, September 29, 2012, was the result of the gracious invitation from then athletic director Michael P. Waddell and associate athletic director Devin Crosby (now at Kent State University) to accompany the Tigers to Baton Rouge as part of a *60 Minutes* piece on college football.

Every on- and off-field scene and all the dialogue depicted in the chapter were personally witnessed and recorded by one of the authors.

Multiple interviews with Waddell put Towson's athletic goals into perspective, as did an interview with David H. Nevins on the team charter. Discussions with Fran S. Soistman, executive vice president of Jessamine Healthcare, and Ross V. Cappuzzo, president of Genesis Eyewear, helped frame the significance of the LSU game to prominent Towson alumni.

Rob Ambrose's personal and professional backstory—including the "Mama" story—was culled from several articles on the athletic department Web site and an interview with the coach.

LSU's prospects for the 2013 NFL draft were the work of Mel Kiper on ESPN.com. The article questioning Towson's decision to play LSU appeared in the *Towerlight,* the campus newspaper, on Thursday, September 27, 2012.

8. OHIO STATE V. MICHIGAN: The return of "The Senator"

The opening section of the chapter—set around the Ohio State–Michigan game—was based upon interviews for this work and the personal observations of James Oldham, a former reporter for the *Lantern.* The authors also conducted interviews with Tim Collins, Cayla Hellwarth and James Larcus.

All of the information quoted in the chapter was pulled from a wide variety of NCAA, public and internal records associated with the "tattoo-gate" scandal. These include: transcripts of NCAA interviews (Jim Tressel and Gene Smith), legal memos, extensive communications (letters) between Bobby DiGeronimo and Smith and e-mails, exhibits and other documents. This information was backed by published reports on *Yahoo! Sports;* detailed reporting by Tim May in the *Columbus Dispatch;* Zack Meissel and James Oldham at the *Lantern;* the *New York Times; Sports Illustrated* magazine (specifically, "The Fall of Jim Tressel," by George Dohrmann with David Epstein); *ESPN the Magazine;* ESPN .com; press releases issued by the university's in-house media relations department; and NCAA.org.

The Jim Tressel recorded interview with NCAA investigators took place on the Ohio State campus on February 8, 2011.

A request to interview Coach Tressel about his relationship with Bobby DiGeronimo and his experience at Ohio State was made via e-mail to the University of Akron athletic department on April 1, 2013. The following day Wayne Hill, the school's associate vice president and chief marketing officer, e-mailed the authors stating Tressel had declined to participate.

Tressel's Response to Notice of Allegations, Case Number M352, was offered by Gene A. Marsh and William H. King III of the Birmingham, Alabama, law firm of Lightfoot, Franklin & White.

One of the authors attempted to speak with Chris Cicero. After a brief phone conversation on October 31, 2012, saying he would like to talk, Cicero declined to respond to further requests for comment. In a March 2011 interview with ESPN's John Barr, Cicero said that in his mind "confidential" meant the media or the public; it was not his intention, he said, to stop Tressel from going to the school or proper authorities. "I wanted him to know that the kids had been hanging out with a person who was the subject of a federal investigation," Cicero told Barr.

9. THE JANITOR: "I fix shit"

The dialogue and discussions depicted during the 2012 national convention of directors of football operations at the Omni Hotel in Fort Worth on May 8, 2012, were witnessed by one of the authors. Multiple follow-up e-mails and interviews with Matt Doyle of Stanford and Zachary Maurides, founder and head of accounts for Logistical Athletic Solutions, formed the basis of both men's profiles.

Doyle's "Duties and Responsibilities" and "A Day in the Life" were provided as attachments to e-mails in May 2012.

The return on investment analysis cited by Maurides was done by LAS in the fall of 2011 and reviewed and approved by Duke University.

The main interview with Cleve Bryant took place at the Four Seasons hotel in Austin, Texas, on October 4, 2011. Both authors were present and took extensive on-the-record notes. Subsequent attempts to follow up with Bryant, who said he was considering writing his own book, were met with limited success. Bryant's background information was available online.

An interview was conducted with Bryant's attorney, Tom Nesbitt. Attorney Gloria Allred declined our request for an interview.

Reporting by Steve Delsohn for ESPN's *Outside the Lines* in September 2011 was critical in detailing the harassment charge by Rachel Arena against Bryant. Equally important was Delsohn's September 15 story posted on ESPN.com in which Arena's formal complaint is quoted at length. Articles in the *Austin American-Statesman* proved important as well, including "Football Aide Cleve Bryant Fighting Dismissal, Lawyer Says" on June 23, 2011.

The three-page University of Texas "Summary of Investigation," dated September 8, 2011, is cited and quoted extensively in this work. It was obtained through an Open Records request filed with the State of Texas. Attempts to obtain Rachel Arena's formal complaint through the same office were resisted by the university's chief legal counsel. According to June Harden, an assistant attorney general in the Open Records Division of the Attorney General's Office, ESPN was able to obtain Arena's complaint because at the time of its request the case was still ongoing and the Summary of Investigation had not been completed. Once it was, by law, the university said, Arena's formal complaint was no longer available. The AG's Office did not necessarily concur.

The University of Texas interview with Cleve Bryant took place in the law office of DeShazo & Nesbitt in Austin on November 3, 2010, and was part of the public record in the case. Bryant's denial of the charges and his attorney Tom Nesbitt's question about the availability of the texts are derived from that source. Follow-up e-mails were exchanged with Nesbitt, and interviews were subsequently conducted with his client's approval.

10. REBUILDING A PROGRAM: "There is no gray with Bronco"

The following individuals were interviewed for this chapter: Bronco Mendenhall, Gary Crowton, Tom Holmoe, Kyle Whittingham, LaVell Edwards, Kyle Van Noy, Kelly Van Noy and McQueen High defensive coordinator Jim Snelling.

One of the authors spent many hours with Kyle Van Noy and Bronco Mendenhall, chronicling their relationship, starting with their initial encounter at a church building in Reno, Nevada. All of the dialogue between them in this chapter comes from interviews with them.

Our reporting on Manti Te'o and BYU's efforts to recruit him was based on interviews with Mendenhall, supplemented by published reports. Our reporting on the arrest of Shiloah Te'o was based on interviews with Mendenhall, supplemented by published reports in the *Deseret News* and the *Salt Lake Tribune*.

11. THE BOOSTER: What $248 million will buy you

The following individuals were interviewed for this chapter: T. Boone Pickens, OSU's athletic director Mike Holder, Robert "Bobby" Stillwell, Chief Justice Steven W. Taylor and OSU's associate AD Jesse Martin.

One of the authors also spent time with the Auburn booster Jimmy Rane and attended his annual charity golf tournament and fund-raising dinner for the Jimmy Rane Foundation on May 17–18, 2012, in Georgia. But after numerous e-mail and personal exchanges over many months, Rane ultimately declined a lengthy on-the-record interview.

Published reports, as well as an independent investigation commissioned by the NCAA, were relied on for information on booster Nevin Shapiro at Miami. The SMU scandal material came from published reports.

All quotations and dialogue pertaining to the hiring of Mike Holder and the financial contributions to Oklahoma State by Boone Pickens are based on interviews conducted by the authors. One exception is the statement "I want us to be competitive . . . I'd bet my ass on it," attributed to Pickens. That appeared in the *New York Times*. Background reporting was also obtained from T. Boone Pickens, *The First Billion Is the Hardest: Reflections on a Life of Comebacks and America's Energy Future* (New York: Three Rivers Press, 2009).

One of the authors spent a weekend traveling with Pickens, which entailed shadowing him at his office, riding in a car with him, flying on his private plane on two occasions and sleeping at his home on his ranch. The author also attended the Oklahoma State–Texas game in Stillwater, Oklahoma, on September 29, 2012. The material from that weekend— all quotations, dialogues and scenes—is based on firsthand observations by one of the authors.

12. THE TUTOR: Friends with benefits

The following individuals were interviewed for this chapter: Teresa Braeckel, Lauren Gavin, Sarah Washington, Derrick Washington, Donald Washington and prosecutor Andrea Hayes. Interviews were also conducted with tutors at Georgia, South Carolina and Miami. Both Braeckel and Gavin gave permission for their names to be used.

Attorneys Christopher Slusher and Bogdan Susan declined to be interviewed. Missouri's football coach Gary Pinkel did not respond to an interview request.

Details of the assault and the events leading up to it were taken from interviews with Teresa Braeckel, Derrick Washington and Lauren Gavin, along with hundreds of pages of court records and trial transcripts. Courtroom scenes and statements attributed to Judge Kevin Crane were obtained from trial transcripts. In all, the authors reviewed more than five hundred pages of court records and trial transcripts.

The information about Missouri basketball player Michael Dixon was obtained from court records and interviews. The domestic violence incident involving Derrick Washington was obtained from court records and published reports. The description of Gary Pinkel's arrest is based on published reports.

13. THE ATHLETIC DIRECTOR: Part I, "We have no money. Nobody is giving money. We are not on TV"

The following individuals were interviewed for this chapter: Bill Moos, Elson Floyd, Kevin Weiberg, Dave Brown and Tom Holmoe.

Dialogue between Bill Moos and Phil Knight is from interviews with Moos. Dialogue between Moos and Floyd is based on multiple interviews with them. The dialogue from the Pac-12 meetings and the negotiations on conference realignment and the new television contract are based on nearly a hundred pages of minutes and notes from the Pac-12 meetings held in 2010 and 2011, along with interviews with Moos and Weiberg.

14. THE INVESTIGATORS: Big-game hunting

Both authors visited NCAA headquarters in Indianapolis on May 23, 2012, and jointly conducted interviews with Rachel Newman Baker, Chance Miller and Brynna Barnhart. President Mark Emmert's quotations and thoughts are derived from numerous public sources and NCAA sources. One of the authors attended the IMG Intercollegiate Athletics Forum in December 2012 in New York, where Mark Emmert participated in a one-on-one discussion moderated by Abraham Madkour, executive editor at Sports BusinessDaily.com. Emmert's NCAA convention speeches were available at NCAA.org and highlighted in *USA Today*.

Reporting on the world of 7-on-7 was centered on one of the authors' three-day visit to the IMG National Championships in the summer of 2012 and a subsequent visit in 2013. Interviews there were conducted with former IMG vice president Odis Lloyd; Chris Ciaccio, then vice president of marketing and outreach for IMG; Chris Weinke, director of football at IMG Academy; performance coach Trevor Moawad; and Josh Clark and Johnny Esfeller of IMG.

A lengthy interview with Coach Dave Schuman, founder of the New Jersey–based National Underclassmen, the largest and most comprehensive touring combine system in high school football, proved invaluable in understanding the growth of scouting combines, camps and the culture of 7-on-7. NUC had grown from just five events in 2007 to more than a hundred events and twenty thousand kids by 2012.

Brett Goetz, founder of South Florida Express, was interviewed multiple times on a variety of 7-on-7 subjects.

The Jimmy D. Smith/James Smith reporting included two interviews with Smith, an NCAA investigator and Charles Fishbein of Elite Scouting Services. It was supplemented with a deep dig into various high school recruiting Web sites. Smith's employment at NOLA.com was confirmed in a September 25, 2012, background interview with James O'Byrne, the *Times-Picayune* editor in charge of high school sports.

From the beginning the Will Lyles story belonged to Charles Robinson and Dan Wetzel at *Yahoo! Sports*. We just followed in their footsteps.

Descriptions of Baron Flenory's power and the rise of New Level Athletics could be found online at "7-on-7: Recruiting's New Battleground," Foxsports.com, March 13, 2011; "Is 7-on-7 King Baron Flenory the Next Sonny Vaccaro?," LostLettermen.com, June 28, 2011; "Flenory on Recruiting Controversy: I Feel Targeted," March 14, 2011, CBSSports .com; and other Web sites, such as oregonlive.com.

The description of the NCAA's investigation into booster Nevin Shapiro and the University of Miami was based largely on the independent report issued by Kenneth L. Wainstein of Cadwalader, Wickersham & Taft LLP on February 17, 2013: "Report on the NCAA's Engagement of a Source's Counsel and Use of the Bankruptcy Process in Its University of Miami Investigation."

Media criticism of Mark Emmert based upon the NCAA's investigation of Miami was best summarized in two articles on SI.com posted on January 24, 2013. One column, written by Andy Staples, was headlined "It's Time for the NCAA to Make Sweeping Changes." The other, by Stewart Mandel, was headlined "Emmert's NCAA Loses More Credibility After Miami Misstep."

The description of certain feelings of frustration and tension inside the NCAA enforcement staff was derived from conversations with members of that staff.

15. THE SYSTEM AT WORK: Ohio State and the consequences of $3.07

Attorney Larry H. James was interviewed at his Columbus law office on May 24, 2012, and several times by telephone. The Cleveland attorney James P. Conroy, a former Buckeye lineman, was also interviewed about Bobby DiGeronimo.

The memorandums cited in the chapter in defense of DeVier Posey and Daniel Herron, and containing things such as the "family tree," a spreadsheet of deposits, time cards and cellular records, were written by Larry James and provided to the authors. They were sent to Doug Archie and either Chance Miller or Tim Nevius. They are dated July 8, 2011, September 26, 27, 30, 2011. The "$3.07" memo was dated October 11, 2011, and sent to Doug Archie at Ohio State.

The recorded Gene Smith interview with investigators took place on October 14, 2011, on the Ohio State campus. A request to interview Smith about his decision to dissociate

Bobby DiGeronimo and discrepancies between Smith's account of their conversations and that of DiGeronimo was made to the Ohio State athletic department via e-mail on April 1, 2013. On April 4, 2013, senior associate athletic director Diane Sabau e-mailed the authors that Smith had respectfully declined the request.

The e-mail from Heather Lyke to Gene Smith was sent on April 20, 2006, at 4:46 p.m.

The 2012 Cornerstone of Hope event, in which some $350,000 was raised, was attended by one of the authors of this book as the guest of DiGeronimo.

The charges against DiGeronimo were outlined in the NCAA's Supplemental Case Summary dated November 21, 2011.

DiGeronimo's controversial "if there's no tattoo-gate, this thing doesn't come out" comments about the case appeared in a story written by Bill Lubinger of the Cleveland *Plain Dealer* on September 15, 2011.

Multiple interviews were conducted with Bobby DiGeronimo at his home, in his car, at lunch and at the 2012 Cornerstone of Hope gala. Subsequent follow-up and fact-checking interviews were conducted over the phone.

In response to a Freedom of Information Act request for Gene Smith's athletic-department-issued cell phone records between April 1 and May 31, 2005, an Ohio State spokeswoman said those records fell outside the university's four-year retention policy and had been destroyed. DiGeronimo said his company phone records from that same period could not be located.

16. THE ATHLETIC DIRECTOR: Part II, "It's going to be expensive"

For this chapter interviews were conducted with Bill Moos, Mike Marlow, Joe Giansante, Gary O'Hagan, Mike Leach, Sharon Leach, Elson Floyd and Guy Bailey. Paul Wulff declined to be interviewed.

All of the dialogue between individuals in this chapter comes directly from interviews with those who are quoted. Details from the meeting in Florida between Moos and Leach were enhanced by receipts, travel documents and calendars provided by Washington State University's athletic department. The dialogue from the press conferences held by Bill Moos and Mike Leach comes from tape recordings of the respective events. Washington State's associate vice president Gil Picciotto and Bill Moos's secretary Debbie Nankivell also provided critical background detail for this chapter.

Information on head coaching salaries was taken from reports in *USA Today* and the *Chronicle of Higher Education.* The authors also had access to the individual employment contracts of many of the head coaches listed in the chapter.

Pricing for premium seating at the upgraded Martin Stadium was taken from "The Cougar Football Project," published by the Cougar Athletic Fund.

Facts and figures pertaining to state budget cuts to Washington State University and the University of Washington were taken from "Wulff's Costly Departure Raises Issues of Priorities," *Tri-City Herald,* December 4, 2011.

17. THE WALK-ON: "I want to play football"

While writing this book, Jeff Benedict profiled Ezekiel "Ziggy" Ansah for *Sports Illustrated* on December 3, 2012. Excerpts from that piece—"The Next Zig Thing"—appear in this chapter.

For this chapter, interviews were conducted with Bronco Mendenhall, Ezekiel "Ziggy" Ansah, Kyle Van Noy, Ken Frei, Chad Lewis and Jordan Johnson. One of the authors was also given access to Ken Frei's journal, which detailed his interaction with Ansah in Africa. Brett Pyne, BYU's sports information director, assisted with our description of Ansah's first game against Wyoming. The description and play-by-play from the BYU–Ole Miss game came from a televised recording of the game.

18. SABAN'S WAY: The New Testament of college football

The story of Nick Saban's hiring at Alabama was predominantly Moore's alone. He told it in his corner office in the athletic department facility in the spring of 2013, just weeks before entering the hospital for a pulmonary condition that took his life. With associate athletics director Jeff Purinton at his side, Moore could not have been more gracious or personable in spinning a tale he obviously wanted to tell.

19. THE WOUNDED: Pain is relative

In this chapter, researchers Timothy Bella and J. J. Feinauer spoke to thirty-four players who responded to a BCS title team survey. The interviews took place between July 2012 and October 2012.

Other interviewees included Marcus Lattimore, the former South Carolina running back; Scott Anderson, president of the College Athletic Trainers' Society; Jim Thornton, president of the National Athletic Trainers' Association; David Bailiff, head coach for Rice University; and Jarad Moon, a former Florida State player whose life has been altered by injuries sustained while at Florida State. Those interviews took place between June 2012 and March 2013.

Lattimore's agent, Pat Dye Jr., was also interviewed about his client's injury, surgery, rehabilitation progress, potential draft status and other subjects.

In terms of the season-ending injuries, we used a number of sources to confirm the injuries, including *USA Today*'s injury tracker, media reports and team reports. We updated our database twice a week, once usually on the Sunday following the Saturday games and once again before the following week's games. The injury period ranged from August 2012 right up to the final regular-season and conference championship games in December 2012.

We also used quotations and information from outside sources, such as the *New Republic*, the *Birmingham News*, *PLOS ONE*, NFL Network, ESPN and 2012 press conferences from University of Washington head coach Steve Sarkisian.

20. THE BLUE-CHIP RECRUIT: The Ricky Seals-Jones sweepstakes

The overwhelming majority of this chapter was based on interviews with the Jones family and personal observation. Chester Jones was interviewed more than a dozen times on various issues related to his son's upbringing, recruitment and injuries, including lengthy interviews in September and November 2012. It was Chester Jones who told one of the authors, and later added detail to, the story of the tragic death of Ricky Seals.

One of the authors saw firsthand the dining room table in the Jones home stacked with recruiting letters. One of the authors also attended the Sealy-Bellville game and sat with Jones.

The injury to Seals-Jones's left knee was witnessed on the ESPNU television broadcast. Subsequent statistics from that game came courtesy of St. Pius X's head football coach, Blake Ware, who called Jones the most gifted high school athlete he'd ever seen.

The charges related to the recruitment of Cam Newton and the subsequent NCAA investigation was pulled from published reports and NCAA.org.

Reporting on the method of under-the-table payments to college football players was provided on a source basis from conversations with boosters, runners, agents and financial planners.

Dialogue as it relates to Seals-Jones's recruitment stems from the memory of Chester Jones and Ricky Seals-Jones.

The information on the $300,000 offer to Chester Jones was originally provided by a secondhand source at a 7-on-7 event. The primary source was named at the time and eventually located and interviewed at length regarding the specifics of the offer, which the individual who heard it confirmed. Following Jones's denial, the source was contacted twice more, the final time during the fact-checking process to triple-check the sourcing and information. The source again confirmed the attribution and the details of the offer.

A request to interview certain members of the University of Texas coaching staff was declined on December 11, 2012, by John Bianco, associate athletic director for media relations. Bianco cited NCAA rules that prohibit comment on prospects or on the recruiting of specific student-athletes.

21. THE COACH: Part III, "The starting lineup is voluntary, too"

One of the authors shadowed Mike Leach during the off-season in 2012. Most of what's reported in this chapter—the practice sessions, workouts and team meetings—was observed firsthand during visits to Pullman, Washington, in 2012. One of the authors was also present during the phone calls Mike Leach had with high school recruits, as well as the car ride and dinner that are described with Sharon and Mike Leach. Additionally, interviews were conducted with Mike Leach, Sharon Leach, Tyler Bruggman, Dave Emerick, Jim Mastro, Nick Galbraith and John Fullington.

22. CRIME AND PUNISHMENT: The SEC leads the nation

In 2011, the authors collaborated on two special reports for *Sports Illustrated* and CBS News. The first—"Criminal Records in College Football"—appeared in the March 7 issue of *SI*. The second—"Straight Outta Compton"—appeared in the December 5 issue. Reports also appeared on the *CBS Evening News* and CBS's *Early Show*. Some reporting from those stories appears in this chapter.

For this chapter, interviews were conducted with Samuel Jurgens, Nick Saban, Scott Decker, Geoff Alpert, Rob Wilson, Tom Seeberg, Keith Donerson, Danielle Farber, Kenneth McGee, Araceli Nogueda, Sergeant Brandon Dean, Lacy Westbrook, Lavell Sanders, Brandon Beaver, Eugene Beaver, Alphonso Marsh, Curley Rachal, Kyle Whittingham, Mike Leach and Delshawn McClellon.

The authors communicated with Caleb Paul after he was assaulted. But he declined our request for an on-the-record interview.

The arrest and conviction statistics for college football players in 2012 are based on the authors' original reporting. The 204 player arrests were confirmed by published reports. The information on James Wilder Jr.'s three arrests was taken from published reports.

The information on the criminal problems with the University of Oklahoma's football program in the 1980s came from "How Barry Switzer's Sooners Terrorized Their Campus," *Sports Illustrated,* February 27, 1989, along with other published reports.

ALABAMA

The primary source for the description of the assault on Samuel Jurgens was our interview with him. We also relied on police records from the case. Our reporting on Nick Saban's response to the arrests was taken almost entirely from a discussion about the subject with Saban.

Jason Neff, a criminal defense attorney for Brent Calloway, was helpful in providing information in the early stages of the criminal case against the four Alabama football players. Reporting on prior arrests at Alabama during Saban's tenure was based on published reports in Alabama newspapers and on ESPN.

NOTRE DAME

One of the authors spent significant time with Tom Seeberg and was given access to e-mails and other correspondence between the family and Notre Dame officials, medical records, text messages and documents. We also relied on a report issued by St. Joseph County prosecutor Michael Dvorak.

PENN STATE

One of the authors covered the Jerry Sandusky child sexual abuse trial and the fallout from the scandal, spending more than a hundred hours on and around the Penn State campus and conducting dozens of interviews. The authors also relied on the 270-plus-page independent report issued by former head of the FBI Louis Freeh and Freeh's subsequent press conference in Philadelphia on July 12, 2012, to announce the findings of the investigation.

ALPHONSO MARSH AT DOMINGUEZ HIGH AND THE UNIVERSITY OF UTAH

The reporting on the Dominguez High School football players is based on multiple trips the authors made to Compton in 2011 and 2012. The authors attended games and practice sessions and conducted interviews with all of the mentioned players, along with their parents. One of the authors also made multiple trips to Salt Lake City to chronicle Alphonso Marsh's arrival and experience during the summer and fall of 2012. The authors also relied on additional reporting from Deanne Fitzmaurice, a photographer who was retained for this book to shadow Alphonso Marsh in Compton and in Salt Lake City. Some information from her observations enriched the reporting. One of the authors also communicated regularly with Marsh and his former teammates at Dominguez High through Facebook and Twitter.

23. THE GAME: "I hate losing more than anything"

Most of what's reported in this chapter—the pregame rituals, the locker room scenes, the games and the postgame material—was observed firsthand by one of the authors during visits to Provo, Salt Lake City and Atlanta in 2012. During these visits, one of the authors shadowed Kyle Van Noy, Mike Leach, Ezekiel "Ziggy" Ansah and Bronco Mendenhall. Photojournalist Deanne Fitzmaurice accompanied one of the authors during the visits to Provo and Salt Lake City. She had access to the players and coaches and was present on the sidelines and in the locker room. Her photography was used to enhance the reporting.

Additionally, one of the authors conducted multiple interviews with Kyle Van Noy, Cody Harris, Mike Leach, Bronco Mendenhall and Ezekiel Ansah. All statements and actions attributed to University of Utah fans during the BYU–Utah game were observed by one of the authors.

Quotations attributed to Max Hall and Austin Collie regarding the BYU–Utah rivalry appeared in the *Salt Lake Tribune* and the *Deseret News*.

24. THE COACH: Part IV, The letter

For this chapter, interviews were conducted with Mike Leach, Bill Moos, Elson Floyd and Tyler Bruggman. Marquess Wilson did not respond to requests for an interview.

All documents referred to in this chapter either are in the possession of the authors or were shown to the authors. Washington State University also provided access to the e-mails and text messages to and from Bill Moos and Elson Floyd, as well as those to and from WSU trustees Ryan Durkan and Scott Carson. The authors also had access to the text message from Marquess Wilson to Bill Moos, as well as Wilson's letter.

Additional sources included WSU's internal review of the football program; the outside review conducted by the Pac-12; published reports of Mike Leach's postgame press conference following the Utah game; a report by Bud Withers in the *Seattle Times* regarding Leach's behavior following the Utah game; Stewart Mandel's reporting on SI.com regarding Leach; a *Los Angeles Times* story, "Ring of Fire," about Barry Alvarez; and published reports on ESPN.com and elsewhere regarding Marquess Wilson's departure from the team.

25. THE DRAFT PICK: To go pro or not to go pro

One of the authors attended the Poinsettia Bowl and was given access to BYU's locker room before and after the game. All scenes and dialogue from the bowl game were observed firsthand. One of the authors also shadowed Kyle Van Noy as he walked alone across the field following the game. Thoughts attributed to Van Noy came from a discussion between the author and Van Noy. Similarly, the thoughts attributed to Ezekiel Ansah, Kyle Van Noy and Bronco Mendenhall in the postgame locker room were told to the author. Interviews were also conducted with Tom Holmoe.

Thoughts attributed to Kyle Van Noy during his decision-making process on whether to remain at BYU for his senior year were told to one of the authors by Van Noy.

The Detroit Lions were helpful in providing background information and photography for the portion of the chapter that chronicles Ezekiel Ansah at the NFL draft.

26. *GAMEDAY*: The genius of ESPN

This chapter was constructed in large measure over the weekend of the SEC Championship game in Atlanta. During that period the authors interviewed Lee Fitting, Chris

Fowler, Lee Corso and, briefly, Tom Rinaldi. In a supplemental interview, Fitting provided additional technical information about the production crew and broadcast.

ESPN's securing the rights to the college football playoff was based upon an interview with Burke Magnus, who declined to comment on specific multimedia rights numbers. Those numbers were obtained from sources within the television industry and later confirmed by a high-ranking member of the BCS coalition.

An all-access spot inside the main production truck provided the real-time feel of the two-hour *GameDay* broadcast. That feel was enhanced by one of the authors watching a DVD copy of the entire two-hour show in order to create a sense of what the viewer was witnessing at home. None of this access or information would have been possible without the help of ESPN's Mike Soltys, the approval of ESPN's president, John Skipper, or, most directly, the assistance of Keri A. Potts, ESPN's senior public relations director of college sports.

27. BUILT BY BAMA: In a class by itself

The information in this chapter came from a wide variety of sources: interviews with Nick Saban and members of his Alabama coaching staff, athletic department personnel and the late athletic director Mal M. Moore. Some of Saban's comments and those of defensive coordinator Kirby Smart were from press conferences at the 2013 BCS national title game. In addition, Saban was observed by one of the authors at practice, before, during and after games and at public and private events, some for this book, some as part of reporting for *60 Minutes,* which featured Saban in a piece on college football in November 2012.

The financial data subsequent to Saban's arrival in Tuscaloosa was the work of associate athletic director Douglas Walker.

It was with Saban's approval that the authors were allowed access to Wesley Neighbors Jr., who was interviewed in person at Alabama on two separate occasions and also over the phone. His personal story was augmented with information from the Alabama football media guide and published reports.

The player interviews with Barrett Jones, Dee Milliner, Damion Square, Eddie Lacy, Cyrus Kouandjio and strength coach Scott Cochran were conducted by one of the authors.

The final scene of the book—Saban on the stage before exiting Sun Life Stadium with his index finger in the air—was observed from the field.

INDEX

ABOUT THE AUTHORS

JEFF BENEDICT is one of the country's top investigative reporters. He is a special features contributor for *Sports Illustrated* and the author of ten critically acclaimed books, including *Pros and Cons* and *Out of Bounds*. His essays and articles have appeared in the *New York Times*, *Newsweek* and the *Los Angeles Times*, among other publications, and have been the basis of segments on CBS's *60 Minutes*, ABC's *20/20*, NBC's *Dateline*, HBO's *Real Sports* and the Discovery Channel. He has a law degree and is a Distinguished Professor of Writing and Mass Media at Southern Virginia University.

ARMEN KETEYIAN is a CBS News correspondent based in New York, a contributing correspondent to *60 Minutes* and the lead correspondent for *60 Minutes Sports* on Showtime. An eleven-time Emmy Award winner, he is widely regarded as one of the finest investigative journalists in the country. He is also the author or co-author of nine previous books, including *Money Players, Raw Recruits* and the autobiographies of Hall of Fame pitcher Catfish Hunter and Hall of Fame linebacker Mike Singletary.